D0064721

Gerontology

Editors

Janet M. Wilmoth, PhD, is Associate Professor of Sociology and Senior Research Associate in the Center for Policy Research at Syracuse University, Syracuse, New York. Her research addresses issues related to the demography of aging and social gerontology, in particular older adult migration, living arrangements, and health status. Her work has been supported by grants from the National Institute on Aging. Her current research examines the impact of military service on health outcomes across the life course.

Wilmoth has published over 25 papers in professional journals or books. Her articles appear in a variety of journals, including the *Journal of Gerontology: Social Sciences, The Gerontologist, Research on Aging, Journal of Marriage and the Family*, and *Teaching Sociology*. She is on the editorial boards of the *Journal of Gerontology: Social Science*, and *Teaching Sociology*, and coedited a special issue of *Research on Aging*.

Kenneth F. Ferraro, PhD, is Professor of Sociology and Director of the Center for Aging and the Life Course at Purdue University, West Lafayette, Indiana. He has conducted research on a number of topics in gerontology, including health status, images of aging, and fear of crime, and his work has been supported by grants from the AARP Andrus Foundation, the National Institute on Aging, and the National Center for Minority Health and Health Disparities. His current research interests focus on health status assessment and ethnic differences in health and health service use across the life course.

Ferraro has published over 80 papers in professional journals or books. His articles appear in a variety of journals, including the *American Sociological Review, Journal of Gerontology: Social Sciences, Journal of Health and Social Behavior, Journal for the Scientific Study of Religion, Public Opinion Quarterly, Research on Aging, Social Forces*, and *Sociological Inquiry*. He has served on several study sections for the National Institutes of Health and on the editorial boards of the *American Sociological Review* and *Journal of Health and Social Behavior*. He is currently the editor of the *Journal of Gerontology: Social Sciences*.

Gerontology

Perspectives and Issues

THIRD EDITION

Janet M. Wilmoth, PhD

Kenneth F. Ferraro, PhD

Editors

SPRINGER PUBLISHING COMPANY

New York

Springer Publishing Company, LLC
11 West 42nd Street
New York, NY 10036

Acquisitions Editor: Sheri W. Sussman
Production Editor: Gail Farrar
Cover design: Mimi Flow
Composition: Publishers' Design and Production Services, Inc.
Cover Photograph by Mark Simons, Purdue University

07 08 09 10 / 5 4 3 2 1

Library of Congress Cataloging-in-Publication Data

Gerontology : perspectives and issues / Janet M. Wilmoth, Kenneth F. Ferraro, editors. — 3rd ed.
    p. cm.
    Includes bibliographical references and index.
    ISBN 0-8261-0230-1
    1. Gerontology—United States. I. Wilmoth, Janet M. (Janet May) II. Ferraro, Kenneth F.

HQ1064.U5G42 2006
305.260973—dc22

2006044366

Printed in the United States of America by Bang Printing.

For my grandmother, Jessie May Sturtevant Stinneford,
who sparked my gerontological imagination.

J. M. W.

Charles M. Barresi
K. F. F.

Contents

Contributors

Brooke N. Baker, MS received her master's degree in child development and family studies from Purdue University. Her research at Purdue focused on the mother-daughter tie in adulthood. She is currently the project coordinator for Indiana University's Paraeducator Support Project, in which her work focuses on improving special education paraeducator training efforts across Indiana.

Thomas R. Cole, PhD, is the director of the John P. McGovern M.D. Center for Health, Humanities, and the Human Spirit at the University of Texas–Houston School of Medicine. He is author of *The Journey of Life: A Cultural History of Aging in America* (Cambridge, 1992) and senior editor of *Handbook of Humanities and Aging* (Springer), whose third edition is now in progress. Cole's forthcoming book, *You Never Knew What Powers Lay Within You: Notes of an Aging Medical Humanist*, will be published by Rowman and Littlefield in 2007.

Dale Dannefer, PhD, received his doctorate in sociology from Rutgers University and is professor of sociology at Case Western Reserve University. His writings on life course theory, sociological perspectives on life span development, and cumulative advantage and disadvantage are widely recognized in the sociology of aging and the life course and related fields.

Kathryn Z. Douthit, PhD, received her doctorate in human development from the University of Rochester and is an assistant professor in counseling and human development at University of Rochester's Warner Graduate School of Education and Human Development. Her work explores the medicalization of mental health issues across the life course.

Ying Fang, PhD, received her doctorate in sociology from Syracuse University. Her research interests are in social gerontology, with a particular focus on living arrangements and health status among older adults in China. She is currently a data analyst/methodologist at New Solutions and Beacon Health Informatics, where she facilitates market research of hospital inpatient data.

Karen L. Fingerman, PhD, received her doctorate in psychology from the University of Michigan and is Berner Hanley Scholar and associate professor of child development and family studies at Purdue University. Her research on social and emotional aspects of aging is widely recognized.

Michael G. Flynn, PhD, received his doctorate in human bioenergetics from Ball State University in 1987. He is a professor of health and kinesiology at Purdue University in West Lafayette, IN. Flynn's primary research interests are exercise and aging and exercise immunology. His research is focused on understanding the mechanisms for the anti-inflammatory effects of exercise training.

Linda K. George, PhD, is professor of sociology and associate director of the Center for the Study of Aging at Duke University. Her major research interests are social factors and illness, the persisting effects of childhood adversity, and the social psychology of health.

Christine L. Himes, PhD, is professor of sociology at the Maxwell School of Citizenship and Public Affairs, Syracuse University, and currently serves as chair of the Department of Sociology. Himes has published numerous scholarly articles on health trends and family care giving, most recently focusing on the effects of obesity for later life health.

Robert B. Hudson, PhD, is professor and chair, Department of Social Welfare Policy, Boston University School of Social Work. He currently serves as editor of *Public Policy and Aging Report*, and his book, *The New Politics of Old Age Policy*, was published by The Johns Hopkins University Press in 2005. He received his doctorate in political science from the University of North Carolina at Chapel Hill.

Charles F. Longino, Jr., PhD, received his doctorate in sociology from the University of North Carolina and is a professor of sociology and public health at Wake Forest University. His work on the demography of aging, especially migration among older adults, is widely recognized.

Douglas K. Miller, MD, received his masters degree from Washington University in St. Louis and is the Richard M. Fairbanks Chair in Aging Research, associate director of the Center for Aging Research at Indiana University and research scientist at the Regenstrief Institute in Indianapolis. He is best known for his work in health disparities experienced by older African Americans and in issues related to age-associated frailty.

Dorothy M. Morré, PhD, is professor of nutrition at Purdue University. Her area of specialization is focused on characterization of an aging-related protein found in serum of older individuals.

Ian Neath, PhD, received his doctorate in Psychology from Yale University and is a professor at Memorial University of Newfoundland, Canada. He is the author of a textbook on human memory and is well known for simulation modeling of immediate memory processes.

Michelle Sierpina, MS, is completing doctoral studies in reminiscence and spirituality. She speaks internationally on topics of creativity and aging. She is founding director of Osher Lifelong Learning Institute at the University of Texas Medical Branch in Galveston.

Timothy M. Smeeding, PhD, is the Maxwell Professor of Public Policy, professor of economics and public administration, associate dean for sponsored programs and director of Maxwell's Center for Policy Research at Syracuse University. He is also the project director of the Luxembourg Income Study and a member of the National Academy of Sciences Advisory Board on Demographics, Behavioral and Social Sciences and Education (DBASSE). Smeeding's research is focused on national and cross-national aspects of economic inequality, poverty, and public policy toward the family and vulnerable groups, such as children, the aged, and the disabled.

Aimée M. Surprenant, PhD, received her doctorate from Yale University and is an associate professor in psychology at Memorial University of Newfoundland, Canada. Her research includes work on the effects of noise and distortion on memory, including effects of age-related hearing loss.

David J. Waters, DVM, PhD, received his BS and DVM from Cornell University and his PhD from the University of Minnesota. He is professor and associate director of the Center on Aging and the Life Course at Purdue University and director of the Gerald P. Murphy Cancer Foundation in West Lafayette, Indiana. Waters's research on the biology of aging focuses on the comparative aspects of aging and cancer in animals and humans.

Fredric D. Wolinsky, PhD, received his doctorate in sociology from Southern Illinois University at Carbondale and is the John W. Colloton Chair in Health Management and Policy at the University of Iowa, and associate director of the Center for the Implementation of Innovative Strategies in Practice (a Veterans Administration national Health Services Research and Development [HSR&D] Center of Excellence) at the Iowa City Veterans Administration Medical Center (VAMC). His work on the measurement (self-report and claims-based) and modeling of health services and health services utilization trajectories is widely recognized.

Preface

The organization and content of the three editions of *Gerontology: Perspectives and Issues* reflect the evolution of the field over the past fifteen years. A primary goal of the first edition, which was published in 1990, was to articulate an overarching paradigm—the *gerontological imagination*—to unite the field and to provide a comprehensive review of theoretical and empirical research in gerontology. The second edition, published in 1997, continued in that vein by offering chapters on a wide range of multidisciplinary topics. Similar to the first and second editions of this text, this book reviews the gerontological concepts and knowledge contained in the theories and research of various disciplines. However, this edition represents a substantial reconceptualization and reorganization that aims to develop the reader's *gerontological imagination* by using an explicitly interdisciplinary approach.

Viewed in its entirety, this edited volume provides a broad overview of gerontological inquiry that focuses on the core questions of gerontology: What is gerontology? How does aging affect the mind and the body? How does social context influence aging and life course development? and What are the needs and interests of an older population? Although the unique contributions of specific disciplines are acknowledged, this book demonstrates that no single discipline can completely answer a core question. A comprehensive understanding of a particular aging topic comes only from integrating knowledge from different disciplines. This type of interdisciplinary inquiry is required for a variety of topics scientists seek to understand. In *Stars and Atoms* (1927) Arthur Eddington noted: "I ask you to look both ways. For the road to knowledge of the stars leads through the atom; and important knowledge of the atom has been reached through the stars."[1] The various facets of aging are like atoms and stars—knowledge about one can be reached through an understanding of the others.

We imagine the book will find a variety of uses. We see it as ideal for multidisciplinary and interdisciplinary courses. But it may also be useful as a supplement for discipline-based courses such as the biology, psychology, or sociology of aging. In those courses we would expect it to stretch the scope of inquiry. Whatever its use, we think the sophistication and clarity of the chapters will make it helpful for audiences at both advanced undergraduate and graduate levels. It is our hope that this book will contribute to the continued development of the *gerontological imagination* among current scholars of aging and the next generation of gerontologists by encouraging a broad, interdisciplinary understanding of aging.

Janet M. Wilmoth   Kenneth F. Ferraro
Syracuse, New York   West Lafayette, Indiana

---

[1]Eddington, A. S. (1927). *Stars and Atoms*. New Haven: Yale University Press.

Acknowledgments

Every book is a collective endeavor. This is particularly true of edited volumes such as this one. Given this, I am indebted to a number of individuals without whom this project would not have been possible.

First, I thank my coeditor, Kenneth Ferraro, who generously provided me with this opportunity, offered conceptual guidance, and supplied professional expertise. He wrote thoughtful substantive reviews and detailed editorial suggestions on all of the chapters. I also thank the chapter authors who graciously adhered to the rigorous deadlines and completed the requested revisions. Their hard work and insight have produced an exceptional set of chapters. Special thanks go to George Maddox, Faculty Emeritus at Duke University, who provided a prompt and thoughtful review of Chapter 2, and the Syracuse University graduate students in my Aging and Society seminar during the spring of 2005, who provided comments on Chapters 1 and 3.

Second, many thanks to the Syracuse University Center for Policy Research and the Purdue University Center on Aging and the Life Course, both of which provided support staff who assisted with producing this book. The lion's share of the administrative work was completed by Kelly Bogart, administrative secretary in the Center for Policy Research at Syracuse University, who carefully copyedited and formatted all of the chapters, handled routine correspondence, and helped keep the project organized. For the Purdue University operations, Ann Howell, secretary of the Center on Aging and the Life Course, provided general administrative assistance and did an outstanding job of copyediting all chapters. Martha Bonney, publications and events coordinator in the Center for Policy Research at Syracuse University, also assisted with copyediting. Maria Brown, graduate assistant in the Syracuse University Social Science

Program, wrote substantive and editorial comments for several of the chapters. Thanks to all of you for your timely and helpful assistance.

Third, I recognize several individuals at Springer Publishing who shepherded this project through the publication process. Helvi Gold, acquisitions editor and out-of-house gerontology editor, saw us through the early stages of the project and the final editing prior to production. Alana Stein, assistant editor, and Sheri W. Sussman, senior vice president, editorial, worked with us as we prepared the manuscript for submission and publication. Each of you provided helpful information that clarified the publication process.

Finally, I acknowledge my husband, Brian Durkin, and daughter, Catherine Jean Durkin, who patiently forfeited family time so that I could write my own chapters and review the chapters contributed by others. Their encouragement and support kept me going throughout this project.

J. M. W.

Introduction

The gerontological imagination is an awareness of the process of human aging that enables one to understand the scientific contributions of a variety of researchers studying aging. In addition, this awareness allows people (not just gerontology scholars) to comprehend the links between biological, behavioral, and social structure factors that influence human aging (Ferraro, 1990, pp. 4–5).[1]

This edited volume seeks to foster the gerontological imagination by using an interdisciplinary conceptual framework, which we refer to in chapter 1 as the fountain of gerontological discovery, to organize the chapters. This framework identifies four broad categories of gerontological inquiry—aging scholarship, physical aspects of aging, social aspects of aging, and public policy—each of which grapples with specific core questions about aging. The corresponding four parts of this book contain chapters that address these core questions from different disciplinary perspectives.

Part I, on aging scholarship, addresses two core questions: What is gerontology? Why should it be studied? In the first chapter, we address the first question by making the case that gerontology is inherently an interdisciplinary endeavor given the multifaceted nature of the aging process. We also advocate an interdisciplinary approach to gerontology

[1]Ferraro, K. F. (1990). *Gerontology: Perspectives and Issues*. New York: Springer Publishing Co.

that synthesizes the contributions of specific disciplines. Kenneth Ferraro provides additional insight into gerontology in chapter 2 by discussing the historical development of the field. He identifies the key players and institutional influences that shaped the field during the 20th century and lead to the emergence of the gerontological imagination. The second core question in this section is addressed by Janet Wilmoth and Charles F. Longino, Jr. in chapter 3, which provides insight into the importance of studying aging from a demographic perspective. It highlights what is known about population aging worldwide and the characteristics of the older adult population in the United States from both formal and social demographic perspectives.

Part II focuses on the physical aspects of aging. Collectively, the chapters in this part address three core questions: Why do we age? How does aging affect the mind and the body? Can age-related changes be mitigated? David Waters provides a biological perspective on the question of why we age in chapter 4. Drawing on a broad array of literature—from evolutionary biology to research on cellular senescence, longevity genes, the endocrine system, caloric restriction, free radicals, Werner's syndrome, and centenarians—he paints a detailed picture of the key concerns of biogerontology. Chapters 5 and 6 address the question of how aging affects the mind and the body. In chapter 5, Aimée Surprenant and Ian Neath consider how aging affects the mind from the perspective of cognitive psychology. After situating the study of cognition within gerontology and reviewing the relevant methodological issues, they provide an overview of research on, explanations of, and interventions for age-related differences in cognitive functioning. Fredric Wolinsky and Douglas Miller draw on their knowledge of public health and medical sciences when examining how aging affects physical functioning in chapter 6. They explicitly focus on conceptualizing and measuring disability in the population and the disablement process. Chapters 7 and 8 consider whether age-related changes can be mitigated. Specifically, in chapter 7 Dorothy Morré discusses the role of nutrition in healthy aging, the nutritional problems encountered in later life, and nutritional interventions for frail older adults. In chapter 8, Michael Flynn considers the effect of exercise on aging. After discussing age-related loss in muscle mass, he considers the various benefits of resistive and endurance exercise and then highlights some practical considerations for older exercisers.

Part III, which examines the social aspects of aging, answers two core questions: How does social context influence aging and life course development? How do history, culture, and biography intersect to create the life course? Each chapter in this part addresses both these questions from different disciplinary perspectives. Chapter 9, by Karen Fingerman and Brooke Baker, addresses these issues from the perspective of developmental psychology. In particular, they focus on the social and emotional aspects of aging, including the complex nature of social ties, emotional development in later life, and the challenges faced by the oldest old. In chapter 10, Linda George provides an overview of the sociological perspective on the life course. She argues that life course perspectives offer a richer, more dynamic way to understand human lives and highlight the role of social structure and social context in aging. This viewpoint is expanded in chapter 11, by Kathryn Douthit and Dale Dannefer. They make a case that cumulative advantage/disadvantage trajectories are collective and cultural phenomena that shape disease risk. Chapter 12, by Thomas Cole and Michelle Sierpina, considers the meaning(s) of age from the perspective of humanist gerontology, a flourishing subfield that involves disciplinary scholarship primarily in history, philosophy, literature, and religious studies, interdisciplinary research drawing on humanistic and social science methods, and practice in the form of bioethics and creative endeavors.

Part IV considers the issues that are directly relevant to public policy. The chapters in this part address two core questions: What are the needs and interests of an older population? How are they created and addressed? Timothy Smeeding presents an economic perspective on financial needs in later life in chapter 13. After reviewing the basic principles and models economists use to understand aging, he considers how private market decisions and public sector policies shape later life financial security. Chapter 14, by Christine Himes and Ying Fang, provides a sociological perspective on social needs in later life. In particular, it considers the social roles that older adults tend to occupy, discusses the living arrangement and care needs of older adults, and reviews the macro-level forces shaping older adults' social needs including demographic shifts, social policy, and cultural norms. In chapter 15, Robert Hudson explores the needs and interests of older adults from the perspective of political science. After providing an overview of American social policy development, he demonstrates how the needs of older people, initially used by policy elites to legitimate establishing social programs, have transformed into interests, which are increasingly organized and politically influential.

The intent of chapters 3 through 15 is not to provide a detailed review of the age-related research in each discipline. Instead, the chapter authors were asked to consider the following questions:

1. How does your discipline approach gerontological inquiry? What types of questions are asked? What topics are of interest? What theories and methods are used?
2. What contribution does your discipline make to gerontological inquiry? Which core questions about aging is your discipline attempting to

answer? What is known and what are the cutting edge topics in this area?

3. How is your disciplinary approach to studying aging similar to and/or different from other disciplinary approaches? Are there similarities in terms of topics of interest? How does the knowledge generated by other disciplines inform your understanding?

These chapters provide a self-reflective discussion that acknowledges the contributions, limitations, and biases of each discipline's approach to aging research. In addition, the chapters offer insight into how researchers in particular disciplines think about aging. Collectively, the chapters highlight the unique contributions particular disciplines make to gerontological inquiry and demonstrate that multiple perspectives are required to answer the core questions in our discipline.

Chapter 16 concludes this endeavor by articulating the major tenets of a gerontological imagination. In doing so, our aim is to aid the development of a paradigm for gerontology and the advancement of gerontology as a discipline.

PART I

Aging Scholarship

CHAPTER 1

The Fountain of Gerontological Discovery

Janet M. Wilmoth
Kenneth F. Ferraro

Gerontology textbooks and edited volumes usually provide a survey of age-related issues that is informed by various disciplinary perspectives. The degree to which disciplinary boundaries are reinforced or integrated in these publications depends on whether the text is based on a multidisciplinary or interdisciplinary approach. Although these terms are often used interchangeably, Ferraro and Chan (1997, p. 374) suggest there is an important distinction between the two approaches:

> A *multidisciplinary* field of study refers to an inquiry involving a plurality of disciplines where disciplinary boundaries are maintained and the unique contributions of each are highlighted. We refer to *interdisciplinary* as an inquiry involving a plurality of disciplines where disciplinary boundaries are often muted and the joint contributions of the synergy are highlighted.

We maintain that most textbooks, edited volumes, and other teaching resources reflect the primarily multidisciplinary approach that is currently pervasive in the field. In this book we provide an interdisciplinary conceptual framework that serves as the foundation of its organization. We then consider the implications of this conceptual framework for the continued evolution of gerontology into a scientific discipline.

MULTIDISCIPLINARY APPROACH IN GERONTOLOGY?

Although gerontologists are increasingly involved in interdisciplinary endeavors, the organization of the academic aging enterprise tends to be multidisciplinary (Ferraro & Chan, 1997; Bass & Ferraro, 2000). The charter of the Gerontological Society of America (2003) "set the tone and composition of the Society as a multidisciplinary enterprise to not only promote the study of aging, but also to encourage exchanges among researchers and practitioners from various disciplines related to gerontology." The society's membership categories and peer-review journals demonstrate this multidisciplinary organization.

Gerontology education also reflects the multidisciplinary organization of the field. Despite their rapid proliferation, gerontology programs are most often housed in particular schools or departments (as opposed to being university-wide) and typically offer specializations, concentrations, minors, or certificates instead of a major in gerontology (Ferraro & Chan, 1997). Although the goal of these programs is to integrate information from various disciplines, the level of explicit integration provided to students through the curriculum and course content varies across institutions (Bass & Ferraro, 2000).

Furthermore, most gerontology textbooks, edited volumes, and other teaching resources reinforce a multidisciplinary approach. Some books provide an in-depth review of the age-related knowledge in a particular discipline (such as Belsky, 1999; Cavanaugh & Blanchard-Fields, 2002; Digiovanna, 2000; Matcha, 1997; Schultz, 2000). Textbooks that are more explicitly multidisciplinary devote entire chapters to reviewing the knowledge from different disciplines (such as Atchley, 2000; Cavanaugh & Whitbourne, 1999; Cox, 2001; Ferraro, 1997; Hooyman & Kiyak, 2002; Kart & Kinney, 2001; Morgan & Kunkel, 2001; Quadagno, 2002; Quadagno & Street, 1996). However, none of these texts is guided by a conceptual framework that facilitates an appreciation for how gerontological questions relate to age-related topics of inquiry or how different disciplines provide insight into those questions.

THE FOUNTAIN OF INTERDISCIPLINARY DISCOVERY IN GERONTOLOGY

An interdisciplinary approach to gerontology should consider the main areas of gerontological inquiry and then focus on the core questions within each of these areas. Figure 1.1 is based on the analogy of a fountain and serves as a heuristic diagram to highlight the process of gerontological discovery. Think of a fountain that is really a system of fountains. The

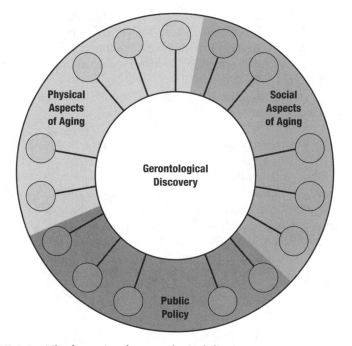

FIGURE 1.1   The fountain of gerontological discovery.

water circulates through all parts, but each part of the fountain directs the water in one direction. At the perimeter of the fountain are many small fountains or jets that propel water at a central fountain. At the base of the central fountain is a trough that catches some of the water from each jet and subsequently directs the water upward. The height of the water projected upward from the central fountain depends on the flow of water from the surrounding jets. The flow from this central fountain cascades down and ultimately returns to the small fountains, which recycle the water and continue the cycle by propelling more water at the central fountain.

The main (central) fountain is the core of gerontological discovery. It represents the basic findings of research on aging and the tenets of the gerontological imagination. It defines the field and thereby raises questions about the field of inquiry such as: What is gerontology? Why should gerontology be studied?

Each small fountain or jet represents a disciplinary approach to the study of aging. Although the disciplines are distinct, some are closer to one another than to other disciplines. The boundaries are blurred, but one may think of three main areas of discovery. The three areas with exemplary questions for gerontological discovery are:

- *Physical aspects of aging.* Why do we age? How does aging affect the body and the mind? Can the effects of aging be mitigated?
- *Social aspects of aging.* How does social context influence aging and life course development? How do history, culture, and biography intersect to create the life course?
- *Public policy.* What are the needs and interests of an older population? How are they created and addressed?

Although some may consider age-related public policy issues to be a subset of the social aspects of aging, this framework places public policy in a separate area to emphasize that it is shaped by information about the physical and social aspects of aging. Together, these three areas of gerontological inquiry define gerontological discovery and provide insight into a wide array of questions about the aging process and older people. Conversely, each discipline is subsequently influenced by the gerontological discovery generated by the flow of knowledge in the other areas. This continuous cycle creates the interdisciplinary flow of knowledge within the field of gerontology.

THE CONTRIBUTIONS OF SPECIFIC DISCIPLINES TO GERONTOLOGICAL DISCOVERY

Figure 1.2 extends the proposed conceptual framework by highlighting the core questions of gerontological discovery and offers some insight into the contributions of each discipline. The first row summarizes the core questions (shown in the rectangles) associated with each area of gerontological inquiry.

The second row of Figure 1.2 provides examples of specific topics that define aging scholarship (shown in the rounded rectangles). The topics are arranged on a continuum from micro-level to macro-level topics. By reading down the figure from top to bottom, you will notice that the specific topics correspond to the core questions listed in the first row. Questions about physical aspects of aging tend to deal with micro-level topics, questions about social aspects of aging span micro- and macro-level topics, and questions about age-related public policy tend to address macro-level topics. For example, the micro-level topics of cellular change, systemic change, disease, nutrition, and exercise address questions related to the physical aspects of aging. Disability, functional limitations, and mental health are at the nexus of questions about physical aging and how aging influences social functioning. Issues related to identity, personal meaning, roles, life events, transitions, and financial status address questions about the social aspects of aging. Topics related to social net-

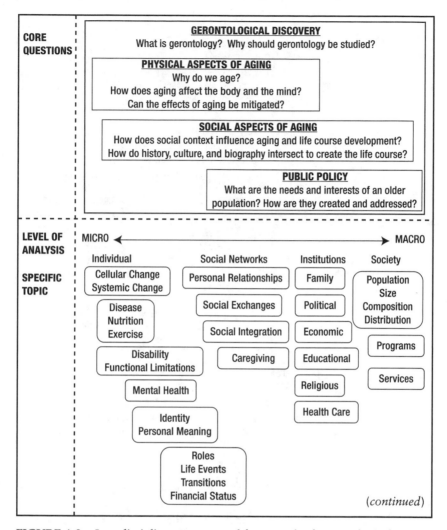

FIGURE 1.2   Interdisciplinary conceptual framework of gerontological inquiry: Core questions, specific topics, and disciplines engaged in those topics.

works typically address questions about social aspects of aging, although they can be used to address questions about age-related public policy. Conversely, more macro-level topics related to institutions and society often address age-related public policy questions but can be used to address questions about the social aspects of aging as well.

The third row of Figure 1.2 lists the disciplines that are, or could potentially be, engaged in gerontological discovery. Specific disciplines

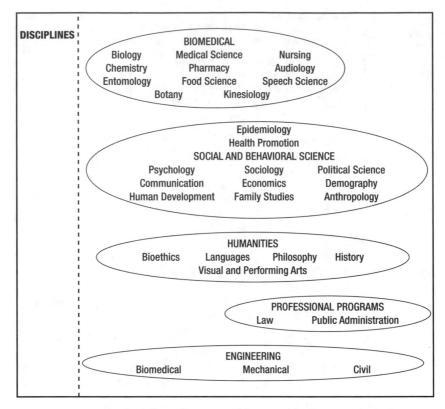

FIGURE 1.2 Interdisciplinary conceptual framework of gerontological inquiry: Core questions, specific topics, and disciplines engaged in those topics.

(shown in the ovals) are organized into five broad categories that reflect their location within academia. The placement of the disciplines across the row indicates the degree to which they are engaged in micro- or macro-level topics. Disciplines on the left side of the row tend to be engaged in micro-level topics, disciplines in the middle of the row address micro- and macro-level topics, and disciplines on the right side of the row tend to address macro-level topics. Of course, this graphical depiction is a simplification of the diversity that exists within a single discipline. Any one discipline can have a variety of subspecialties that study a range of micro- and macro-level topics. The intent of Figure 1.2, however, is to characterize the general type of contribution the discipline makes toward understanding the core questions of gerontology.

Reading down (or up) the entire length of Figure 1.2, from top to bottom (or from bottom to top), provides some insight into how different areas of academic inquiry make contributions to the aging enterprise.

For example, biomedical disciplines seek answers to questions regarding the physical aspects of aging. Specific disciplines, such as biology, chemistry, entomology, and botany, address micro-level topics regarding cellular and systemic change. Medical science, pharmacy, food science, and kinesiology are more concerned with topics such as disease, nutrition, exercise, and disability. Nursing, audiology, and speech science are also interested in topics such as disease and disability but often examine how those issues relate to social interactions.

The social and behavioral science disciplines address a range of micro- and macro-level topics that inform our understanding of the physical and social aspects of aging, as well as age-related public policy. Epidemiology and health promotion address biomedical concerns more than the other social and behavioral science disciplines by examining micro- and macro-level issues related to disease and prevention. Psychology and human development tend to be more micro in their orientation, addressing issues such as cognition or personality over the life course. At the other end of the continuum is demography, which is more macro in orientation given its concern about the implications of changing population age structure. The disciplines in the middle address a variety of micro- and macro-level topics depending on the specific subspecialty within the discipline. For example, a political scientist might be interested in the individual-level determinants of voting behavior or cross-national differences in the formation of income security programs.

The humanities also span micro- and macro-level topics but primarily address issues related to the social aspects of aging. History is an exception, given that it can be concerned with the historical development of age-related policy. Professional programs, such as law and public administration, tend to focus on macro-level issues related to the social aspects of aging and age-related public policy. Finally, engineering speaks to a variety of topics at the micro- and macro-levels. Biomedical engineers typically address micro-level topics regarding physical aging. Mechanical engineers often design products and civil engineers design environments that are more suited to the needs and functional capacity of older adults.

DEVELOPING AN INTERDISCIPLINARY UNDERSTANDING OF GERONTOLOGICAL TOPICS: AN EXAMPLE

This conceptual framework can be a powerful tool for developing an interdisciplinary understanding of specific gerontological topics. Consider, for example, how it could be used to highlight the disciplines that examine informal caregiving. Given that this topic falls under the area of social aspects of aging, the flow of knowledge about informal caregiving tends to come from disciplines in the social and behavioral sciences and the humanities. Psychologists are often interested in the mental health outcomes of providing care. Sociologists view caregiving as a social role that is constrained by competing demands and shaped by institutional arrangements. Economists are typically concerned with the costs of providing informal care and how care provision is related to other forms of intergenerational transfers. Demographers document the characteristics of care providers and care recipients. Anthropologists focus on understanding cross-cultural differences in caregiving. Scholars in the humanities explore the experience of providing care in written work, film, performances, and historical documents. In addition, select researchers in biomedical sciences, professional programs, and engineering address informal caregiving issues from their disciplinary perspectives. However, the flow of knowledge about informal caregiving from these disciplines is not as profuse. The knowledge generated about informal caregiving by the disciplines concerned with the social aspects of aging spills over into areas that are primarily focused on the physical aspects of aging and age-related public policy. This flow of ideas among academic disciplines provides rich insight into informal caregiving. It also contributes to our general understanding of aging and the development of gerontology as a field.

As the example demonstrates, this conceptual framework recognizes the knowledge generated by a specific discipline but shifts the focus toward developing an interdisciplinary understanding of aging issues that transcends disciplinary boundaries. It reminds us that no single discipline is equipped to fully address a particular age-related topic, but that various disciplines speak to specific issues and together provide a more complete understanding of aging.

IMPLICATIONS FOR DEVELOPING A DISCIPLINE

Instead of maintaining and reinforcing disciplinary boundaries, the proposed framework focuses on the core questions of gerontology and the topics of inquiry that address those questions. It recognizes the unique contributions of specific disciplines, but it also acknowledges that no single discipline can answer the core questions that gerontologists address. This conceptual framework cultivates the gerontological imagination by explicitly integrating knowledge from different disciplines (Ferraro, 1997).

Actively encouraging the development of this type of integrated intellectual view on aging is essential for the continued development of gerontology as a scientific field. Achenbaum (1995) noted that

Gerontology will continue to open new frontiers of knowledge as long as highly trained scholars are willing to cross the boundaries of their own scientific training and appreciate the rewards of broadening their fields of vision. (p. 268)

But as an emerging field, gerontology should not only entice promising scientists who have been trained in traditional disciplines to pursue age-related research agendas. We need to cultivate an interdisciplinary gerontological imagination among the "third generation of gerontologists" (Bass & Ferraro, 2000). By developing an appreciation of the rewards of this broader view earlier in their careers, future scholars of aging will be poised to make unique scientific contributions to, and advocate for institutional arrangements within academe that will lead to the development of gerontology as a new discipline.

REFERENCES

Achenbaum, W. A. (1995). *Crossing frontiers: Gerontology emerges as a science*. Cambridge: Cambridge University Press.

Atchley, R. C. (2000). *Social forces and aging: An introduction to social gerontology* (9th ed.). Belmont, CA: Wadsworth.

Bass, S. A., & Ferraro, K. F. (2000). Gerontology education in transition: Considering disciplinary and paradigmatic evolution. *Gerontologist, 40,* 97–106.

Belsky, J. (1999). *The psychology of aging: Theory research, and interventions* (3rd ed.). Pacific Grove, CA: Brooks/Cole.

Cavanaugh, J. C., & Blanchard-Fields, F. (2002). *Adult development and aging* (4th ed.). Belmont, CA: Wadsworth.

Cavanaugh, J. C., & Whitbourne, S. K. (1999). *Gerontology: An interdisciplinary perspective*. New York: Oxford University Press.

Cox, H. (2001). *Later life: The realities of aging* (5th ed.). Upper Saddle River, NJ: Prentice Hall.

Digiovanna, A. G. (2000). *Human aging: Biological perspectives* (2nd ed.). New York: McGraw-Hill.

Ferraro, K. F. (1997). *Gerontology: Perspectives and issues* (2nd ed.). New York: Springer Publishing.

Ferraro, K. F., & Chan, S. R. (1997). Is gerontology a multidisciplinary or interdisciplinary field of study? Evidence from scholarly affiliations and educational programming. In K. F. Ferraro (Ed.), *Gerontology: Perspectives and issues* (pp. 373–387). New York: Springer Publishing.

Gerontological Society of America. (2003). A brief history. Retrieved from http://www.geron.org/history.htm

Hooyman, N. R., & Kiyak, H. A. (2002). *Social gerontology: A multidisciplinary perspective* (6th ed.). Boston: Allyn and Bacon.

Kart, C. S., & Kinney, J. M. (2001). *The realities of aging: An introduction to gerontology.* Boston: Allyn and Bacon.

Matcha, D. A. (1997). *The sociology of aging: A social problems perspective.* Boston: Allyn and Bacon.

Morgan, L., & Kunkel, S. (2001). *Aging: The social context* (2nd ed.). Thousand Oaks, CA: Pine Forge.

Quadagno, J. (2002). *Aging and the life course: An introduction to social gerontology* (2nd ed.). New York: McGraw-Hill.

Quadagno, J., & Street, D. (1996). *Aging for the twenty-first century: Readings in social gerontology.* New York: St. Martin's Press.

Schultz, J. H. (2000). *The economics of aging.* Westport, CT: Auburn House.

CHAPTER 2

The Evolution of Gerontology as a Scientific Field of Inquiry

Kenneth F. Ferraro

Aging, like life itself, doesn't belong to one academic discipline. As an object of study, it is interdisciplinary by its very nature. . . . This is good for the students because truth is too big and gets caught in the cracks between disciplinary paradigms.

Charles F. Longino, Jr.

Gerontology as a field of study is a relatively recent phenomenon. Reflections on what it means to grow older as well as the search for youthfulness have been documented from the earliest historical records. The scientific study of aging, however, was not observed until about a century ago. Many disciplines such as biology, psychology, and sociology have long been interested in aging, but gerontology as a field draws from these and other disciplines to systematically study the aging process (Katz, 1996). In this chapter, I seek to describe how gerontology began and identify some of the key elements of its evolution during the 20th century.

At the heart of this inquiry is a question of how scholars view the aging process. What are the fundamental images of aging that have shaped scientific inquiry? Do gerontologists have a paradigm that helps define the field and articulate streams of basic and applied research? Are there concepts, principles, or approaches that scholars from varied disciplines share in the study of aging?

In considering these questions, it is important to note that paradigms—how scientists view their subject matter—are the product of a community of scientists seeking the cumulative development of knowledge on a subject. All too often, the human side of science is ignored, but science is more than theories, methods, and hypothesis testing; science is also shaped by social and political forces. Evans and Scott (1978, p. 711) helped illuminate these influences and to "bring humans back in" to our conceptions of scientific evolution. They remind us that

> it is easy to forget that science is also a congery of people, often acting out of personal pique or institutional jealousies having nothing to do with the "understanding of the nature of things." The politics of science is often as important a part of its history as the concepts produced.

My purpose is not to detail these social and political developments in gerontology over the past century. Achenbaum (1995) has already provided a splendid account of the history of this young science (see also Schaie & Achenbaum, 1993). Instead, the purpose is to briefly describe the evolution of the field in order to better understand the roots of an emerging paradigm on aging and why certain concepts and perspectives are given priority in this field of study.

METCHNIKOFF'S OPTIMISTIC GERONTOLOGY

It could be argued that the process of growing older has long been viewed in one of two basic ways. On the one hand, as evidenced in literature and some religions, aging has been considered an unpleasant phenomenon. A cursory review of famous quotations reveals the pessimistic view of aging (e.g., Giga Quotes, 2006). Marie Ebner-Eschenbach claimed that "age either transfigures or petrifies," and Swift stated that "every man desires to live long; but no man would be old." Advanced years have been seen by many as an empty success: the person survived but is left in a diminished state. According to Shakespeare, "when age is in, the wit is out." And in many minds, aging and dying are inseparable: "Old age is an incurable disease," wrote Seneca. For Buddha, old age, sickness, and death were closely related and exemplified suffering in life. Given these pejorative views of aging, it is not surprising that millions, including Ponce de Leon, have been looking for a fountain of youth. As Rowe and Kahn (1998) observed, the goal of aging for many people is to imitate youth.

On the other hand, history is replete with positive or noble images of growing older. Robert Browning, in the poem, "Rabbi Ben Ezra," exhorted, "Grow old along with me! The best is yet to be, the last of life, for which the first was made." Joubert asserted that "old age takes from the man of intellect no qualities save those that are useless to wisdom." Plato described a form of compensation with aging: "The spiritual eyesight improves as the physical eyesight declines." These voices acknowledge the many challenges of aging, but conclude that growing older is still a good thing.

Although both the negative and positive images of aging have been lodged in literature, philosophy, and religion for centuries, both of these views of aging have also been expressed to some degree in science, including medical science. Consider the perspective expressed in *The Household Physician*, published during the early 20th century (Buffum et al., 1929, p. 550):

> Growth, maturity, and decline are the three periods which divide and measure human life.
>
> During growth, the deposit of new matter takes place more rapidly than the decay or waste which is also going on.
>
> During healthy maturity, waste and increase are exactly equal, the one taking place just as rapidly as the other.
>
> The decline of old age reverses the order of growth, and waste outstrips addition. The newly deposited matter comes, but not so rapidly as it is cast away.

This text also characterized periods of the aging process ranging from "declining age" (50 to 60 years old) to the stage of "decrepitude or second infancy" (80 years old to the end of life).

Most contemporary gerontologists scoff at such descriptions of the aging process and characterizations of life stages. Those views are now not only regarded as inaccurate but with disdain, because the image of aging during the first half of the 20th century was often anchored in a decremental model. Recall, however, that only about 4 percent of the U.S. population was 65 years of age or older at the beginning of the 20th century. Indeed, if one examines human history around the globe, the demography of aging is qualitatively different now than it was in times past, and this demographic destiny has helped to fuel the engine of gerontology: the scientific study of aging.

Later life was widely viewed by scientists and physicians of the time as a period of major and inexorable decline in physical and mental function. A Russian-born zoologist and professor at the Pasteur Institute recognized the substance of the decline but led the early charge to question the inexorability of it. Elie Metchnikoff (1903) described old age as a period of time when "the body becomes an easy prey to pernicious influences and diseases" (p. 229), but he staunchly questioned the inevitability of old age as a period of decline. In many ways, he may be considered the father of gerontology, for he argued that "scientific study of old age and of the means of modifying its pathological character will make life longer and happier. Although modern knowledge is still imperfect, there is no reason to be pessimistic on the subject of old age" (p. 261). Metchnikoff was a realist but not a pessimist. The tenor of his book *The Nature of Man* was not that science needs to cure aging by stopping its progression, but that science can help the process of aging by both extending life and improving the quality of it.

It is not surprising that gerontology was born in Europe at the hands of Metchnikoff. Medicine was much more advanced in Europe than in the United States at the turn of the 20th century. European scientists such as Cheyne, Charcot, Morgagni, and Carlisle rapidly advanced the field of pathology, often by studying case histories of older patients. Metchnikoff's career was launched in Russia, but matured with scientists in Messina, Italy, and later in Paris (Achenbaum, 1995). He drew from these experiences to advance his own theory of how phagocytes (leukocytes) defend the body from acute infection. This work garnered praise from Virchow and Pasteur and set the stage for his later research.

Metchnikoff (1903) valued the later years of life and argued that a science of aging could pay huge dividends to humanity: "I think it extremely probable that the scientific study of old age and of death, two branches of science that may be called *gerontology* and *thanatology*, will bring about great modifications in the course of the last period of life" (pp. 297–298). Thus, Metchnikoff embraced the scientific progress in pathology and immunology but pushed for more direct interest in aging.

A later book, *The Prolongation of Life* (1910), developed Metchnikoff's theory of natural death, treating it as analogous to sleep. His thesis was not that biological declines rob the individual of life but that there is a death instinct: "It would be natural if, just as in sleep there is an instinctive desire for rest, so also the natural death of man were preceded by an instinctive wish for it" (p. 125). Metchnikoff saw aging and death as intertwined and that science should work to both understand the processes and intervene when appropriate. His theory of natural death was soon dismissed, and even his *Nature of Man* was harshly criticized (Small, 1904). Still, Metchnikoff left a legacy sufficient to launch gerontology. He felt there ought to be a science of aging—it deserved systematic study—and he was optimistic that it could serve humanity by extending and enhancing the second half of life.

TAKING ROOT IN AMERICA

I. L. Nascher (1909), a physician, sparked American interest in the systematic study of aging by naming a new medical specialty, *geriatrics*. He saw "senility," or old age, as a distinct phase of the life course that merited careful examination. Five years later, he published *Geriatrics: The Diseases of Old Age and Their Treatment, Including Physiological Old Age, Home and Institutional Care, and Medico-Legal Relations* (1914). He founded the New York Geriatrics Society in 1915. Although *Geriatrics* covered all of the topics described in its long title, over 80 percent of its pages were devoted to "pathological old age." Nascher saw old age as rife with disease, but he attempted to distinguish aging from disease processes. He also argued that social context was important to understanding aging, an insight that helped to launch geriatrics and gerontology in a multidisciplinary posture. In a sense, Nascher was echoing the axiom of Rudolph Virchow, the nineteenth-century German pathologist, that "medicine is a social science." Nascher's interest, however, was developing the field of geriatrics with sensitivity to what social science and social epidemiology could contribute.

In the next decade, G. Stanley Hall, a psychologist, played a pivotal role in establishing the field of gerontology in the United States. Hall was best known for his work *Adolescence*, published in 1904, but his interest in later life swelled over the years, culminating in the publication of *Senescence: The Last Half of Life* during 1922. The book also expressed Hall's personal reflections on aging—he was 78 years of age when *Senescence* was published (Achenbaum, 1995). Since then, scores of scientists, especially in psychology, have launched their careers by studying child development and moved on to studying later life during their middle or later years. (Recall that Metchnikoff's research interest in aging grew during middle age.) Hall (1922, p. vii) described his odyssey in the introduction:

> My own life work, such as it is, as a genetic psychologist was devoted for years to the study of infancy and childhood, then to the phenomena of youth, later to adulthood and the stage of sex maturity. To complete a long-cherished program I have now finally tried, aided by the first-hand knowledge that advancing years have brought, to understand better the two last and closing stages of human life.

The two last and closing stages of human life according to Hall were senescence, "which begins in the early forties, or before in woman," and "senectitude, the post-climacteric or old age proper" (p. vii). Hall developed his views on aging from the writings of some of Europe's best scholars interested in aging, most notably Charcot; his own personal observations; and "questionnaire returns" from "mostly eminent and some very distinguished old people, both acquaintances and strangers" (p. 321). Hall weaves both the pessimistic and optimistic views of aging into the book. On the one hand, he frequently laments life for "the old." "Disguise it as we will, old age is now only too commonly a hateful and even ghastly thing" (p. 195). He asserts that the period between 45 and 65 "has very new and great temptations" (pp. 24–25) because people are forced to confront their own finitude and the "great fatigue" (p. 366). On the other hand, Hall experimented with health promotion during his years of retirement and concluded that "old age may become the most satisfying and deeply enjoyable stage of life" (p. 379). He also suggests that aging may lead to a more optimistic orientation (p. 382):

> How different we find old age from what we had expected or observed it to be; how little there is in common between what we feel toward it and the way we find it regarded by our juniors; and how hard it is to conform to their expectations of us! . . . Instead of descending toward a deep, dark valley we stand, in fact, before a delectable mountain, from the summit of which, if we can only reach it, we can view the world in a clearer light and in truer perspective than the race has yet attained. It is all only a question of strength and endurance.

Thus, Hall inventoried a litany of physical and mental illnesses and peculiarities, but asserted that later life can be quite fulfilling, even liberating in some respects. Thomas Cole (1993) argued that this tension reflects the emerging dualism of gerontology that captured morbidity and frailty on the one hand, and wisdom and serenity on the other. Indeed, it could be argued that an essential component of the gerontological imagination is an awareness of the many challenges posed by growing older coupled with an appreciation for varied ways in which people face and adapt to the challenges.

THE INSTITUTIONAL SUBSTRATE

Achenbaum (1995) argued that much of gerontology's early growth was the result of a set of individuals exploring and raising interest in the systematic study of aging. Beginning in the 1930s, however, an institutional matrix developed to greatly accelerate the growth of gerontology. To begin, many foundations committed to research on social and behavioral aspects of human development were launched between 1905 and 1930 (e.g., Milbank Memorial, Carnegie, Rockefeller, and Kellogg). The year

1930 saw the establishment of both the National Institute of Health (later renamed the National Institutes of Health) and the Josiah Macy, Jr., Foundation. The early focus of most of these organizations was real-life problems, and much of the interest centered on child development (from infancy to youth). The Macy Foundation took a broader perspective, including the study of aging and the diseases of later life. In 1931, the foundation contacted Edmund Vincent Cowdry, an anatomist at Washington University, for scientific guidance on its philanthropic initiatives (Achenbaum, 1995). After several years of investigating arteriosclerosis and editing a handbook bearing that name, Cowdry suggested that the Macy leadership support the fledgling field of gerontology. The foundation agreed and did so in several ways.

While Cowdry was primarily interested in the biology of aging, especially the aging of tissue fluids, John Dewey, a board member of the Macy Foundation, argued for a more multidisciplinary approach to gerontology. Of course, a multidisciplinary approach was evident in the thinking of Nascher and Hall, but Dewey urged Cowdry to make sure it manifested itself at the foundation. Cowdry sought assistance in this endeavor, and Lawrence K. Frank, an economist, joined the foundation in 1936.

Cowdry (1939) edited the first systematic anthology for gerontology, *Problems of Ageing: Biological and Medical Aspects*, with the support of the Josiah Macy, Jr., Foundation. Lawrence Frank wrote the Foreword and Dewey the Introduction to the first edition. A good indication of Dewey's argument to link biological and cultural analyses is found in his introduction to *Problems of Ageing* (Cowdry, 1939, p. xxvi):

> Biological processes are at the roots of the problems and of the methods of solving them, but the biological processes take place in economic, political and cultural contexts. They are inextricably interwoven with these contexts so that one reacts upon the other in all sorts of intricate ways. We need to know the ways in which social contexts react back into biological processes as well as to know the ways in which the biological processes condition social life. This is the problem to which attention is invited.

Cowdry selected a distinguished set of contributors to review the extant body of knowledge. There were a couple of chapters on personality and psychological aspects, but the bulk of the book focused on anatomical systems. Thus, it possessed enough breadth to call it multidisciplinary—ranging from biology to demography—but the coverage of the social and behavioral sciences was modest. It became the major handbook for gerontology through several editions and demonstrated the interest in the biological and medical sciences. Most of its content was framed in a problem orientation, as manifest in its title. The problem orientation was not surprising given Cowdry's interest in the biology of aging and his previous book, *Arteriosclerosis* (1933). The problem orientation in the volume intensified in later editions as new chapters on arteriosclerosis and cancer were added (Lansing, 1952). Social and economic issues were covered more extensively in later editions, but again the emphasis was on the problems of aging.

While the problem orientation became strong after Cowdry's book, it is clear that some scholars of the time questioned the problem orientation (see, e.g., Lawton, 1943). Lawton's anthology included chapters by E. T. Hall ("Creative Urge in Older People") and his own "Aging Mental Abilities and Their Preservation." Lawrence Frank's (1946, p. 8) observation a few years later in the inaugural issue of the *Journal of Gerontology* was another indication that the study of aging should not focus on the problems of aging: "There is a widespread feeling of defeatism about old age as if the last years of life, the period of later maturity, were inevitably a barren, tragic time of decline and frustration."

It is clear that Cowdry eventually moved beyond the problem orientation as witnessed by the title of his book *Aging Better*, published in 1972. More generally, the field of gerontology made the transition from an orientation based on the premise that aging is a social problem to an orientation that aging is a topic for scientific investigation (Maddox & Wiley, 1976).

PARADIGM PIONEERS AND INSTITUTIONAL LEADERS

One year after the first edition of *Problems of Ageing* was published, the U.S. Public Health Service (PHS), with assistance from the Macy Foundation, hired a specialist for aging research. Edward Stieglitz held the position for only a year before Nathan Shock joined the PHS. Shock's studies in organic chemistry at Purdue University and in biochemistry and psychology at the University of Chicago prepared him well for discussing aging with scientists from a variety of fields. Shock soon became the director of the Gerontology Research Center, a position he held for over 30 years. He may be best known as the principal investigator of the Baltimore Longitudinal Study (BLSA), begun in 1958. He was a key actor in developing the intellectual and institutional fabric from which gerontology was woven.

Besides being an advocate for the systematic study of aging and directing the Gerontology Research Center at the National Institute on Aging (NIA), Shock's scientific contributions were paradigm defining. He was a prolific author, with over 350 publications. His research findings became some of the fundamental building blocks of the emerging paradigm for gerontology. Shock provided compelling evidence that all biological functions do not diminish with age (Shock et al., 1984), countering the problem orientation to the study of aging. Psychologists with the BLSA, especially Costa, McCrae, and Arenberg (1983), showed that there is considerable personality stability over the life course. Shock's distinguished career helped separate aging from disease processes and define what is now known as "normal aging." A few months before his death in 1989, Shock composed six axioms for aging research (Baker & Achenbaum, 1992, p. 262; see also Achenbaum, 1995).

1. Give me a testable hypothesis. It is worth a thousand theories.
2. Formulate questions to address basic mechanisms of aging and design scientifically rigorous protocols to examine those questions.
3. Focus research on the processes of aging over the entire life span. Studies on older individuals may tell one much about diseases in later life but are not likely to yield information about the basic mechanisms of aging.
4. Aging and disease are not synonymous. There are processes of aging and etiologies of disease. The relationships between the two are important but not inevitable.
5. Aging is a dynamic equilibrium. The rates of aging differ for various systems in any given organism, however, it is the whole organism that ages and dies.
6. Well-documented observations and good scientific data are timeless. Also, don't overlook studies in other scientific fields. Much of our knowledge in gerontology today is a by-product of nonaging research.

Some of these axioms reflect his view of science more generally, but all are instructive for understanding how he influenced the field and was influenced by it. Shock was undeniably a positivist who saw the importance of the cumulative development of science (Shock, 1951a). He welcomed cross-disciplinary research, especially if it was linked to the biological or medical sciences, but he also saw the need for social gerontology to grow. "Although research in the biological field, particularly on the cellular and biochemical aspects of aging, is in need of expansion, encouragement of research on the psychological and sociological aspects of aging is in even greater need of augmentation" (Shock, 1951b, p. 125). In both his intellectual and institution-building endeavors, his interest and passion was a life span perspective on normal aging, viewed as a dynamic equilibrium.

Perhaps the most paradigm-defining discovery in gerontology, especially biological gerontology, was derived from the work of Leonard Hayflick. After a two-year fellowship in infection and immunity at the

University of Texas Medical Branch at Galveston, Hayflick joined the Wistar Institute of Anatomy and Biology in 1958 (Achenbaum, 1995). The prevailing understanding of the time was that senescence occurred at the tissue and organ levels and that there was no intrinsic process to cause cell death. Hayflick and Morehead (1961) questioned this understanding through experiments on normal diploid human cells. They observed that regardless of the age of the donor, such cells could proliferate in culture only for a finite number of times; they have a limited capacity to divide and function. They described this work in a manuscript and submitted it to the prestigious *Journal of Experimental Medicine*. The manuscript was rejected, and one "reviewer commented, 'The inference that the death of cells . . . is due to "senescence at the cellular level" seems notably rash'" (Hayflick, 1994, p. 123). Apparently Hayflick and Morehead were pricking a sacred scientific cow.

Undeterred, they submitted the manuscript to *Experimental Cell Research*, which published it in 1961. It took years for the scientific community to accept the conclusion that cells are not immortal. The axiom had always been that it was aging per se that was related to cell structure and reproduction. Hayflick and Morehead (1961) showed that aging was not the cause of cell death, but that the number of passages such cells underwent was the key. In other words, there is a limit on the number of cell doublings in vitro, implying that there is a "clock" within cells governing longevity. The article is now considered a classic, for it showed that cell reproduction is governed by a process independent of changes occurring with time (Hayflick, 1965, 1994). Indeed, there are over 3,000 citations to the 1961 article (Hayflick & Morehead, 1961) and over 2,600 to the 1965 paper (Hayflick, 1965).

While Shock and Hayflick were key to developments in the biology of aging after World War II, interest in the social and behavioral science of aging grew during this time as well. The Committee on Human Development at the University of Chicago, launched during the 1930s, played a pivotal role in its ascendancy. Ruth Shonle Cavan, a sociologist, worked with Ernest Burgess, Robert Havighurst, and Herbert Goldhamer (all of the University of Chicago) to produce *Personal Adjustment in Old Age* (1949). Just as the Macy Foundation helped spur Cowdry's *Problems of Ageing*, the Social Science Research Council's Committee on Social Adjustment helped birth *Personal Adjustment in Old Age*.

Cavan and colleagues developed inventories to measure activities and attitudes of older people by studying over 3,000 subjects 60 years or older. The inventories garnered some use over the years, but one of the major contributions of the research was to define personal adjustment as a global but multifaceted phenomenon. Personal adjustment involves social activity, satisfaction with relationships, happiness, wish fulfillment, and "the absence of non-adjustive behavior" (Cavan et al., 1949, p. 103). (Nonadjustive behavior included psychopathology, irrational fears, and psychosomatic illness.) This was the first of several University of Chicago studies that sparked systematic interest in the social side of gerontology. It helped launch research on how social relationships change in later life, as well as the consequences of such changes for well-being. In the process, it helped build a social gerontology laboratory at the University of Chicago. A virtual who's who of social gerontologists worked at the university in the next decade, including Bernice Neugarten and Ethel Shanas, two of the first students to earn a doctorate from the Committee on Human Development.

In addition to community studies in the Chicago area, a collaborative undertaking in Kansas City proved to be quite consequential. The Kansas City Study of Adult Life was a team effort involving Burgess, Havighurst, Neugarten, and Shanas, as well as Everett Hughes, W. Lloyd Warner, and William E. Henry. While Havighurst and Neugarten emphasized the importance of activity to well-being, William Henry and Elaine Cumming focused on the process of disengagement. What emerged was the great debate in social gerontology, initially begun between University of Chicago investigators.

Cumming and Henry's (1961) controversial, almost inflammatory, theory of disengagement in *Growing Old* set the stage for the debate. They argued that disengagement was a normal and inevitable part of growing older. Social withdrawal was a natural response to the expectation of death and decreased ego energy. Havighurst, Neugarten, and Tobin (1968) countered that while it may be normal for some, it was clearly not inevitable. Disengagement was seen as an ageist theory because social withdrawal was viewed as satisfying and universal. Many chapters, articles, and books were oriented to discrediting disengagement theory during the 1960s and 1970s (e.g., Hochschild, 1975; Maddox, 1964). To call it a revolution in the structure of scientific thought on aging seems to inflate the scope of the tension, but social gerontology's fundamental image of study underwent serious change.

The year 1961 was an intellectual turning point for gerontology. During that year, Hayflick and Morehead published their classic work on cell reproduction and death, and Cumming and Henry published their book on disengagement. Both were greeted with concern, and some staunch skepticism, but each shaped the fledgling field of gerontology. Hayflick and Morehead's work was eventually accepted, while Cumming and Henry's was refuted. The concept of normal aging became the reigning view in the ensuing decade, creating a distinction between disease and simply growing older.

NORMALIZING AGING IN A
MULTIDISCIPLINARY FRAME

Two universities played major roles in shaping the emerging paradigm in a normal aging perspective and assuring that gerontology would span more than one or two disciplines. Ewald Busse led the charge at Duke University. Busse, a physician, studied central nervous system functioning in normal elderly patients at the University of Colorado until he moved to Duke in 1953 (Achenbaum, 1995). He established a University Council on Aging at Duke in 1955 and launched the Duke Longitudinal Studies of Normal Aging in the same year. Duke was also designated by NIH in 1957 as one of five regional centers for the study of aging.

Busse continued his investigation of the brain waves of elderly subjects in the Duke Longitudinal Studies and invited scientists from other fields to collaborate (Busse & Maddox, 1985). George Maddox and Erdman Palmore investigated social aspects of aging, while Ilene Siegler, Gail Marsh, and Robert Nebes investigated cognitive aspects of aging. Good science and the multidisciplinary approach meant that the studies attracted a distinguished array of graduate students and postdoctoral fellows to help anchor gerontology in the normal aging paradigm. What resulted was a reorientation to the study of aging as a normal process that entailed so much more than inexorable losses of function (Maddox, 1987). It became axiomatic that human aging poses problems and challenges, but that it also offers certain advantages to the individual and society (Palmore, 1979). Also with this shift came an emphasis on studying the process of aging, not just the characteristics of older people.

Besides the Duke influence, the University of Southern California played an important role in shaping the field of gerontology. James Birren worked under Nathan Shock at the Gerontology Research Center from 1947 to 1950 and later served as the chief of the division on aging at the National Institute of Mental Health. He moved to the University of Southern California in 1965 to build a center on aging. What began with a contract from the Rossmoor Corporation eventually turned into the Ethel Percy Andrus Gerontology Center with a major gift from the American Association of Retired Persons (Achenbaum, 1995). Birren maintained his research on the aging of the nervous system, but masterfully built the Andrus Center with solid links to the primary disciplines. As a result, USC's Andrus Gerontology Center was able to attract outstanding scholars at varying ranks and fashion a truly multidisciplinary program. Unlike Duke, USC created a distinctive model for gerontology education. The Leonard Davis School of Gerontology was one of the first universities to offer degrees in gerontology, rather than minors or options, and it emerged as the leading professional school for gerontology. The fact that students had to gain some mastery of biological, psychological, and sociological aspects of aging was significant in establishing those disciplines as pillars of the new field of gerontology.

Sociological analyses of aging were shaped in important ways by Matilda White Riley and colleagues, especially Anne Foner, at Rutgers University. A three-volume work, *Aging and Society*, published between 1968 and 1972, provided an inventory of research findings related to age and society (Riley, & Foner, 1968), identified links between aging and the professions (Riley, Riley, & Johnson, 1969), and sketched out the age stratification perspective (Riley, Johnson, & Foner, 1972). Riley argued forcefully for viewing aging as growing older—not growing old— and articulated that age is a property of social structures (Dannefer, Uhlenberg, Foner, & Abeles, 2005; Riley, 1987). In doing so, Riley et al. (1972) also linked aging to history: "Age also serves as an important link, on the one hand, between the individual and his biological life cycle and, on the other hand, between society and its history" (p. 4).

Matilda White Riley not only made important intellectual contributions to the study of aging, but also became NIA's first associate director for behavioral and social research (BSR) in 1979. For more than a decade, she directed the development of BSR, attracting many scholars to the scientific study of aging, especially the links between aging and society (Behavioral and Social Sciences Research Coordinating Committee, 2006).

INTELLECTUAL CAPITAL IN GERONTOLOGY?

By many standards, gerontology is a young field. Metchnikoff coined the name *gerontology* for this field of inquiry in 1903. Gerontology attracted attention from scholars around the globe and resulted in some important publications in the next four decades, especially Nascher's *Geriatrics* (1914), Hall's *Senescence* (1922), and Cowdry's *Problems of Aging* (1939). Gerontology also developed an institutional structure of support from private foundations and the federal government. Gerontology as a field, however, experienced its most rapid growth after World War II. The Gerontological Society of America (GSA) was created in 1946, and major initiatives to scientifically study aging were launched at the Gerontology Research Center of NIH and the Committee on Human Development at the University of Chicago. Further definition of the emerging paradigm during the 1950s and 1960s was evident by the work of Shock, Hayflick, Busse, Maddox, Birren, Riley, and Neugarten, to name a few.

The youth of the field and its vitality can be seen in a survey of its intellectual capital. GSA has grown to more than 5,000 members, and gerontology has established itself on college and university campuses around the world. The Association for Gerontology in Higher Education indicates that there are now over 1,000 educational programs identified with studies of aging, housed in over 500 institutions of higher education (Stepp, 2000). There are over 150 graduate gerontology education programs in the United States alone.

While GSA and other organizations have advanced gerontology during the past fifty years, the study of aging has also been merged into the institutional fabric of many disciplines as a recognized specialty. Sections of major professional societies are devoted to the study of aging (e.g., Division 20 of the American Psychological Association).

The creation of the NIA in 1975 was a watershed for the development of both gerontology and geriatrics. Given the obvious links between health and aging, NIA has supported a wide range of research projects and laboratories related to aging. Some of these initiatives have aging as a central focus, while others are more directly linked to specific diseases (e.g., Alzheimer's). Regardless, gerontology and geriatrics have prospered under NIH support, especially from the NIA.

Intellectual capital ultimately rests on a community of scholars: Achenbaum and Albert (1995) identified some of the leaders in the field of gerontology in a biographical inventory, providing brief profiles on about 300 key researchers, teachers, and practitioners on aging. A review of these profiles reveals the breadth of intellectual interests, ranging from molecular biology to social work. Notably, most of the gerontologists profiled, especially those who received their degree prior to 1980, received their training in a single discipline, often integrating what they could from related fields. Tomorrow's leaders may well have more experience in integrating information across the disciplines studying aging.

Publications are a major product of intellectual communities, and published reports on the science of aging have mushroomed since the 1970s. The Handbook of Aging series (originally published by Van Nostrand Reinhold) helped diagram the architecture of the field during the 1970s (Binstock & Shanas, 1976; Birren & Schaie, 1977; Finch & Hayflick, 1977). While the number of published monographs and anthologies on aging continues to grow, so have journals. Using recent issues of Magazines for Libraries, Table 2.1 displays over 60 journals related to gerontology and geriatrics created since 1946. The Gerontological Society of America (GSA) launched the Journal of Gerontology at the society's inception, which has evolved into four highly respected journals.

Scholarly interest in gerontology and geriatrics mushroomed during the mid-1970s. Indeed, 11 journals were created in the 1970s, and 31 journals were launched in the 1980s. (These numbers would be much higher if magazines and newsletters related to aging were also included.) The pace of growth is remarkable, and the breadth of disciplinary interests

TABLE 2.1   Inception of Gerontology/Geriatric Journals

Year	Journal Title
1946	*Journal(s) of Gerontology* *Geriatrics*
1951	*Aging*
1953	*Journal of the American Geriatrics Society*
1957	*Gerontologia/Gerontology*
1958	*Gerontology and Geriatrics*
1960	*Gerontologist*
1961	*Experimental Gerontology*
1962	*Journal of Geriatric Psychiatry*
1963	*Industrial Gerontology*
1964	*Aged Care and Services Review/Clinical Gerontologist*
1965	*Mechanisms of Ageing and Development* *Age and Ageing*
1973	*International Journal of Aging and Human Development*
1974	*Ageing International*
1975	*Experimental Aging Research* *Journal of Gerontological Nursing*
1976	*Educational Gerontology* *Generations*
1977	*Clinical Gerontologist*
1978	*Journal of Gerontological Social Work* *Aging and Work*
1979	*Research on Aging* *Journal of Clinical and Experimental Gerontology*
1980	*Journal of Nutrition for the Elderly* *Geriatric Nursing* *Aging* *Activities, Adaptation and Aging* *Gerontology and Geriatrics Education* *Neurobiology of Aging* *Physical and Occupational Therapy in Geriatrics*
1981	*Gerontology and Geriatrics Education* *Journal of Applied Gerontology* *Ageing and Society*
1982	*Archives of Gerontology and Geriatrics* *Geriatric Consultant* *Canadian Journal on Aging*
1983	*Journal of Housing for the Elderly*

(*continued*)

TABLE 2.1   Inception of Gerontology/Geriatric Journals (Continued)

Year	Journal Title
1984	*Journal of Religion and Aging* *Journal of Religious Gerontology*
1985	*Clinics in Geriatric Medicine* *Death Studies* *Gerodontics* *Topics in Geriatric Rehabilitation*
1986	*Journal of Geriatric Drug Therapy* *Loss, Grief, and Care* *Psychology and Aging*
1987	*Journal of Aging Studies*
1988	*Journal of Geriatric Psychiatry and Neurology* *Journal of Elder Abuse and Neglect* *Journal of Aging and Health* *Journal of Aging and Social Policy* *Journal of Aging Studies* *Journal of Women and Aging* *Behavior, Health, and Aging*
1993	*American Journal of Geriatric Psychiatry* *Assisted Living Today* *Contemporary Gerontology* *Journal of Aging and Physical Activity*
1995	*Journal of Mental Health and Aging* *Today's Caregiver*
1996	*Journal of Aging and Ethnicity*
2005	*Journal of Religion, Spirituality, and Aging*

Notes: Compiled from *Magazines for Libraries* (1992, 1995, 2004). Excluded are magazines, newsletters, electronic-only periodicals, or publications not indexed in one or more of the following: *Abstracts in Social Gerontology, AGELINE, Index Medicus, Physical Education Index, Psychological Abstracts, or Sociological Abstracts.*

is also impressive. The field has attracted scholars from many disciplines, and many of the more recent journals tend to be more specialized (e.g., *Gerodontics* and *Journal of Religion and Aging*). Some of the relatively recent journals manifest considerable interdisciplinary activity (e.g., *Journal of Aging and Health*), but others are more clearly based in a single discipline (e.g., *Psychology and Aging*).

As one surveys publications on the science of aging, funding sources for gerontological research, and gerontology programs in higher education, some conclusions are worth articulating here. First, there is bull-market orientation to the field of gerontology. With the demographic destiny facing modern nations, interest in this field is high. Gerontology has attracted scores of promising young and midlevel scientists, but is also attracting interest from more senior investigators. Although some of the more senior investigators may be lured by the appeal of funding for their research, many may also be experiencing the same phenomenon as Metchnikoff, Hall, and Dewey: a growing interest synchronized with their own sense of senescence. Whatever the case, the study of aging is valued, and it is attracting career investments from scientists of various fields.

Second, no one discipline owns gerontology. The field emerged from the biological and medical sciences, and three sections were identified in the GSA by-laws: medical research, biological research, and general (Achenbaum, 1995). There has always been strong interest in clinical medicine among the members, but the growth in the behavioral and social sciences has been dramatic, now accounting for about half of the membership of GSA (L. K. Harootyan to the author, January 2006). Although one should not put too much stock in membership numbers, it is clear that gerontology spans a number of disciplines. At the outset of the field, the disciplines coexisted in a multidisciplinary orientation, but there are ample manifestations of moving to a more interdisciplinary, or new discipline approach within the field.

Third, while a paradigm for gerontology is in the making, it has not yet been widely recognized. Nathan Shock's axioms for the study of aging showed that a paradigm was within reach. In previous editions of this book, I articulated what is meant by *gerontological imagination* (Ferraro, 1990, 1997). The elements of the emerging paradigm continue to be discussed and debated, most recently at the 2006 annual meeting of the GSA where the theme was "education and the gerontological imagination."

The tenets of what I refer to as the gerontological imagination reflect many of the themes and questions raised by Metchnikoff, Nascher, Shock, Busse, Riley, and others who pioneered the development of scientific research on aging. They are also manifest throughout this book. Indeed, the chapter authors were asked to emphasize how gerontologists think as they address the basic questions of aging research such as: Why do we age? How does aging affect the mind and the body? Can age-related changes be mitigated? What are the needs and interests of an older population? Answering these questions often requires expertise from more than one discipline, but how much expertise is enough to meaningfully reach beyond one's primary disciplinary training? The gerontological imagination is designed to identify the core of a paradigm for aging research and thereby set reasonable standards for interdisciplinary breadth (Bass & Ferraro, 2000).

GERONTOLOGICAL IMAGINATION

The gerontological imagination is an awareness of the process of aging that enables one to understand the scientific contributions of a variety of researchers studying aging. This awareness allows scholars in any field to comprehend the links among biological, behavioral, and social structural factors that influence aging. As such, it is consistent with the biopsychosocial model of human development and aging (Engel, 1996). Placing the information from the various disciplines in a larger context illuminates findings in a revealing way (Boyer, 1990). It also helps one to see the "disciplinary intersection" for the study of aging.

What intellectual ground is shared by gerontologists of varied disciplinary backgrounds? Do biologists and sociologist agree on anything besides the importance of studying aging? Do psychologists and economists share any intellectual capital as they study aging? I think there is common intellectual ground shared by scholars from such diverse fields of study, but it may not be readily apparent, especially for scholars new to the study of aging. I will mention the tenets that capture the interests of gerontologists briefly here and more systematically in the final chapter of this book. I ask readers to ponder these tenets throughout the book; then the final chapter can serve as a capstone for the emerging paradigm.

The gerontological imagination entails a multidisciplinary sensitivity to aging that incorporates the common stock of knowledge from the core disciplines engaged in research on aging. The basic elements of the gerontological imagination can be viewed as representative of a culture of scientific thinking on aging. There are seven key tenets:

1. *Causality.* Aging is not a cause of all age-related phenomena. Gerontology leads to a healthy skepticism for what are attributed to be "age" effects.
2. *Multifaceted Change.* Aging involves biological, psychological, and social changes in individuals at varying rates. The aging process is complex because it entails a host of biopsychosocial processes, including the expression of genes, the influence of social structures, and the functional capacity of the individual.
3. *Genetic Influences on Aging.* The imprint of genetics on aging is substantial. Genetics influences not only longevity but biological and behavioral processes across the life course.
4. *Heterogeneity.* Age is positively associated with heterogeneity in a population. Gerontologists understand the diversity of the older adult population, and this understanding is closely related to their skepticism about age effects.

5. *Cumulative Disadvantage.* Advantage can accumulate over the life course, thereby differentiating a cohort over time.
6. *Ageism.* There is a propensity toward ageism in modern societies whereby beliefs about aging tend to be disproportionately negative; ageism may also exist among older people or those who work with or for older people.
7. *Life Course Analysis.* Aging is a life-long process, and using a life course perspective helps advance the scientific study of aging.

These seven tenets of the gerontological imagination surface repeatedly throughout this book. Empirical evidence continues to illuminate and refine the tenets, showing that aging is much more than the "great fatigue." Gerontology has accomplished much in the past century, and the empirical evidence reveals that it can do much more. Contemporary gerontology sees aging as normal—distinct from pathology—and opens the door to optimizing the experience of growing older.

REFERENCES

Achenbaum, W. A. (1995). *Crossing frontiers: Gerontology emerges as a science.* New York: Cambridge University Press.

Achenbaum, W. A., & Albert, D. M. (1995). *Profiles in gerontology: A biographical dictionary.* Westport, CT: Greenwood.

Baker, G. T. III, & Achenbaum, W. A. (1992). A historical perspective of research on the biology of aging from Nathan W. Shock. *Experimental Gerontology, 27,* 261–273.

Bass, S. A., & Ferraro, K. F. (2000). Gerontology education in transition: Considering disciplinary and paradigmatic evolution. *The Gerontologist, 40,* 97–106.

Behavioral and Social Sciences Research Coordinating Committee. (2006). *Matilda White Riley, 1911–2004, Founding chair of BSSR CC.* Retrieved January 24, 2006, from http://obssr.od.nih.gov/bssrcc/MWR.htm

Binstock, R. H., & Shanas, E. (Eds.). (1976). *Handbook of aging and the social sciences.* New York: Van Nostrand Reinhold.

Birren, J. E., & Schaie, K. W. (Eds.). (1977). *Handbook of the psychology of aging.* New York: Van Nostrand Reinhold.

Boyer, E. J. (1990). *Scholarship reconsidered: Priorities of the professoriate.* Princeton, NJ: Carnegie Foundation for the Advancement of Teaching.

Buffum, H. E., Lovering, A. T., Warren, I., Small, A. E., Thorndike, W., Smith, J. H., et al. (1929). *The household physician.* Buffalo, NY: Brofly Press.

Busse, E. W., & Maddox, G. L. (1985). *The Duke Longitudinal Studies of Normal Aging, 1955–1980.* New York: Springer Publishing.

Cavan, R. S., Burgess, E. W., Havighurst, R. J., & Goldhamer, H. (1949). *Personal adjustment in old age*. Chicago: University of Chicago Press.

Cole, T. R. (1993). The prophecy of senescence. In K. Warner Schaie & W. Andrew Achenbaum (Eds.), *Societal impact on aging: Historical perspectives*. New York: Springer Publishing.

Costa, P. T., Jr., McCrae, R. R., & Arenberg, D. (1983). Recent longitudinal research on personality and aging. In K. W. Schaie (Ed.), *Longitudinal studies of adult psychological development*. New York: Guilford.

Cowdry, E. V. (Ed.). (1933). *Arteriosclerosis*. New York: Macmillan.

Cowdry, E. V. (Ed.). (1939). *Problems of ageing: Biological and medical aspects*. Baltimore: Williams & Wilkins.

Cowdry. E. V. (1972). *Aging better*. Springfield, IL: Charles C. Thomas.

Cumming, E., & Henry, W. E. (1961). *Growing old: The process of disengagement*. New York: Basic Books.

Dannefer, D., Uhlenberg, P., Foner, A., & Abeles, R. P. (2005). On the shoulders of a giant: The legacy of Matilda White Riley for gerontology. *Journal of Gerontology: Social Sciences, 60*, S296–S304.

Engel, G. L. (1996). From biomedical to biopsychosocial: I. Being scientific in the human domain. *Families, Systems and Health, 14*, 425–433.

Evans, R. B., & Scott, F. J. D. (1978). The 1913 International Congress of Psychology: The American Congress that wasn't. *American Psychologist, 33*, 711–723.

Ferraro, K. F. (Ed.). (1990). *Gerontology: Perspectives and issues*. New York: Springer Publishing.

Ferraro, K. F. (Ed.). (1997). *Gerontology: Perspectives and issues* (2nd ed.). New York: Springer Publishing.

Finch, C. E., & Hayflick, L. (Eds.). (1977). *Handbook of the biology of aging*. New York: Van Nostrand Reinhold.

Frank, L. K. (1946). Gerontology. *Journal of Gerontology, 1*, 4–8.

Giga Quotes. (2006). *Age*. Retrieved January 20, 2006, from http://www.giga-usa.com/index.html

Hall, G. S. (1904). *Adolescence: Its psychology and its relations to physiology, anthropology, sociology, sex, crime, religion and education*. New York: Appleton.

Hall, G. S. (1922). *Senescence: The last half of life*. New York: Appleton.

Havighurst, R. J., Neugarten, B. L., & Tobin, S. L. (1968). Disengagement and patterns of aging. In B. L. Neugarten (Ed.), *Middle age and aging* (pp. 161–172). Chicago: University of Chicago Press.

Hayflick, L. (1965). The limited in vitro lifetime of human diploid cell strains. *Experimental Cell Research, 37*, 614–636.

Hayflick, L. (1994). *How and why we age*. New York: Ballantine Books.

Hayflick, L., & Morehead, P. S. (1961). The serial cultivation of human diploid cell strains. *Experimental Cell Research, 25*, 585–621.

Hochschild, A. (1975). Disengagement theory: A critique and proposal. *American Sociological Review, 40*, 553–569.

Katz, S. (1996). *Disciplining old age: The formation of gerontological knowledge*. Charlottesville, VA: University of Virginia Press.

Lansing, A. I. (Ed.). (1952). *Cowdry's problems of ageing: Biological and medical aspects* (3rd ed.). Baltimore: Williams & Wilkins.

Lawton, G. (1943). *New goals for old age*. New York: Columbia University Press.

Maddox, G. L. (1964). Disengagement theory: A critical evaluation. *Gerontologist, 4*, 80–82.

Maddox, G. L. (1987). Aging differently. *Gerontologist, 27*, 557–564.

Maddox, G. L., & Wiley, J. (1976). Scope, concepts, and methods in the study of aging. In R. H. Binstock & E. Shanas (Eds.), *Handbook of aging and the social sciences*. New York: Van Nostrand Reinhold.

Magazines for libraries. (1992, 1995, 2004). New Providence, NJ: Bowker.

Metchnikoff, E. (1903). *The nature of man*. New York: Putnam.

Metchnikoff, E. (1910). *The prolongation of life*. New York: Putnam.

Nascher, I. L. (1909). Geriatrics. *New York Medical Journal, 90*, 358.

Nascher, I. L. (1914). *Geriatrics: The diseases of old age and their treatment, including physiological old age, home and institutional care, and medico-legal relations*. Philadelphia: P. Blakiston's Son & Co.

Palmore, E. (1979). Advantages of aging. *Gerontologist, 19*, 220–223.

Riley, M. W. (1987). On the significance of age in sociology. *American Sociological Review, 52*, 1–14.

Riley, M. W., & Foner, A. (1968). *Aging and society: Vol. 1. An inventory of research findings*. New York: Russell Sage Foundation.

Riley, M. W., Johnson, M., & Foner, A. (1972). *Aging and society: Vol. 3. A sociology of age stratification*. New York: Russell Sage Foundation.

Riley, M. W., Riley, J. W., Jr., & Johnson, M. (Eds.). (1969). *Aging and society: Vol. 2. Aging and the professions*. New York: Russell Sage Foundation.

Rowe, J. W., & Kahn, R. L. (1998). *Successful aging*. New York. Pantheon.

Schaie, K. W., & Achenbaum, W. A. (Eds.). (1993). *Societal impact on aging: Historical perspectives*. New York: Springer Publishing.

Shock, N. W. (1951a). *A classified bibliography of gerontology and geriatrics*. Stanford, CA: Stanford University Press.

Shock, N. W. (1951b). *Trends in gerontology*. Stanford, CA: Stanford University Press.

Shock, N. W., Greulich, R. C., Costa, P. T., Jr., Andres, R., Lakatta, E. G., Arenberg, D., et al. (1984). *Normal human aging: The Baltimore Longitudinal Study of Aging*. Washington, DC: U. S. Department of Health and Human Services.

Small, A. W. (1904). A review of *The nature of man*. *American Journal of Sociology, 9*, 580, 582.

Stepp, D. D. (2000). *Directory of educational programs in gerontology and geriatrics* (7th ed.). Washington, DC: Association for Gerontology in Higher Education.

CHAPTER 3

Demographic Perspectives on Aging

Janet M. Wilmoth
Charles F. Longino, Jr.

In order to understand the contribution demography of aging makes to gerontological inquiry, it is necessary to first appreciate the subject matter of demography. Demography is the scientific study of human populations. Similar to gerontology, it is a both a multidisciplinary and interdisciplinary endeavor that encompasses a variety of disciplines, including sociology, economics, statistics, geography, and anthropology. Formal demographers are primarily concerned with documenting the changing size, age-sex structure, and geographic distribution of the population, which are influenced by fertility, mortality, and migration rates. For example, a formal demographer might examine how shifts in the causes of mortality influence the age structure of a population. Social demographers focus on the social causes and consequences of demographic trends. For example, a social demographer might consider how the changing age structure of a population alters intergenerational relationships.

Both formal and social demographers employ empirical methods of inquiry that rely on data from vital statistic registries, censuses, and surveys. Often demographers analyze secondary data, which have been collected by another researcher or agency. But, they also collect primary data using standard social science research methods. Traditionally demographic data collection and analysis has relied primarily on a quantitative approach. However, qualitative methodologies are increasingly used, particularly mixed-modes of inquiry that combine qualitative and quantitative methods.

Although issues related to the age structure of the population are an inherent part of demographic inquiry, the demography of aging did not begin to emerge as a distinct subfield until the second half of the 20th century, when low fertility and mortality rates were creating dramatic shifts in the age structure of developed countries. Demographers who began to consider the causes of this shift demonstrated that, contrary to popular notions, the aging of the population was influenced more by changes in fertility rates than dropping mortality rates (Coale, 1964). By 1980, demographers were studying various age-related topics in sufficient depth for Jacob Siegel to devote his presidential address to the Population Association of America to the topic of demography of aging, which he indicated "brings demographers to focus holistically on a population group, the elderly, and a demographic process, aging" (Siegel, 1980, p. 345).

By 1980, researchers in the demography of aging were in the early stages of defining old age and aging, documenting changes in the age structure, identifying mortality trends, describing the health status of older adults, explaining the geographic distribution and mobility of older adults, understanding the life course and cohort flow, and exploring living arrangements, family support, and retirement trends (Siegel, 1980). Although these continue to be topics of interest, demographers have become increasingly concerned with the implications of population aging in developed and developing countries, particularly as it relates to social transfer programs, social institutions such as the economy and the family, and the overall quality of life for different age groups (e.g., children, working-age adults, older adults) (Preston & Martin, 1994).

The remainder of this chapter briefly reviews what is known about population aging worldwide and the demographic characteristics of the older population in the United States. This is not intended to be a comprehensive review of the literature in the demography of aging but rather illustrative of the contributions demography makes to gerontological inquiry.

POPULATION AGING WORLDWIDE

Formal Demography Perspectives

The first contribution demography makes to gerontology is documenting worldwide trends in population aging. Demographic transition theory explains the shifting fertility and mortality rates that accompany economic development (Teitelbaum, 1975). This transition has three distinct phases. The first is characterized by high, fluctuating mortality rates and high, stable fertility rates. Under such demographic circumstances, the age structure of the population is young, and life expectancy at birth is low. In the second phase, mortality rates begin to drop, particularly among children and childbearing-age women. Infectious disease rates drop, and life expectancy at birth increases. Drops in fertility typically lag behind reductions in mortality, causing population growth and a reduction in the average age of the population. The final stage of the demographic transition is characterized by additional improvements in mortality, particularly mortality related to man-made (e.g., cardiovascular disease and cancer) and degenerative diseases that disproportionately affect older adults. Fertility fluctuates but remains low, often below replacement levels (i.e., total fertility rate below 2.1 children per woman). It is during this last stage that the population ages. Specifically, the average age of the population increases as the proportion of the population that is older increases. There is emerging evidence that this stage has been followed by a reemergence of infectious disease, particularly in developing countries (Cook & Dummer, 2004).

Historical evidence suggests this demographic transition occurred slowly in most developed countries as the industrial revolution spurred economic development that raised the standard of living. Consequently developed countries, particularly in Western Europe and North America, experienced gradual population aging during the second half of the twentieth century. The highest rates of growth in developed countries among the older adult population (ages 65 and over), which were approximately 2.5% per year, occurred in the late 1960s and early 1970s (United Nations, 1999). In contrast, developing countries are going through this demographic transition at a quicker pace. Consequently, their populations are projected to age at a more rapid rate. The annual growth in the older adult population in developing nations is expected to be over 4% by 2020 (United Nations, 1999). Currently, relatively wealthy industrialized nations with well-developed welfare states in Europe and North America have populations with the greatest percentage of older adults. However, those percentages are increasing rapidly in developing countries, particularly in Asia and South America (see Table 3.1).

The aggregate percentages shown in Table 3.1 mask the variation in the percentage of the population ages 65 and over across specific countries. For example, Japan's population is already quite old: 17% of the population was age 65 or older in 2000, and 34.3% is projected to be elderly by 2050. In contrast, only 3% of Cambodia's population was age 65 or older in 2000, and that percentage will increase to only 9.9% by 2050 (U.S. Census Bureau, 2004). There is also considerable variation in the distribution of older adults within specific countries. Urbanization, a

TABLE 3.1   Percentage of the Population Ages 65 and Older

	2000	2025	2050
World total	6.9	10.7	16.6
Developed countries	14.3	21.0	26.2
Developing countries	5.1	8.7	15.1
Regions			
Europe	14.7	21.2	28.7
North America	9.9	14.9	19.3
South America	5.8	10.8	19.7
Oceania	10.1	15.1	20.1
Asia	5.9	10.1	17.7
Africa	3.2	4.3	6.9

Source: U.S. Census Bureau (2004).

hallmark of economic development, has affected the distribution of young and older adult populations in developed and developing countries. Approximately two-thirds of older adults live in urban areas in developed countries compared to one-third in developing countries (United Nations, 1991). The percentage of the older adult population living in urban areas is increasing worldwide, but the rate of increase is occurring fastest in Asia.

Table 3.1 also does not convey the magnitude of increase in the number of older adults many countries will experience. For example, the percentage of Brazil's population age 65 and older will increase from 5.3% to 21.9% between 2000 and 2050, which corresponds to an increase from approximately 9 million older adults to over 50 million older adults (U.S. Census Bureau, 2004). But Table 3.1 does demonstrate the dramatic aging of the world population that will continue throughout the twenty-first century.

Another contribution demographers make to gerontology is documenting national changes in mortality, morbidity, and disability. Mortality rates are related to life expectancy. Life expectancy at birth is currently 76 years in developed countries and 65 in developing countries, although there is substantial variation across regions and specific countries. Life expectancy at birth is quite low in African countries, such as Sierra Leone and Zambia where it is 35 years, and consistently high in European countries, like Norway, Sweden, and Italy where it is 80 years, and some Asian countries, most notably Japan where it is 82 years (Population Reference Bureau, 2004). Improvements in life expectancy at birth have been slowing, particularly in developed countries, as the gains due to improved standards of living and health care have been realized and mortality rates due to infectious disease have decreased. However, in many countries, improvements in life expectancy at age 65 continue as mortality rates among the oldest old decline (U.S. Census Bureau, 2004). Life expectancy at age 65 tends to be highest in developed countries with more equitable wealth distributions, a higher percentage of gross domestic product that is allocated to old age benefits and health care expenditures, and lower rates of tobacco consumption (Munnell, Hatch, & Lee, 2004).

Increasing life expectancy, particularly at age 65, raises questions about the quality of life during these additional years lived. Are older adults living longer, healthier lives, or living longer in poor health? The answer to this question depends on healthy life expectancy, which is a function of mortality, morbidity, and disability. Healthy life expectancy is the number of years lived, on average, without disease or functional limitations. It increases when improvements in morbidity and disability keep pace with, or exceed, improvements in mortality. In this scenario, morbidity is compressed into a shorter period of the life span such that older adults, on average, live longer and in better health.

Estimates of healthy life expectancy are typically based on calculations of active (or disability-free) life expectancy, which are derived from cross-sectional (Sullivan, 1971) and longitudinal methods (Rogers, Rogers, & Belanger, 1990; Laditka & Wolf, 1998). Although considerable strides have been made in understanding changes in healthy life expectancy over the past 10 years, it is difficult to make cross-national comparisons due to differences in concepts, definitions, measures, and computational techniques across studies. The Global Burden of Disease Study attempts to overcome some of these limitations by using various data sources to estimate regional differences in mortality and disability (Murray & Lopez, 1996). The data suggest that there is a positive relationship between mortality and disability; regions such as subSaharan Africa, Latin America, India, and Asia (excluding China and other established market economies) that have the highest mortality rates also have high disability rates. Consequently, these regions tend to have the lowest levels of disability-free life expectancy, even after adjusting for disability severity (Murray & Lopez, 1997a). There is also emerging evidence based on a variety of published studies that disability rates among older adults in industrialized countries are declining (Waidmann & Manton, 2000).

Overall, the evidence supports the compression of morbidity hypothesis. However, the future prospects for continued disability decline are unclear, although a shift in the causes of disability is likely. Murray and Lopez (1997b) project that disability due to infectious and parasitic diseases will drop, while those due to noncommunicable diseases like cancer, heart disease, and neuropsychiatric disorders will increase. This shift will be particularly noteworthy in developing countries that are experiencing rapid population aging.

Social Demography Perspectives

The increase in the percentage and number of older adults worldwide raises various questions about the consequences of population aging. Social demographers have attempted to address a range of issues related to population aging with international data (Martin & Kinsella, 1994). Two commonly addressed topics related to international population aging are the need for informal and formal care provision and the economic implications of an aging population.

Informal and Formal Care Provision

Worldwide the family is a primary source of support for older adults, providing material, instrumental, and emotional assistance. One area of extensive demographic research related to family support is older adult living arrangements. This research indicates that multigenerational households are more common, and living alone is less common, among older adults in Asia, Central and South America, and Eastern Europe than in Western Europe or North America (De Vos, 1990; Knodel & Ofstedal, 2002; Wolf, 1990, 1995). Although the percentage of older adults living alone tends to increase over time as a country experiences economic development, the variation in older adult living arrangements across countries is not simply due to the stage of a country's development. It can be attributed to cultural and religious beliefs that shape intergenerational relationships, norms pertaining to the appropriate living arrangement of older adults, the availability of housing, and the level of state-supported social services (Logan, Bian, & Bian, 1998; Markides & Mindel, 1987; Sokolovsky, 1990).

Demographers have also systematically considered the influence of modernization on the availability of family members as care providers. Several social changes that accompany modernization can undermine traditional family care arrangements. For example, later marriage and delayed childbearing substantially alter family structure by decreasing the number of family members in each subsequent generation. In addition, the number of generations within families increases due to mortality improvements (Bengston, Rosehthal, & Burton, 1995). The net result is fewer younger family members to care for an increasing number of older family members. Numerous studies across various cultures consistently indicate women are the "kin keepers" within families, doing the everyday work required to maintain family relationships and providing direct personal care to family members (Hagestad, 1986). However, the number of available female care providers is reduced by women's increased labor force participation, which diverts women's time and energy away from traditional caregiving roles. Urbanization further reduces the availability of family caregivers by enticing younger family members to move from rural to urban areas in search of employment opportunities. This internal migration tends to leave older family members behind in rural areas to age in place, with occasional monetary provisions, but no personal care support, from children.

These fundamental shifts in the availability of family care providers, particularly female care providers, increase the need for more formal care options in the community (e.g., community-based services for older adults) and institutionalized settings (e.g., assisted living and nursing homes). Cultural norms regarding the role of family members in providing care begin to change, and increasing pressure is placed on the public sector to develop alternative care arrangements. The exact form of these public care arrangements varies across countries, depending primarily on the organization and financing of long-term care services (Ribbe et al., 1997). Regardless of the type of public care programs available to older adults, the expansion of public programs that subsidize or directly provide formal care raises concerns about the economic implications of increasing public expenditures for elder care.

The concerns about the increasing cost of elder care are due in part to the cost of health care. Although there is no clear relationship between age and the general use of health care, there is a stronger relationship between age and hospitalization (Martin & Kinsella, 1994). Thus, the growth of the older adult population is likely to increase demand for hospital-based care as the absolute number of people who need to be served increases. In addition, the demand for treatment of noncommunicable diseases and chronic conditions is likely to increase (Murray & Lopez, 1997b). This type of care is typically more technologically intensive and occurs over a longer period of time, which also will contribute to increased health care costs. Given that the health care systems in many developing countries have been organized to address infectious disease and conditions that affect children and childbearing-age women, considerable resources will have to be devoted to developing health care services that meet the needs of older adults (Ofstedal et al., 2002). Thus, it is expected that the costs of providing care to older adults will increase as the population ages, family structure continues to shift, the public sector becomes more involved in care provision, and health care services for older adults are expanded.

Economic Implications of Population Aging

Many social scientists assert that population aging will lower economic growth for a variety of reasons, including increasing public debt, a shrinking labor force, labor shortages, rising wages, erosion of the workforce skill base, a drop in the pace of living standard improvements, and lower rates of saving and investment (England, 2002; Hateley & Tan, 2003). However, the projected negative impact of population aging on economic growth is not inevitable. This economic slowdown could be offset by high labor force participation rates, productivity gains (particularly gains due to the new economy related to information technology), increased foreign investment on the part of developed nations, stabilization of national debt, and reform of public pension systems (England, 2002).

Many demographers challenge the notion that population aging leads to slower economic growth. Mullan (2000) argues that the precise mechanisms through which population aging effects economic growth are rarely explicated, calling into question the validity of the causal connection between population aging and slowing economic growth. This notion of a weak causal connection is supported by research that shows no historical evidence that population aging has slowed economic growth in advanced industrialized nations (Easterlin, 1991; Mullan, 2000). Despite dire predictions, which are often used to justify dismantling the welfare state, a National Research Council panel chaired by economist F. Thomas Juster concluded there is "ample reason to believe that nations will be able to cope with current and projected demographic changes provided policy makers have access to information about the emerging economic and social forces that will shape future society well-being" (National Research Council, 2001, p.17). Thus, while some researchers warn of the potential negative economic impact of population aging, demographers tend to emphasize the malleability of outcomes.

DEMOGRAPHIC CHARACTERISTICS OF THE OLDER ADULT POPULATION IN THE UNITED STATES

Formal Demography Perspectives

Another contribution of demography to gerontological inquiry is that it documents in detail the trends in population aging that have occurred in the United States. These demographic facts are often used by gerontologists to justify researching a particular age-related topic. For example, increases in the number and percentage of the population age 65 and older are commonly cited in gerontological research. As shown in Figure 3.1, the population age 65 or older in the United States increased from roughly 3 million in 1900 to nearly 35 million in 2000, and it is projected to almost triple to approximately 90 million by 2060. More important, the percentage of the population age 65 or older increased from 4.1% in 1900 to 12.4% in 2000 and will be over 20% by 2060 (Himes, 2001).

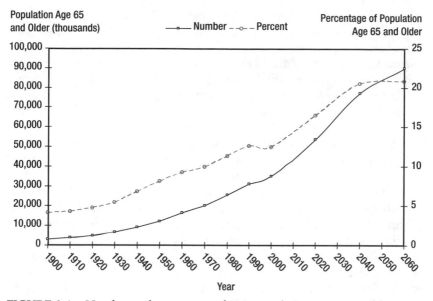

Population Age 65 and Older (thousands)   ——□—— Number – –○– – Percent   Percentage of Population Age 65 and Older

Year

FIGURE 3.1   Number and percentage of U.S. population age 65 or older, 1900–2060.

Source: Himes (2001).

Furthermore, the fastest-growing segment of the older adult population is among the oldest old, who are age 85 and over. The percentage of older Americans who are age 85 and older increased from only 5% in 1900 to 12% in 2000, and is expected to increase to 23% by 2050 (Himes, 2001).

The older adult population in the United States is not equally distributed across geographic areas. Some areas of the United States, including parts of the Midwest and Northeast, have high concentrations of older adults due to the out-migration of young adults and the aging in place of older adults. Other areas of the United States, notably states in the southeastern and western regions such as Florida, California, Arizona, Texas, and North Carolina, are popular destination states for older migrants (Longino & Bradley, 2003). These demographic processes place different demands on programs and services offered to older adults in particular local areas.

There have been substantial decreases in mortality and concurrent increases in life expectancy in the United States. Life expectancy at birth is now 74.3 years for men and 79.7 for women (National Vital Statistics, 2004). Similar to the concerns expressed about worldwide improvements in life expectancy, these trends have raised questions about the quality of these added years among older Americans. Are Americans living longer lives in better health, or living more years in worse health? In answering these questions, demographers have focused on documenting morbidity and disability among older adults with a variety of nationally representative data sets, including the Longitudinal Study on Aging, the National Health and Nutrition Examination Surveys, the Established Populations for Epidemiological Studies of the Elderly, and the Health and Retirement Study/Assets and Health Dynamics Among the Oldest-Old.

The leading causes of death in the United States continue to be due to degenerative diseases associated with aging, include heart disease, cancer, and stroke (Centers for Disease Control, 2003). Although Alzheimer's disease is not a leading cause of death, it currently affects up to 4 million Americans, and its prevalence increases systematically with age (Sloane et al., 2002). Chronic conditions are generally not immediately life threatening, but they do increase the risk of functional limitations and mortality over time. Approximately 105 million Americans have a chronic condition, the most common of which are arthritis, hypertension, hearing impairments, heart disease, diabetes, and cataracts (Robert Wood Johnson Foundation, 1996). Almost 45% of older adults are limited in activities because of a chronic condition (National Academy on an Aging Society, 1999)

Recent evidence suggests there have been improvements in some types of functioning (i.e., instrumental activities of daily living and functional limitations) among older Americans (Freedman, Martin, & Schoeni, 2002). But it is unclear whether these observed trends will continue for future cohorts. Given the uncertainty about disability trends, we do not have a clear understanding of recent or future changes in active life expectancy among older Americans. There is agreement that the percentage of active life decreases with age, is higher for men than women, and varies between and within race/ethnic groups (Crimmins, Hayward, & Satio, 1996; Hayward & Heron, 1999; Manton & Stallard, 1991). However, estimates of active life expectancy in the American population vary across studies, and there is some speculation that older adults may be surviving longer than expected without serious disability (Manton & Land, 2000). Overall, demographic research on the health of older adults suggests Americans are living longer in better health.

Social Demography Perspectives

A core concept in gerontology is heterogeneity among the older adult population, which is substantiated by demographic research on gender, racial, ethnic, and socioeconomic variation among older Americans. Demographic research also makes a contribution to gerontology by systematically considering the consequences of population aging in the United States, particularly as it relates to labor force participation and retirement, family ties, and intergenerational transfers.

Demographic Variation Among Older Adults

In terms of gender, the ratio of men to women in later life is quite unbalanced and decreases dramatically with age. Due to gender differences in mortality rates, there are 70 males for every 100 females over the age of 65. Among those age 85 and older, there are only 41 males for every 100 females (U.S. Census Bureau, 2000a). Consequently, many of the issues that gerontologists are interested in studying are disproportionately experienced by women whose life course experiences shape their later life outcomes, including health conditions, economic status, and social relationships.

Demographic research has demonstrated that these outcomes also vary by race and ethnicity. The older U.S. population is increasingly racially and ethnically diverse: 83% is currently non-Hispanic White, but only 64% will be by 2050. Although the representation of all minority groups is increasing among the older adult population, rates of growth are fastest among older Hispanic and Asian populations. For example, in 2000, 5.6% of adults aged 65 and older were Hispanic; that percentage will increase to 16.4% by 2050. Over the same period, the percentage of older adults who are Asian will increase from 2.4% to 6.5% (Federal Interagency Forum on Aging-Related Statistics, 2000). This growth is due primarily to immigration trends, including the shift in immigrant streams to Latin American and Asian countries, changing preferences for entry into the United States based on family status, and increases in the number of immigrants age 60 or older.

Demographers have noted that some of the differences in later-life outcomes across race and ethnic groups can be attributed to differences in socioeconomic status. One indicator of socioeconomic status is educational attainment. Although the percentage of older adults with a bachelor's degree or high school diploma increased from 20% in 1950 to over 60% by 1998, nonHispanic White older adults are more likely to have completed high school (72%) than African American (42%) or Hispanic (29%) older adults (Federal Interagency Forum on Aging-Related Statistics, 2000). Given the close connection between education attainment and income, it is not surprising that non-Hispanic White older adults are less likely to be in poverty, and have more wealth in later life, than other race and ethnic groups. For example, although poverty rates among older adults have decreased in the past 40 years, over 20% of the Black and Hispanic older adult population is in poverty compared to only 8% of nonHispanic White and Asian older adults (U.S. Census Bureau, 2002). The median total wealth among nonHispanic White older adult is approximately $350,000, while for Black and Hispanic older adults, it is approximately $230,000 and $199,000, respectively (Choudhury, 2003). At all income and educational levels, nonHispanic White older adults are more likely than minority older adults to own a variety of assets, including high-risk investments that can yield higher returns (Choudhury, 2003). Perhaps more important, there is evidence that economic disparities across racial and ethnic groups are increasing (Utendorf, 2002). This demographic variation among the older adult population sets the stage for diversity in the aging experience, which is documented by a variety of gerontologists.

Labor Force Participation and Retirement

Over the past 50 years, labor force participation among middle-aged and older men has dropped, while for middle-aged and older women, labor force participation has increased (Federal Interagency Forum on Aging-Related Statistics, 2001). For both men and women, the age at retirement has declined. Among men, the average age at retirement decreased from over 67 years in 1950–1955 to 62 years in 1995—2000. Among women, that average decreased from almost 68 years to approximately 62 years over the same time period (Gendell, 2001). Interestingly, there is evidence that the average age at retirement is younger than the average age of first receipt of Social Security benefits, particularly for African Americans (Gendell & Siegel, 1996; Hayward, Hardy, & Grady, 1989). These trends have encouraged social demographers to consider the factors that influence retirement decisions, particularly the incentives for early retirement that are built into Social Security and defined benefit employer pension plans (Quinn & Burkhauser, 1994).

This trend toward early retirement, in combination with increasing life expectancy, has substantially increased the average number of years retirees collect benefits: for men, the average life expectancy at the median age of retirement in the early 1950s was 12 years but had increased to 18 years by the late 1990s, and among women, the average life expectancy at the median age of retirement increased from nearly 14 years to 22 years during the same time period (Gendell, 2001). However, there is disagreement over whether these trends will continue. Some economists indicate that the trend toward early retirement, which has been flat since 1985, is starting to reverse due to changes in private and public sector policies (Clark & Quinn, 2002). Others suggest early retirement will continue to be an attractive and affordable option for many older adults (Costa, 1998). Demographers speculate that even if age at retirement were to remain stable or increase somewhat, the average length of retirement is likely to increase due to projected improvements in life expectancy (U.S. Census, 2000b). This will place additional pressure on the Social Security system by increasing the number of years payments are made to recipients at the same time that the ratio of recipients to workers paying into the system is declining. Therefore social demographers, whether they are formally trained as economists or in other social science disciplines, contribute to our understanding of past and future retirement trends among older Americans. In doing so, they provide insight into potential policy options for addressing the fiscal challenges faced by Social Security.

Family Ties

Given that family members are a primary source of support to older adults, social demographers are also concerned with documenting family ties and considering how demographic changes are restructuring American families in ways that could alter the support provided to older adults. Most demographic research in this area, which is typically conducted by researchers with training in sociology, indicates the majority of older Americans are embedded in a web of family relationships despite the increasing propensity to live independently.

Over the twentieth century, the percentage of older Americans living with family declined dramatically. This trend toward independent living is often attributed to preferences for living alone that have been realized through the improved economic and health status of the older population, as well as changes in norms and values concerning nonfamily living arrangements (Kramarow, 1995; Michael, Fuchs, & Scott, 1980). Another contributing factor is improvement in life expectancy, which has increased the percentage of older adults who are married (and therefore living with a spouse). Approximately 73% of older men live with a spouse, and 17% live alone. Among older women, approximately 41% live with a spouse, and 41% live alone (Federal Interagency Forum on Aging-Related Statistics, 2000). The likelihood of living alone tends to be lower among older adults who are minority group members or immigrants, are in poorer health, have fewer financial resources, and have more children (Angel, 1991; Himes, Hogan, & Eggebeen, 1996; Soldo, Wolf, & Agree, 1990; Wilmoth, 2001).

Although living arrangements in later life tend to be relatively stable (Mutchler, 1992), the degree of stability depends on the age of the older adult and the living arrangement being considered (Wilmoth, 1998). Living arrangement transitions are particularly likely when exchanges with family and friends become unbalanced (Wilmoth, 2000). Therefore, demographic research indicates that informal networks play an important role in older adults' living arrangements, and living arrangements themselves represent an important exchange of resources between family members.

Although older adults are not likely to live with family, they tend to be in frequent contact with and live in close proximity to at least some family members. For example, retirement-aged adults (ages 55–74) report seeing their children four times a month and are in contact by phone or letters with their children about four and a half times a month (Szinovacz & Davey, 2001) Approximately 40% of adults aged 70 or older who have a child live with or within 10 minutes of at least one adult child, 33% live between 10 to 59 minutes, and only 27% live more than 60 minutes from a child. Proximity to children tends to be stable over time, and when changes in proximity occur, older parents and adult children tend to become geographically closer (Silverstein, 1995). Convergence in geographic proximity is more likely among older adults who experience declining health, increasing functional limitations, lower income, and death of a spouse (Silverstein, 1995; Rogerson, Burr, & Lin, 1997). Changes in proximity occur when an adult child or an older adult moves. Although we are not aware of any specific estimates for the prevalence of an adult child moving to be geographically closer to aging parents, there is evidence older adults are often motivated to move to be closer to family, particularly in later life when health declines (Litwak & Longino, 1987; DeJong, Wilmoth, Angel, & Cornwell, 1997). In fact, location of children is an influential factor in older adult migration, particularly among older adults who are White, unmarried, and over the age of 75 (Liaw, Frey, & Lin, 2002).

Current cohorts of older adults had relatively high marriage and fertility rates and therefore have relatively large family networks from which to draw support (Himes, 1992). However, the trend toward lower fertility in combination with longer life expectancy is substantially restructuring American families. Similar to other countries, average family size in the United States is decreasing, and multigenerational families are more prevalent (Bengston et al., 1995). Consequently, middle-aged Americans are more likely to have surviving parents and grandparents in addition to their own children and grandchildren, which increases the burden of care, particularly for middle-aged women.

The complexity of family structure has been compounded in the United States by rising divorce rates, falling remarriage rates, and increases in the proportion of population who have never married. This retreat from marriage has created a range of blended, alternative, and step-family arrangements. The long-term implications of the restructuring of the American family for family relationships and caregiving in later life have yet to be determined. But some research suggests that divorce undermines affection and exchanges between parents and children, particularly between fathers and children (Amato & Booth, 1996). Thus, future cohorts of older adults may not be able to rely as much on spouses and children for support.

Intergenerational Transfers

Social demographers often point out that older adults are not always on the receiving end of social exchanges. In fact, most older adults are not routinely involved in exchanges with their children (Eggebeen 1992). Generally, the flow of resources across generations consists of long-term downward transfers of support (e.g., emotional, instrumental, financial, educational) and inheritance. There is debate as to whether transfers from older to younger generations are motivated by altruism or are used to compensate younger family members for their support of older family members. In either case, this transfer of private resources substantially contributes to the economic well-being of younger generations (Holtz-Eakin & Smeeding, 1994).

The transfer of resources across generations does not only take place within families. Intergenerational transfers also occur through the private market and the public sector (Lee, 1994). Increasingly, social demographers have been interested in understanding the impact of population aging on transfers within the public sector. From this perspective, which is heavily influenced by economics, labor income exceeds consumption from midlife until retirement. This enables the working-age population to support public programs for children (e.g., public education), older adults (e.g., Social Security, Medicare), and disadvantaged populations (e.g., Medicaid) via federal, state, and local taxes. These public programs represent a macro-level redistribution of resources across generations and socioeconomic groups. Given the dependence of this system on the productivity of working-age population, public sector transfer programs are particularly vulnerable to shifts in the population age structure. An aging population potentially slows economic growth, which can further suppress government revenues used to finance public programs. However, many demographers are skeptical of alarmist predictions about the negative effects of population aging in developed countries (Friedland & Summer, 1999; Easterlin, 1991; Schultz, 1999). The extent of the impact of population aging will depend in part on future changes in public policy and trends in fertility, mortality, morbidity, and migration (Bongaarts, 2004; Lee & Skinner, 1999; Lee, 2000).

CONTRIBUTIONS OF DEMOGRAPHY
TO GERONTOLOGY

As this review of the literature demonstrates, the demography of aging is unique in that it provides a justification for studying older adults and the aging process by documenting the growth, and changes in the characteristics, of the older adult population. Beyond providing basic descriptive statistics about the older adult population, demographic research examines the social causes and consequences of population aging. In doing so, it offers insight into gerontological questions such as: what causes a population to grow older, are older adults living longer and healthier lives, how have changes in family structure affected care provision and family ties, and what are the economic implications of population aging? Answers to such questions not only help us understand the dynamics of an aging population but also provide information that can inform public policy decision making and assist in planning future services for the older adult population. Therefore, the demography of aging serves the other disciplines involved in gerontological inquiry by providing a detailed understanding of the demographic characteristics of the older adult population, the social causes of changes in the age structure, and the various consequences of population aging.

REFERENCES

Amato, P., & Booth, A. (1996). A prospective study of divorce and parent-child relationships. *Journal of Marriage and the Family, 58,* 356–365.

Angel, J. (1991). *Health and living arrangements of the elderly.* New York: Garland Publishing.

Bengston, V., Rosenthal, C., & Burton, L. (1995). Paradoxes of families and aging. In R. Binstock & L. George (Eds.), *Handbook of aging and the social sciences* (4th ed., pp. 254–282). San Diego: Academic Press.

Bongaarts, J. (2004). Population aging and the rising cost of public pensions. *Population Development and Review, 30*(1), 1–23.

Centers for Disease Control and Prevention. (2003). *Chartbook on trends in the health of Americans.* Retrieved April 6, 2004, from http://www.cdc.gov/nchs/data/hus/hus03cht.pdf

Choudhury, S. (2003). Race and ethnic differences in wealth and asset choices. *Social Security Bulletin, 64*(4), 1–15.

Clark, R., & Quinn, J. (2002). Patterns of work and retirement for a new century. *Generations, 26,* 17–24.

Coale, A. (1964). How a population ages or grows younger. In R. Freedman (Ed.), *Population: The vital revolution.* Garden City, NY: Anchor Books.

Cook, I. G., & Dummer, T. J. (2004). Changing health in China: Re-evaluating the demographic transition model. *Health Policy, 67,* 329–343.

Costa, D. (1998). *The evolution of retirement.* Chicago: University of Chicago Press.

Crimmins, E., Hayward, M., & Saito, Y. (1996). Differentials in active life expectancy in the older population of the United States. *Journal of Gerontology: Social Sciences, 51B,* S111–S120.

De Jong, G., Wilmoth, J., Angel, J., & Cornwell, G. (1995). Motives and the geographic mobility of the very old. *Journal of Gerontology: Social Sciences, 50,* S395–S404.

De Vos, S. (1990). Extended family living among older people in six Latin American countries. *Journal of Gerontology: Social Sciences, 45,* S87–S94.

Easterlin, R. (1991). The economic impact of prospective population changes in advanced industrial countries. *Journal of Gerontology: Social Sciences, 46,* S299–S309.

Eggebeen, D. (1992). Family structure and intergenerational exchanges. *Research on Aging, 14,* 427–447.

England, R. S. (2002). *The macroeconomic impact of global aging: A new era of economic frailty?* Washington, DC: Center for Strategic and International Studies Press.

Federal Interagency Forum on Age-Related Statistics. (2000). *Older Americans: 2000: Key indicators of well-being.* Washington, DC: U.S. Government Printing Office.

Freedman, V. A., Martin, L., & Schoeni, R. (2002). Recent trends in disability and functioning among older adults in the United States: A systematic review. *Journal of the American Medical Association, 288,* 3137–3146.

Friedland, R., & Summer, L. (1999). *Demography is not destiny.* Washington, DC: National Academy on an Aging Society.

Gendell, M. (2001). Retirement age declines again in the 1990s. *Monthly Labor Review, 124,* 12–21.

Gendell, M., & Siegel, J. (1996). Trends in retirement age in the United States, 1955–1993, by sex and race. *Journals of Gerontology: Social Sciences, 51B,* S132–S139.

Hagestad, G. (1986). Family: Women and grandparents as kin-keepers. In A. Pifer & L. Bronte (Eds.), *Our aging society: Paradox and promise* (pp. 141–160). New York: Norton.

Hateley, L., & Tan, G. (2003). *The graying of Asia: Causes and consequences of rapid aging in Asia.* New York: Eastern Universities Press.

Hayward, M., Hardy, M., & Grady, W. (1989). Labor force withdrawal patterns among older men in the United States. *Social Science Quarterly, 70,* 425–448.

Hayward, M., & Heron, M. (1999). Racial inequality in active life among adult Americans. *Demography, 36,* 77–91.

Himes, C. (1992). Future caregivers: Projected family structures of older persons. *Journal of Gerontology, 47,* S17–S26.

Himes, C. (2001). Elderly Americans. *Population Bulletin, 54*(4). Washington, DC: Population Reference Bureau.

Himes, C. L., Hogan, D. P., & Eggebeen, D. J. (1996). Living arrangements of minority elders. *Journal of Gerontology: Social Sciences, 51B*, S42–S48.

Holtz-Eakin, D., & Smeeding, T. (1994). Income, wealth, and intergenerational economic relations of the aged. In L. Martin & S. Preston (Eds.), *Demography of aging* (pp. 102–145). Washington, DC: National Academy Press.

Knodel, J., & Ofstedal, M. B. (2002). Patterns and determinant of living arrangements. In A. Hermalin (Ed.), *The well-being of the elderly in Asia: A four-country comparative study* (pp. 143–184). Ann Arbor: University of Michigan Press.

Kramarow, E. (1995). The elderly who live alone in the United States: Historical perspectives on household change. *Demography, 32*, 335–352.

Laditka, S. B., & Wolf, D. A. (1998). New methods for analyzing active life expectancy. *Journal of Aging and Health, 10*, 214–241.

Lee, R. (1994). The formal demography of population aging, transfers, and the economic life cycle. In L. Martin & S. Preston (Eds.), *Demography of aging* (pp. 8–49). Washington, DC: National Academy Press.

Lee, R. (2000). Long-term population projections and the U.S. Social Security System. *Population Development and Review, 26*, 137–144.

Lee, R., & Skinner, J. (1999). Will aging baby boomers bust the federal budget? *Journal of Economic Perspectives, 13*, 117–140.

Liaw, K. L., Frey, W., & Lin, J. P. (2002). Location of adult children as an attraction for black and white elderly primary migrants in the United States. *Environment and Planning, 34*, 191–216.

Litwak, E., & Longino, C. F. Jr. (1987). Migration patterns among the elderly: A developmental perspective. *Gerontologist, 27*, 266–272.

Logan, J., Bian, F., & Bain, Y. (1998). Tradition and change in the urban Chinese family: The case of living arrangements. *Social Forces, 76*, 851–882.

Longino, C. F. Jr., & Bradley, D. E. (2003). A first look at retirement migration trends in 2000. *Gerontologist, 43*, 904–907.

Manton, K., & Land, K. (2000). Active life expectancy estimates for the U.S. elderly population: A multidimensional continuous-mixture model of functional change applied to completed cohorts, 1982–1996. *Demography, 37*, 253–265.

Manton, K., & Stallard, E. (1991). Cross-sectional estimates of active life expectancy for U.S. elderly and oldest-old populations. *Journals of Gerontology, 46*, S170–S182.

Markides, K. S., & Mindel C. H. (1987). *Aging and ethnicity*. Newbury Park, CA: Sage.

Martin, L., & Kinsella, K. (1994). Research on the demography of aging in developing countries. In L. Martin & S. Preston (Eds.), *Demography of aging* (pp. 356–403). Washington, DC: National Academy Press.

Michael, R., Fuchs, V., & Scott, S. (1980). Changes in the propensity to live alone: 1950–1976. *Demography, 17*, 39–58.

Mullan, P. (2000). *The imaginary time bomb: Why an ageing population is not a social problem*. New York: I. B. Tauris.

Munnell, A. H., Hatch, R. E., & Lee, J. G. (2004). *Why is life expectancy so low in the United States?* Chestnut Hill, MA: Center for Retirement Research, Boston College.

Mutchler, J. (1992). Living arrangements and household transitions among the unmarried in later life. *Social Science Quarterly, 73,* 565–580.

Murray, C. J. L., & Lopez, A. D. (1996). *The global burden of disease: A comprehensive assessment of mortality and disability from diseases, injuries, and risk factors in 1990 and projected to 2020.* Cambridge, MA: Harvard University Press.

Murray, C. J. L., & Lopez, A. D. (1997a). Regional patterns of disability-free life expectancy and disability-adjusted life expectancy: Global burden of disease study. *Lancet, 349,* 1347–1352.

Murray, C. J. L., & Lopez, A. D. (1997b). Alternative projections of mortality and disability by cause, 1990–2020: Global Burden of Disease study. *Lancet, 349,* 1498–1504.

National Academy on an Aging Society. (1999). Chronic conditions: A challenge for the 21st century. *Data Profile, 1*(1). Washington, DC: National Academy on an Aging Society.

National Research Council. (2001). *Preparing for an aging world: The case for cross-national research.* Washington, DC: National Academy Press.

National Vital Statistics. (2004). Table 12: Estimated life expectancy at birth in years, by race and sex. Retrieved April 6, 2004, from http://www.cdc.gov/nchs/data/dvs/nvsr52_14t12.pdf

Ofstedal, M. B., Chan, A., Chayovan, N., Chauang, Y.-L., Perex, A., Mehta, K., et al. (2002). Policies and programs in place and under development. In A. Hermalin (Ed.), *The well-being of the elderly in Asia: A four-country comparative study* (pp. 65–99). Ann Arbor: University of Michigan Press.

Population Reference Bureau. (2004). 2004 world population data sheet. Retrieved August 17, 2004, from http://www.prb.org/pdf04/04WorldDataSheet_Eng.pdf

Preston, S., & Martin, L. (1994). Introduction In L. Martin & S. Preston (Eds.), *Demography of aging* (pp. 1–7). Washington, DC: National Academy Press.

Quinn, J., & Burkhauser, R. (1994). Retirement and labor force behavior of the elderly. In L. Martin & S. Preston (Eds.), *Demography of aging* (pp. 50–101). Washington, DC: National Academy Press.

Ribbe, M., Ljunggren, G., Steel, K., Topinkova, E., Hawes, C., Ikegami, N., et al. (1997). Nursing homes in 10 nations: A comparison between countries and settings. *Age-and-Ageing, 26,* 3–12.

Robert Wood Johnson Foundation. (1996). *Chronic care in America: A 21st century challenge.* Princeton, NJ: Author.

Rogers, A., Rogers, R. G., & Belanger, A. (1990). Longer life but worse health? Measurement and dynamics. *Gerontologist, 30,* 640–649.

Rogerson, P. A., Burr, J. A., & Lin, G. (1997). Changes in geographic proximity between parents and their adult children. *International Journal of Population Geography, 3,* 121–136.

Schultz, J. H. (1999). Population aging: Economic growth and generational transfers. In R. Cliquet & M. Nizamuddin (Eds.), *Population ageing: Challenges for policies and programmes in developed and developing countries* (pp. 123–140). New York: United Nations.

Siegel, J. (1980). On the demography of aging. *Demography, 17,* 345–364.

Silverstein, M. (1995). Stability and change in temporal distance between the elderly and their children. *Demography, 32,* 29–45.

Sloane, P., Zimmerman, S., Suchindran-Chirayath, R., Peter, W., Lily, B.-M., & Shudha, S. (2002). Public health impact of Alzheimer's disease, 2000–2050: Potential implications of treatment advances. *Annual Review of Public Health, 23,* 213–231.

Sokolovsky, J. (Ed.). (1990). *The cultural context of aging: Worldwide perspectives.* New York: Bergin and Garvey.

Soldo, B., Wolf, D., & Agree, E. (1990). Family, households, and care arrangements of frail older women: A structural analysis. *Journal of Gerontology: Social Sciences, 45,* S238–S249.

Sullivan, D. F. (1971). A single index of mortality and morbidity. *HSMHA Health Report, 86,* 347–354.

Szinovacz, M., & Davey, A. (2001). Retirement effects on parent-child contacts. *Gerontologist, 41,* 191–200.

Teitelbaum, M. S. (1975). Relevance of demographic transition theory for developing countries. *Science, 188,* 420–425.

United Nations. (1991). *World population prospects 1990.* New York: Author.

United Nations. (1999). *The sex and age distribution of the world populations, 1998 revision.* New York: Author.

U.S. Census Bureau. (2000a). QT-P1. *Age groups and sex: 2000.* Retrieved April 8, 2004, from http://factfinder.census.gov/

U.S. Census Bureau. (2000b). *Projections of the total resident population by 5-year age groups, race, and Hispanic origin with special age categories: Middle series, 1999 to 2070.* Retrieved April 8, 2004, from http://www.census.gov/population/www/projections/natsum-T3.html

U.S. Census Bureau. (2002). *Table 3. Poverty status of people, by age, race, and Hispanic origin: 1959–2002.* Retrieved April 9, 2004, from http://www.census.gov/hhes/poverty/histpov/

U. S. Census Bureau. (2004). *International Data Base.* Retrieved August 3, 2004, from http://www.census.gov/ipc/www/idbnew.html

Utendorf, K. (2002). The upper part of the earnings distribution in the United States: How has it changed? *Social Security Bulletin, 64*(3), 1–11.

Waidmann, T. A., & Manton, K. G. (2000). *Measuring trends in disability among the elderly: An international review.* Washington, DC: Urban Institute.

Wilmoth, J. (1998). Living arrangement transitions among America's older adults. *Gerontologist, 38,* 434–444.

Wilmoth, J. (2000). Unbalanced social exchanges and living arrangement transitions in later life. *Gerontologist, 40,* 64–74.

Wilmoth, J. (2001). Living arrangements among immigrants in the United States. *Gerontologist, 41,* 228–238.

Wolf, D. (1990). Household patterns of older women: Some international comparisons. *Research on Aging, 12,* 463–486.

Wolf, D. (1995). Changes in the living arrangements of older women: An international study. *Gerontologist, 35,* 724–731.

PART II

Physical Aspects of Aging

CHAPTER 4

Cellular and Organismal Aspects of Senescence and Longevity

David J. Waters

This chapter presents a contemporary perspective on the biology of aging, focusing on fundamental questions that reflect some of the most critical gaps in our understanding of organismal senescence and human longevity. In this chapter, organismal senescence is used to describe the deteriorative changes that result in decreased viability and ultimately an increase in an organism's risk for mortality. In contrast, the term *aging* refers to any time-dependent changes that occur during the life course of an organism. Thus, aging encompasses changes that are good (e.g., increased wisdom), bad (e.g., arteriosclerosis), or indifferent (e.g., baldness) in terms of their effect on viability and survival (Finch, 1990). It is an unfortunate reality that scientists and the public often use these terms interchangeably, resorting to using the term *aging* synonymously with *deterioration*.

Not all organisms undergo senescence at the same tempo (Finch, 1990). Humans exhibit gradual senescence (deterioration over decades), whereas other species, such as bamboo, have very rapid senescence (deterioration over days). There is an eclectic group of organisms that exhibit negligible senescence; age-related deteriorative changes are virtually imperceptible in these species. Not surprisingly, organisms with negligible senescence, including rockfish and bristlecone pine, are currently the subject of great scientific interest (Finch, 1998; Finch & Austad, 2001).

Understanding the mechanisms of organismal senescence and how morbidity can be compressed, culminating in extension of a healthy life span, is the goal embraced by most biogerontologists (Olshansky, Hayflick, & Carnes, 2002; Fries, 2003). These aims must be clearly articulated to the public (Binstock, 2004). It is also critical that the public understands what are not the goals of biogerontology research. For example, reversal of aging and achieving immortality are not considered tenable objectives. Including these metrics in the scientific dialogue serves only to compromise the public's understanding of the purpose and value of biogerontology research. Basic and applied scientists are working diligently to understand the processes of cellular and organismal senescence and to identify the determinants of human longevity. Some of the diverse and complementary scientific approaches being used are discussed in the sections that follow.

LESSONS FROM EVOLUTIONARY BIOLOGY

It has been argued that longevity, not aging or senescence per se, is under genetic control (Martin, Austad, & Johnson, 1996). These so-called longevity genes extend longevity by increasing physiological reserve or increasing disease resistance rather than having a direct effect on the intrinsic rate of aging. Evolutionary biologists would concur that genes that regulate late-life deterioration would not be under the influence of natural selection. Instead, natural selection favors genes that influence the likelihood of reproductive success, because organisms rely on the successful completion of development and reproduction to perpetuate the species. During the postreproductive period, however, the force of natural selection quickly diminishes, rendering organisms ill equipped to protect themselves against the age-related accumulation of molecular damage. Seldom is this an important consequence to animals living in the wild because, in general, they experience relatively brief postreproductive life spans owing to their vulnerability to predators, accidents, or infectious diseases. In contrast, humans and other highly protected, domesticated animals encounter the manifestations of organismal senescence, including cancer and other age-related degenerative diseases.

When it comes to age-related deterioration and disability, two tenets of evolutionary theory would suggest that humans and other domesticated species are indeed hard-wired for postreproductive calamity. First, the disposal soma hypothesis (Kirkwood, 1977, 1990) states that after reproduction, the soma (body) can be thrown away. Second, genes that confer an advantage early in life may also exert detrimental effects in the postreproductive period—the theory of antagonistic pleiotropy (Williams,

1957). The incidence of several age-related diseases is likely to be under the control of such antagonistically pleiotropic genes. For example, genes that stimulate abundant blood vessel formation within the placenta (favoring successful reproduction early in life) might be considered detrimental later in life if they promote a rich supply of blood vessels to rapidly growing tumors. Moreover, it is expected that the frequency of alleles that exert these late-life detrimental effects would be maintained or even increased in the population owing to their early-life benefit.

In his famous treatise, *An Unsolved Problem of Biology*, Nobel laureate Sir Peter Medawar noted that in order to understand the consequences of senescence and age-related diseases, one would have to study the aging process of "protected" species (Medawar, 1952). In a classic thought experiment in which Medawar considered the aging of test tubes, he pointed out that in order to observe the consequences of aging, test tubes would have to be "domesticated"—that is, kept sheltered from damage in a little box so they would not suffer an early "death" by rolling off the laboratory bench.

Thus, organismal senescence and accompanying age-related diseases are an inevitable by-product of domestication (see Figure 4.1). An organism is not built with any regard for optimizing aging. Instead, an organism is designed to successfully and advantageously complete its maturation and reproduction. As a consequence, one expects to see an accumulation

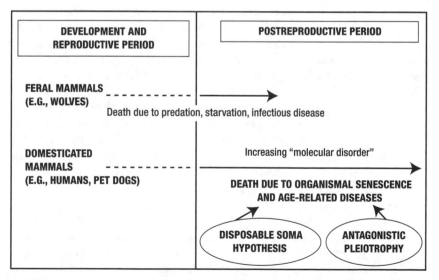

FIGURE 4.1   Domestication's curse: Organismal senescence and the incidence of age-related diseases.

of molecular disorder (Hayflick, 1998) in species attaining a prolonged postreproductive life span. This progressive increase in molecular disorder leads to organismal senescence: physiological deterioration, an increased risk for age-related diseases, and an increased mortality rate.

CELLULAR SENESCENCE: AGING IN THE CELL CULTURE LABORATORY

More than 40 years ago, Hayflick and Moorhead (1961) advanced the notion that normal somatic cells have a finite replicative life span in cell culture. Prior to this, it was believed that normal cells in culture, if cared for properly, could divide indefinitely. Subsequent studies have provided solid support for the concept of replicative senescence, whereby normal diploid cells have a limited number of population doublings (now known as the *Hayflick limit*).

The process of in vitro replicative senescence has been studied extensively in normal fibroblasts and other cell types in cell culture (Campisi, 1996; Cristofalo & Pignolo, 1993). Not only do senescent cells suffer irreversible loss of their ability to replicate, they undergo other phenotypic changes. For example, senescent cells increase their production of matrix metalloproteinase enzymes, which might be expected to alter the function of tissues by favoring the turnover of extracellular matrix and tissue remodeling. Importantly, senescent cells retain their viability (they do not die); in fact, they are actually resistant to apoptotic cell death.

The in vitro replicative life span of normal cells is based on the number of population doublings rather than elapsed time in culture. The number of potential population doublings that a cell can undergo is determined by the length of telomeres, the structures that cap the ends of chromosomes (Kim, Kaminker, & Campisi, 2002). When normal cells undergo cell division, each replication witnesses a shortening of the telomere. When telomeric shortening reaches a critical threshold, the ability to replicate is lost; this signal is presumably mediated by a cellular DNA damage response (Dimri, 2005). In contrast, stem cells and most tumor cells possess the enzyme telomerase, which effectively maintains telomere length and allows these cells to escape the rules of replicative senescence (Granger, Wright, & Shay, 2002).

If replicative senescence reflects cellular aging, it provides scientists with a unique vantage point for studying deteriorative processes that may, to some extent, parallel the age-related changes that actually occur in vivo. This experimental approach also provides the advantage that specific mechanisms can be investigated under carefully controlled, albeit artificial, conditions.

There are at least two lines of evidence that make it attractive to consider that aging in the cell culture laboratory is indeed relevant to organismal senescence. First, when one looks across different species, the population doubling potential for cultured normal fibroblasts is proportional to the maximum life span potential of animals (Hayflick, 1976). Second, in studies with human fibroblasts, there is an inverse correlation between the age of the donor and replicative life span of cultured cells (Martin, Sprague, & Epstein, 1970). However, a more recent study by Cristofalo and colleagues (Cristofalo, Allen, Pignolo, Martin, & Beck, 1998) challenged this notion by showing no significant relationship between donor age and the replicative potential of human fibroblasts. One possible explanation of these contradictory results is that in vivo aging does not result in a global, uniform age-related loss of proliferative capacity. Instead, in vivo aging might be characterized by mosaicism—with old tissues representing a mosaic of senescent and "youthful" cells. If true, then even old hosts have populations of youthful fibroblasts with a replicative life span comparable to that of cells retrieved from young hosts.

However, it is still not clear whether senescent cells actually accumulate in vivo in older individuals. Using the enzyme senescence-associated beta-galactosidase (SAβgal) as a marker of cellular senescence, Dimri and colleagues (1995) found more senescent cells in the skin of elderly humans than in younger subjects. Although the species and tissue specificity of SAβgal activity are yet to be determined, these exciting findings take an important step toward addressing the critical need for biomarkers of senescence so that we can determine whether the accumulation of senescent cells causes the functional decline seen in old tissues and old organs.

If cellular senescence is actually an in vivo phenomenon, then it is intriguing to consider that cellular senescence might not be all bad; this process might actually be beneficial to an organism. To this end, Campisi (2003) has proposed that replicative senescence is an example of antagonistic pleiotropy. By limiting the proliferative potential of cells, replicative senescence might serve as a potent cancer-suppressive mechanism in young adults. Later in life, however, the accumulation of senescent cells might contribute to functional deterioration by limiting the capacity of tissues to respond to insults. Furthermore, accumulation of senescent cells might create a cancer-permissive neighborhood—one that promotes the progression of transformed cells into clinically important cancers by enhancing the turnover of the surrounding extracellular matrix, thereby enhancing the local concentration of stimulatory growth factors (Krtolica, Parrinello, Lockett, Desprez, & Campisi, 2001). These effects would facilitate the proliferation and metastatic escape of tumor cells.

In addition to replicative senescence, it is now evident that cells can reach senescence by another pathway: in response to exposure to sublethal stress. Stress-induced premature senescence (SiPS) is triggered by a variety of sublethal exposures (e.g., H_2O_2, hyperoxia, cancer chemotherapy agents) and represents a potentially important mechanism by which senescent cells might accumulate in vivo. Cells in replicative senescence or SiPS share common morphologic features, telomere shortening, SAβgal activity, and changes in gene expression (Toussaint, Medrano, & von Zglinicki, 2000). At present, it is not clear whether replicative senescence and SiPS are identical, and the extent to which either contributes to in vivo organismal senescence is not known (Marcotte & Wang, 2002; Touissant et al., 2000; Rubin, 2002).

THE DETERMINANTS OF LIFE SPAN: GENES, ENVIRONMENT, AND CHANCE

Evolutionary theory teaches us there are no genes whose purpose is to cause or accelerate the aging process. In that sense, senescence is not programmed, but rather a passive by-product of an organism's genetic hardwiring. That genes influence life span is not subject to debate: no amount of environmental protection or enrichment can produce a rat that lives as long as the average human. Specific genes have been identified that regulate life span in worms (*C. elegans*) (Morris, Tissenbaum, & Ruvkun, 1996; Kimura, Tissenbaum, Liu, & Ruvkun, 1997), flies (*Drosophila*) (Clancy et al., 2001; Lin, Seroude, & Benzer, 1998), and mice (Migliaccio et al., 1999). What remains enigmatic is whether any of these genes actually prolongs life span by slowing down the rate of aging.

Data from twin studies (McGue, Vaupel, Holm, & Harvald, 1993; Ljungquist, Berg, Lanke, McClearn, & Pedersen, 1998) suggest that 25 to 30 percent of the variation in life span among individuals can be attributed to genetic factors. In other words, there is considerable plasticity to life span. This means lifestyle is important—both the external environment (e.g., diet, exposure to chemicals) and the internal environment (e.g., hormones, oxidative stress) significantly influence an individual's life span.

Recently, the widely accepted idea that gene-environment interactions are the major determinant of all complex traits, including longevity, has made room for a third element: chance. That chance has an important impact on life span is supported by observations that genetically identical organisms raised under identical conditions have differences in life span—all of the individuals do not drop dead on the same day. It is a complex choreography of genes, environment, and chance that orchestrates a vast array of biological outcomes (reviewed in Finch & Kirkwood, 2000).

Although several organismal models suggest that life span is indeed under genetic control, there are differing views about how many genes regulate longevity and how those genes should be classified. Martin (1978) estimates as many as 7,000 genes may regulate life span, suggesting that longevity is under polygenic control. However, some scientists favor the idea of oligogenic control—that a few critical genes may account for the lion's share of the 25% to 30% portion of human life span that is heritable. This view is supported by a considerable body of evidence from *C. elegans* in which single gene mutations can significantly prolong life span (Morris et al., 1996; Kimura et al., 1997).

There are two major classes of genes whose action escapes the force of natural selection and therefore could modulate the collection of senescent phenotypes that we call aging (Martin et al., 1996): (1) constitutive genetic variations, which do not manifest any deleterious effects until late in life, and (2) constitutive genetic variations, which are selected because of their association with increased early fitness but exert deleterious effects late in life. In the first category, the bad genes—for example, genes responsible for early-onset Alzheimer's disease—are neutral early in life. The second category of genes follows the theory of antagonistic pleiotropy proposed by Williams (1957). For example, $\in 4$ is the bad allele of apolipoprotein E, which is underrepresented among centenarians (Schachter et al., 1994). However, individuals with apolipoprotein E$\in 4$ may benefit early in life from better response to stress (Ravaja, Raikkonen, Lyytinen, Lehtimaki, & Keltikangas-Jarvinen, 1997) or protection from parasitic diseases (Martin, 1999). More recently, this classification scheme has been expanded by Martin (2002) to include six categories of gene action.

The search continues for genes that can persist within populations and increase life span by decreasing the rate of aging. Although unproven, the existence of such genes is supported by the profound within-species difference in life span observed in island- versus mainland-dwelling opossums (Austad, 1993), selective breeding experiments in flies (Arking, 1987), and the natural evolution of dog breeds (Patronek, Waters, & Glickman, 1997; Deeb & Wolf, 1994). These so-called longevity assurance genes (Hodes, McCormick, & Pruzan, 1996; Butler et al., 2003) are assumed to influence the rate of aging because they are beneficial to the organism, for example, by regulating antioxidant defenses or DNA repair. But scientists in hot pursuit of candidate longevity assurance genes are bound to uncover some unexpected results, because these genes are likely to have tissue-specific effects that may manifest themselves differently during different periods of the life course. Furthermore, nonlinear dose responses and threshold effects, in which further increases in gene action do not enhance the organism's viability, may befuddle investigators.

Perhaps the richest treasure of all in the hunt for longevity genes will be finding the genes responsible for the differences in life span between different species. To date, none have been identified. However, it is believed that this approach will likely lead to the discovery of *pacemaker genes*—a small collection of master regulatory genes that controls the tempo of age-related erosion of homeostasis and organismal decline across species (Miller, 1999). It is tempting to consider that the life span–extending effect of caloric restriction might indeed be attributable to its effect on these pacemaker genes.

Evolutionary theory predicts that life span, which may be regulated by pacemaker genes, is the indirect result of an organism's schedule of reproduction. Because reproduction is under neural and endocrine control, it is plausible that whole animal aging is regulated by genes acting on, or expressed by, particular neural cells (Finch & Ruvkun, 2001). Studies in *C. elegans* support the importance of neuroendocrine factors in the regulation of life span (Wolkow, Kimura, Lee, & Ruvkun, 2000). Consistent with this thinking, Finch and Ruvkun (2001) have proposed that free radicals produced by neurons regulate mammalian aging, a notion that fits with the free radical theory of aging. Identifying these pacemaker cells and their associated life span regulatory networks will be an important step toward unraveling the genetic basis for senescence and longevity. This task may not be particularly easy because these key regulatory genes may be tissue-specific. If investigators analyze the wrong tissue, they will miss the regulators.

It is clear from this discussion that heritable shortening of life span should not be considered equivalent to genes accelerating the aging process (Finch & Ruvkun, 2001). Ultimately, biogerontologists must define the extent to which particular genetic and environmental factors slow down or speed up the intrinsic rate of aging. To date, this has been exceedingly difficult because of the lack of validated biomarkers of senescence. Thus, for the time being, age at death (life span) and the incidence of particular age-related diseases will continue to be used as surrogates, albeit imperfect ones, for the rate of organismal senescence.

HORMONES AND AGING: NOTHING IS RAGING

The endocrine system, a major contributor to the host's internal environment, is profoundly and predictably affected by aging. An age-related decline in hormone production results in lower circulating levels of growth hormone/insulin-like growth factor-I (somatopause), estrogen (menopause), testosterone (andropause), and DHEA (adrenopause) (Lamberts, van den Beld, & van der Lely, 1997). The age-associated decline in these regulators of homeostasis has several important biological and clinical implications.

Although unproven, the idea that alterations in hormone levels cause organismal senescence, including the physiological deterioration seen in older adults, is supported by clinical observations. For example, loss of estrogen action in postmenopausal women has been associated with an increased risk for cardiovascular disease, accelerated loss of bone mass, and a decline in cognitive function (Love et al., 1992). Also, individuals suffering from inherited growth hormone deficiency show many signs that mimic normal aging, such as thinning skin and decreased bone and muscle mass (Rudman et al., 1990). It follows from these observations that hormone supplementation might prove a useful intervention to decrease significantly the rate of age-associated physiological decline.

However, from a biological standpoint, there are several issues that transform successful hormonal replacement from a straightforward proposition to a formidable task. First, one must decide whether to use a replacement dose (i.e., restoring circulating hormone concentrations in older adults to normal youthful levels) or supraphysiologic dose (i.e., achieving high-circulating hormone concentrations that exceed normal levels). Other issues, such as timing of hormone administration during the life course (Bartke et al., 1998), use of a single hormone or a combination of them (Tang et al., 1996; Shumaker et al., 2003), and sex-specific effects (Blackman et al., 2002), add another layer of complexity.

Second, hormones have tissue-specific actions—some desirable, some undesirable. For example, testosterone supplementation may decrease frailty in older men by increasing muscle mass and muscle strength (Krause, Mueller, & Mazur, 2005). However, an expected downside of testosterone supplementation is an increased incidence of prostatic disease. Because of potentially troubling trade-offs, scientists are developing hormonal agents with tissue-selective actions. For example, selective estrogen receptor modulators (SERMs), such as tamoxifen, exert beneficial effects on particular target organs (e.g., brain, blood vessels, bone) without detrimental stimulatory effects on cancer cells in the breast or uterus (Jordan, 2004).

Finally, it will be important to develop reliable biomarkers that can identify those individuals who will benefit most from hormone supplementation. By accomplishing this, it will be possible to finger hormone supplementation regimens that have the best risk-benefit profile.

However, it is not clear whether an age-related decline in circulating hormones is truly a bad thing. For example, if decreased growth hormone contributes significantly to the age-related decline in muscle mass and bone density, then a decline in circulating growth hormone levels would be considered maladaptive. On the other hand, the age-associated drop in growth hormone production might serve as a favorable anticancer mechanism. Decreased growth hormone production translates into lower levels of circulating IGF-I, a peptide that stimulates the survival and proliferation of most human breast, prostate, and colon cancers (Chan et al., 1998; Giovannucci et al., 2000; Schernhammer, Holly, Pollak, & Hankinson, 2005). Experimentally, carcinogen-treated mice with growth hormone deficiency are cancer resistant; growth hormone infusions render these mice more vulnerable to cancer development (Ramsey et al., 2002). Taken together, sustained growth hormone production throughout the life course might actually be undesirable because it would favor an increased incidence of cancer.

Another key issue is whether interventions, other than taking hormone supplements, can restore youthful levels of circulating hormones in older adults. Recent experimental evidence suggests two possibilities: caloric restriction and sleep. In nonhuman primates, 40% caloric restriction almost completely abrogates the age-associated decline in plasma levels of the adrenal hormone DHEA (Roth, Ingram, & Lane, 2001). Now scientists are working to determine whether caloric restriction mimetics or intermittent caloric restriction can similarly modulate hormone levels. In terms of sleep, we know that approximately 60 to 70% of growth hormone is released during sleep, and recent evidence suggests that reduced growth hormone secretion seen in older adults may be the consequence of age-related reductions in slow wave sleep (Van Cauter, Leproult, & Plat, 2000). This raises the intriguing possibility that instead of administering growth hormone supplements, one could attempt to restore youthful hormone levels by restoring youthful sleep quality. Someday, in the not-too-distant future, to optimize your health you might have to make a decision: take a pill, take a snooze, or take a pill that helps you snooze like a young person.

CALORIC RESTRICTION: IMPRACTICAL INTERVENTION, INVALUABLE RESEARCH TOOL

In 1935, McCay and colleagues reported that restricting food intake delayed the onset of age-related diseases and extended the life span of rodents (McCay, Crowell, & Maynard, 1935). Seventy years later, caloric restriction (also called undernutrition without malnutrition or dietary restriction) is regarded as the only experimental intervention that consistently retards aging in rodents (Masoro, 2003). The beneficial effects of caloric restriction (CR) on life span extension and cancer suppression are observed when total energy intake is curtailed to 20 to 40% less than the caloric intake of ad libitum fed animals. The experimental paradigm of CR is distinct from starvation: CR animals receive fewer calories but nutritionally adequate levels of all essential nutrients.

Most CR experiments employ life-long CR in rodents initiated soon after weaning. More recently, life span extension in mice has been documented when CR was initiated at middle age (approximately 12 months old) (Pugh, Oberley, & Weindruch, 1999). Critical studies in nonhuman primates are in progress, but have yet to yield an answer to whether CR can extend survival. However, CR monkeys and CR rodents show significant improvements in several physiological parameters, including decreased fasting blood glucose and insulin levels (Roberts et al., 2001).

The mechanism by which CR extends life span has not been determined but is under intense investigation. By identifying key targets modulated by CR, scientists hope to identify critical regulatory points that control senescence and longevity. One thing is certain: CR exerts pleiotropic effects, significantly altering numerous biochemical, immunologic, and hormonal networks.

To determine whether CR extends life span by slowing the accumulation of irreversible damage, scientists measured the change in age-specific mortality rate in full-fed fruit flies and after flies were switched to CR (Mair, Goymer, Pletcher, & Partridge, 2003). The experiments yielded an intriguing, clear-cut result: full-fed and CR flies accumulated irreversible damage at the same rate. However, for each given level of damage, CR flies had a significant survival advantage over full-fed flies. Apparently CR allows an organism to cope with the cellular damage that accumulates with aging, which translates into a reduced risk for mortality. Interestingly, these fruit fly results are consistent with mortality data from mice in which CR was initiated at middle age (Pugh et al., 1999). These remarkable findings have important implications because they predict that CR initiated at any time during the life course will have immediate beneficial effects, regardless of the organism's previous caloric history.

The search for the mechanistic basis for the longevity-enhancing effects of CR is more than just an academic exercise. Scientists are avidly seeking to develop CR mimetics because 20 to 40% CR is an impractical intervention strategy to implement in humans (Hass et al., 1996). The discovery of effective CR mimetics would allow individuals to reap the benefits of CR without the undesirable effects of severe food restriction. However, because of our rudimentary understanding of how CR really works, there is considerable scientific debate as to what kind of agents will be the most effective CR mimetics. For example, if changes in circulating hormone levels or hormone action induced by CR are responsible for CR's effect on life span, then agents that mimic these neuroendocrine responses might be expected to extend life span. Alternatively, it is possible that CR works in a different way—by protecting critical neuroendocrine cells from age-related impairment in hormone production (Mobbs et al., 2001). Clearly, a more complete mechanistic understanding of CR will provide much-needed guidance in developing useful first-generation CR mimetic agents.

Taken together, future research on CR will undoubtedly yield new insights into better understanding the aging process, as well as developing practical interventions that increase healthy life span. There are several important unresolved questions about CR currently under investigation. For example, very little is known about the response of CR animals to infection because most rodent experiments are performed under highly artificial, pathogen-free conditions (Weindruch et al., 2001). Therefore it is not clear whether CR animals are able to mount a more effective immune response to bacterial or viral pathogens compared to age-matched controls. This has important implications because if CR augments immune function, then CR animals might fall victim to their own overexuberant immune responses, resulting in an increase in the incidence of life-threatening inflammatory conditions or autoimmune diseases.

Finally, as an alternative to sustained CR or CR mimetic agents, intermittent CR might provide a more practical lifestyle modification. Currently, it is unclear whether intermittent CR would effectively mimic the beneficial effects of CR. Moreover, rats exposed to a dietary regimen of cyclic fasting and refeeding had enhanced sensitivity to developing chemically induced cancers (Premoselli, Sesca, Binasco, Caderni, & Tessitore, 1998; Tagliaferro et al., 1996). Clearly, further studies are needed to rule out the possibility that intermittent CR has deleterious health consequences in humans.

RUSTING OUT: THE OXIDATIVE STRESS HYPOTHESIS

In 1956, Denham Harman proposed that endogenous products of aerobic metabolism are a major determinant of organismal senescence (Harman, 1956). Harman's free radical theory of aging predicted that organisms would inevitably suffer age-related accumulation of macromolecular damage induced by reactive oxygen species (ROS), leading to physiological decline and increased risk of mortality. During the ensuing 50 years, substantial correlative data have been collected from animal studies that support this popular hypothesis, although definitive evidence that oxidant stress causes organismal senescence is lacking. Elucidating the precise role of oxidative stress in the aging process is complicated by the fact that the impact of oxidative stress on an organism's well-being depends on (1) the amount of ROS production, (2) the vulnerability of macromolecules to ROS-induced damage, which reflects cellular antioxidant defenses, and (3) the capacity to repair oxidative damage (Beckman & Ames, 1998).

Sources of Reactive Oxygen Species

The mitochondria represent the most important cellular source of ROS. The electron transport chain within mitochondria generates the adenosine triphosphate (ATP) necessary to power the cell, but is an imperfect system, resulting in the generation of ROS (especially hydroxyl radical). Oxidative damage to mitochondrial DNA leads to the production of defective mitochondrial proteins, which favors impaired electron transfer and a resultant increase in ROS production. According to the mitochondrial theory of aging (Miquel, 1992), the age-related accumulation of mitochondrial DNA mutations contributes significantly to organismal senescence by driving a vicious cycle of mitochondrial dysfunction and cellular energetic collapse. There are also important nonmitochondrial sources of oxidants, including beta oxidation of fatty acids, cytochrome p450 enzyme, and the oxidative burst used by phagocytic cells to destroy pathogens.

Macromolecular Targets of Oxidative Stress

Lipids, proteins, and nucleic acids are vulnerable to damage by oxidative stress. Lipid peroxidation leads to changes in membrane fluidity that can corrupt the cell's signal transduction—that is, how a cell processes information from its environment and interacts with other cells (Monteiro & Stern, 1996). The level of F_2 isoprostanes or malondialdehyde is commonly used to assess the extent of lipid peroxidation.

Protein oxidation disrupts homeostasis by inactivating essential enzymes and altering the cell's ability to recognize and dispose of worn-out proteins. Moribund flies ("crawlers") have increased protein oxidation compared with age-matched flies that are still viable "fliers" (Sohal, Agarwal, Dubey, & Orr, 1993). Scientists measure the level of protein carbonyls or advanced glycation end products to assess the amount of oxidative protein damage.

Oxidative damage to nucleic acids can lead to deleterious mutations, which may diminish cellular function or contribute to cancer development. The extent of oxidative lesions in mitochondrial DNA exceeds those seen in nuclear DNA by 10 to 1, suggesting that oxidative stress significantly contributes to disruption of mitochondrial function. The oxidative DNA adduct, 8-hydroxyguanosine, is the biochemical marker most widely used to measure the extent of oxidative DNA damage (Wu, Chiou, Chiang, & Wu, 2004).

Cellular Antioxidant Defenses

Cellular protection from oxidative stress relies on enzymes that speed up ROS detoxification and on the activity of free radical scavengers. The antioxidant enzyme superoxide dismutase (SOD) catalyzes the conversion of superoxide anion to hydrogen peroxide; then hydrogen peroxide is converted to water by the enzymes catalase or glutathione peroxidase to complete the detoxification process. There are two distinct forms of SOD: CuZnSOD, which is cytoplasmic and constitutively expressed, and MnSOD, which is mitochondrial and inducible. SOD activity is highly conserved across species, and interspecies comparisons show a strong positive correlation between SOD activity and maximum life span potential (Sohal, Sohal, & Brunk, 1990). Free radical scavengers that are hydrophilic, such as ascorbate, urate, and glutathione, operate within the cell cytoplasm. Lipophilic scavengers, such as carotenoids (e.g., beta-carotene, lycopene) and tocopherols (e.g., vitamin E), provide valuable protection against peroxidation of membrane lipids.

Defining the precise role that a particular antioxidant defense enzyme plays in the aging process can be difficult for several reasons. First, some enzymes have sequential activity; SOD alone cannot drive the complete detoxification of superoxide anion to water. Also, there is functional redundancy built into the system: two different enzymes, catalase and glutathione peroxidase, can complete the detoxification process of hydrogen peroxide to water. Furthermore, the inducibility of enzyme systems renders ambiguous the interpretation of "low" versus "high" enzyme activities. For example, high activity might reflect innately strong defenses or instead induced activity because the organism is under siege by overwhelming oxidative stress. Clearly, more studies are needed that not only measure baseline antioxidant enzyme activities but also assess cells after oxidative challenge.

Age-Related Changes in Oxidative Damage

In general, older hosts appear to be more susceptible to oxidative injury. For example, old mice exposed to low-dose (2Gy) irradiation had a twofold greater increase in oxidative DNA damage in the liver, brain, and heart than young mice after radiation exposure (Hamilton et al., 2001). In that study, evaluation of repair kinetics showed no difference in the capacity for young or old mice to repair oxidative DNA lesions (Hamilton et al., 2001). Studies probing whether age-related increases in oxidative damage reflect increased ROS production, diminished antioxidant defenses, or decreased repair of oxidative damage have yielded inconsistent results (Blumberg, 2000).

Caloric Restriction, Replicative Senescence

Additional supportive evidence for the importance of oxidant stress as a determinant of life span comes from caloric restriction studies. The life span–extending effect of 40% caloric restriction in mice is associated with a significant decrease in protein carbonyls and increased levels of SOD and catalase (Wachsman, 1996; Yu, 1996). Oxidative stress may also contribute to in vitro cellular senescence by accelerating the shortening of telomeres, thereby decreasing the population doubling required for cells to reach replicative senescence (von Zglinicki, Burkle, & Kirkwood, 2001).

Interventional Studies

The evidence is mixed regarding whether manipulation of antioxidant defenses influences longevity. Transgenic flies that overexpress both CuZn-SOD and catalase show increased maximum life span (Orr & Sohal, 1994). Selective overexpression of CuZnSOD in motor neurons also increases the maximum life span of flies (Parkes et al., 1998). However, upregulation of CuZnSOD activity in transgenic mice to levels up to five times greater than those seen in normal mice failed to increase life span (Huang, Carlson, Gillespie, Shi, & Epstein, 2000).

Perhaps the most convincing evidence to support the oxidative stress hypothesis comes from the work of Melov and colleagues (2000) in *C. elegans*. Experimentally, the antioxidant defenses of worms were boosted by exposing them to a synthetic SOD mimetic in their culture media, while control worms were exposed to vehicle alone. Worms exposed to the SOD mimetic had a significant 44% increase in mean life span. Furthermore, when genetically altered short-lived worms were exposed to the SOD mimetic, normal life span was restored in these short-lived mutants.

Unfortunately, direct evidence is lacking to support the hypothesis that increasing the dietary intake of antioxidants can increase life span in mammals. A synthetic free radical spin trap compound called PBN (N-tert-butyl α phenylnitrone) decreased brain protein oxidation (Carney et al., 1991) and increased life span of mice in some experiments and is currently under investigation (Floyd, Hensley, Forster, Kelleher-Andersson, & Wood, 2002).

In summary, a vast library of experimental observations lends support to the notion that oxidative stress significantly contributes to organismal senescence. For example, the intriguing differences between ROS production in short-lived and long-lived species—the mitochondria of birds have a ten-times lower rate of ROS generation than shorter-lived mammals of the same body size (Barja, Cadenas, Rojas, Perez-Campo, & Lopez-Torres, 1994)—provide tantalizing clues to the potential importance of oxidative stress in organismal senescence. However, new research continues to challenge old thinking. In fact, emerging data now call into question whether mitochondrial generation of oxidants is actually strongly correlated with metabolic rate (Speakman et al., 2004). It follows that definitive conclusions about the causal role of oxidative stress in mammalian aging must await the results of additional carefully controlled mechanistic and interventional studies.

LESSONS FROM STUDYING THE YOUNGEST-OLD AND THE OLDEST-OLD HUMANS

The Youngest-Old

Humans with Werner's syndrome show a phenotype that in many ways looks like aging in fast motion (Finch, 1990). Affected individuals develop skin and muscle atrophy, graying of hair and hair loss, atherosclerosis, and osteoporosis before the fourth decade of life and usually succumb to cancer or myocardial infarction before the age of 50. Interestingly, the histologic spectrum of their cancers is very different from that seen in the general population; nonepithelial cancers (e.g., sarcoma, melanoma) predominate in Werner's syndrome in contrast to the carcinomas of the breast, prostate, colon, and lung that most commonly affect the general population (Lebel & Leder, 1998). Werner's syndrome is considered a segmental progeroid syndrome because not all systems are affected; the central nervous system is spared.

Werner's syndrome is an autosomal recessive disorder associated with loss of function of the wrn DNA helicase. Cells from affected individuals show an increased number of spontaneous chromosome breaks, enhanced sensitivity to mutagens, and an increased rate of telomere shortening. Findings from humans with Werner's syndrome and from mutant mice with accelerated aging phenotypes (e.g., klotho, KU-80 mutant mice) suggest that longevity is strongly dependent on the quality of an organism's genome maintenance, indicating that organismal senescence is driven by DNA damage and the cellular response to DNA damage (Hasty & Vijg, 2004). Whether studying accelerated aging in humans or short-lived mutant mice moves us substantially closer to understanding the mechanisms of normal aging or the gene-environment interactions that determine human longevity has been questioned (Miller, 2004).

The Oldest-Old

Centenarians provide a potentially valuable natural experiment of highly successful aging. To date, the search for specific environmental exposures or lifestyle factors (e.g., diet, education, physical activity) that confer an increased likelihood of living to be 100 has not been fruitful (Perls, Levensen, Regan, & Puca, 2002). Among centenarians, females outnumber males by more than two to one. Among women, successful late reproduction—live childbirth at age 40 years or more—is a strong predictor of exceptional longevity (Perls, Alpert, & Frett, 1997). Larger particle size of high- and low-density lipoproteins (Barzilai et al., 2003) and higher plasma antioxidant capacity (Hyland et al., 2002) have also been associated with exceptional longevity.

Siblings of centenarians are 15 times more likely to live to be 100 compared with the general population (Perls, Wilmoth, et al., 2002a). The mortality advantage seen in siblings of centenarians is sustained throughout the life course, suggesting that their good fortune may be more strongly influenced by genetics than by environmental factors (Perls, Wilmoth, et al., 2002). A few genes have already been implicated as candidate longevity-enabling genes because the bad polymorphic variants of these genes are underrepresented in centenarians. These sinister variants include the apolipoprotein E$\in$4 allele and the angiotensin-converting enzyme D allele (Schacter et al., 1994). Also, genetic linkage analysis has provided evidence that a gene or several genes on human chromosome 4 significantly contribute to exceptional longevity (Puca et al., 2001). It should be noted that the genetic factors that contribute to exceptional longevity may be different from the genetic determinants of average life span. In addition, men and women may follow different trajectories to achieve exceptional longevity; male centenarians are less heterogeneous and healthier than female centenarians (Franceschi et al., 2000).

Centenarians outlive most of us, but just how healthy are centenarians? When it comes to vulnerability to major age-related diseases, a recent study of lifetime medical histories suggests there are three types of centenarians: (1) survivors (38%)—individuals with onset of at least one major disease prior to 80 years of age; (2) delayers (43%)—individuals who are free of all major diseases until after 80 years of age; and (3) escapers (19%)—individuals who are free of all major diseases until after 100 years of age (Evert, Lawler, Borgan, & Perls, 2003). This important study confirmed that centenarians are indeed a highly heterogeneous population. It is apparent that strong disease resistance, however, is a characteristic shared by the majority of centenarians; almost two-thirds of centenarians remained free of all major diseases until after the median age at death for their birth cohort. An analysis of exceptional longevity in pet dogs reached a similar conclusion: 76% of oldest-old dogs delayed the onset of major diseases, and more than half of extreme aged dogs had profound disease resistance (Cooley, Schlittler, Glickman, Hayek, & Waters, 2003). In humans, mortality from cancer, a disease strongly associated with aging, actually declines in the tenth decade of life—a puzzling paradox (Smith, 1996; Stanta, Campagner, Cavallieri, &

Giarelli, 1997; Miyaishi, Ando, Matsuzawa, Kanawa, & Isobe, 2000) (see Figure 4.2A). Like the oldest-old humans, extreme aged pet dogs also experience a significant decline in cancer-related mortality (Perls & Hutter-Silver, 1999; Cooley et al., 2003) (Figure 4.2B).

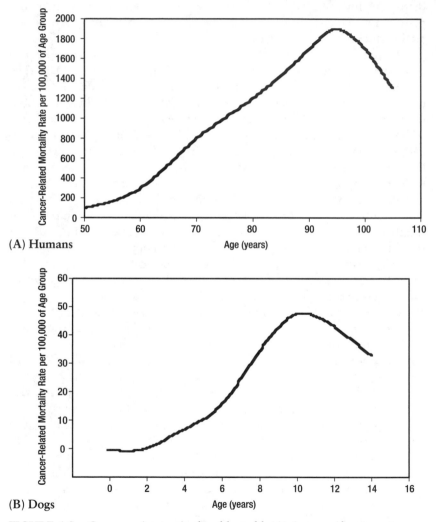

(A) Humans

(B) Dogs

FIGURE 4.2 Cancer resistance in the oldest-old. (A) Age-specific cancer mortality rate in humans (Vital Statistics of the United State, 1994). (B) Age-specific cancer-related mortality rate in 345 Rottweiler dogs (Cooley et al., 2003). Rottweiler dogs older than 13 years are equivalent to human centenarians. Cancer mortality rate begins to decline at 10.5 years in Rottweiler dogs, an age equivalent to 85 years in humans.

Undoubtedly, exceptional longevity is a complex trait reflecting genetic, environmental, and stochastic influences. Based on our current understanding of extreme aged humans and pet dogs, we posited that disease resistance is a central and essential determinant of exceptional longevity (Cooley et al., 2003) (see Figure 4.3). In the extreme aged, strong disease resistance may be manifested as disease avoidance, delayed onset of clinical disease, or decreased mortality from specific diseases. Recent findings in *C. elegans* lend further support to the important contribution of disease resistance to exceptional longevity (Garsin et al., 2003). High physiologic reserve likely contributes to exceptional longevity, because it may delay the clinical onset of diseases or ameliorate the deleterious effects of comorbid conditions. It remains unproven, however, whether the rate of organismal senescence is a significant determinant of exceptional longevity. To date, there are no definitive data from humans supporting the hypothesis that a slow rate of physiologic decline is essential to achieving exceptional longevity. Future studies are needed to collect longitudinal

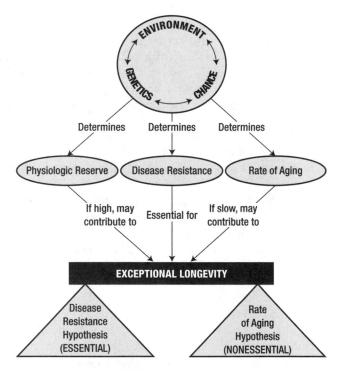

FIGURE 4.3   A conceptual model of factors that contribute to exceptional longevity.

Source: Modified from Cooley et al., 2003.

data on an array of age-sensitive physiologic parameters so that we can determine whether individuals reaching extreme age demonstrate a significantly slower rate of physiologic decline than individuals with usual longevity. The compressed life span of dogs compared to humans makes such studies more feasible in pet dogs that share the same environment as humans (Cooley et al., 2003).

Indeed, several aspects of studying human centenarians present problematic hurdles for researchers: the issue of age validation, stochastic influences, concurrent disease, selection of adequate controls for comparison, and long-term recall, diet and other lifestyle factors. Notwithstanding these challenges, human centenarians remain one of the most highly relevant animal models to probe for the genetic and environmental determinants of successful aging.

THE FRONTIER OF BIOGERONTOLOGIC DISCOVERY: CRITICAL KNOWLEDGE GAPS

During the next decade, basic and applied scientists working in the field of biogerontology will seek to describe the mechanisms of organismal senescence so that prudent public health policies can be developed that will reduce age-related disability and promote healthy life span. Successful resolution of the most important knowledge gaps in the biology of aging will demand the expertise of scientists who possess a wide range of skills and experience—from molecular and cell biology to epidemiology and geriatrics. The next generation of biogerontologists must be transdisciplinarians who excel in their home discipline yet are conversant in related areas of inquiry (Waters, Cooley, Hyner, & Ferraro, in press).

There is a critical need to identify biomarkers that can accurately identify individuals who are aging at significantly different rates. The validation of such biomarkers is an essential step toward the rigorous evaluation of interventions to slow the rate of organismal senescence (Nakamura, Lane, Roth, & Ingram, 1998). Without them, investigators will have to rely on life span as an end point—making studies in long-lived species like humans impractical. Moreover, in the absence of validated biomarkers of senescence, the public will continue to be bombarded by unsubstantiated claims from peddlers of antiaging interventions.

There is genuine concern about the relevance of the model systems used to study aging. At best, animal and cellular models are imitations of human aging. It is imperative that investigators understand and freely communicate the strengths and limitations of the experimental model systems they use. Animal models should never drive the research questions. Instead, the particular research question should determine the selection of the most appropriate animal model (Waters, Bostwick, & Murphy, 1998). There is a recognized need for development of a broader array of model systems, including birds (Holmes & Austad, 1995), marsupials (Austad, 1997), and other mammals (Miller et al., 1999), to test important hypotheses relevant to human aging.

There is need for a coherent theoretical framework that can be used to test important hypotheses. Useful conceptual models should distinguish between senescence and longevity. Development of a consensus framework would undoubtedly help investigators posit hypotheses and propose experiments to answer the most fundamental of all questions: why old tissues have increased vulnerability to disease (Hayflick, 1998). This should also enable the formal testing of the hypothesis that a slower rate of aging is, in fact, an important determinant of exceptional longevity.

It makes good sense to apply a life course perspective to studying the determinants of life span. Biogerontology should not be confined to the study of old cells, old animals, or old people because the origins of many adult health outcomes are shaped significantly by early life events and experiences. For example, the risk of older people to suffer pathologic bone fractures secondary to osteoporosis is strongly dependent on the peak bone mass established in the second and third decades of life. A contemporary approach to finding the determinants of exceptional longevity must also integrate how psychosocial factors modify physiologic homeostasis and the rate of age-related functional decline. The wisdom of using this integrative approach is illustrated by the groundbreaking work documenting that adverse childhood events have a significant impact on adult health outcomes (Felitti et al., 2003).

Clearly, there are many unresolved questions relevant to the question of why we age. Biogerontologists are rolling up their sleeves and getting to work. More than ever before, they are taking an active role in shaping the public dialogue about the goals of aging research: the compression of morbidity and extension of healthy life span. Today, there is great optimism that the frontier of biogerontologic discovery is an exciting place where answers to many questions will be revealed so that these goals can be realized.

REFERENCES

Arking, R. (1987). Successful selection for increased longevity in *Drosophila: Analysis of the survival data and presentation of a hypothesis on the genetic regulation of longevity. Experimental Gerontology, 22,* 199–220.

Austad, S. N. (1993). Retarded senescence in an insular population of Virginia opossums. *Journal of Zoology* (London), *229,* 695–708.

Austad, S. N. (1997). Comparative aging and life histories in mammals. *Experimental Gerontology, 32,* 23–38.

Barja, G., Cadenas, S., Rojas, C., Perez-Campo, R., & Lopez-Torres, M. (1994). Low mitochondrial free radical production per unit O_2 consumption can explain the simultaneous presence of high longevity and high aerobic metabolic rate in birds. *Free Radical Research, 21,* 317–327.

Bartke, A., Brown-Borg, H. M., Bode, A. M., Carlson, J., Hunter, W. S., & Bronson, R. T. (1998). Does growth hormone prevent or accelerate aging? *Experimental Gerontology, 33,* 675–687.

Barzilai, N., Atzmon, G., Schechter, C., Schaefer, E. J., Cupples, A. L., Lipton, R., et al. (2003). Unique lipoprotein phenotype and genotype associated with exceptional longevity. *Journal of the American Medical Association, 290,* 2030–2040.

Beckman, K. B., & Ames, B. N. (1998). The free radical theory of aging matures. *Physiological Reviews, 78,* 547–581.

Binstock, R. H. (2004). Anti-aging medicine and research: A realm of conflict and profound societal implications. *Journal of Gerontology Series A: Biological Sciences and Medical Sciences, 59,* B523–B533.

Blackman, M. R., Sorkin, J. D., Munzer, T., Bellantoni, M. F., Busby-Whitehead, J., Stevens, T. E., et al. (2002). Growth hormone and sex steroid administration in healthy aged women and men: A randomized controlled trial. *Journal of the American Medical Association, 288,* 2282–2292.

Blumberg, J. B. (2000). Free radical theory of aging. In J. E. Morley, H. J. Armbrecht, R. M. Coe, & B. Vellas (Eds.), *The science of geriatrics, Vol. 1* (pp. 57–74). New York: Springer Publishing.

Butler, R. N., Austad, S. N., Barzilai, N., Braun, A., Helfand, S., Larsen, P. L., et al. (2003). Longevity genes: From primitive organisms to humans. *Journal of Gerontology Series A: Biological Sciences and Medical Sciences, 58,* 581–584.

Campisi, J. (1996). Replicative senescence: An old lives' tale? *Cell, 84,* 497–500.

Campisi, J. (2003). Cellular senescence and apoptosis: How cellular responses might influence aging phenotypes. *Experimental Gerontology, 38,* 5–11.

Carney, J. M., Starke-Reed, P. E., Oliver, C. N., Landum, R. W., Cheng, M. S., Wu, J. F., et al. (1991). Reversal of age-related increase in brain protein oxidation, decrease in enzyme activity, and loss in temporal and spatial memory by chronic administration of the spin-trapping compound N-tert-butyl-alpha-phenylnitrone. *Proceedings of the National Academy of Sciences of the United States of America, 88,* 3633–3636.

Chan, J. M., Stampfer, M. J., Giovannucci, E., Gann, P. H., Ma, J., Wilkinson, P., et al. (1998). Plasma insulin-like growth factor-I and prostate cancer risk: A prospective study. *Science, 279,* 563–566.

Clancy, D. J., Gems, D., Harshman, L. G., Oldham, S., Stocker, H., Hafen, E., et al. (2001). Extension of life-span by loss of CHICO, a Drosophila insulin receptor substrate protein. *Science, 292,* 104–106.

Cooley, D. M., Schlittler, D. L., Glickman, L. T., Hayek, M., & Waters, D. J. (2003). Exceptional longevity in pet dogs is accompanied by cancer resistance and delayed onset of major diseases. *Journal of Gerontology Series A: Biological Sciences and Medical Sciences, 58,* B1078–B1084.

Cristofalo, V. J., Allen, R. G., Pignolo, R. J., Martin, B. G., & Beck, J. C. (1998). Relationship between donor age and the replicative lifespan of human cells in culture: A reevaluation. *Proceedings of the National Academy of Sciences of the United States of America, 95,* 10614–10619.

Cristofalo, V. J., & Pignolo, R. J. (1993). Replicative senescence of human fibroblast-like cells in culture. *Physiological Reviews, 73,* 617–638.

Deeb, B. J., & Wolf, N. S. (1994). Studying longevity and morbidity in giant and small breeds of dogs. *Veterinary Medicine* (Suppl.), *89,* 702–713.

Dimri, G. P. (2005). What has senescence got to do with cancer? *Cancer Cell, 7,* 505–512.

Dimri, G. P., Lee, X., Basile, G., Acosta, M., Scott, G., Roskelley, C., et al. (1995). A biomarker that identifies senescent human cells in culture and in aging skin in vivo. *Proceedings of the National Academy of Sciences of the United States of America, 92,* 9363–9367.

Evert, J., Lawler, E., Bogan, H., & Perls, T. (2003). Morbidity profiles of centenarians: Survivors, delayers, and escapers. *Journal of Gerontology Series A: Biological Sciences and Medical Sciences, 58,* 232–237.

Felitti, V. J., Anda, R. F., Nordenberg, D., Williamson, D. F., Spitz, A. M., Edwards, V., et al. (1998). Relationship of childhood abuse and household dysfunction to many of the leading causes of death in adults. The Adverse Childhood Experiences (ACE) Study. *American Journal of Preventive Medicine, 14,* 245–258.

Finch, C. E. (1990). *Longevity, senescence and the genome.* Chicago: University of Chicago Press.

Finch, C. E. (1998). Variations in senesence and longevity include the possibility of negligible senescence. *Journal of Gerontology Series A: Biological Sciences and Medical Sciences, 53A,* 232–237.

Finch, C. E., & Austad, S. N. (2001). History and prospects: Symposium on organisms with slow aging. *Experimental Gerontology, 36,* 593–597.

Finch, C. E., & Kirkwood, T. B. L. (2000). *Chance, development and aging.* New York: Oxford University Press.

Finch, C. E., & Ruvkun, G. (2001). The genetics of aging. *Annual Review of Genomics and Human Genetics, 2,* 435–462.

Floyd, R. A., Hensley, K., Forster, M. J., Kelleher-Andersson, J. A., & Wood, P. L. (2002). Nitrones, their value as therapeutics and probes to understand aging. *Mechanisms of Ageing and Development, 123,* 1021–1031.

Franceschi, C., Motta, L., Valensin, S., Rapisarda, R., Franzone, A., Berardelli, M., et al. (2000). Do men and women follow different trajectories to reach extreme longevity? *Aging* (Milano), *12,* 77–84.

Fries, J. F. (2003). Measuring and monitoring success in compressing morbidity. *Annals of Internal Medicine, 139,* 455–459.

Garsin, D. A., Villanueva, J. M., Begun, J., Kim, D. H., Sifri, C. D., Calderwood, S. B., et al. (2003). Long-lived *C. elegans* daf-2 mutants are resistant to bacterial pathogens. *Science, 300,* 1921.

Giovannucci, E., Pollak, M. N., Platz, E. A., Willett, W. C., Stampfer, M. J., Majeed, N., et al. (2000). A prospective study of plasma insulin-like growth factor-1 and binding protein-3 and risk of colorectal neoplasia in women. *Cancer Epidemiology, Biomarkers and Prevention, 9,* 345–349.

Granger, M. P., Wright, W. E., & Shay, J. W. (2002). Telomerase in cancer and aging. *Critical Reviews in Oncology/Hematology, 41,* 29–40.

Hamilton, M. L., Van Remmen, H., Drake, J. A., Yang, H., Guo, Z. M., Kewitt, K., et al. (2001). Does oxidative damage to DNA increase with age? *Proceedings of the National Academy of Sciences of the United States of America, 98,* 10469–10474.

Harman, D. (1956). Aging: A theory based on free radical and radiation chemistry. *Journal of Gerontology, 11,* 298–300.

Hass, B. S., Lewis, S. M., Duffy, P. H., Ershler, W., Feuers, R. J., Good, R. A., et al. (1996). Dietary restriction in humans: Report on the Little Rock Conference on the value, feasibility, and parameters of a proposed study. *Mechanisms of Ageing and Development, 91,* 79–94.

Hasty, P., & Vijg, J. (2004). Accelerating aging by mouse reverse genetics: A rational approach to understanding longevity. *Aging Cell, 3,* 55–65.

Hayflick, L. (1976). The cell biology of human aging. *New England Journal of Medicine, 295,* 1302–1308.

Hayflick, L. (1998). How and why we age. *Experimental Gerontology, 33,* 639–653.

Hayflick, L., & Moorhead, P. S. (1961). The serial cultivation of human diploid cell strains. *Experimental Cell Research, 25,* 585–621.

Hodes, R. J., McCormick, A. M., & Pruzan, M. (1996). Longevity assurance genes: How do they influence aging and life span? *Journal of the American Geriatric Society, 44,* 988–991.

Holmes, D. J., & Austad, S. N. (1995). Birds as animal models for the comparative biology of aging: A prospectus. *Journal of Gerontology Series A: Biological Sciences and Medical Sciences, 50,* B59–B66.

Huang, T. T., Carlson, E. J., Gillespie, A. M., Shi, Y., & Epstein, C. J. (2000). Ubiquitous overexpression of CuZn superoxide dismutase does not extend life span in mice. *Journal of Gerontology Series A: Biological Sciences and Medical Sciences, 55,* B5–B9.

Hyland, P., Duggan, O., Turbitt, J., Coulter, J., Wikby, A., Johansson, B., et al. (2002). Nonagenarians from the Swedish NONA Immune Study have increased plasma antioxidant capacity and similar levels of DNA damage in peripheral blood mononuclear cells compared to younger control subjects. *Experimental Gerontology, 37,* 465–473.

Jordan, V. C. (2004). Selective estrogen receptor modulation: Concept and consequences in cancer. *Cancer Cell, 5,* 207–213.

Kim Sh, S. H., Kaminker, P., & Campisi, J. (2002). Telomeres, aging and cancer: In search of a happy ending. *Oncogene, 21,* 503–511.

Kimura, K. D., Tissenbaum, H. A., Liu, Y., & Ruvkun, G. (1997). daf-2, an insulin receptor-like gene that regulates longevity and diapause in *Caenorhabditis elegans. Science, 277,* 942–946.

Kirkwood, T. B. (1977). Evolution of ageing. *Nature, 270,* 301–304.

Kirkwood, T. B. (1990). The disposable soma theory of aging. In D. E. Harrison, (Ed.), *Genetic effects on aging* (Vol. 2, pp. 9–19). Caldwell, NJ: Telford Press.

Krause, W., Mueller, U., & Mazur, A. (2005). Testosterone supplementation in the aging male: Which questions have been answered? *Aging Male, 8,* 31–38.

Krtolica, A., Parrinello, S., Lockett, S., Desprez, P. Y., & Campisi, J. (2001). Senescent fibroblasts promote epithelial cell growth and tumorigenesis: A link between cancer and aging. *Proceedings of the National Academy of Sciences of the United States of America, 98,* 12072–12077.

Lamberts, S. W., van den Beld, A. W., & van der Lely, A. J. (1997). The endocrinology of aging. *Science, 278,* 419–424.

Lebel, M., & Leder, P. (1998). A deletion within the murine Werner syndrome helicase induces sensitivity to inhibitors of topoisomerase and loss of cellular proliferative capacity. *Proceedings of the National Academy of Sciences of the United States of America, 95,* 13097–13102.

Lin, Y. J., Seroude, L., & Benzer, S. (1998). Extended life-span and stress resistance in the *Drosophila* mutant methuselah. *Science, 282,* 943–946.

Ljungquist, B., Berg, S., Lanke, J., McClearn, G. E., & Pedersen, N. L. (1998). The effect of genetic factors for longevity: A comparison of identical and fraternal twins in the Swedish Twin Registry. *Journal of Gerontology Series A: Biological Sciences and Medical Sciences, 53,* M441–M446.

Love, R. R., Mazess, R. B., Barden, H. S., Epstein, S., Newcomb, P. A., Jordan, V. C., et al. (1992). Effects of tamoxifen on bone mineral density in postmenopausal women with breast cancer. *New England Journal of Medicine, 326,* 852–856.

Mair, W., Goymer, P., Pletcher, S. D., & Partridge, L. (2003). Demography of dietary restriction and death in *Drosophila. Science, 301,* 1731–1733.

Marcotte, R., & Wang, E. (2002). Replicative senescence revisited. *Journal of Gerontology Series A: Biological Sciences and Medical Sciences, 57,* B257–B269.

Martin, G. M. (1978). Genetic syndromes in man with potential relevance to the pathobiology of aging. In D. Bergsma & D. E. Harrison (Eds.), *Genetic effects on aging* (Vol. 14, pp. 5–39). New York: Alan R. Liss.

Martin, G. M. (1999). APOE alleles and lipophylic pathogens. *Neurobiology of Aging, 20,* 441–443.

Martin, G. M. (2002). Gene action in the aging brain: An evolutionary biological perspective. *Neurobiology of Aging, 23,* 647–654.

Martin, G. M., Austad, S. N., & Johnson, T. E. (1996). Genetic analysis of ageing: Role of oxidative damage and environmental stresses. *Nature Genetics, 13,* 25–34.

Martin, G. M., Sprague, C. A., & Epstein, C. J. (1970). Replicative life-span of cultivated human cells. Effects of donor's age, tissue, and genotype. *Laboratory Investigation, 23,* 86–92.

Masoro E. J. (2003). Subfield history: Caloric restriction, slowing aging, and extending life. *Scientific Aging Knowledge Environment, 8,* RE2. Review.

McCay, C. M., Crowell, M. F., & Maynard, L. A. (1935). The effect of retarded growth upon the length of life span and upon the ultimate body size. *Journal of Nutrition, 10,* 63–79.

McGue, M., Vaupel, J. W., Holm, N., & Harvald, B. (1993). Longevity is moderately heritable in a sample of Danish twins born 1870–1880. *Journal of Gerontology, 48,* B237–B244.

Medawar, P. (1952). *An unsolved problem of biology.* London: H. K. Lewis.

Melov, S., Ravenscroft, J., Malik, S., Gill, M. S., Walker, D. W., Clayton, P. E., et al. (2000). Extension of life-span with superoxide dismutase/catalase mimetics. *Science, 289,* 1567–1569.

Migliaccio, E., Giorgio, M., Mele, S., Pelicci, G., Reboldi, P., Pandolfi, P. P., et al. (1999). The p66shc adaptor protein controls oxidative stress response and life span in mammals. *Nature, 402,* 309–313.

Miller, R. A. (1999). Kleemeier award lecture: Are there genes for aging? *Journal of Gerontology Series A: Biological Sciences and Medical Sciences, 54,* B297–B307.

Miller, R. A. (2004). "Accelerated aging": A primrose path to insight? *Aging Cell, 3,* 47–51.

Miller, R. A., Austad, S., Burke, D., Chrisp, C., Dysko, R., Galecki, A., et al. (1999). Exotic mice as models for aging research: Polemic and prospectus. *Neurobiology of Aging, 20,* 217–231.

Miquel, J. (1992). An update on the mitochondrial-DNA mutation hypothesis of cell aging. *Mutation Research, 275,* 209–216.

Miyaishi, O., Ando, F., Matsuzawa, K., Kanawa, R., & Isobe, K. (2000). Cancer incidence in old age. *Mechanisms of Ageing and Development, 117,* 47–55.

Mobbs, C. V., Bray, G. A., Atkinson, R. L., Bartke, A., Finch, C. E., Maratos-Flier, et al. (2001). Neuroendocrine and pharmacological manipulations to assess how caloric restriction increases life span. *Journal of Gerontology Series A: Biological Sciences and Medical Sciences, 56,* 34–44.

Monteiro, H. P., & Stern, A. (1996). Redox modulation of tyrosine phosphorylation-dependent signal transduction pathways. *Free Radical Biology and Medicine, 21,* 323–333.

Morris, J. Z., Tissenbaum, H. A., & Ruvkun, G. (1996). A phosphatidylinositol-3-OH kinase family member regulating longevity and diapause in *Caenorhabditis elegans. Nature, 382,* 536–539.

Nakamura, E., Lane, M. A., Roth, G. S., & Ingram, D. K. (1998). A strategy for identifying biomarkers of aging: Further evaluation of hematology and blood chemistry data from a calorie restriction study in rhesus monkeys. *Experimental Gerontology, 33,* 421–443.

Olshansky, S. J., Hayflick, L., & Carnes, B. A. (2002). Position statement on human aging. *Journal of Gerontology Series A: Biological Sciences and Medical Sciences, 57,* B292–B297.

Orr, W. C., & Sohal, R. S. (1994). Extension of life-span by overexpression of superoxide dismutase and catalase in *Drosophila melanogaster. Science, 263,* 1128–1130.

Parkes, T. L., Elia, A. J., Dickinson, D., Hilliker, A. J., Phillips, J. P., & Boulianne, G. L. (1998). Extension of *Drosophila* lifespan by overexpression of human SOD1 in motorneurons. *Nature Genetics, 19,* 171–174.

Patronek, G. J., Waters, D. J., & Glickman, L. T. (1997). Comparative longevity of pet dogs and humans: Implications for gerontology research. *Journal of Gerontology Series A Biological Sciences and Medical Sciences, 52,* B171–B178.

Perls, T., Alpert, L., & Frett, R. (1997). Middle aged mothers live longer. *Nature, 389,* 133.

Perls, T., & Hutter-Silver, M. (1999). *Living to 100: Lessons in living to your maximum potential at any age.* New York: Basic Books.

Perls, T., Levenson, R., Regan, M., & Puca, A. (2002). What does it take to live to 100? *Mechanisms of Ageing and Development, 123,* 231–242.

Perls, T. T., Wilmoth, J., Levenson, R., Drinkwater, M., Cohen, M., Bogan, H., Joyce, E., et al. (2002). Life-long sustained mortality advantage of siblings of centenarians. *Proceedings of the National Academy of Sciences of the United States of America, 99,* 8442–8447.

Premoselli, F., Sesca, E., Binasco, V., Caderni, G., & Tessitore, L. (1998). Fasting/refeeding before initiation enhances the growth of aberrant crypt foci induced by azoxymethane in rat colon and rectum. *International Journal of Cancer, 77,* 286–294.

Puca, A. A., Daly, M. J., Brewster, S. J., Matise, T. C., Barrett, J., Shea-Drinkwater, M., et al. (2001). A genome-wide scan for linkage to human exceptional longevity identifies a locus on chromosome 4. *Proceedings of the National Academy of Sciences of the United States of America, 98,* 10505–10508.

Pugh, T. D., Oberley, T. D., & Weindruch, R. (1999). Dietary intervention at middle age: Caloric restriction but not dehydroepiandrosterone sulfate increases lifespan and lifetime cancer incidence in mice. *Cancer Research, 59,* 1642–1648.

Ramsey, M. M., Ingram, R. L., Cashion, A. B., Ng, A. H., Cline, J. M., Parlow, A. F., et al. (2002). Growth hormone-deficient dwarf animals are resistant to dimethylbenzanthracine (DMBA)-induced mammary carcinogenesis. *Endocrinology, 143,* 4139–4142.

Ravaja, N., Raikkonen, K., Lyytinen, H., Lehtimaki, T., & Keltikangas-Jarvinen, L. (1997). Apolipoprotein E phenotypes and cardiovascular responses to experimentally induced mental stress in adolescent boys. *Journal of Behavioral Medicine, 20,* 571–587.

Roberts, S. B., Pi-Sunyer, X., Kuller, L., Lane, M. A., Ellison, P., Prior, J. C., et al. (2001). Physiologic effects of lowering caloric intake in nonhuman primates and nonobese humans. *Journal of Gerontology Series A: Biological Sciences and Medical Sciences, 56,* 66–75.

Roth, G. S., Ingram, D. K., & Lane, M. A. (2001). Caloric restriction in primates and relevance to humans. *Annals of the New York Academy of Sciences, 928,* 305–315.

Rubin, H. (2002). The disparity between human cell senescence in vitro and life-long replication in vivo. *Nature Biotechnology, 20,* 675–681.

Rudman, D., Feller, A. G., Nagraj, H. S., Gergans, G. A., Lalitha, P. Y., Goldberg, A. F., et al. (1990). Effects of human growth hormone in men over 60 years old. *New England Journal of Medicine, 323,* 1–6.

Schachter, F., Faure-Delanef, L., Guenot, F., Rouger, H., Froguel, P., Lesueur-Ginot, L., et al. (1994). Genetic associations with human longevity at the APOE and ACE loci. *Nature Genetics, 6,* 29–32.

Schernhammer, E. S., Holly, J. M., Pollak, M. N., & Hankinson, S. E. (2005). Circulating levels of insulin-like growth factors, their binding proteins, and breast cancer risk. *Cancer Epidemiology, Biomarkers and Prevention, 14,* 699–704.

Shumaker, S. A., Legault, C., Rapp, S. R., Thal, L., Wallace, R. B., Ockene, J. K., et al. (2003). Estrogen plus progestin and the incidence of dementia and mild cognitive impairment in postmenopausal women: The Women's Health Initiative Memory Study: A randomized controlled trial. *Journal of the American Medical Association, 289,* 2651–2662.

Smith, D. W. E (1996). Cancer mortality at very old ages. *Cancer, 77,* 1367–1372.

Sohal, R. S., Agarwal, S., Dubey, A., & Orr, W. C. (1993). Protein oxidative damage is associated with life expectancy of houseflies. *Proceedings of the National Academy of Sciences of the United States of America, 90,* 7255–7259.

Sohal, R. S., Sohal, B. H., & Brunk, U. T. (1990). Relationship between antioxidant defenses and longevity in different mammalian species. *Mechanisms of Ageing and Development, 53,* 217–227.

Speakman, J. R., Talbot, D. A., Selman, C., Snart, S., McLaren, J. S., Redman, P., et al. (2004). Uncoupled and surviving: Individual mice with high metabolism have greater mitochondrial uncoupling and live longer. *Aging Cell, 3,* 87–95.

Stanta, G., Campagner, L., Cavallieri, F., & Giarelli, L. (1997). Cancer of the oldest old. What we have learned from autopsy studies. *Clinics in Geriatric Medicine, 13,* 55–68.

Tagliaferro, A. R., Ronan, A. M., Meeker, L. D., Thompson, H. J., Scott, A. L., & Sinha, D. (1996). Cyclic food restriction alters substrate utilization and abolishes protection from mammary carcinogenesis female rats. *Journal of Nutrition, 126,* 1398–1405.

Tang, M. X., Jacobs, D., Stern, Y., Marder, K., Schofield, P., Gurland, B., et al. (1996). Effect of oestrogen during menopause on risk and age at onset of Alzheimer's disease. *Lancet, 348,* 429–432.

Toussaint, O., Medrano, E. E., & von Zglinicki, T. (2000). Cellular and molecular mechanisms of stress-induced premature senescence (SIPS) of human diploid fibroblasts and melanocytes. *Experimental Gerontology, 35,* 927–945.

Van Cauter, E., Leproult, R., & Plat, I. (2000). Age-related changes in slow wave sleep and REM sleep and relationship with growth hormone and cortisol levels in healthy men. *Journal of the American Medical Association, 284,* 861–868.

von Zglinicki T., Burkle, A., & Kirkwood, T. B. (2001). Stress, DNA damage and ageing—an integrative approach. *Experimental Gerontology, 36,* 1049–1062.

Wachsman, J. T. (1996). The beneficial effects of dietary restriction: Reduced oxidative damage and enhanced apoptosis. *Mutation Research, 350,* 25–34.

Waters, D. J., Bostwick, D. G., & Murphy, G. P. (1998). Conference summary: First International Workshop on Animal Models of Prostate Cancer. *Prostate, 36,* 47–48.

Waters, D. J., Cooley, D. M., Hyner, G. C., & Ferraro, K. F., (in press). Training the next generation of biogerontologists: Opportunities and challenges. *Experimental Gerontology.*

Weindruch, R., Keenan, K. P., Carney, J. M., Fernandes, G., Feuers, R. J., Floyd, R. A., et al. (2001). Caloric restriction mimetics: Metabolic interventions. *Journal of Gerontology Series A: Biological Sciences and Medical Sciences, 56,* 20–33.

Williams, G. (1957). Pleiotropy, natural selection, and the evolution of senescence. *Evolution, 11,* 398–411.

Wolkow, C. A., Kimura, K. D., Lee, M. S., & Ruvkun, G. (2000). Regulation of *C. elegans* life-span by insulinlike signaling in the nervous system. *Science, 290,* 147–150.

Wu, L. L., Chiou, C. C., Chang, P. Y., & Wu, J. T. (2004). Urinary 8-OHdG: A marker of oxidative stress to DNA and a risk factor for cancer, atherosclerosis and diabetics. *Clinical Chimica Acta, 339,* 1–9.

Yu, B. P. (1996). Aging and oxidative stress: Modulation by dietary restriction. *Free Radical Biology and Medicine, 21,* 651–668.

CHAPTER 5

Cognitive Aging

Aimée M. Surprenant
Ian Neath

When people think of growing older, they not only express concerns over losing their abilities to think, reason, and remember as well as they used to, but they increasingly worry that these changes will have a profound impact on all aspects of their lives (Centofanti, 1998). Research suggests that these concerns are not unfounded: decreases in cognitive functioning have been associated with significant increases in depression and can have a great impact on quality of life (Comijs et al., 2004). Individuals experiencing cognitive decline lose relationships even with members of their own family, a change that does not occur with physical decline alone (Aartsen, van Tilburg, Smits, & Knipscheer, 2004). Recent research has established close links among cognitive, physical, social, and emotional health and has shown that they rely on one another to an astonishing degree (Baltes & Lindenberger, 1997; Colcombe & Kramer, 2003; Gallo, Rebok, Tennsted, Wadley, & Horgas, 2003). Findings such as these reinforce the notion that age-related differences in cognitive functioning do not occur in a vacuum: the entire person needs to be considered in order to develop a comprehensive theory of cognitive aging.

As the most recent edition of the *Handbook of Aging and Cognition* (Craik & Salthouse, 2000) illustrates, cognitive aging encompasses a wide

Preparation of this chapter was sponsored by National Institute on Aging Grant AG021071 awarded to both authors. Portions of this chapter were written while the authors were Visiting Fellows at the Department of Psychology, City University, London, UK. The authors are now at Memorial University of Newfoundland, St. John's, NL, Canada, A1B 3X9.

range of topics, including memory, attention, language, human factors, intelligence, and changes in the brain. One chapter cannot hope to survey all of the topics in cognitive aging. Rather, we situate the field of cognitive aging within gerontology, discuss how cognitive psychologists investigate the fundamental processes underlying the aging of the mind, and identify the most promising theoretical frameworks driving the research. Finally, we briefly touch on some new developments in the area of cognitive neuroscience and aging, and effects of training interventions on retaining or slowing declines in cognitive abilities in older adults.

COGNITION AND GERONTOLOGY

It has been suggested that the field of gerontology has been shifting to a focus on life course analysis that encompasses the entire developmental history of the individual (Ferraro, 1997). In addition, the field has been emphasizing a multidisciplinary approach, including investigating the biological, behavioral, and social structural factors that influence aging and their interactions. To a certain extent, this is also true among researchers interested in cognitive aging. For example, there is an increasing body of research using large-scale cross-sectional and longitudinal methods to examine the psychological, social, health, biological, economic, and other factors that might have an impact on cognitive functioning. These studies include, among others, the Seattle Longitudinal Study (Schaie, 2004), the Berlin Aging Study (Baltes & Meyer, 1999), the Longitudinal Aging Study Amsterdam (Deeg, Knipscheer, & van Tilburg, 1993), and the Victoria Longitudinal Aging study (Hultsch, Hertzog, Dixon, & Small, 1998). All of these studies include multiple measures of each cognitive construct, as well as demographic, health, and other social, economic, and behavioral measures.

These large-scale studies are excellent resources and give an important overview of many aspects of cognitive aging. However, in some senses, these reports are unsatisfying because they are correlational and tend to be rather atheoretical in nature. In addition, the sheer amount of information collected tends to make it difficult to abstract a general message. On the other hand, these studies are valuable in that they can help focus and narrow down the important variables that can then be tested empirically. As such, they can pave the way toward an integration of longitudinal models with experimental tests of the multiple alternative explanations that exist for such data (Hertzog, 2004).

In addition to these large-scale studies, there has been an increasing sensitivity to the importance of considering a broad range of factors in more traditional cognitive aging research. This shift in thinking is illustrated by the contributions in *New Frontiers in Cognitive Aging* (Dixon,

Bäckman, & Nilsson, 2004). This edited book includes chapters discussing new theoretical and methodological orientations and sets the field of cognitive aging more firmly in the gerontological arena. In particular, cognition is placed in the context of everyday functioning in familiar environments, something that is often missing from traditional laboratory-based measures of cognition. In contrast to many other compendia on cognition and aging, the book includes an entire section on biological and health effects on cognitive aging.

Thus, it seems that the context of cognitive aging has been broadening considerably, along with the rest of gerontology. These investigations help us determine what empirical effects to search for, the types of dependent variables to be examined, and the methods that will be used to search for explanations. The interplay of theory, method, and the choice of the constructs or underlying effects that are investigated determine, to some extent, the conclusions that are drawn from them (Light, 2004).

METHODOLOGICAL ISSUES

Psychometric (Macro) Versus Experimental (Micro) Approaches

The study of cognitive aging is divided, like many other areas of gerontological inquiry, into researchers who are interested in issues involved with aging in particular and researchers who wish to use the aging population to help develop models of cognition in general. Salthouse (2000) places the psychometric and experimental approaches into two general categories: macro (broad and integrative) and micro (analytical and specific).

The macro approach focuses on a broad range of cognitive processing abilities that differ as a function of age and generally uses correlational or psychometric techniques. In this method, the researcher is interested in identifying commonalities among tasks in terms of the underlying abilities they tap. The ultimate goal is to determine the fundamental cognitive abilities that are different as a function of age. This approach assumes that there are a limited number of general effects of aging that are shared among a variety of tasks. Typically, researchers adopting this method use an individual differences or psychometric design in which each participant is given multiple tasks. The underlying constructs controlling performance in the tasks are identified by using statistical procedures that identify shared variances (see, e.g., Salthouse & Ferrer-Caja, 2003). Using such designs, one can identify the number of age-related influences that operate on the cognitive variables being measured. Mediating variables that interact with the latent variables can also be identified.

In contrast, the micro approach focuses on describing specific tasks and processes that differ as a function of age and generally uses an experimental manipulation of independent variables. This method is a common one in information processing, still the dominant paradigm in cognitive psychology (see, e.g., Fisk & Rogers, 1991; Fisher & Glaser, 1996): A task is decomposed into subtasks, each relatively independent of the others. In terms of aging, the magnitude of the age-related influence on each aspect of a task can be measured. As an example of this type of approach, consider a simple reaction time task in which the subject is asked to respond as quickly as possible to the presentation of a stimulus, perhaps by pressing a key. The time it takes to respond is measured. In a more complex version of the task, the subject may be asked to identify the stimulus and choose among a number of alternative responses. Analytically, the time to complete the second task can be decomposed into the simple task plus the time it takes to identify the stimulus and make a choice. This type of approach lends itself naturally to an experimental design in which the experimenter varies the parameters of a single task to try to determine effects of aging on each aspect of the task.

A relatively recent approach to the study of cognitive aging uses the logic of simulation modeling to investigate very complex interactions among variables. This can be seen as a middle ground between the macro and micro approaches. There are many advantages in using a formal model to help guide interpretation of the data (Neath, 1999). It has become increasingly obvious that the effects of aging on cognition are extremely complex and are caused by multiple interactions among factors. A formal computational model allows for the exploration of higher-order interactions that simply could not be worked through with a less detailed verbal model. In addition, clear and testable predictions can be made from a formal model in which psychologically plausible parameters are mapped on to particular human processes. The drawback to computational modeling, of course, is that it is merely an existence proof; it shows that if we manipulate the parameters in such a way, the proper pattern of data emerges. If the parameters do not map on to real properties of the organism, it can become merely an exercise in fitting data.

Cross-Sectional versus Longitudinal Designs

Much of the research in cognitive aging uses a cross-sectional design. In these investigations, the performance of a group of individuals from one age range is compared to that of a group from another age range. There are numerous difficulties in drawing conclusions about the effects of chronological age per se from such a design. There are a substantial number of uncontrolled covariates, including cohort effects, motivation, and health status, to name just a few (for a review, see Salthouse, 1991).

However, these designs can be very informative in identifying specific areas of differences between groups of older and younger adults. There are a number of ways in which researchers overcome or work around the difficulties embodied in cross-sectional designs. For example, many studies use a cross-sectional design but several different kinds of older subject groups (see, e.g., Craik, Byrd, & Swanson, 1987).

In contrast to cross-sectional designs, longitudinal research involves following particular individuals over a period of time and testing them repeatedly (see, e.g., Hultsch et al., 1998; Hertzog, 2004). These designs allow the researcher to estimate individual changes in particular abilities rather than inferring changes based on differences among disparate groups. These sorts of designs control for the covariates that are unconstrained in cross-sectional designs, particularly effects of early experience. However, these designs are costly, and once the study has begun, it is difficult to incorporate new techniques and tasks to test new hypotheses.

Although it may often be argued that the ideal case for studying cognition and aging is a longitudinal design, each approach brings with it difficulties and limitations. As noted nearly 50 years ago (Garner, Hake, & Eriksen, 1956), researchers must be cautious in forming conclusions based on data from just one methodology. Instead, the strategy of looking for converging operations from multiple paradigms results in the most powerful conclusions (e.g., Bromley, 1990; Salthouse, 2000). The idea is that to the extent that one finds a similar pattern of results using a number of different perspectives, the results are less likely to be due to the adoption of one particular method. Hertzog (1996) recommends a three-stage approach. First, one might test participants in an extreme-group cross-sectional study to establish that there is an age-related effect (e.g., young versus older adults). This can then be followed by a larger cross-sectional study involving a continuous range of ages to gain an idea of the magnitude of the effect and at what age it begins to become apparent. Finally, longitudinal studies can be conducted to determine the predictors and other factors that go along with and may be a cause of those changes.

Meta-Analysis

Meta-analysis is a tool for combining results from multiple experiments in order to take advantage of the increased number of observations to determine the true size of an effect. This method can be used to integrate disparate findings and summarize an entire body of research. For example, using such a technique, Light and her colleagues (Light, Prull, La Voie, & Healy, 2000) were able to resolve a long-standing controversy over whether there was a difference in implicit memory performance between older and younger adults.

AGE-RELATED DIFFERENCES IN COGNITIVE FUNCTIONING

The primary question posed by researchers in cognitive aging concerns the specific differences in cognitive functioning between older and younger adults. Is it the case that performance declines only on particular tasks, with some abilities spared, or, as Rabbitt (1993) put it, "Does it all go together when it goes?"

Perceptual Deficits

Both visual and auditory processing abilities decline substantially as a function of increasing age. Age-related hearing loss, or presbycusis, is experienced by as many one-third of adults over the age of 70. In addition, about 14% of individuals from 70 to 75 years old experience trouble seeing even with glasses; that number increases to 32 percent for those over age 85 (Desai, Pratt, Lentzner, & Robinson, 2001). Age-related declines in perceptual abilities are not restricted solely to increases in sensory thresholds: complex processing, including frequency discrimination, temporal processing, gap detection, and sound localization, is also generally affected in older adults. Understanding speech in noise is particularly difficult for older adults, even when they have normal hearing for their age group. This can lead older adults to avoid situations in which conversation will be difficult, thus reducing the number of social activities, for example. Light sensitivity, visual acuity, color vision, and contrast sensitivity are all worse in the older eye. (See Schneider & Pichora-Fuller, 2000, for a comprehensive review of perceptual deterioration as a function of age.) These types of deficits can lead to an unwillingness to drive or travel, again limiting social interaction.

In addition to the social and health implications of these deficits, there are serious cognitive consequences. Efficient perceptual processing is essential for navigating through the world, following discourse, and integrating information from multiple sources. Speech perception, in particular, relies on the rapid processing of auditory input and may be substantially affected by hearing loss.

Memory

Memory is an area of great concern for many older adults, but the correlation between actual memory ability and self-judged memory ability can be quite low (Hertzog, 2002). For example, Rabbitt and Abson (1991) found that older subjects' estimates of their performance were uncorrelated with their actual performance on recognition, memory span, recall, and cumulative learning tasks. Interestingly, there were significant correlations between estimated memory ability and reports of depression: people who thought their memory abilities were poor or declining were more likely to report feeling depressed.

Older adults generally perform worse than younger adults on memory tests in which there are few environmental cues. Thus, they perform worse on recall tests but equivalently on recognition tests (Naveh-Benjamin, Hussain, Guez, & Bar-On, 2003) and worse on explicit than implicit tasks (La Voie & Light, 1994; Light & La Voie, 1993). In immediate memory, older adults perform worse on tasks that require the active manipulation of information but only slightly worse on measures of simple memory span (Zacks, Hasher, & Li, 2000).

Prospective memory refers to remembering to perform some action at some point in the future. There are two different ways in which prospective memory tasks can be categorized. In a time-based task, the subject must perform some activity at a certain time; in an event-based task, the subject must perform the activity when a certain event occurs. Examples are remembering to take a pill every 8 hours versus remembering to give a neighbor a message when you see her. Comparing young college-age individuals and older adults (age 70 to 78), Einstein, McDaniel, Richardson, Guynn, and Cunfer (1995) found no age-related differences on an event-based prospective memory task, but did find age-related differences on a time-based task. Interestingly, older adults are often better than younger adults in remembering to perform real-life tasks, perhaps due to greater motivation (Rendell & Thomson, 1999). Anderson and Craik (2000) argue that the self-initiated activities that show a large decline with aging in the prospective memory literature are the same as those that show a decline in recall and context; both are sensitive to the amount of environmental support available in the situation.

A burgeoning area of research on memory and aging is often referred to as false memories (although the word *false* is a misnomer; see Neath & Surprenant, 2003, for a discussion). In this type of illusory recollection, individuals "remember" an event that never happened. This phenomenon is common in younger people and surprisingly easy to demonstrate in laboratory conditions (Hyman & Billings, 1998). Older adults seem particularly susceptible to such illusions (Dywan & Jacoby, 1990). This susceptibility has been interpreted as being due to a difficulty in identifying the origin of a memory or source monitoring. For example, older adults have more trouble determining whether an item was earlier seen or imagined (Henkel, Johnson, & De Leonardis, 1998), even when overall recall rates are equivalent to those of young adults. This difference can be eliminated with strategies such as using a distinctiveness heuristic, such as saying the target out loud at encoding. Then, at retrieval, the individual can search for the distinctive information (his or her own voice) in order to identify the source (Dodson & Schacter, 2002).

Intelligence

There are a variety of differences in intellectual functioning between older and younger adults. The typical finding is that older adults score lower on tests designed to tap what is called *fluid intelligence* but perform just as well or even better than younger adults on measures of *crystallized intelligence*. The definitions of these intelligences are not always precise but tasks that involve quick thinking, manipulation of information, and performing multiple activities that require the allocation and reallocation of attention are generally considered to rely mainly on fluid intelligence. Those that tap well-learned skills, language, and retrieval of well-learned material are generally considered to rely more on crystallized intelligence.

Thus, aspects of intelligence such as vocabulary and knowledge are relatively unaffected by increasing age (and, in fact, often increase with age), but tasks such as reasoning, mental calculations, and free recall tend to decrease as a function of age (Salthouse, 1991). In a recent study looking at cognitive performance in over 5,000 20- to 50-year-old adults, Schroeder and Salthouse (2004) reported that scores on composite tests of memory, spatial relations, and reasoning decreased by about 0.02 standard deviation units per year. At the same time, scores on a vocabulary test increased (again, rather steadily) by 0.05 standard deviation units per year. Schroeder and Salthouse speculated that the reason this decline in fluid abilities is not noticeable in our early 40s and 50s is that it is such a very small decline that the cumulative effect is generally not noticed for quite some time. Moreover, these small declines can be offset by increases in knowledge and experience (crystallized intelligence). To a certain extent, one can compensate for decreased abilities in one domain with increased abilities in another.

EXPLANATIONS OF AGE-RELATED DIFFERENCES

There are currently at least four major explanations of the cause of decreases in cognitive abilities as a function of age: (1) slowed speed of processing, (2) lack of inhibitory control, (3) reductions in processing resources or working memory capacity, and (4) reductions in perceptual processing efficiency. The models that are chosen are critical in driving the field toward particular methods, constructs, and dependent variables. The assumptions and premises taken to be given by the researcher determine, to some extent, the questions that will be asked.

Slowed Speed of Processing

One of the dominant explanations of cognitive aging is that declines in performance accompanying normal aging are due to a reduced capacity caused by a general slowing of processing speed (Birren, 1965; Salthouse, 1985). Speed of processing has been shown to be a general factor that underlies performance in a wide variety of cognitive tasks, including attention, memory, reasoning, and language (Salthouse & Ferrer-Caja, 2003). On relatively direct measures of processing speed such as reaction times, older adults do perform more slowly than younger adults. These measures share variance with other measures of cognitive functioning such as episodic memory and fluid intelligence scores. In addition, it has frequently been reported that when individual differences in speed of processing are partialed out statistically, age by itself no longer accounts for significant variance (Salthouse, 1996). It has been suggested that speed is a primary ability, and decreases in speed underlie most of the age-related declines in cognitive functioning. This is consistent with the finding that tasks using crystallized intelligence are relatively unaffected by aging: they rely very little on quick processing and more on very well-learned responses.

Although the construct "speed of processing" has been a powerful motivator in a great deal of research, it has not been immune to criticism. The most basic criticism (Collins, 1994; Kramer & Larish, 1996) is that speed may very well play a central role in most cognitive tasks, but that is a description, not an explanation: the mechanisms by which speed may affect performance have not been specified (Craik & Anderson, 1999). Indeed, even if one accepts the conclusion that slowing of processing can account for the majority of the variance in performance, what causes the slowing (Collins, 1994)?

Inhibition and Control

The impaired-inhibition view (Hasher & Zacks, 1988) is in some ways similar to the reduced-speed-of-processing view. Both focus on processing differences between younger and older subjects, and both posit a reduction in one general ability that contributes to performance on a wide variety of tasks. According to the inhibitory view, deficits seen in performance by elderly subjects are due to a difficulty in inhibiting irrelevant information, the consequences of which are increased interference and reduced processing resources.

Hasher, Zacks, and May (1999) have suggested that inhibitory processes could decline at three points: (1) inhibiting access of information to immediate memory, (2) deleting information from immediate memory, and (3) inhibiting output of irrelevant responses. Although separating out these possibilities is difficult, there is some evidence for deficits in each of those functions. The inhibitory view predicts not only worse performance on a variety of memory tasks but also an improvement under certain circumstances. For example, one major prediction is that older adults will have more difficulty eliminating information from working memory when it is activated but is irrelevant. Thus, they should show better memory for irrelevant information than younger adults. Dywan and Murphy (1996) reported that when younger and older adults were given a surprise recognition test on irrelevant information, the younger adults remembered more of the distracting information than the older adults did. One interpretation is that both older and younger adults process irrelevant information, but the younger adults are better at assigning the source of the irrelevant information and can inhibit these responses at output. A summary of this approach is offered by Stoltzfus, Hasher, and Zacks (1996; see also Hasher et al., 1999).

Processing Resources and Environmental Support

One of the great debates in cognitive research during the 1990s concerned whether memory (and cognition in general) is better thought of from a systems view or a processing view (see, e.g., Foster & Jelicic, 1999). Although the dominant view posits multiple systems (Schacter, Wagner, & Buckner, 2000; Tulving, 1999), the processing account (described below) better explains the pattern of data found in research on cognitive aging.

Historically the systems approach grows out of the structuralist tradition in which the purpose of the science of psychology is to analyze and describe the basic elements of cognition and discover how those elements work together (Tichener, 1898; Tulving, 1983). Within this sort of framework, development can be seen as a process of the maturation of those structures in childhood and the deterioration of those systems in older adulthood. This is implicitly (if not explicitly) the viewpoint of researchers who investigate how brain lesions affect performance. Essentially, they assume that a particular function is localized in one area of the brain so that damage in a particular area can be correlated with a particular loss of function. This viewpoint also suggests that specific types of function can be lost without all functioning being compromised. Finally, this system or structural way of partitioning cognition could be interpreted as predicting that the process of aging will be like reverse development: structures that mature latest should be most vulnerable to the detrimental effects of aging and should start to show deterioration first (Tulving, 1983).

A very different view is embodied in what has been called a process-ing approach to aging, argued by Craik (1986). Although Craik generally restricts himself to discussing memory functioning, his viewpoint can be extended and elaborated to encompass all of cognitive aging (Salthouse, 2001). When Craik looked at the pattern of differences between older and younger adults, he found that the magnitude of the age difference in-creased in a systematic way—but not in the way that would be predicted by structural theories. Instead, it seemed that the more cues there were available in the environment and the less the individual was forced to rely on self-initiated processing in order to do the task, the smaller the age dif-ference was in the task. But as the amount of environmental support de-creased and the more self-initiated processing was necessary in order to perform the task, the larger the age-related difference was. Tasks that were supposedly controlled by one structure or another in the structural theory varied within this taxonomy. In addition, tasks that were suppos-edly controlled by different structures showed similar patterns.

Craik (1986) argues that memory and cognition are better described in terms of processes rather than in terms of structures or systems. The in-teraction of the environment at encoding, the environment at retrieval, and the individual is the key to predicting what tasks will show age-related declines. For example, within the systems view, recognition and recall are both explicit memory tasks that rely on the episodic memory system (Tulving, 1983). However, free recall performance is worse for older and younger adults and recognition performance is the same, even when overall difficulty is controlled (Craik & McDowd, 1987).

The processing view suggests that one of the effects of aging is to re-duce the resources available to do the memory task (Craik, 1986; Craik & Byrd, 1982; Craik, Anderson, Kerr, & Li, 1995) rather than the selec-tive degradation of one system over another. This is supported by studies showing that dividing attention in younger adults seems to simulate the effects of aging. In addition, aging and divided attention both result in re-duced frontal lobe activity when measured by neuropsychological mea-sures such as positron emission tomography or functional magnetic resonance imaging. Attention is needed in order to initiate a strategy and make use of elaborate, deep encoding. Thus, older adults are at a disad-vantage in using context or identifying the source of the information. This viewpoint incorporates aspects of the transfer-appropriate process-ing view in that environmental support provided at retrieval can interact with internal cues to make up for the deficit, which is why cued recall is better than free recall, and recognition is better than cued recall (Craik, 1986; Craik & Anderson, 1999). The processing view suggests that the combination of the person, the task, and the environment are all needed in order to explain age-related changes in memory.

Declining Sensory Abilities as a Function of Age

Recent reports have demonstrated strong relationships between basic sensory/perceptual capabilities and cognitive functioning. For example, (Baltes and Lindenberger 1997; Lindenberger & Baltes, 1994) reported that up to 70% of the variance in measures of intellectual ability for subjects ranging in age from 25 to 101 years could be accounted for by a composite score that included age, vision, and hearing abilities. In a separate study, speed of processing effects on intelligence was entirely mediated by vision and hearing scores (Lindenberger & Baltes, 1994).

The other cognitive explanations described above could be reinterpreted in the light of these results. For example, it is possible that speed of processing slows because basic input processes result in impoverished input that then takes more time to identify and interpret. In addition, difficulties in perceptual processing could take away resources that normally would be devoted to higher-level processing such as rehearsal or elaboration, resulting in reduced abilities to make use of contextual information. Reduced inhibitory control could be an after-effect of reduced perceptual processing: the ability to focus on one stimulus while filtering out irrelevant information is reduced in the auditory system by the upward spread of masking found in hearing loss and in the visual system by loss of contrast information. More recent experiments and reviews have further supported the substantial relations between sensory and cognitive functioning (e.g., Scialfa, 2002; Schneider, Daneman, & Pichora-Fuller, 2002). This sort of direct effect of perceptual difficulties on cognitive processing has been called the information-degradation hypothesis (Schneider & Pichora-Fuller, 2000).

However, given the correlational nature of the previous studies, the direction of causality cannot be conclusively determined. Lindenberger and Baltes (1994), for example, suggested that a third factor, widespread neural degeneration, might cause both perceptual and cognitive deterioration (the common cause hypothesis). Another logical possibility actually reverses the causality and suggests that cognitive declines could cause a depletion of resources at a higher level, which takes away resources that would normally be devoted to the perceptual system (the cognitive load on perception hypothesis). In addition, the effects of perceptual deterioration could act gradually on cognitive processing and result in long-term changes in the cognitive system (the sensory deprivation hypothesis). Based on an extensive review of this literature with these possibilities in mind, Schneider and Pichora-Fuller (2000) concluded that there is likely to be a very complex relationship between perception and cognition because the two systems are highly integrated and interdependent. They proposed an integrated system model of shared resources in which the flexible allocation of resources is a key ingredient. This essentially combines all of the above hypotheses and suggests that each one could play a role at any point in cognitive aging.

Biological Aspects of the Aging Brain

Advances in noninvasive neuro-imaging techniques have provided a window into physical differences in brain structure and function between older and younger brains. Unfortunately, the techniques are not yet precise enough to give more than a relatively gross description of functional and structural aspects of the aging brain. Nonetheless, two major differences have been found between the brains of older adults and those of younger adults: absolute brain volume and frontal lobe functioning. Changes that reduce total brain volume would seem to predict global rather than specific age-related changes in cognitive functioning. As we have seen above, that is not what is found in the behavioral data. However, Raz (2000) suggests that this difficulty can be overcome by positing a threshold model in which age-related cognitive deficits become apparent only after a certain amount of deterioration has occurred. Certain functions that rely on more distributed areas of the brain (such as those involved in combining multiple cues) may thus be differentially affected by a general change in brain volume.

It is clear that although all areas of the brain appear to be smaller in the older brain compared to the younger, the brain does not age uniformly. Aging seems to have a particular effect on the frontal lobe, whereas the primary sensory cortices seem to remain structurally unchanged. In one of the few longitudinal studies using brain imaging, Raz and his colleagues (Raz et al., 2003) reported significant shrinkage in specific areas of the brain, particularly in the frontal lobes, over a five-year period in a sample of healthy adults ranging in age from 26 to 82 years old.

However, relating brain changes to specific cognitive deficits has been difficult. In terms of relating specific functions to brain changes, the clearest case is found by examining the blood flow to different areas of the brain while engaging in a variety of tasks. Although there is age-related shrinking of the frontal lobes, there is an actual increase in prefrontal activation in older as compared to younger adults. There have been speculations (Grady et al., 1994; Raz, 2000) that this may be due to the older adult's making an effort to recruit general resources in order to compensate for reduced processing efficiency at lower levels of processing. This analysis dovetails nicely with the research on the relationship between sensory processing and cognition: the older adult is diverting resources to deciphering the incoming information, which then takes away from more higher-level processing resources. In the younger adult, the initial encoding is generally more effortless and automatic.

Anderson et al. (2000) measured brain activity in both younger and older adults when they were performing a paired-associate task under conditions of full or divided attention. They found reduced activity in the left frontal lobe during encoding in older adults as well as in the younger adults, but only when they were performing the primary task while doing a secondary task. They suggest that older adults might be essentially operating with reduced attentional resources all the time, which would affect memory processing. This fits in with the hypothesis that the frontal lobes are involved in strategic, self-initiated aspects of memory (Kapur et al., 1995) and that the difficulty of older adults to retrieve context may be due to a difficulty in the encoding and retrieval of associative information, which is known as the *associative deficit hypothesis* (Naveh-Benjamin, 2000).

IMPROVING COGNITIVE ABILITIES IN OLDER ADULTS

Is there anything to be done to reduce or slow the progress of age-related declines in cognition? The findings on this point have been mixed and are often difficult to interpret, partly because some studies suffer from basic methodological flaws. However, there are at least three areas in which interpretable research can be summarized: experience, cognitive training, and improving vascular fitness through fitness training. A brief review follows (for a more in-depth review, see Kramer & Willis, 2004).

Expertise

It is possible that individuals who are very experienced in a task or are experts in a particular domain might show little or no age-related decline in those consolidated abilities. The available research on this question is quite mixed. In particular, it has been found that some well-learned skills (typing, complex game playing, piloting) can be maintained at very high levels even in very old adults. However, the abilities that are spared are specific to the area of expertise and do not generalize to other tasks or domains. In addition, the maintenance of such skills is probably due to a variety of compensatory strategies that the individual uses (Bosman, 1993, 1994). However, along with studies showing spared abilities, there are numerous studies that have shown that age differences can be found among experts in complex domains such as music-related tasks (Halpern, Bartlett, & Dowling, 1995). The discrepancies between such findings and the ones on typing might be due to differences in the demands of the task or the components of each task (Kramer & Willis, 2004). Thus, although it seems that some age-related declines can be reduced or at least compensated for with experience or expertise, the effects are very domain specific and may not generalize to very complex tasks.

Cognitive Training

What is the effect of deliberate training in cognitive skills? As in the preceding section, the available data show variable results. It is clear that older adults can benefit from practice on specific tasks (such as visual search, recognition, and recall) and that they show approximately the same amount of gain as younger adults. However, as in the expertise literature, the training effects are quite specific to the task that is trained and tend not to generalize to other tasks. Thus, if an individual is trained in using a particular mnemonic technique, memory and cognitive performance in general do not improve as well (Verhaeghen & Marcoen, 1996). As a result, the usefulness of such training in everyday life is somewhat open to question. Because it is clear that older adults can benefit from cognitive training on specific tasks, if not overall, there should be some benefit to developing training programs and targeting them at important domains of performance.

Fitness Training

Due to the numerous studies showing a positive link between fitness and cognitive abilities (e.g., Colcombe & Kramer, 2003), an obvious question is whether increasing an older adult's level of fitness will increase that person's cognitive functioning. As with the other possibilities considered in this section, the answer is a qualified yes. Colcombe and Kramer (2003) carried out a meta-analysis including a great many studies on whether fitness training has an effect on cognitive functioning. They found that, overall, improving fitness has a significant effect on cognitive functioning and, moreover, the effects were largest on tasks that entailed executive control processes such as planning, task coordination, and working memory. In other studies Colcombe and colleagues (Colcombe et al., 2003; Kramer et al., 2003) suggested that the effects of fitness training on cognition were due mainly to increases in cardiovascular fitness. They suggested that older adults with good cardiovascular fitness lost less brain tissue than those with poor cardiovascular fitness.

SUMMARY AND CONCLUSIONS

Age-related changes are slight in measures of crystallized intelligence such as vocabulary or knowledge tests. In contrast, age-related losses are sizable when measured by tasks tapping fluid intelligence such as reasoning and divided-attention tasks. The latter tasks generally require the manipulation of information or the coordination of multiple tasks. Performance on tasks that offer sufficient retrieval cues and performance on indirect tasks frequently show no age-related impairment. That is, to the extent that self-initiated processes are important, there will probably be age-related differences; to the extent that the task provides sufficient cues or relies on well-learned behaviors, there will probably be few or no age-related differences.

Explanations of age-related differences in cognitive processing as a function of age have focused on speed of processing, increased inhibition, reduced processing resources, and self-initiated processing and reduced sensory capabilities. In the end, most or all of these explanations will be needed to a certain extent, depending on the particular task at hand. New research using noninvasive imaging technology is still in its infancy but shows the promise of providing converging evidence to the behavioral data.

Decline in cognitive abilities has been shown to have wide social and emotional consequences and has been linked to reductions in effective social functioning, diminished psychological well-being, difficulties in personal relationships, lower self-esteem, and a reduction in general quality of life. Declines in physical health also have a significant impact on cognitive processing. Even worrying about declines in cognitive functioning can have a negative effect on health and relationships. Some declines may be ameliorated with cognitive and fitness training, although the generality of such training is limited. Cognitive aging researchers have only just begun to incorporate such social and biological effects into their theories, and much work is yet to be done in this area.

The field of cognitive aging is not a cohesive one. There are clear disagreements in the methodology, theoretical constructs, and even what questions are the important ones. However, the debates are healthy and vigorous and have resulted in an increasing amount of imaginative research that may not have been possible without these types of challenges.

REFERENCES

Aartsen, M. J., van Tilburg, T. G., Smits, C. H. M., & Knipscheer, C. P. M. (2004). A longitudinal study on the impact of physical and cognitive decline on the personal network in old age. *Journal of Social and Personal Relationships, 21,* 249–266.

Anderson, N. D., & Craik, F. I. M. (2000). Memory in the aging brain. In E. Tulving & F. I. M. Craik (Eds.), *The Oxford handbook of memory* (pp. 411–425). New York: Oxford University Press.

Anderson, N. D., Iidaka, T., Cabeza, R., Kapur, S., McIntosh, A. R., & Craik, F. I. M. (2000). The effects of divided attention on encoding- and retrieval-related brain activity: A PET study of younger and older adults. *Journal of Cognitive Neuroscience, 12,* 775–792.

Baltes, P. B., & Lindenberger, U. (1997). Emergence of a powerful connection between sensory and cognitive functions across the adult life span: A new window to the study of cognitive aging? *Psychology and Aging, 12,* 12–21.

Baltes, P. B., & Mayer, K. U. (Eds.). (1999). *The Berlin Aging Study: Aging from 70 to 100.* New York: Cambridge University Press.

Birren, J. E. (1965). Age changes in speed of behavior: Its central nature and physiological correlates. In A. T. Welford & J. E. Birren (Eds.), *Behavior, aging and the nervous system* (pp. 191–216). Springfield, IL: Charles C. Thomas.

Bosman, A. A. (1993). Age-related difference in the motoric aspects of transcription typing skills. *Psychology and Aging, 8,* 87–102.

Bosman, A. A. (1994). Age and skill differences in typing related and unrelated reaction time tasks. *Aging and Cognition, 1,* 310–322.

Bromley, D. B. (1990). *Behavioural gerontology: Central issues in the psychology of ageing.* New York: Wiley.

Centofanti, M. (1998). Fear of Alzheimer's undermines health of elderly patients. *APA Monitor, 29,* 33.

Colcombe, S. J., Erickson, K. I., Raz, N., Webb, A. G., Cohen, N. J., McAuley, E., et al. (2003). Aerobic fitness reduced brain tissue loss in aging humans. *Journal of Gerontology: Medical Sciences, 58,* 176–180.

Colcombe, S., & Kramer, A. F. (2003). Fitness effects on the cognitive function of older adults: A meta-analytic study. *Psychological Science, 14,* 125–130.

Collins, L. M. (1994). Comment on "How many causes are there of aging-related decrements in cognitive functioning?" *Developmental Review, 14,* 438–443.

Comijs, H. C., van Tilburg, T., Geerlings, S. W., Jonker, C., Deeg, D. J. H., van Tilburg, W., et al. (2004). Do severity and duration of depressive symptoms predict cognitive decline in older persons? Results of the Longitudinal Aging Study Amsterdam. *Aging, Clinical and Experimental Research, 16,* 226–232.

Craik, F. I. M. (1986). A functional account of age differences in memory. In F. Klix & H. Hagendorf (Eds.), *Human memory and cognitive capabilities* (pp. 409–422). Amsterdam: Elsevier.

Craik, F. I. M., & Anderson, N. D. (1999). Applying cognitive research to problems of aging. In D. Gopher & A. Koriat (Eds.), *Attention and performance XVII* (pp. 583–615). Cambridge, MA: MIT Press.

Craik, F. I. M., Anderson, N. D., Kerr, S. A., & Li, K. Z. H. (1995). Memory changes in normal ageing. In A. D. Baddeley, B. A. Wilson, & F. N. Watts (Eds.), *Handbook of memory disorders* (pp. 211–241). New York: Wiley.

Craik, F. I. M., & Byrd, M. (1982). Aging and cognitive deficits: The role of attentional resources. In F. I. M. Craik & S. Trehub (Eds.), *Aging and cognitive processes* (pp. 191–211). New York: Plenum.

Craik, F. I. M., Byrd, M., & Swanson, J. M. (1987). Patterns of memory loss in three elderly samples. *Psychology and Aging, 2,* 79–86.

Craik, F. I. M., & McDowd, J. M. (1987). Age differences in recall and recognition. *Journal of Experimental Psychology: Learning, Memory, and Cognition, 13,* 474–479.

Craik, F. I. M., & Salthouse, T. A. (Eds.). (2000). *The handbook of aging and cognition.* Mahwah, NJ: Erlbaum.

Deeg, D. J. H., Knipscheer, C. P. M., & van Tilburg, W. (Eds.). (1993). *Autonomy and well-being in the aging population: Concepts and design of the Longitudinal Aging Study Amsterdam.* Bunnik, Netherlands: Netherlands Institute of Gerontology.

Desai, M., Pratt, L. A., Lentzner, H., & Robinson, K. N. (2001). Trends in vision and hearing among older Americans. In *Aging trends, No. 2* (pp. 1–8). Hyattsville, MD: National Center for Health Statistics.

Dixon, R. A., Bäckman, L., & Nilsson, L. G. (Eds.). (2004). *New frontiers in cognitive aging.* New York: Oxford University Press.

Dodson, C. S., & Schacter, D. L. (2002). Aging and strategic retrieval processes: Reducing false memories with a distinctiveness heuristic. *Psychology and Aging, 17,* 405–415.

Dywan, J., & Jacoby, L. L. (1990). Effects of aging on source monitoring: Differences in susceptibility to false fame. *Psychology and Aging, 5,* 379–387.

Dywan, J., & Murphy, W. E. (1996). Aging and inhibitory control in text comprehension. *Psychology and Aging, 11,* 199–206.

Einstein, G. O., McDaniel, M. A., Richardson, S. L., Guynn, M. J., & Cunfer, A. R. (1995). Aging and prospective memory: Examining the influences of self-initiated retrieval processes. *Journal of Experimental Psychology: Learning, Memory, and Cognition, 21,* 996–1007.

Ferraro, K. F. (1997). The gerontological imagination. In K. F. Ferraro (Ed.), *Gerontology: Perspectives and issues* (pp. 3–18). New York: Springer Publishing.

Fisk, A. D., & Rogers, W. (1991). Toward an understanding of age-related memory and visual search effects. *Journal of Experimental Psychology: General, 120,* 131–149.

Fisher, D. L., & Glaser, R. A. (1996). Molar and latent models of cognitive slowing: Implications for aging, dementia, depression, development, and intelligence. *Psychonomic Bulletin and Review, 3,* 458–480.

Foster, J. K., & Jelicic, M. (1999). *Memory: Systems, process, or function?* New York: Oxford University Press.

Gallo, J. J., Rebok, G. W., Tennsted, S., Wadley, V. G., & Horgas, A. (2003). Linking depressive symptoms and functional disability in late life. *Aging and Mental Health, 7,* 469–480.

Garner, W. R., Hake, H. W., & Eriksen, C. W. (1956). Operationism and the concept of perception. *Psychological Review, 63,* 149–158.

Grady, C. L., Maisog, J. M., Horwitz, B., Ungerleider, L. G., Mentis, M. J., Salerno, J. A., et al. (1994). Age-related changes in cortical blood flow activation during visual processing of faces and location. *Journal of Neuroscience, 14,* 1450–1462.

Halpern, A. R., Bartlett, J. C., & Dowling, W. J. (1995). Aging and experience in the recognition of musical transpositions. *Psychology and Aging, 10,* 325–342.

Hasher, L., & Zacks, R. T. (1988). Working memory, comprehension, and aging: A review and a new view. In G. H. Bower (Ed.), *The psychology of learning and motivation* (Vol. 22, pp. 193–225). San Diego, CA: Academic Press.

Hasher, L., Zacks, R. T., & May, C. P. (1999). Inhibitory control, circadian arousal, and age. In D. Gopher & A. Koriat (Eds.), *Attention and performance XVII* (pp. 653–675). Cambridge, MA: MIT Press.

Henkel, L. A., Johnson, M. K., & De Leonardis, D. M. (1998). Aging and source monitoring: Cognitive processes and neuropsychological correlates. *Journal of Experimental Psychology: General, 127,* 251–268.

Hertzog, C. (1996). Research design in studies of aging and cognition. In J. E. Birren & K. W. Schaie (Eds.), *Handbook of the psychology of aging* (4th ed., pp. 24–37). San Diego: Academic Press.

Hertzog, C. (2002). Metacognition in older adults: Implications for application. In T. J. Perfect & B. L. Schwartz (Eds.), *Applied metacognition* (pp. 169–196). New York: Cambridge University Press.

Hertzog, C. (2004). Does longitudinal evidence confirm theories of cognitive aging derived from cross-sectional data? In R. A. Dixon, L. Bäckman, & L-G. Nilsson (Eds.), *New frontiers in cognitive aging* (pp. 40–64). New York: Oxford University Press.

Hultsch, D. F., Hertzog, C., Dixon, R. A., & Small, B. J. (1998). *Memory change in the aged.* New York: Cambridge University Press.

Hyman, I. E., Jr., & Billings, F. J. (1998). Individual differences and the creation of false childhood memories. *Memory, 6,* 1–20.

Kapur, S., Craik, F. I. M., Jones, C., Brown, G. M., Houle, S., & Tulving, E. (1995). Functional role of the prefrontal cortex in retrieval of memories: A PET study. *Neuroreport, 6,* 1880–1884.

Kramer, A., Colcombe, S., McAuley, E., Eriksen, K., Scalf, P., Jerome, G., et al. (2003). Enhancing brain and cognitive function of older adults through fitness training. *Journal of Molecular Neuroscience, 20,* 213–222.

Kramer, A. F., & Larish, J. L. (1996). Aging and dual-task performance. In W. A. Rogers, A. D. Fisk, N. Walker (Eds.), *Aging and skilled performance: Advances in theory and applications* (pp. 83–112). Mahwah, NJ: Erlbaum.

Kramer, A. F., & Willis, S. L. (2004). Cognitive plasticity and aging. *Psychology of Learning and Motivation, 43,* 267–302.

La Voie, D. J., & Light, L. L. (1994). Adult age differences in repetition priming: A meta-analysis. *Psychology and Aging, 9,* 539–553.

Light, L. L. (2004). Commentary: Measures, constructs, models, and inferences about aging. In R. A. Dixon, L. Bäckman, & L-G. Nilsson (Eds.), *New frontiers in cognitive aging* (pp. 89–112). New York: Oxford University Press.

Light, L. L., & La Voie, D. (1993). Direct and indirect measures of memory in old age. In P. Graf (Ed.), *Implicit memory: New directions in cognition, development, and neuropsychology* (pp. 207–230). Hillsdale, NJ: Erlbaum,

Light, L. L., Prull, M. W., La Voie, D. J., & Healy, M. R. (2000). Dual-process theories of memory in old age. In T. J. Perfect & E. A. Maylor (Eds.), *Models of cognitive aging: Debates in psychology* (pp. 238–300). New York: Oxford University Press.

Lindenberger, U., & Baltes, P. B. (1994). Sensory functioning and intelligence in old age: A strong connection. *Psychology and Aging, 9,* 339–355.

Naveh-Benjamin, M. (2000). Adult age differences in memory performance: Tests of an associative deficit hypothesis. *Journal of Experimental Psychology: Learning, Memory, and Cognition, 26,* 1170–1187.

Naveh-Benjamin, M., Hussain, Z., Guez, J., & Bar-On, M. (2003). Adult age differences in episodic memory: Further support for an associative-deficit hypothesis. *Journal of Experimental Psychology: Learning, Memory, and Cognition, 29,* 826–837.

Neath, I. (1999). Computer simulations of global memory models. *Behavior Research Methods, Instruments, and Computers, 31,* 74–80.

Neath, I., & Surprenant, A. M. (2003). *Human memory: An introduction to research, data, and theory* (2nd ed.). Belmont, CA: Wadsworth.

Rabbitt, P. M. A. (1993). Does it all go together when it goes? The Nineteenth Bartlett Memorial Lecture. *Quarterly Journal of Experimental Psychology, 46A,* 385–434.

Rabbitt, P. M. A., & Abson, V. (1991). Do older people know how good they are? *British Journal of Psychology, 82,* 137–151.

Raz, N. (2000). Aging of the brain. In F. I. M. Craik & T. A. Salthouse (Eds.), *The handbook of aging and cognition* (pp. 1–90). Mahwah, NJ: Erlbaum.

Raz, N., Rodrigue, K. M., Kennedy, K. M., Dahle, C., Head, D., & Acker, J. D. (2003). Differential age-related changes in the regional metencephalic volumes in humans: A 5-year follow-up. *Neuroscience Letters, 349,* 163–166.

Rendell, P. G., & Thomson, D. M. (1999). Aging and prospective memory: Differences between naturalistic and laboratory tasks. *Journals of Gerontology, Psychological Sciences and Social Sciences, 54B,* 256–269.

Salthouse, T. A. (1985). *A theory of cognitive aging.* Amsterdam: North-Holland.

Salthouse, T. A. (1991). *Theoretical perspectives on cognitive aging.* Hillsdale, NJ: Erlbaum.

Salthouse, T. A. (1996). The processing speed theory of adult age differences in cognition. *Psychological Review, 103,* 403–428.

Salthouse, T. A. (2000). Methodological assumptions in cognitive aging research. In F. I. M. Craik & T. A. Salthouse (Eds.). *The handbook of aging and cognition* (2nd ed., pp. 467–498). Mawah, NJ: Erlbaum.

Salthouse, T. A. (2001). The broader context of Craik's self-initiated processing hypothesis. In M. Naveh-Benjamin, M. Moscovitch, & H. L. Roediger III (Eds.), *Perspectives on human memory and cognitive aging: Essays in honour of Fergus Craik* (pp. 277–297). New York: Psychology Press.

Salthouse, T. A., & Ferrer-Caja, E. (2003). What needs to be explained to account for age-related effects on multiple cognitive variables? *Psychology and Aging, 18,* 91–110.

Schacter, D. L., Wagner, A. D., & Buckner, R. L. (2000). Memory systems of 1999. In E. Tulving & F. I. M. Craik (Eds.), *The Oxford handbook of memory* (pp. 627–643). New York: Oxford University Press.

Schaie, K. W. (2004). *Developmental influences on adult intelligence: The Seattle Longitudinal Study.* New York: Oxford University Press.

Scialfa, C. T. (2002). The role of sensory factors in cognitive aging research. *Canadian Journal of Experimental Psychology, 56,* 153–163.

Schneider, B. A., Daneman, M., & Pichora-Fuller, M. K. (2002). Listening in aging adults: From discourse comprehension to psychoacoustics. *Canadian Journal of Experimental Psychology, 56,* 139–152.

Schneider, B. A., & Pichora-Fuller, M. K. (2000). Implications of perceptual deterioration for cognitive aging research. In F. I. M. Craik & T. A. Salthouse (Eds.), *The handbook of aging and cognition* (2nd ed., pp. 155–219). Mahwah, NJ: Erlbaum.

Schroeder, D. H., & Salthouse, T. A. (2004). Age-related effects on cognition between 20 and 50 years of age. *Personality and Individual Differences, 36,* 393–404.

Stoltzfus, E. R., Hasher, L., & Zacks, R. T. (1996). Working memory and aging: Current status of the inhibitory view. In J. T. E. Richardson (Ed.), *Working memory and human cognition* (pp. 66–68). New York: Oxford University Press.

Titchener, E. B. (1898). The postulates of a structural psychology. *Philosophical Review, 7,* 449–465

Tulving, E. (1983). *Elements of episodic memory.* New York: Oxford University Press.

Tulving, E. (1999). Study of memory: Processes and systems. In J. K. Foster & M. Jelicic (Eds.), *Memory: Systems, process, or function?* (pp. 11–30). New York: Oxford University Press.

Verhaeghen, P., & Marcoen, A. (1996). On the mechanisms of plasticity in young and older adults after instruction in the method of loci: Evidence for an amplification model. *Psychology and Aging, 11,* 164–178.

Zacks, R. T., Hasher, L., & Li, K. Z. H. (2000). Human memory. In T. A. Salthouse & F. I. M. Craik (Eds.), *Handbook of aging and cognition* (2nd ed., pp. 293–357). Mahwah, NJ: Erlbaum.

CHAPTER 6

Disability Concepts and Measurement

Contributions of the Epidemiology of Disability to Gerontological Inquiry

Fredric D. Wolinsky
Douglas K. Miller

In 1976, the sociologist Saad Nagi coined the phrase "the epidemiology of disability." His article began with this statement: "Despite its significance as a health and social problem, it is only recently that disability has attracted attention as an object of epidemiological analysis" (Nagi, 1976, p. 439). Three decades later, a considerable number of scholars are actively interested in understanding disability. Although some are formally trained as epidemiologists, others come from a variety of disciplines, including sociology, demography, medicine, and public health. Together they have contributed to gerontological inquiry by articulating the disablement process and documenting the prevalence of disability in the population. The knowledge generated from their studies has fueled debates about disability trends in the older adult population and provided

This work was supported by NIH grant R01 AG-022913 to Fredric D. Wolinsky and by NIH grant R01 AG-10436 to Douglas K. Miller. The opinions expressed here are those of the authors and do not necessarily reflect those of the NIH or any of the academic or governmental institutions involved.

conflicting evidence about whether older adults are living longer, healthier lives (Crimmins, 2004; Crimmins, Reynolds, & Saito, 1999; Freedman et al., 2004; Manton & Gu, 2001; Manton & Land, 2000). This conflicting evidence is due in large part to the ongoing confusion regarding the core disablement concepts and their measurement (Nagi, 1976; Verbrugge & Jette, 1994; Jette et al., 2002).

Given this situation, the purpose of this chapter is to (1) review the conceptual model that Nagi originally presented, as well as his responses to subsequent criticism concerning that model; (2) review the clarifications and dynamic recasting of the Nagi model provided by Lois Verbrugge and Alan Jette; (3) consider recent conceptual and measurement innovations offered by Jette and his colleagues, as well as by Linda Fried and her colleagues; and (4) consider recent conceptual and methodological developments for determining when meaningful change in an individual's score on a functional limitation or disability measure has occurred.

What warrants such an extended consideration of disability concepts and their measurement in this chapter? The answer lies in the prevalence of these conditions among older adults. To illustrate the disability burden that older adults face, data from the Survey on Assets and Health Dynamics Among the Oldest Old (AHEAD) study, are presented in Table 6.1. Conducted by the University of Michigan's Survey Research Center for the National Institute on Aging, the AHEAD study included 7,447 respondents from a nationally representative sample whose baseline interviews were conducted in 1993–1994. The percentage of these older adults who reported having selected examples of active pathology, impairments, functional limitations, and disability are shown in Table 6.1 by age. These data underscore the fact that the prevalence of disease is considerable, sensory and organic impairments are frequent, functional limitations abound, and disability is all too common. Moreover, with the exception of some decreases associated with survivor bias among the oldest age groups, the prevalence of these conditions clearly increases with age. As both the number and proportion of older adults continue to increase, so will these prevalence estimates. Thus, an extended discussion of disability concepts and their measurement is critically important for furthering the process of informed gerontological inquiry.

NAGI'S CONCEPTUAL MODEL

Nagi's conceptual model of disability is contained in four principal publications (Nagi, 1965, 1969, 1976, 1991) that have been cited by other scholars over a thousand times. To facilitate a basic understanding of the conceptual model, Figure 6.1 contains an overly simplistic diagram. As

TABLE 6.1   Percentage of Active Pathology, Impairment, Functional
Limitation, and Disability, by Age Group, Among the 7,447 Older Adults
Participating in the Baseline (1993) Round of Interviews for the Survey on
Assets and Health Dynamics among the Oldest Old

Age Groups	70–75	76–80	81–85	86 and Over	Total
Active pathology					
Arthritis	22.7	27.0	25.6	28.6	25.0
Cancer	11.8	13.5	14.0	12.0	12.7
Diabetes	14.2	14.0	10.9	8.0	12.9
Heart disease	25.9	28.9	35.0	32.2	29.1
Hypertension	45.6	48.4	47.1	41.0	46.1
Lung disease	9.3	9.7	9.7	5.8	9.1
Stroke	7.7	10.5	12.1	14.6	10.0
Impairments					
Depressive symptoms (mean; range = 0–8)	1.4	1.7	1.9	1.9	1.6
Cognitive ability (mean; range = 0–15)	12.4	11.8	11.0	10.0	11.8
Self-reported poor health	10.6	13.3	18.6	17.5	13.5
Self-reported poor hearing	3.5	5.8	8.7	16.9	6.6
Self-reported poor memory	4.1	7.6	9.9	12.9	7.1
Self-reported poor vision	5.0	8.4	12.8	21.0	9.1
Functional limitations (Difficulties with . . .)					
Picking up a dime	6.4	7.5	12.3	15.2	8.8
Lifting and carrying 10 pounds	25.4	34.0	41.2	50.5	33.4
Pushing or pulling heavy objects	28.5	35.0	40.0	49.4	34.6
Walking up one flight of stairs	21.7	28.6	36.0	49.3	29.2
Disability (Difficulties with one or more of five . . .)					
Activities of daily living (ADLs; e.g., dressing)	14.0	20.0	25.8	37.6	20.4
Instrumental ADLs (IADLs; e.g., meal preparation)	19.3	26.9	36.7	58.3	28.8

shown, there are four main concepts: active pathology, impairment, functional limitation, and disability. These four concepts represent the distinct
but interrelated core components of the disablement process. The sequencing and direction of the arrows indicate that active pathology may

Active Pathology ⟶ Impairment ⟶ Functional Limitation ⟶ Disability

FIGURE 6.1   A simplistic representation of the main pathway is Nagi's (1965,
1969, 1976, 1991) conceptual scheme for the epidemiology of disability.

result in impairment, that impairment may result in functional limitation, and that functional limitation may result in disability. In fact, this progressive stream from left to right represents the principal pathway by which disability develops. As we shall see, however, the representational diagram in Figure 6.1 has fueled the productive debate over whether the disablement process should be viewed as linear, fixed, and unrecoverable (Verbrugge & Jette, 1994).

According to Nagi (1991), *active pathology* results from either internal sources, such as metabolic imbalance or degenerative disease, or from external sources like trauma and infection. Regardless of the source, active pathology interrupts or interferes with normal functioning and stimulates the organism to attempt recovery. *Impairment* indicates functional decrement of an anatomical, physiological, mental, or emotional nature. Impairments can involve residual losses or abnormalities that linger after recovery, or they may involve congenital defects. Like impairments, *functional limitations* involve the ability to perform at normal levels. The difference, however, is that functional limitations occur (or manifest) at the level of the whole organism. Furthermore, functional limitations are the direct link through which impairments may lead to disability. In contrast, *disability* refers to social functioning, and it involves an inability or limitation in performing socially defined roles and tasks. However, not all impairments or functional limitations lead to disability, and similar disability patterns may result from different types of impairments and functional limitations.

Further understanding of the distinctions among these four concepts can be found among the indicators that Nagi and others have used to operationalize them. In the absence of physician examination and laboratory testing, the most common indicators of active pathology have been taken from self-reported disease history. Respondents in social and epidemiologic surveys are typically asked whether a doctor has ever told them that they have a particular disease, such as angina, arthritis, asthma, cancer, coronary artery disease, congestive heart failure, chronic obstructive pulmonary disease, diabetes, a heart attack, hypertension, kidney disease, or a stroke. Each individual disease reported by the subject, or their simple sum, can be used as an indicator of active pathology.

Impairments involve dysfunctional or structural abnormalities in one or more body systems. They may be measured by a variety of methods, including self-reported symptoms (such as dizziness or shortness of breath) or self-rated global health assessments, clinical examinations, or laboratory or epidemiologic field testing (such as range of motion, gait speed, standing balance, grip strength, or peak expiratory flow). Basically, impairments are decrements to normal functional abilities that have yet to progress to the stage where they affect how the individual performs, even though he or she may recognize that the deficit exists. For example, a respondent may have significantly less balance, quadricep strength, and digital dexterity than age and sex norms would suggest, but these impairments may not pose difficulties in terms of her or his ability to perform routine functions, such as bending over to pick up a dime.

Functional limitations emerge when impairments can be seen at the individual level. They refer to limitations in cognitive functional ability, such as memory and processing speed, and in sensory-motor functional ability, such as walking, stair climbing, and reaching out to grab an object. Nagi's (1976) indicators asked the respondents to indicate if they had no, some, or great difficulty in standing for long periods, lifting or carrying weights of approximately 10 pounds, going up and down stairs, walking, stooping-bending-kneeling, using hands and fingers, and reaching out with either or both arms. It is important to note here that Nagi advocated using both upper-body and lower-body functional limitation items, although he did not construct separate scales (Wolinsky & Johnson, 1991).

The most widely used (Jette et al., 2002) functional limitation measure is the Physical Function Index (PFI) contained in the MOS 36-item short-form health survey (SF-36) (Ware, Kosinski, & Dewey, 2000). The PFI asks respondents whether they are limited a lot, limited a little, or have no difficulty in performing 10 functions: vigorous activities, moderate activities, lifting or carrying groceries, climbing several flights of stairs, climbing one flight of stairs, bending-stooping-kneeling, walking more than a mile, walking several hundred yards, walking 100 yards, and bathing or dressing. As we shall see, however, the last PFI item is empirically problematic and has repeatedly been shown psychometrically to balk at being included with the other functional status items (Dexter, Stump, Tierney, & Wolinsky, 1996; Wolinsky, Miller, Andresen, Malmstrom, & Miller, 2004; Wolinsky & Stump, 1996). Moreover, the vigorous activities, moderate activities, and bathing or dressing items are conceptually problematic; according to Nagi's (1976) conceptualization, they are actually measures of disability (Jette et al., 2002).

To fully understand what separates disability from the other concepts in the model, Nagi makes the point that the latter are all attributes or properties of the individual. As such, active pathology, impairment, and functional limitations can be measured within the individual, in isolation from other individuals. This is not the case for disability, which is essentially a social phenomenon involving the performance of task and role assignments. Thus, Nagi relies on his sociological training in role theory and role sets to differentiate disability as an extraindividual concept.

According to Nagi, disability exists in two main dimensions: work and independent living. The work dimension has traditionally posed a bit of a problem inasmuch as measuring work for older adults, especially those who are either fully or partially retired, is quite complicated. Therefore, to simplify things, Nagi (1976) originally restricted his analyses to respondents between the ages of 18 and 64. He then developed the Work Disability Index, which ultimately classified respondents into one of three categories. In the first category, he placed those who had no work disability, as indicated by regularly working in jobs of 36 hours per week or more, including housekeeping or school work, and who reported no health limitations in their current or previous positions. The second category included persons who were limited in their work roles and activities by their health. People in this category were working regularly but reported some difficulties in the performance of their jobs due to health reasons. Individuals who were no longer in the labor force due to health limitations were placed in the third category, which Nagi labeled the *vocationally disabled*.

The second, and most commonly used, disability domain involves limitations in independent living. For the most part, measures of independent living tap activities of daily living (ADLs). There are two main types of ADLs. The first involves personal care activities and has been variously referred to simply as ADLs (Katz, Ford, Moskowitz, Jackson, & Jaffe, 1963), personal ADLs (PADLs; Lawton, 1972), or basic ADLs (BADLs; Verbrugge & Jette, 1994; Wolinsky & Johnson, 1991). ADLs are measured by asking respondents whether they have difficulty (yes/no), due to health reasons, in performing specific personal care activities, such as bathing or showering, dressing, eating, getting in or out of a bed or a chair, walking across a room, getting outside, or using the toilet. Typically, respondents who indicate that they have difficulty with a particular task are then asked how much difficulty they have, with the response options being some difficulty, a lot of difficulty, or that they are unable to perform the task at all. There is no clear consensus, however, about how to incorporate this severity information. Indeed, in practice, the ADL measure that is most commonly used is simply the number of ADLs for which the respondent reports difficulty (Jette, 1994; Weiner, Hanley, Clark, & Van Nostrand, 1990). When respondents indicate that they do not do a particular task because of something other than a health reason (i.e., someone else does it), they are asked whether they would have difficulty if they tried to do the task.

The second main type of ADLs are instrumental ADLs (IADLs; Duke University, 1978; Lawton, 1972; Rosow & Breslau, 1966). Like ADLs, IADLs are measured by asking respondents whether they have difficulty (yes/no), due to health reasons, in performing specific activities that go beyond personal care. Such activities include meal preparation, shopping for groceries or personal items, keeping track of expenses and paying bills, using the telephone, doing light housework (e.g., dishes or straightening up), doing heavy housework (e.g., scrubbing floors or washing windows), or managing medications. Respondents who express difficulty in performing one of these activities are then asked how much difficulty they have, using the same response options as in ADL items. Because of the gender stratification in American society, where money management may be considered "a man's task" and meal preparation may be considered "a woman's task," it is especially important with IADL items to determine whether the respondent would have difficulty if he or she tried to do the task (Lawton, 1972).

CLARIFYING AND DYNAMICALLY RECASTING THE MODEL

The purpose of Nagi's (1965, 1969, 1976, 1991) conceptualization of disability was to identify and frame the primary pathway through which disease diminishes the individual's functional abilities to perform his or her task and role assignments—that is, to outline the way that disease may ultimately result in disability. Verbrugge and Jette (1994) provide a thorough and thoughtful review and update by recasting this conceptualization as a dynamic approach, with special emphasis on identifying factors that may either accelerate or inhibit progress along that primary pathway. They accomplish this by reframing Nagi's focus on disability to a focus on the disablement process, in which *disablement* refers to the impact of acute and chronic conditions on an individual's ability to function, and *process* refers to the dynamics of disablement, including the direction, pace, and patterns of change.

Before describing Verbrugge and Jette's (1994) dynamic recasting of the disability process, it is important to note the lengths that they go to in order to clarify how disability differs from functional limitation and how disability should be measured. Basically, they underscore the fact that "disability is difficulty doing activities in one's regular milieu" (Verbrugge & Jette, 1994, p. 5), and thus is essentially activity associated with one's social roles. In contrast, functional limitation reflects the individual's capability to execute the physical actions (or tasks) that may be required for performing that role. As such, Verbrugge and Jette are consistent with La Plante's (1990) prior pair-wise differentiations of functional limitations versus disability using the contrasts of action versus activity and task versus role, or the similar contrast used by others of can do versus do do.

According to Verbrugge and Jette (1994), the correct and standard way to measure disability is as indicated above: one asks individuals whether they have any difficulty in performing specific ADL or IADL activities. If they do, the degree of difficulty is ascertained. Several alternative approaches that involve performance-based assessment of disability have been developed in which the individual is observed and timed doing ADL or IADL activities (Diehl, Willis, & Schaie, 1995; Marsiske & Willis, 1995; Willis 1996). These alternative approaches, however, are rather time-consuming and require laboratory-like settings for standardization. As a result, they are infrequently used.

Some researchers (e.g., Gill, Robinson, & Tinetti, 1998; Gill & Kurland, 2003) have suggested an alternative strategy to measuring disability that they refer to as the *dependency approach*. In it, *dependency* is defined as needing or having help to do an activity. The proponents of this approach believe that it provides a more fundamental and objective measure of disability that is clinically relevant because it reflects a more severe state of disability. Verbrugge and Jette (1994), however, reject this approach as ill advised, because it causes further confusion in that dependency actually measures the presence of supportive mechanisms that act as a buffer to disability rather than disability itself. That is, the buffer may simply reflect whether someone lives with the respondent and can provide help or if the respondent can hire help.

Verbrugge and Jette's (1994) model of the disablement process is essentially the same as that shown in Figure 6.1, with the addition of three sets of factors that moderate the flow and rate of progression through the main pathway: risk factors, extraindividual factors, and intraindividual factors. Consistent with longstanding epidemiologic traditions (Berkman & Kawachi, 2000; Brownson & Petitti, 1998; Lilienfeld & Stolley, 1994), risk factors are long-term, if not permanent, behaviors or attributes of the individual or place that increase the odds of developing functional limitations or disabilities. These include biological, sociodemographic, psychosocial, and environmental characteristics that exist prior to or concomitantly with the initiation of the disablement process. In contrast, the extraindividual and intraindividual factors enter the model at the point where functional limitations are manifest and reflect the traditional effects of moderators (Aneshensel, 2002; Bollen, 1989; Heise, 1975). These factors can be initiated earlier, as in the case of primary prevention.

Ideally, the function of these moderators is to buffer progression through the main pathway, although sometimes there is backlash, or exacerbation. *Buffering* involves interventions designed to avoid the onset of disability, retard its progression, or return the individual to a fully functioning state. These can either be located within the individual (intra-; such as lifestyle or behavioral modification, enhanced coping skills, or personal activity accommodation), or be effected upon the individual (extra-; such as medical care, pharmaceutical therapy, standby assistance or help, or environmental modifications). *Exacerbation* can also stem from within or outside the individual and may occur when the side effects of an intervention result in greater harm than good, when individuals exhibit atrophic or failure to thrive, vicious-cycle responses to their functional limitations and disabilities, or when inflexible societal demands emerge as barriers to avoiding, retarding, or resolving the disablement process.

The intervention and exacerbation concepts highlight another important contribution made by Verbrugge and Jette (1994). This involves clarification of the dynamic nature of their reformulation. Rather than simply assuming that disability is a single process that is linear, fixed, and unrecoverable, they note that the disablement process includes the potential for feedback loops from any current position in the main pathway back to the starting point (complete recovery or reversal), back to any prior point (rehabilitation), or arrested progression (stabilization).

Three further notions are implied, if not actually embedded, in this dynamic conceptualization. One is that each individual may have two or more active pathologies, two or more impairments, two or more functional limitations, and two or more disabilities occurring at any given time. Thus, several layers of the disablement process may be, and in reality usually are, operating at the same time. A second notion is that these different layers are not isolated or unrelated. Indeed, interventions targeted to improve one layer may help improve another layer, or they may exacerbate the other layer of the disablement process. Thus, the layers of the disablement process should not be considered independently. Third, the different layers may interact in such a fashion as to produce an acceleration of the disablement process. That is, in combination, multiple layers may result in negative synergy, or the rapid downward spiral at the end of the life course referred to variously as the "terminal drop," "one hoss shay," "circling the drain," or "tornado" effect (Ferraro & Kelley-Moore, 2001; Fries, 1980; Wolinsky, Armbrecht, & Wyrwich, 2000).

Another clarification made by Verbrugge and Jette (1994) is their distinction between intrinsic and actual disability. In general, most research has focused on the former. *Intrinsic disability* is measured by setting the context for the ADL items to be asked with a preceding statement, such as, "By yourself, and without using any special equipment, do you have any difficulty bathing or showering?" Thus, what is obtained is whether, unassisted by aids (devices) or aides (people), the respondent has difficulty doing the ADL item. In contrast, to capture *actual disability*, the context-setting statement is not used.

The value of the distinction between intrinsic and actual disability is that their difference represents the success of the respondent in overcoming ADL limitations by relying on assistance from devices or people, or both. In that sense, actual disability can be seen as an indicator of unmet need. The notion of unmet need helps to clarify Verbrugge and Jette's (1994) perspective that disability can be seen as a person-environmental-fit failure. That is, society has not adequately helped the individual fulfill his or her normal role expectations and obligations. This perspective shifts the "blame" for disability from the individual to the societal level, and echoes the emphasis in the voice of persons with life-long disabilities who admonish society to "change the milieu, not me!" Subsequent work by Susan Allen and her colleagues (Allen, Foster, & Berg, 2001; Allen & Mor, 1997; Lima & Allen, 2001) has further clarified and expanded the notion of unmet need from the person-environmental-fit perspective.

The last two contributions arising from Verbrugge and Jette's (1994) conceptualization of the disablement process involve the specification of subsequent outcomes and the recognition of feedback loops resulting in secondary conditions or dysfunctions. In terms of the former, it is noted that disability has sequelae and that these often involve serious and global outcomes. The negative consequences of disability include reduced quality of life, depression, short- or long-term institutionalization, and death. Such outcomes would be placed in Figure 6.1 after an arrow flowing out of disability. The notion of feedback loops represents an expansion of the recognition suggested above that one layer of the disablement process may affect another. More to the point is the recognition that a specific disability (or functional limitation) may initiate the onset of secondary disability (or functional limitation). Determining which are the primary and which are the secondary disabilities, however, requires timing information. This is complicated by the reversibility of disabilities and functional limitations due to effective interventions over the life course. Indeed, standard protocols for obtaining disability histories do not yet exist, and substantially more theoretical and empirical work is needed on this topic.

FURTHER CONCEPTUAL AND
MEASUREMENT INNOVATIONS

The two major problems that continue to plague the epidemiology of disability are measurement and conceptual refinement (Jette, 1994, 1999, 2003; Jette & Keysor, 2003). In terms of measurement, it has been shown that even apparently modest variations in the way that disability is measured lead to rather significant differences in estimates of prevalence and incidence rates (Jette, 1994; Rodgers & Miller, 1997; Weiner et al., 1990). This was first demonstrated using several different national samples in which the way that the disability questions were asked varied in terms of the duration of the disability (short term versus lasting three months or more), whether the focus was on intrinsic or actual disability, and if, and how, the degree of difficulty was considered (Weiner et al., 1990). Because of concerns that compositional differences resulting from variations in the sampling designs of these national studies could account for some of the observed differences in disability prevalence and incidence rates, subsequent studies (Jette, 1994; Rodgers & Miller, 1997) focused on using the same sample but asking the disability questions in multiple and different ways. Although this controls for compositional change, it introduces other potential problems related to respondent burden and ordering effects.

Nonetheless, in both a regional probability sample of six New England states (Jette, 1994) and a national sample of older adults (Rodgers & Miller, 1997), results similar to those reported by Weiner et al. (1990) were observed. That is, different approaches to measuring disability lead to substantial variations in estimated prevalence and incidence rates. Not surprisingly, both of these more recent studies demonstrated that the use of dependency (received personal assistance) measures substantially underestimated the extent of disability. In a similar vein, Gill and Kurland (2003) have more recently shown that disability incidence rates are significantly underestimated in longitudinal studies that have follow-up periods longer than six months because of the high rate of recovery from disability, even among older adults. Accordingly, the search for the right way to measure disability continues.

Current efforts to correctly measure disability range from the relatively straightforward and parsimonious to the more detailed and time-consuming. In terms of simplicity, Verbrugge, Merrill, and Liu (1999) have endeavored to develop a single-item, self-rated disability question as an analogue to the popular self-rated health item ("How would you rate your health? Would you say it is excellent, very good, good, fair, or poor?"). The underlying motivation here involves both the remarkably predictive value of the self-rated health question in terms of subsequent mortality and the use of health services (Idler & Kasl, 1991; Idler, 1992; Wolinsky & Johnson, 1992), as well as the desire to find a parsimonious measure of disability that could be included in omnibus surveys.

Verbrugge et al.'s (1999) focus was on the global question from the Centers for Disease Control's (CDC) Behavioral Risk Factor Surveillance System Survey (BRFSS), which asks respondents: "During the past 30 days, for about how many days did your poor physical or mental health keep you from doing your usual activities, such as self-care, work, or recreation?" Using data from three nationally representative studies—the Health and Retirement Study (HRS), the AHEAD, and BRFSS—Verbrugge et al. (1999) found that when the response to this global question was dichotomized to reflect 0 versus 1 to 30 days, it was comparable to that measured by dichotomizing responses to a more detailed set of questions where 0 equals no disability and 1 equals disability on one or more ADL and IADL items. Furthermore, when dichotomized as less than 10 disability days versus 11 or more, the global question correlated well with specific disabilities and dependencies. The global disability question, however, is not a panacea. Although it provides a parsimonious estimate of the prevalence of any disabilities, it is not suitable for use in identifying specific disabilities or the onset of new or recovery from old disabilities. Thus, global disability measures are best suited for estimating crude prevalence rates or the association of having any disability with other outcomes.

Among the more detailed and time-consuming approaches to disability measurement is the recent and provocative work of Jette and colleagues (Jette et al., 2002; Haley et al., 2002) resulting in the Late-Life Function and Disability Instrument (Late-Life FDI). Proceeding by the book (DeVellis, 2003) for the development of new indicators, Jette and colleagues developed a novel questionnaire that is an expansion of the traditional ADLs and IADLs. This questionnaire addresses both the frequency of and limitation in performing 25 life activities, as well as the extent of difficulty in performing 48 common functional tasks. The first phase of their developmental work involved a detailed review of existing measures from which to select or generate items, expert panel evaluation of those items, and suggestions from a series of focus group evaluations by older adults themselves. The second phase involved the collection of detailed data on a targeted convenience sample of 150 older adults who collectively provided a wide range of functional and disability levels.

Extensive psychometric evaluation of the data using exploratory factor analysis and item response theory techniques reduced the number of disability items to 16 and the number of common functional tasks to 32. Two questions are asked for each of the disability items: (1) "How often do you *do a particular task*?" and (2) "To what extent do you feel limited *in doing a particular task*?" Two underlying dimensions emerged for the frequency aspect reflecting social role versus personal role components (similar to the extra- versus intraindividual distinction discussed above). Two dimensions also emerged from the limitation aspect reflecting instrumental role versus management role components. The instrumental role component included items such as traveling out of town and working at a volunteer job, while the management role included items such as taking care of one's own health and taking care of household business and finances. The four resulting disability dimensional scales had good reliability and validity (Jette et al., 2002). Only one question was asked for each of the common functional tasks: "How much difficulty do you have *doing a particular activity* without the help of someone else or the use of assistive devices?" (Haley et al., 2002). Three functional dimensions emerged, reflecting upper extremity movements, basic lower extremity movements, and advanced (i.e., vigorous or strenuous) lower extremity movements. The three resulting functional dimension scales also had good reliability and validity.

The most promising feature of the Late-Life FDI is that it was built from the ground up for the purpose at hand. That is, it is theoretically consistent with the disablement process model developed by Nagi (1965, 1969, 1976, 1991) and clarified and elaborated by Verbrugge and Jette (1994). Moreover, it takes into consideration the frequency of performance and extent of limitation in the disability items. In addition, it considerably expands the range of intensity and duration of the functional activities under consideration. Finally, the use of item response theory methods provides a weighting metric reflecting the importance of each item. These strengths, however, are offset by two major weaknesses. First, it took the respondents about 25 minutes on average to complete the functional limitation and disability components of the Late-Life FDI. This poses considerable respondent burden and substantially diminishes the possibility that the Late-Life FDI will be included in large-scale studies. Second, the 150-person developmental sample was obtained by convenience in two regions of one state. As a result, generalizability is limited, and population norms for the Late-Life FDI do not exist. These weaknesses notwithstanding, the Late-Life FDI is a promising development.

Important contributions to refining the conceptualization and measurement of disability have also been made by Fried and her colleagues. Noting that the traditional approach for ascertaining physical disability based on reported difficulty captures only the tip of the iceberg and misses adaptations that respondents have made along the way that make the task easier and thus prevent a sense of difficulty (Fried, Herdman, Kuhn, Rubin, & Turano, 1991), they proposed measuring subclinical difficulty as an early warning sign that the disablement process was underway (Fried et al., 1996). Basically, Fried and colleagues view subclinical disability as an intermediary stage along the disability continuum. Although they did not explicitly attempt to integrate the subclinical disability concept into Verbrugge and Jette's (1994) model of the disablement process, it might logically be positioned between functional limitation and disability.

This represents a conceptual deviation, inasmuch as Fried's subclinical disability concept would seem to be equivalent to "activity accommodation." This deviation becomes clearer in the context of the ascertainment methods for subclinical disability, which involve asking two additional questions for each ADL or IADL activity. One question focuses on modifying the method of task performance (e.g., "Because of health or physical problems, have you changed the method you use to bathe or shower?"), and the other focuses on modifying the frequency of task performance (e.g., "Because of health or physical problems, do you bathe or shower less often now?"). This approach facilitates the identification of respondents who report no difficulty with task performance, but have compensated for their functional decrement by modifying the method or frequency of task performance.

Cross-sectional data support the reliability and construct validity of the subclinical difficulty concept (Freid et al., 1996), and longitudinal data have demonstrated its predictive validity in terms of incident disability in older women (Fried, Bandeen-Roche, Chaves, & Johnson, 2000). Indeed, using data on 436 community-dwelling women who were 70 to 80 years old at baseline in the Women's Health and Aging Study, subclinical disability in two tasks—walking a half-mile or more and climbing up 10 steps—were significant predictors of incident disability in those tasks 18 months later. From the standpoint of the disablement process defined by Nagi (1965, 1969, 1976, 1991) and Verbrugge and Jette (1994), however, these two tasks are actually functional limitations rather than disabilities.

Longitudinal analysis of data from the 998 respondents in the African American Health study (Miller et al., 2004; Wolinsky, Miller, Andresen, Malmstrom, & Miller, 2005a, 2005b) has further demonstrated the reliability and contextual validity of subclinical measures for both functional limitation and disability, and has convincingly shown that subclinical measures at baseline are very robust predictors of the onset of the respective functional limitation or disability within two years of follow-up. Thus, ascertainment of subclinical levels of functional limitation and disability appears to be an effective way to provide a promising early warning system for targeting individuals most likely to benefit from interventions to prevent, delay, or even reverse the disablement process. Similar to the promising work of Jette and colleagues on the Late-Life FDI (Haley et al., 2002; Jette et al., 2002), however, the main limitation with the subclinical ascertainment approach is respondent burden and the time consumed in asking two additional questions for each task of those respondents who report no task difficulty.

DETERMINING WHEN MEANINGFUL CHANGE HAS OCCURRED

The underlying goal of aging and life course studies is to examine changes over time. Doing so requires a framework for determining when a meaningful change has occurred. This is relatively straightforward in the case of reliably and validly measured dichotomies, such as whether the respondent has any difficulty performing a particular functional task or role activity. In that case, meaningful change has occurred whenever the respondent's answer changes over time from not having difficulty to having difficulty, or vice versa. It is not so straightforward, however, when one moves beyond the simplicity of whether difficulty exists with a particular item, to either the degree of difficulty with that item or summary measures that combine responses to sets of ADLs or IADLs (Wolinsky et al., 2000). Moreover, although this issue has recently been recognized as one of the two most serious problems in the disability literature (Jette, 2003), it has not received adequate attention.

Considerable work has been done on determining whether meaningful change has occurred with respect to health-related quality of life (HRQoL) measures, and it is instructive to consider those methods here, especially because HRQoL has been identified by Verbrugge and Jette (1994) as an important sequela of disability. At the root of the problem is the well-known fact that all measures have two variance components: true score and error (DeVellis, 2003; Nunnally, 1967). There are two types of error: random error, which diminishes reliability, and systematic error, which diminishes validity. Using the illustrative notion of shooting a gun at a target composed of progressively larger concentric circles, the tightness of the cluster of shots represents reliability, and the proximity of the center of that cluster to the bull's eye represents validity. Ideally, the cluster should be tight and centered on the bull's eye.

Using the concentric circle analogy, the issue of determining whether meaningful change has occurred involves comparing cluster centers obtained from the same shooter at two different points in time, where the individual bullet holes represent the response to specific ADL or IADL activities. If the cluster centers (i.e., scale scores) are different, the problem is knowing whether the difference is due to the size of the clusters (i.e., reliability), or whether the bull's eye has been moved (i.e., validity). There are two major approaches for determining whether meaningful change has occurred: distributional and anchor methods. *Distributional methods* rely on information contained in the frequency distribution of the measure under consideration. The most widely recognized approach derives from Jacob Cohen's (1969) classic work on effect size. What Cohen suggested was that the magnitude of intervention and control group-level differences could best be gauged by (1) obtaining the average change from baseline to the end of the study in each group, (2) subtracting the average change in the control group from the average change in the intervention group, and (3) dividing the result by the pooled standard deviation obtained from both groups at baseline. The result is *effect size*, a measure of the average change attributable to the intervention expressed relative to an estimate of the amount of variation in the population.

Based on decades of intervention studies in education, Cohen (1969) suggested that effect sizes of .20 or greater were small, effect sizes of .50 or greater were medium, and effect sizes of .80 or greater were large. The main problem with the effect size approach is that the categorization of levels is arbitrary. Indeed, others have argued for different categorical cut-offs, relying on similarly arbitrary arguments. Interestingly, the most widely cited of the arbitrarily argued meaningful categorical cut-offs are very close to Cohen's .50 level (Feinstein, 1999; Sloan, Loprinzi, & Kuross, 1988; Testa, 1987). Moreover, in a recent meta-analysis, Norman, Sloan, and Wyrwich (2003) reviewed 38 studies that yielded 68 effect size estimates and found that the mean estimated meaningfully important difference (MID) was .495. Furthermore, if there are seven response options for each question on the scale, an effect size of .50 is remarkably close to estimates of human abilities to discriminate between two feeling states (Miller, 1956). And if the reliability (internal consistency or test-retest) of the scale is about .75, then an effect size of .50 is equivalent to one standard error of measurement (1-SEM), which Wyrwich et al. have shown corresponds to typical anchor-based MID assessments (Wyrwich, Nienaber, Tierney, & Wolinsky, 1999; Wyrwich, Tierney, & Wolinsky, 1999, 2002).

Anchor-based approaches to establishing MIDs rely on some external criterion. For example, in addition to being asked the set of HRQoL questions at baseline and follow-up, subjects would also be asked whether there had been a meaningful change in their life condition over that period of time, and if so, whether that change was small, medium, or large. The average difference between the baseline and follow-up HRQoL scores within each of the seven resulting groups on the retrospective change measure (a large difference for the worse, no change, or a large difference for the better) would then be construed as the HRQoL thresholds defining the levels of meaningful change. As indicated above, Wyrwich and colleagues (Wyrwich, Nienaber, et al., 1999; Wyrwich, Tierney, et al., 1999; Wyrwich et al., 2002) have shown that the minimally important change approximates 1-SEM, which is generally equivalent to an effect size of .50. The principal problem with the anchor-based methods is selecting the appropriate anchor. In the case of patients and their HRQoL, should the anchor come from the patients, their primary care providers, or an independent panel of expert physicians (Wyrwich, Tierney, Babu, Kroenke, & Wolinsky, 2005)? The answer depends on whether one is looking for the minimally detectable difference for the patient, the amount of change required for the primary care physician to initiate a change in the treatment regimen, or a more universal guideline devoid of situational context.

Although this section has focused on work done in HRQoL, similar issues apply in evaluating meaningful change in the disablement process.

For example, how much recovery must occur to demonstrate that a disability reduction intervention has been successful? Or how much progression must occur to warrant an increase in reimbursement for home health care or eligibility for institutional placement? Although the work done on assessing meaningful change in HRQoL provides a valuable template for discussing these difficult issues, it does not resolve them. Moreover, it is clear that longitudinal models using three or more waves of data are becoming more common in gerontological studies (Ferraro & Kelley-Moore, 2003). Therefore, further work is needed to generalize the essence of meaningful change in the disablement process into more sophisticated multiwave analyses using Markov models or latent growth curve approaches (Mendes de Leon, Glass, & Berkman, 2003; Mendes de Leon, Guralnik, & Bandeen-Roche, 2002; McArdle, Ferrer-Caja, Hamagami, & Woodcock, 2002; McArdle et al., 2004).

CONCLUSION

The purpose of this chapter was to provide an organizing framework for the study of functional limitations and disability in older adults. We began by reviewing the conceptual model that Nagi (1965, 1969, 1976) originally presented, as well as his responses to subsequent criticism concerning that model (Nagi, 1991). This was followed by a review of the clarifications and dynamic recasting of Nagi's model provided by Verbrugge and Jette (1994). Conceptual and measurement innovations offered by Jette and his colleagues (the Late-Life FDI; Haley et al., 2002; Jette et al., 2002), as well as by Fried and her colleagues (subclinical disability; 1991, 1996, 2000), were then considered. The final section briefly reviewed conceptual and methodological developments for determining when meaningful change in an individual's score on a functional limitation or disability measure has occurred (Norman et al., 2003). Many of the major issues identified early on in the epidemiology of disability—conceptual confusion, inappropriate and inadequate measurement, and the lack of consensus on knowing when important changes in levels of functional limitations or disability have occurred—continue to exist. Further coordinated conceptual and methodological development is needed if advances are to be made in the epidemiology of disability.

REFERENCES

Allen, S. M., & Mor, V. (1997). The prevalence and consequences of unmet need: Contrasts between older and younger adults with disability. *Medical Care, 35*, 1132–1148.

Allen, S. M., Foster, A., & Berg, K. (2001). Receiving help at home: The interplay of human and technological assistance. *Journal of Gerontology: Social Sciences, 56B*, S374–S382.

Aneshensel, C. S. (2002). *Theory-based data analysis for the social sciences.* Thousand Oaks, CA: Pine Forge Press.

Berkman, L. F., & Kawachi, I. (2000). *Social epidemiology.* New York: Oxford University Press.

Bollen, K. A. (1989). *Structural equations with latent variables.* San Francisco: Jossey-Bass.

Brownson, R. C., & Petitti, D. B. (1998). *Applied epidemiology: Theory to practice.* New York: Oxford University Press.

Cohen, J. (1969). *Statistical power analysis for the behavioural sciences.* London: Academic Press.

Crimmins, E. M. (2004). Trends in the health of the elderly. *Annual Review of Public Health, 25*, 79–98.

Crimmins, E. M., Reynolds, S. L., & Saito, Y. (1999). Trends in health and ability to work among the older working age population. *Journal of Gerontology: Social Sciences, 54*, S31–S40.

DeVellis, R. F. (2003). *Scale development: Theory and applications.* Thousand Oaks, CA: Sage.

Dexter, P. R., Stump, T. E., Tierney, W. M., & Wolinsky, F. D. (1996). The psychometric properties of the SF-36 health survey among older adults in clinical settings. *Journal of Clinical Geropsychology, 2*, 225–237.

Diehl, M., Willis, S. L., & Schaie, K. W. (1995). Everyday problem solving in older adults: Observational assessment and cognitive correlates. *Psychology and Aging, 10*, 478–491.

Duke University Center for the Study of Aging and Human Development. (1978). *Multidimensional functional assessment: The OARS methodology.* Durham, NC: Duke University.

Feinstein, A. R. (1999). Indexes of contrast and quantitative significance for comparisons of two groups. *Statistics in Medicine, 18*, 2557–2581.

Ferraro, K. F., & Kelley-Moore, J. A. (2001). Self-rated health and mortality among black and white adults: Examining the dynamic evaluation thesis. *Journal of Gerontology: Social Sciences, 56B*, S195–S205.

Ferraro, K. F., & Kelley-Moore, J. A. (2003). A half-century of longitudinal methods in social gerontology: Evidence of change in the journal. *Journal of Gerontology: Social Sciences, 58B*, S264–S270.

Freedman, V. A., Crimmins, E. M., Schoeni, R. F., Spillman, B. C., Aykan, H., Kramarow, E., et al. (2004). Resolving inconsistencies in trends in old-age disability: Report from a technical working group. *Demography, 41*, 417–441.

Fried, L. P., Bandeen-Roche, K., Chaves, P. H. M., & Johnson, B. A. (2000). Preclinical mobility disability predicts incident mobility disability in older women. *Journal of Gerontology: Medical Sciences, 55A*, M43–M52.

Fried, L. P., Bandeen-Roche, K., Williamson, J. D., Prasada-Rao, P., Chee, E., Tepper, S., et al. (1996). Functional decline in older adults: Expanding methods of ascertainment. *Journal of Gerontology: Medical Sciences, 51A,* M206–M214.

Fried, L. P., Herdman, S. J., Kuhn, K. E., Rubin, G., & Turano, K. (1991). Preclinical disability: Hypotheses about the bottom of the iceberg. *Journal of Aging and Health, 3,* 285–300.

Fries, J. F. (1980). Aging, natural death, and the compression of morbidity. *New England Journal of Medicine, 303,* 130–135.

Gill, T. M., & Kurland, B. (2003). The burden of patterns of disability in activities of daily living among community-living older persons. *Journal of Gerontology: Medical Sciences, 58A,* 70–75.

Gill, T. M., Robinson, J. T., & Tinetti, M. E. (1998). Difficulty and dependence: Two components of the disability continuum among community-living older persons. *Annals of Internal Medicine, 128,* 96–101.

Haley, S. M., Jette, A. M., Coster, W. J., Kooyoomjian, J. T., Levenson, S., Heeren, T., et al. (2002). Late life function and disability instrument: II. Development and evaluation of the function component. *Journal of Gerontology: Medical Sciences, 57A,* M217–M222.

Heise, D. (1975). *Causal analysis.* New York: Wiley-Interscience.

Idler, E. M. (1992). Self-assessed health and mortality: A review of studies. In S. Maes, H. Leventhal, & M. Johnston (Eds.), *International review of health psychology* (pp. 35–54). New York: Wiley.

Idler, E. L., & Kasl, S. V. (1991). Health perceptions and survival: Do global evaluations of health status really predict mortality? *Journal of Gerontology, 46,* S55–S65.

Jette, A. M. (1994). How measurement techniques influence estimates of disability in older populations. *Social Science and Medicine, 38,* 937–942.

Jette, A. M. (1999). Disentangling the process of disablement. *Social Science and Medicine, 48,* 471–472.

Jette, A. M. (2003). Assessing disability in studies on physical activity. *American Journal of Preventive Medicine, 25,* 122–128.

Jette, A. M., Haley, S. M., Coster, W. J., Kooyoomjian, J. T., Levenson, S., Heeren, T., et al. (2002). Late life function and disability instrument: I. Development and evaluation of the disability component. *Journal of Gerontology: Medical Sciences, 57A,* M209–M216.

Jette, A. M., & Keysor, J. J. (2003). Disability models: Implications for arthritis exercise and physical activity interventions. *Arthritis and Rheumatism, 49,* 114–120.

Katz, S., Ford, A., Moskowitz, R., Jackson, B., & Jaffe, M. (1963). Studies of illness in the aged. The Index of ADL: A standardized measure of biological and psychological function. *Journal of the American Medical Association, 185,* 914–919.

La Plante, M. P. (1990). Who counts as having a disability? Musings on the meaning and prevalence of disability. *Disability Studies Quarterly, 10,* 15–17.

Lawton, M. P. (1972). Assessing the competence of older people. In D. Kent, R. Kastenbaum, & S. Sherwood (Eds.), *Research planning and action for the elderly.* New York: Behavioral Publications.

Lilienfeld, D. E., & Stolley, P. D. (1994). *Foundations of epidemiology* (3rd ed.). New York: Oxford University Press.

Lima, J. C., & Allen, S. M. (2001). Targeting risk for unmet need: Not enough help versus no help at all. *Journal of Gerontology: Social Sciences, 56B,* S302–S310.

Manton, K. G., & Gu, X. (2001). Changes in the prevalence of chronic disability in the United States black and nonblack population above age 65 from 1982 to 1999. *Proceedings of the National Academy of Sciences, 98,* 6354–6359.

Manton, K. G., & Land, K. C. (2000). Active life expectancy estimates for the U.S. elderly population: A multidimensional continuous-mixture model of functional change applied to completed cohorts, 1982–1996. *Demography, 37,* 253–265.

Marsiske, M., & Willis, S. L. (1995). Dimensionality of everyday problem solving in older adults. *Psychology and Aging, 10,* 269–283.

McArdle, J. J., Ferrer-Caja, E., Hamagami, F., & Woodcock, R. W. (2002). Comparative longitudinal structural analyses of the growth and decline of multiple intellectual abilities over the life span. *Developmental Psychology, 38,* 115–142.

McArdle, J. J., Hamagami, F., Jones, K., Jolesz, F., Kikinis, R., Spiro, A., et al. (2004). Structural modeling of dynamic changes in memory and brain structure using longitudinal data from the Normative Aging Study. *Journal of Gerontology: Psychological Sciences, 59B,* P294–P304.

Mendes de Leon, C. F., Glass, T. A., & Berkman, L. F. (2003). Social engagement and disability in a community population of older adults: The New Haven EPESE. *American Journal of Epidemiology, 157,* 633–642.

Mendes de Leon, C. F., Guralnik, J. M., & Bandeen-Roche, K. (2002). Short-term change in physical function and disability: The Women's Health and Aging Study. *Journal of Gerontology: Social Sciences, 57B,* S355–S365.

Miller, D. K., Malmstrom, T. K., Joshi, S., Andresen, E. M., Morley, J. E., & Wolinsky, F. D. (2004). Clinically relevant levels of depressive symptoms in community-dwelling middle aged African Americans. *Journal of the American Geriatrics Society, 52,* 741–748.

Miller, G. A. (1956). The magic number seven plus or minus two: Some limits on our capacity for processing information. *Psychological Review, 63,* 81–97.

Nagi, S. Z. (1965). Some conceptual issues in disability and rehabilitation. In M. B. Sussman (Ed.), *Sociology and rehabilitation* (pp. 100–113). Washington, DC: American Sociological Association.

Nagi, S. Z. (1969). *Disability and rehabilitation: Legal, clinical, and self concepts and measurement.* Columbus: Ohio State University Press.

Nagi, S. Z. (1976). An epidemiology of disability among adults in the United States. *Milbank Memorial Fund Quarterly/Health and Society, 54,* 439–467.

Nagi, S. Z. (1991). Disability concepts revisited: Implications for prevention. In A. M. Pope & A. R. Tarlov (Eds.), *Disability in America: Toward a national agenda for prevention* (pp. 309–327). Washington, DC: National Academy Press.

Norman, G. R., Sloan, J. A., & Wyrwich, K. W. (2003). Interpretation of changes in health related quality of life: The remarkable universality of half a standard deviation. *Medical Care, 41,* 582–592.

Nunnally, J. C. (1967). *Psychometric theory.* New York: McGraw-Hill.

Rodgers, W., & Miller, B. (1997). A comparative analysis of ADL questions in surveys of older people. *Journal of Gerontology: Social Sciences, 52B,* S325–S335.

Rosow, I., & Breslau, N. (1966). A Guttman health scale for the aged. *Journal of Gerontology, 21,* 556–559.

Sloan, J. A., Loprinzi, C. L., & Kuross, S. A. (1988). Randomized comparison of four tools measuring overall quality of life in patients with advanced cancer. *Journal of Clinical Oncology, 16,* 3662–3673.

Testa, M. A. (1987). Interpreting quality of life clinical trial data for use in the clinical practice of antihypertensive therapy. *Journal of Hypertension, 5,* S9–S13.

Verbrugge, L. K., & Jette, A. M. (1994). The disablement process. *Social Science and Medicine, 38,* 1–14.

Verbrugge, L. K., Merrill, S. S., & Liu, X. (1999). Measuring disability with parsimony. *Disability and Rehabilitation, 21,* 295–306.

Ware, J. E., Kosinski, M., & Dewey, J. E. (2000). *How to score Version 2 of the SF-36 health survey.* Boston: QualityMetric.

Weiner, J., Hanley, R., Clark, R., & Van Nostrand, J. (1990). Measuring the activities of daily living: Comparisons across national surveys. *Journal of Gerontology: Social Sciences, 45,* S229–S237.

Willis, S. L. (1996). Everyday cognitive competence in elderly persons: Conceptual issues and empirical findings. *Gerontologist, 36,* 595–601.

Wolinsky, F. D., Armbrecht, E. S., & Wyrwich, K. W. (2000). Rethinking functional limitation pathways. *Gerontologist, 40,* 137–146.

Wolinsky, F. D., & Johnson, R. J. (1991). The use of health services by older adults. *Journal of Gerontology: Social Sciences, 46,* S345–S357.

Wolinsky, F. D., & Johnson, R. J. (1992). Perceived health status and mortality among older men and women. *Journal of Gerontology: Social Sciences, 47,* S304–S312.

Wolinsky, F. D., Miller, D. K., Andresen, E. M., Malmstrom, T. K., & Miller J. P. (2004). Health related quality of life in middle aged African Americans. *Journal of Gerontology: Social Sciences, 58B,* S118–S123.

Wolinsky, F. D., Miller, D. K., Andresen, E. M., Malmstrom, T. K., & Miller, J. P. (2005a). Reproducibility of physical performance and physiologic assessments. *Journal of Aging and Health, 17,* 111–124.

Wolinsky, F. D., Miller, D. K., Andresen, E. M., Malmstrom, T. K., & Miller, J. P. (2005b). Further evidence for the importance of sub-clinical functional limitation and sub-clinical disability assessment in gerontology and geriatrics. *Journal of Gerontology: Social Sciences, 60B,* S146–S151.

Wolinsky, F. D., & Stump, T. E. (1996). A measurement model of the MOS 36-Item Short Form Health Survey (SF-36) in a clinical sample of disadvantaged, older, Black and White men and women. *Medical Care, 34,* 537–548.

Wyrwich, K. W., Nienaber, N. A., Tierney, W. M., & Wolinsky, F. D. (1999). Linking clinical relevance and statistical significance in evaluating intra-individual changes in health-related quality of life. *Medical Care, 37,* 469–478.

Wyrwich, K. W., Tierney, W. M., Babu, A. N., Kroenke, K., & Wolinsky, F. D. (2005). A comparison of clinically important differences in health-related quality of life for patients with asthma, lung disease, or heart disease. *Health Services Research, 40,* 577–592.

Wyrwich, K. W., Tierney, W. M., & Wolinsky, F. D. (1999). Further evidence supporting a SEM-based criterion for identifying meaningful intra-individual changes in health-related quality of life instruments. *Journal of Clinical Epidemiology, 52,* 861–873.

Wyrwich, K. W., Tierney, W. M., & Wolinsky, F. D. (2002). Using the standard error of measurement to identify important intra-individual change on the Asthma Quality of Life Questionnaire. *Quality of Life Research, 11,* 1–7.

CHAPTER 7

The Role of Nutrition in the Older Individual

Dorothy M. Morré

Given the demographic trends documented in chapter 2, there is increased susceptibility to age- and diet-related diseases that can increase the risk of mortality. The role of nutrition in the aging process continues to attract public interest in the hope that specific nutrients can decrease mortality risk, prevent the development of chronic diseases, and perhaps slow aging itself. In addition, nutrition services play a key role in the treatment and reduction of costly complications associated with age-related diseases (Committee on Nutrition Services for Medicare Beneficiaries, 2000).

The majority of nutritional scientists who examine age-related issues tend to focus on uncovering the nutritional problems older adults face and designing nutrition-based interventions for frail older adults. Less emphasis is placed on understanding how nutrition contributes toward the well-being of healthy older individuals. Nutritional scientists should take an interdisciplinary approach that addresses the person holistically. For example, one may ask what factors contribute to inadequate food consumption, not strictly from a nutritional viewpoint but also from maintaining social contact with others. Another logical question that should be addressed is what effect early-initiated and subsequent nutritional intervention will have on ameliorating or slowing aging-related changes that ultimately occur in the majority of elderly people.

This chapter reviews the contributions of nutrition to gerontological knowledge. The role of nutrition will be considered in the aging process of healthy older individuals, as well as older individuals who face nutritionally related problems such as anorexia, sarcopenia, cachexia, and nutritional frailty. Among other topics, interactions between drugs and nutrients, caloric restriction, food assistance programs, and food safety will be discussed.

NUTRITION FOR HEALTHY AGING

Because aging is a complex process that involves the whole body, it is unlikely that a single product, pill, or potion could provide one with a long and healthy life. Research addressing the dietary needs of independent healthy older populations is essential to understand challenges that will be presented in the future (Foote, Giuliano, & Harris, 2000). Until the 1950s, nutritional research was dominated by nutrient deficiencies. More recently, the emphasis has gradually shifted from cardiovascular diseases to the impact of nutrition on cancer and then to nutrition of the elderly. Besides the ongoing effort to change food habits, attention has begun to focus on the promotion of nutritional health through the use of novel but functional foods such as lactose replacement products and eggs containing extra vitamins and omega-3 fatty acids.

As one ages, the realization that poor health is not an inevitable consequence of aging becomes apparent to many older individuals, although there are some nutritional and metabolic differences between young and old humans. The variability in nutrient needs becomes wider rather than narrower with age, so it is difficult to generalize about the nutritional needs of the older individuals (Russell, 2000). Research has shown that some bodily functions, such as cardiac output, lung capacity, and kidney filtration, decline with advancing aging (Geokas, Laktta, Makinodan, & Timiras, 1990). The intestinal functions for macronutrients are generally well preserved with aging, but the aging gastrointestinal tract becomes less efficient in absorbing some of the micronutrients, such as vitamin B_{12}, vitamin D, and calcium.

Although keeping oneself healthy and preventing chronic diseases begins early in life by such simple approaches as eating a varied diet with plenty of fruits and vegetables, maintaining a healthy weight, regular physical activity, and seeking prompt medical care when ill or injured, the aging-related changes become enough of a reality to motivate aging adults to seek advice on good nutritional practices. Aging individuals are particularly concerned about how nutrition can help them remain mentally and physically healthy. A paradox that needs to be refuted is that one diet fits all. There is too much heterogeneity among the aging population for one diet to fit the nutritional needs and health concerns of all older individuals.

A very recent guide, *MyPyramid 2005* (U.S. Department of Agriculture, 2005), incorporates the recommendations from the 2005 Dietary

Guidelines for Americans released by the U.S. Department of Health and Human Services and U.S. Department of Agriculture in January 2005. It emphasizes the need for a more individualized approach to improving diet and lifestyle and provides a web-based interactive food guidance system based on both the 2005 Dietary Guidelines for Americans and the Dietary Reference Intakes (DRI) from the Food and Nutrition Board, National Academy of Sciences, Institute of Medicine. After plugging in the age, gender, and level of activity, MyPyramid gives a suggested number of servings in the grains, vegetables, fruits, milk, meats, and beans groups, and then one can access tips for what is included in the individual groups. While this is helpful for someone who is adept at using a computer, it may not be accessible for many of the older individuals who wish to know what is an ideal diet plan for them.

A friendlier aid to promote routine nutrition screening and better nutrition care in America's health care system is the Nutrition Screening Initiative (1991). This five-year multifaceted effort is a project of the American Academy of Family Physicians, American Dietetic Association, and the National Council on Aging (American Academy of Family Physicians, 2005). The Nutrition Screening Manual for Professional Caring for Older Americans (1991) includes a "Determine Your Nutritional Health" checklist and two levels of screens to help quickly identify individuals who may require nutrition counseling, social or health services, or medical and nutritional intervention. The checklist uses a simple mnemonic, DETERMINE, based on a number of warning signs of poor nutritional health status that can be self-administered by anyone who interacts with older individuals. DETERMINE stands for Disease, Eating poorly, Tooth loss/mouth pain, Economic hardship, Reduced social contact, Multiple medicines, Involuntary weight loss/gain, Needs assistance in self care, and Elderly years above age 80.

Nutrition for Disease Prevention

Traditionally, prevention programs to reduce chronic disease risks have focused on children and younger adults; however, with the increase in the number of older adults and the attendant increase in medical expenditures with the onset of several major chronic diseases, researchers are beginning to focus their interests and attention on older adults. Nutritionists need to consider more broadly and creatively how nutrition may help to prevent or delay progression of typically age-related diseases.

Substantial scientific evidence exists to support the effectiveness of nutrition intervention in the prevention and treatment of chronic diseases, such as cardiovascular disease, hypertension, diabetes mellitus, and obesity related to poor nutrition and reduced physical activity (Ponza, Ohls, & Millen, 1996; Millen, Ohls, Ponza, & McCool, 2002). It is estimated that the condition of nine out of ten individuals with chronic disease could be improved by nutrition intervention (Food Security Institute, 2003). Because of older Americans' vulnerability to disease and conditions that may impair their health, it is critical that they obtain adequate nutrition. The Committee on Nutrition Services for Medicare Beneficiaries of the Institute of Medicine (2000) estimates that nearly 90% of the older population has one or more chronic conditions in which nutritional interventions may be beneficial.

Caloric Restriction

Unlike obesity, where the intake of calories exceeds the output of energy, caloric restriction (CR) refers to a diet containing 30 to 40% fewer calories than typically consumed but containing all the necessary nutrients and vitamins to support life. In the 1930s, evidence for the phenomenon of slowing the aging process by restricting caloric intake emerged when scientists learned that underfed rodents lived up to 40 percent longer than their well-fed counterparts (McCay, Crowell, & Maynard, 1935). Since then, the results have been duplicated in worms, fruit flies, spiders, insects, and other lab animals where CR has been shown to increase both the average and the maximal life spans (Weindruch & Walford, 1988; Weindruch & Sohal, 1997). Data on extension of life span by CR in humans are not available, although life expectancy for humans has consistently increased with each generation without strong evidence that CR played a major role. Comparisons of dietary intake and longevity data have not produced consistent correlations. Two major negative effects of CR are a reduced ability to deal with hypothermia (lowered body temperature), possibly associated with lower body fat content, and wounds that do not heal as quickly in CR animals as in normal-fed laboratory animals (Reed et al., 1996). Because of limited studies, we do not know how people respond to CR. There has been interest in developing mimetics— compounds that would produce in humans the positive effects of CR while evading side effects such as muscle wasting and infertility (Roth et al., 2002).

Osteoporosis

Osteoporosis is one of the chronic conditions in which regular physical activity and an adequate diet (Nieves, 2002) during the early years are important lifestyle contributors to bone health and the maintenance later in life. Osteoporosis is a chronic multifactorial disease that usually occurs following menopause in women and a decade or so later in men. It is characterized by low bone mass and increased risk of fractures (Nieves, 2005). After the onset of menopause in women and later in men, more rapid bone loss due to reductions in both bone mineral content and density occurs in response to imbalances in the remodeling of the skeleton. In addition to the postmenopause decline in estrogen in women and likely decline in androgens in men, dietary risk factors operating throughout the life cycle may have adverse effects on skeletal tissue. These include inadequate consumption of calcium and phosphorus, a low intake of vitamin D–containing foods and/or low exposure to sunlight, a high-animal protein intake, and a high intake of sodium resulting in renal losses of calcium. Inadequate intake of calcium or vitamin D, or both, will influence the adaptation of the calcium regulatory system in an attempt to preserve skeletal structure for its functional uses. Insufficient adaptation leads to reduced calcium absorption and lower circulating ionized calcium and, in turn, results in loss of both bone mass and density (Anderson & Ontjes, 2004). Calcium and vitamin D supplementation and appropriate exercise may be easily modifiable approaches to prevent osteoporosis. The recommended elemental calcium intake for elderly Americans is 1200 milligrams a day or more and at least 600 IU per day of vitamin D, although higher doses of vitamin D (800–1,000 IU per day) in the elderly (65 years and over) may be required for optimal bone growth (Nieves, 2002, 2003).

Osteoarthritis and Rheumatoid Arthritis

Two other bone-related diseases are osteoarthritis and rheumatoid arthritis. They affect about half of persons 65 years and older, leading to impaired mobility and increasing the risk of developing osteoporosis, aerobic and muscular deconditioning, and pressure sores (National Institute of Arthritis and Musculoskeletal and Skin Diseases, 2002). While numerous unorthodox cures involving nutrition have been suggested, there is no reliable treatment available to cure arthritis. Rest, exercise, consuming a well-balanced diet, and using medications to help control pain are still the usual recommendations. In addition to physical and occupational therapy, diet and exercise play an extremely important role; thus, patient education in these areas is of great importance.

Diabetes Mellitus

Patient education and compliance are important for older individuals with diabetes. The Expert Committee on the Diagnosis and Classification of Diabetes Mellitus (1997) reported that the signs and symptoms of diabetes in the older adult may not be recognized since they are often different from those in younger adults and include involuntary weight loss, fatigue, anorexia, incontinence, disturbed sleep, or cognitive disturbances. Chronic complications of diabetes tend to be more severe in older adults (Morley, 1998), who are at excess risk for disability associated with cardiovascular disease, peripheral vascular disease, stroke, vision loss, and neuropathy (Jette & Branch, 1985; Gregg et al., 2000). The American Diabetes Association estimates there are two cases of prediabetes waiting to be found for every diagnosed case. Failure to diagnose and manage diabetes, especially in frail older adults, leads to poor outcomes when a patient is hospitalized (Hirsch, 2002).

A position statement issued by the American Diabetes Association (2004) states that since research focused on aging subjects with diabetes is limited, nutrition recommendations must be extrapolated from what is known about the general population. However, based on observations in long-term care facilities that the older adult with diabetes tends to be underweight rather than overweight, caution should be exercised when prescribing weight loss diets. Restrictive diets with decreased food choices can make meals unappealing and may lead to malnutrition and dehydration, with accompanying weight loss. Medical nutrition therapy in general for patients with diabetes involves a plan to ensure daily consistent distribution of a specified amount of carbohydrates. For example, if sucrose-containing foods are added to the usual carbohydrate allowance rather than substituted, the person needs to counteract the extra carbohydrate with insulin or medication depending on the particular treatment regimen (Yim, 2002).

Hypertension

Although pharmacological treatment of hypertension has been very effective, lifestyle modifications have been efficient prevention or adjunct treatment strategies that are appropriate for adults of all ages (Alaimo et al., 1994). In the United States, 70 to 80% of heart failure cases result from chronic hypertension and coronary heart disease (Levy et al., 1996; Gottdiener et al., 2000). Morbidity due to heart failure is significant among the elderly, with a higher mortality rate than that of many cancers. Appropriate, aggressive treatment, while keeping a watchful eye on maintaining a good electrolyte and lipid balance, reduces functional decline, hospitalization, and mortality rates.

Decline in Energy Expenditure

For some, aging is associated with impaired ability to regulate food intake and a decline in energy expenditure. Some older individuals lack the ability to maintain a constant energy balance that would enable them to care for themselves. Older individuals are more susceptible to undernutrition due to aging-related changes, resulting in decreased appetite, metabolic disorders, medications that cause the body to burn more calories, or their living situation, which, for example, may be such that they are living alone and may be less motivated to prepare and eat meals, or they have limited funds or are unable to shop for or prepare foods. Dehydration may result if insufficient fluids are consumed due to impaired sensing and response to thirst. Coupling that with a depressed sensation of hunger during episodes of negative energy balance can result in weight loss. Even when weight is maintained during aging, the basal metabolic rate (BMR), defined as the minimum caloric requirement needed to sustain life in a resting individual, normally declines approximately 1 to 2% each decade, due partially to reduction in fat-free mass and changes in body fat composition (Piers, Soares, McCormack, & O'Dea, 1998). BMR is the largest factor in determining overall metabolic rate and the number of calories required to maintain, lose, or gain weight. During starvation or if there is an abrupt reduction in calories, BMR can be reduced by up to 30%. Consumption of too little food or calories, eating foods that lack the needed nutrients, particularly protein, vitamins, and minerals, or the inability of the body to absorb the nutrients from foods can lead to undernutrition. However, undernutrition and weight loss do not always go together. Some individuals can be undernourished without losing weight, be overweight and undernourished, or lose weight without being undernourished. Weight loss, especially if involuntary, is not a normal part of aging and usually signals some underlying disease process (Bales & Ritchie, 2002). Weight loss with loss of both muscle and fat mass, even in those who are obese or overweight, suggests that weight loss may not be beneficial.

Depression may be a leading cause of weight loss by blunting the desire to consume adequate nutrients to maintain the energy level needed for normal functioning. Life-altering events, for example, the death of a spouse, loneliness, or social isolation, frequently result in significantly greater rates of depression in the elderly compared to rates observed in younger age groups (Huffman, 2002). Successful treatment of depression-related anorexia of aging requires early detection and treatment. Pathological conditions, such as Alzheimer's disease (AD) or Parkinson's disease (PD), may also result in decreased food intake (Young, Greenwood, van Reekum, & Binns, 2004). The person with AD may forget to eat or eat less during mealtime due to a heightened degree of distraction. The ability to recognize the appropriate appetite signals may vary depending on time of day, level of behavioral difficulties, and body weight status (Young & Greenwood, 2001; Young, Binns, & Greenwood, 2001). PD patients may have altered taste and smell perception and insufficient motor skills necessary for eating. Also, certain medications decrease hunger. The persistent tremors associated with PD and often constant pacing of patients with AD require the expenditure of energy above what is normally expended.

Supplements

Although good nutrition and appropriate lifestyle habits must be initiated early in life to achieve a healthy old age, it is necessary to make certain dietary modifications in later life to adjust to the physical and metabolic changes that occur with aging. For example, it may be necessary to supplement with vitamins and minerals in order to offset some of the nutritional deficiencies that occur in some elderly (Donald et al., 1992). Twenty years ago, it was thought that all older people malabsorbed most nutrients. Now we know that some nutrients are absorbed better than others with aging, for example, vitamin A. Feskanich and colleagues (Feskanich, Singh, Willett, & Colditz, 2002) found an association between vitamin A supplementation and increased hip fractures. However, the need for selected nutrients does increase with aging. For example, the need for vitamin D appears to be greater based on a number of literature reports that vitamin D deficiency is a major unrecognized epidemic in the older adult population (Semba, Garret, Johnson, Guralnik, & Fried, 2000). Conditions such as gastritis atrophy, bacterial overgrowth, and malabsorption syndromes increase the need for many of the vitamins, especially vitamin B_{12} and folate; however, healthy older individuals do not require most of the vitamins at drastically different levels from those of younger individuals. In the early 20th century, a number of nutrients were identified, isolated, and purified, raising the possibility that optimal health conditions may be attained through nutrient supplementation. Recent attempts to alleviate cardiovascular disease and lung cancer by supplementation with vitamin E and beta carotene have not achieved these effects (Lichtenstein & Russell, 2005). Unexpectedly, during some of the intervention studies with nutrient supplementations, there was evidence of nutrient toxicity and nutrient interactions (Lichtenstein & Russell, 2005).

Another concern is that older individuals are particularly prone to suffering from nutrient-drug or drug-drug interactions, partly due to an increased practice of taking prescription medications along with over-the-counter products such as vitamins or herbal supplements. A typical older adult's regimen may comprise 10 or more medications and supplements. Age-related changes in the pharmacokinetics of the absorption, distribution, metabolism, and excretion of a drug may influence how a food interacts with the drug (Thomas & Burns, 1998). Coexisting disease states may exaggerate the action of the drug and be a confounding factor in drug-nutrient interactions. Health care professionals, including nutritionists, are concerned with the increasing use of over-the-counter drugs and herbal supplements, primarily because they are not regulated and may contain so-called hidden ingredients that may exacerbate or interfere with the benefits of nutrients and the actions of prescribed medications.

NUTRITIONAL PROBLEMS IN LATER LIFE

The overall nutritional status of older individuals must take into consideration genetic and environmental factors, including hunger, poverty, inadequate food and nutrient intake, social isolation, poor dentition and oral health, difficulty in chewing and swallowing, diet-related diseases and disorders, chronic medication use, advanced age, and living alone. Knowledge of the biological, physiological, and social changes likely to occur with aging aids in understanding the nutritional consequences of reduced functional abilities.

Functional impairments such as limitations on physical mobility or cognitive losses (Johnson & Fischer, 2004) may interfere with the well-being of an elderly person to the degree that shopping without assistance for food and then preparing it for consumption exceeds the person's abilities. The common age-related decline in vision, including decline in contrast sensitivity, glare sensitivity, dark adaptation, and depth (Pitts, 1982), can have adverse effects on an older person's ability to perform activities of daily living. Being unable to detect relevant visual stimuli and perceive spatial relationships can affect balance and predispose to falls. Loss of teeth can be a major problem leading to malnutrition. The person may have impaired chewing ability and therefore avoid foods that are difficult to chew, such as fruits, vegetables, and whole grains that are nutrient dense. In turn, this may ultimately lead to clinically important outcomes, such as poor diet quality and poor nutritional status (Hung et al., 2003).

Anorexia of Aging

One biological manifestation of the aging process, the anorexia of aging, appears to be an age-related progressive decrease in hunger and energy intake (Morley, 1997; Wilson & Morley, 2003) with associated secondary problems, such as sarcopenia (Evans & Campbell, 1993; Morley, Baumgartner, Roubenoff, Mayer, & Nair, 2001), impaired immunity (Thompson, Robbins, & Cooper, 1987), physical frailty (Fried et al., 2001; Gillick, 2001; Morley, 2001; Wilson & Morley, 2003), functional impairment (Newman et al., 2001), and mortality (Liu, Bopp, Roberson, & Sullivan, 2002; Newman et al., 2001). Mean energy intake is reduced by up to 1200 kilocalories in men and 800 kilocalories in women between ages 20 and 80 (Vellas et al., 1996; Wakimoto & Block, 2001). Virtually every large-scale study of healthy community-dwelling elderly individuals has documented this age-related reduction in energy intake (Vellas et al., 1996; Wakimoto & Block, 2001). Some of the causes for this reduction most likely are due to reduced physical activity, decrease in resting energy expenditure, and loss of lean body mass, which lead to a decrease in demand for calories (food intake) (Klausen, Toubro, & Astrup, 1997; Hunter, Weinsier, Gower, & Wetzstein, 2001).

Physiological mechanisms, as well as psychological states, influence energy regulation and age-related anorexia. Generally older individuals feel satiated sooner during meals compared to younger individuals. The feeling of fullness may be due to slowing of gastric emptying time (Clarkston, 1997; Evans, Triggs, Broe, & Creasey, 1981). Regulatory signals from the gut are suggested to stimulate the satiety center of the brain. Possible hormonal causes of the anorexia of aging include increased activity of cholecystokinin (CCK) (Sturm et al., 2004), leptin (Chapman, 2004), and various cytokines.

Obesity

In contrast to undernutrition, one of the most common nutritional disorders among the elderly is obesity and is now the major contributor to morbidity and mortality in older adults (Wilson & Kannel, 2000). In 1991, 14.7% of United States adults 60–69 years of age and 11.4% of those over 70 were obese (with a body mass index of more than 30 kilograms per square meter). Ten years later, the prevalence of obesity in these age groups increased 22.9% and 15.5%, respectively, representing increases of 56% and 36%, respectively (Mokdad, Bowman, Ford, Vinicor, Marks, & Koplan, 2001). Many obese older adults were obese as middle-aged adults and even as children. Up to the age of 80, obesity may be more common, after which time there is a decline likely reflecting both weight loss and mortality. Assessment of obesity using the waist circumference and waist-to-hip ratio are useful because an android pattern of abdominal adiposity closely correlates with comorbidities like cardiovascular disease, diabetes, and hypertension (Kissebah & Krakower, 1994). Waist circumference is measured at its narrowest point and the hip circumference at its widest point with the person standing. Guidelines published by the National Institutes of Health (1998) state there are increased health risks for comorbid conditions such as hypertension, diabetes, and cardiovascular disease with a waist circumference of 35 inches or more in females and 40 inches or more in males or with an abdominal fat distribution indicated by a waist-to-hip ratio of more than 0.80 for females and more than 0.95 for males.

Sarcopenia

Generally, total body fat increases and lean body mass (muscle mass) and muscle strength decrease during aging in humans (Guo, Zeller, Chumlea, & Siervogel, 1999). Sarcopenia is the loss of muscle mass with a corresponding reduction in muscle strength (Rosenberg, 1989; Roubenoff,

2001), as well as a decline in muscle efficiency (muscle strength/unit of muscle mass) and a decrease in protein synthesis (Short & Nair, 2000). Mobility and overall functioning are affected by sarcopenia (Morley et al., 2001), which appears to be an age-related phenomenon exacerbated by a sedentary lifestyle, nutritional factors, and chronic disease. Some elderly individuals consume insufficient amounts of protein or adequate calories to meet their caloric and protein needs, both of which lead to muscle catabolism (Evans, 1997).

Cachexia

Cachexia is a clinical phenomenon that presents as a combination of weight loss, lipolysis, loss of muscle and visceral protein, anorexia, chronic nausea, and weakness (Bruera, 1997). Aggressive caloric supplementation does not prevent the loss of lean body mass, and if there is any weight gain, it is due to increased fat accumulation, since the increase in protein degradation is greater than the increase in protein synthesis. Appetite stimulants, used as an alternative way to increase caloric intake, are better tolerated than tube feeding.

In contrast to starvation, which is characterized by pure caloric deficiency, cachexia is associated with chronic inflammatory or neoplastic conditions that elicit an acute-phase response. An involuntary loss of lean body mass with little or no weight loss occurs in individuals with a cytokine-mediated inflammatory or injury response (conditions such as rheumatoid arthritis, congestive heart failure, and, in some cases, cancer). The cytokines commonly involved in cachexia are interleukin-1 (IL-1), interleukin-6 (IL-6), and tumor necrosis factor-α (TNF-α). Both IL-1 and TNF-α increase IL-6, which is associated with anorexia in older individuals (Martinez, Arnalich, & Hernanz, 1993). Targeting these cytokines in older adults may be a way to counter cachexia and nutritional frailty.

Nutritional Frailty

Unlike sarcopenia or cachexia, *nutritional frailty* is used to define the condition of rapid, unintentional loss of body weight and accompanying disability that often signals the beginning of a terminal decline in an elderly individual (Bales & Ritchie, 2002). Nutritional frailty is characterized by an acute, dramatic reduction in appetite as well as food consumption. This wasting syndrome of advanced age leaves a person vulnerable to falls, functional decline, morbidity, and mortality (Walston & Fried, 1999). The symptoms of weight loss, depressed appetite, poor nutrition, and inactivity accompanied by dehydration, depressive symptoms, impaired immune function, and low cholesterol are commonly observed in the last year of life in many elderly individuals

It is extremely important to detect the onset of frailty as early as possible. Some signs and symptoms to watch for during the clinical examination are fatigue, weakness, change in ability to taste and smell, any gastrointestinal complaints such as poor appetite, oral problems, nausea, vomiting, diarrhea, and constipation, as well as changes in mental or emotional status (Fabiny & Kiel, 1997). Signs of protein deficiency may include alopecia, edema, glossitis, desquamation of skin, and hair depigmentation. The most important strategy for evaluating nutritional adequacy in the frail older adult is measurement of body weight, although it may not be easy to obtain regular body weights in the frail patient. A chair or bed scale may be used if the individual is unable to stand on an upright balance-beam scale. Ideally, when using body height in calculating body mass index (BMI), the person's height before age 50 years should be used as the reference height to avoid the effects of kyphosis (curvature of the spine) due to osteoporosis (Thomas et al., 2002).

NUTRITIONAL INTERVENTION FOR FRAIL OLDER INDIVIDUALS

Providing more food rarely reverses the progression of nutritional frailty primarily because most of the factors responsible for producing nutritional frailty are not related to food access. Approaches used to slow or reverse the development of nutritional frailty include using the enteral route of feeding to provide more calories and protein or by tube feedings if there is an intestinal obstruction or the person is unable to ingest sufficient calories. Orexigenic drugs, such as the synthetic progestin megestrol acetate (Yeh et al., 2000, 2001; Karcic, Philpot, & Morley, 2002), have been used as an appetite enhancer. However, the weight gain of cancer and HIV patients on these drugs tends to be due to increases in fat (Mantovani et al., 1995; Kotler, 2000). Other efforts to enhance consumption of food include adding food flavors such as roast beef, ham, natural bacon, maple, and cheese to the diet (Schiffman & Warwick, 1992).

Since nutritional frailty rarely has only one cause, guidelines for planning and prioritizing appropriate interventions have been developed by an expert panel of medical caregivers and academicians (Council for Nutrition, Clinical Strategies in Long-Term Care) for the diagnosis and treatment of involuntary weight loss in the long-term care setting (Clinical Guide to Prevent and Manage Malnutrition in Long-Term Care; see Thomas et al., 2000). The guidelines consider the following three indicators of nutritional frailty: (1) involuntary weight loss of 5% in 30 days or 10% in 180 days or less, (2) a BMI of 21 kilograms per square meter or more, or (3) 25% or more of food uneaten for two-thirds of meals over 7 days.

Food Assistance Programs

Four food assistance programs available to elderly households include the Food Stamp Program, senior meals (Meals on Wheels or meals served at a senior center), food pantries, and community-based emergency soup kitchens. The Administration on Aging's Elderly Nutrition Program (Administration on Aging, 2003) provides grants to support nutrition services to older adults throughout the country. The program authorized under Title III, Grants for State and Community Programs on Aging, and Title VI, Grants for Native Americans, under the Older Americans Act, is intended to improve the dietary intake of adults age 60 years and older. Emphasis is given to individuals at greatest risk of developing nutrition problems. Numerous services provided by this program emphasize preventive intervention programs through the use of nutrition screening and education, as well as other health-related and social support (Millen et al., 2002). This program, the largest U.S. community nutrition program for older adults, provides meals and other nutrition services in a variety of group settings, such as senior centers, schools, and private homes. Meals served under the program must provide at least one-third of the recommended dietary allowances established by the Food and Nutrition Board of the Institute of Medicine of the National Academy of Sciences, as well as the Dietary Guidelines for Americans issued by the Secretaries of Departments of Health and Human Services and Agriculture (U.S. Department of Health and Human Services, 2005).

The Elderly Nutrition Program (National Council on Aging) provides congregate and home-delivered meals, as well as support services, such as nutrition screening, assessment, education, and counseling to help meet health and nutrition needs. Special health assessments for diseases such as hypertension and diabetes are also available. The services are targeted to older adults with the greatest economic or social need, with special attention given to low-income minorities and rural older adults. About 7% of the older population overall and 20% of low-income older people receive congregate and home-delivered meals and the other services (Millen et al., 2002). Often important constraints to healthful eating for rural elderly include lack of nearby supermarkets with an adequate selection of healthful foods or access to support programs such as Meals on Wheels.

Food Safety

In November 2004, a fact sheet was developed by the Food Safety Information Council advising people preparing food for elderly to be extra careful, as poor preparation could result in serious illness. Some of the changes with aging, such as a decrease in gastric acid secretion and decline in functioning of the immune system, can lessen the body's ability to remain free from foodborne illnesses. Although many spoilage agents cause unpleasant odors that serve as a warning that the food is unfit to eat, the less acute sense of smell worsened by medication or illness may decrease the ability of the older person to detect when a food product is spoiled. Due to financial constraints, the elderly may be reluctant to dispose of food that may be unsafe to consume.

Food Insecurity

A close association exists between inadequate income, limited mobility, level of education, poor health, and hunger and food insecurity. In 2001, various levels of poverty were defined as *severe poverty* (below the 50% level of the poverty threshold of $4,241 per person), *near poor* (income between 100% and 125% of poverty), and *nonpoor* (income 125% of the poverty threshold). The Center on Hunger and Poverty reported that the United States has the second highest elderly poverty rate among the 19 industrialized countries, just behind Australia. This suggests that many older individuals in America are at risk of both hunger and food insecurity (Radimer, Olson, Greene, Campbell, & Habicht, 1992). High health care costs make it difficult for many on limited funds to afford adequate food. Low-income elderly receiving monthly checks may face a monthly financial cycle resulting in less food insecurity and anxiety at the beginning of the month, which increases as the money is spent during the month (Wolfe, Olson, Kendall, & Frongillo, 1996). Some low-income elderly become so accustomed to this monthly cycle that they do not discuss this problem with others.

Social support and food insecurity interact in complex ways that are neither well understood nor easy to study (Lee & Frongillo, 2001). To assess and interpret what low-income persons are experiencing requires an understanding of the biological, psychological, and social dynamics of their help-seeking behavior. Often innovative approaches are used to compensate for dwindling funds toward the end of the month. For example, for dinner, less expensive foods such as cereal or canned food are substituted for more expensive foods such as meats or other fresh foods. There is extensive food sharing among the older individuals, especially if they are living in congregate housing. Some older individuals eat less varied diets, participate in federal assistance programs, or get emergency foods from community food pantries.

SUMMARY

No one doubts that diet and exercise have an important positive and preventive influence on health in later life. Aging-related research has demonstrated that nutritional and metabolic differences do exist between young and old humans. Increasingly, studies are being refined to show that distinct metabolic characteristics in older adults alter their requirements for specific nutrients. To achieve this, studies of aging and nutritional metabolism must include not only healthy elderly adults but also those who are affected by disease and physical stress. An upcoming area in aging-related research that is focusing on life extension while maintaining a productive quality of life must include nutrition as an integral part in order to maximize the chances of individuals' living longer healthier lives while minimizing the public costs of aging-related diseases.

REFERENCES

Administration on Aging. (2002). *Services for seniors.* Retrieved December 15, 2005, from http://www.aoa.gov/eldfam/Service_Options/Service_Options.asp

Alaimo, K., McDowell, M., Briefel, R., Bischof, A., Caughman, C., Loria, C., et al. (1994). Dietary intake of vitamins, minerals and fiber of persons ages 2 months and over in the United States: Third National Health and Nutrition Examination Survey, Phase 1, 1988–1991. *Advance Data from Vital and Health Statistics, 258.*

American Academy of Family Physicians. (2005). Determine your nutritional health. Retrieved January 10, 2006, from http://www.aafp.org/x16138.xml

American Diabetes Association. (2004). Position statement. *Diabetes Care, 27,* S54.

Anderson, J. B., & Ontjes, D. A. (2004). Nutritional and pharmacological aspects of osteoporosis. In C. W. Bales & C. S. Ritchie (Eds.), *Handbook of clinical nutrition and aging* (pp. 639–653). Totowa, NJ: Humana Press.

Bales, C. W., & Ritchie, C. S. (2002). Sarcopenia, weight loss and nutritional frailty in the elderly. *Annual Review Nutrition, 22,* 309–323.

Bruera, E. (1997). ABC of palliative care. Anorexia, cachexia and nutrition. *British Medical Journal, 315,* 1219–1222.

Chapman, I. M. (2004). Endocrinology of anorexia of ageing. *Best Practice and Research, Clinical Endocrinology and Metabolism, 18,* 437–452.

Clarkston, W. K., Pantano, M. M., Morley, J. E., Horowitz, M., Littlefield, J. M., & Burton, F. R. (1997). Evidence for the anorexia of aging: Gastrointestinal transit and hunger in healthy elderly vs. young adults. *American Journal of Physiology, 272,* R243–R248

Committee on Nutrition Services for Medicare Beneficiaries. (2000). *The role of nutrition in maintaining health in the nation's elderly: Evaluating coverage of nutrition services for the Medicare population.* Washington, DC: National Academy Press.

Donald, E. A., Basu, T. K., Hargreaves, J. A., Thompson, G. W., Overton, T. R., & Peterson, R. D. (1992). Dietary intake biochemical status of a selected group of older Albertans taking or not taking micronutrient supplements. *Journal of the Canadian Dietetics Association, 53,* 39–43.

Evans, W. (1997). Functional and metabolic consequences of sarcopenia. *Journal of Nutrition, 127,* 998S–1003S.

Evans, W. J., & Campbell, W. W. (1993). Sarcopenia and age-related changes in body composition and functional capacity. *Journal of Nutrition, 123,* 465–846.

Evans, M., Triggs, E., Broe, G. A., & Creasey, H. (1981). Gastric emptying rate in the elderly: Implications for drug therapy. *Journal of the American Geriatrics Society, 29,* 201–205.

Expert Committee on the Diagnosis and Classification of Diabetes Mellitus. (1997). Report on the diagnosis and classification of diabetes mellitus. *Diabetes Care, 20,* 1183–1197.

Fabiny, A. R., & Kiel, D. P. (1997). Assessing and treating weight loss in nursing home patients. *Clinics in Geriatric Medicine, 4,* 737–751.

Feskanich, D., Singh, V., Willett, W. C., & Colditz, G. A. (2002). Vitamin A intake and hip fractures among postmenopausal women. *Journal of the American Medical Association, 287,* 47–54.

Food Security Institute, Center on Hunger and Poverty, Heller Graduate School for Social Policy and Management, Brandeis University (2003, February). *Hunger and food insecurity among the elderly.* Retrieved April 1, 2003, from http://www.centeronhunger.org/pdf/Elderly.pdf

Foote, J. A., Giuliano, A. R., & Harris, R. B. (2000). Older adults need guidance to meet nutritional recommendations. *Journal of the American College of Nutrition, 19,* 628–640.

Fried, L. P. Tangen, C. M., Walston, J., Newman, A. B., Hirsch, C., Gottdiener, J., et al. (2001). Frailty in older adults: Evidence for a phenotype. *Journals of Gerontology, Series A: Biological Sciences and Medical Sciences, 56A,* M146–M156.

Geokas, M. C., Laktta, E. G., Makinodan, T., & Timiras, P. S. (1990). The aging process. *Annuals of Internal Medicine, 113,* 455–466.

Gillick, M. (2001). Pinning down frailty. *Journals of Gerontology, Series A: Biological Sciences and Medical Sciences, 56,* M134–M135.

Gottdiener, J. S., Arnold, A. M., Aurigemma, G. P., Polak, J. F., Tracy, R. P., Kitzman, D. W., et al. (2000). Predictors of congestive heart failure in the elderly. The Cardiovascular Health Study. *Journal of the American College of Cardiology, 35,* 1628–1637.

Gregg E. W., Beckles, G. L., Williamson, D. F., Leveille, S. G., Langlois, J. A., Engelgau, M. M., et al. (2000). Diabetes and physical disability among older U.S. adults. *Diabetes Care, 23,* 1272–1277.

Guo, S. S., Zeller, C., Chumlea, W. C., & Siervogel, R. M. (1999). Aging, body composition and lifestyle: The Fels Longitudinal Study. *American Journal of Clinical Nutrition, 70,* 405–411.

Hirsch, I. B. (2002). Editorial: In-patient hyperglycemia—are we ready to treat it yet? *Journal of Clinical Endocrinology and Metabolism, 87,* 975–977.

Huffman, G. B. (2002). Evaluating and treating unintentional weight loss in the elderly. *American Family Physician, 65,* 640–650.

Hung, H. C., Willett, W., Ascherio, A., Rosner, B. A., Rimm, E., & Joshipura, K. J. (2003). Tooth loss and dietary intake. *Journal of the American Dental Association, 134,* 1185–1192.

Hunter, G. R., Weinsier, R. L., Gower, B. A., & Wetzstein, C. (2001). Age-related decrease in resting energy expenditure in sedentary white women: Effects of regional differences in lean and fat mass. *American Journal of Clinical Nutrition, 73,* 333–337.

Jette, A. M., & Branch, L. G. (1985). Impairment and disability in the aged. *Journal of Chronic Diseases, 38,* 59–65.

Johnson, M. A., & Fischer, J. G. (2004). Eating and appetite: Common problems and practical remedies. *Generations, 28,* 11–17.

Karcic, E., Philpot, C., & Morley, J. E. (2002). Treating malnutrition with megestrol acetate: Literature review and review of our experience. *Journal of Nutrition, Health and Aging, 6,* 191–200.

Kissebah, A. H., & Krakower, G. R. (1994). Regional adiposity and morbidity. *Physiological Reviews, 74,* 761–811.

Klausen, B., Toubro, S., & Astrup, A. (1997). Age and sex effects on energy expenditure. *American Journal of Clinical Nutrition, 65,* 895–907.

Kotler, D. P. (2000). Nutritional alterations associated with HIV infection. *Journal of Acquired Immune Deficiency Syndromes, 25,* S81–S87.

Lee, J. S., & Frongillo, E. A. (2001). Understanding needs is important for assessing the impact of food assistance program participation on nutritional and health status in U.S. elderly persons. *Journal of Nutrition, 131,* 765–773.

Levy, D., Larson, M. G., Vasan, R. S., Kannel, W. B., & Ho, K. K. (1996). The progression from hypertension to congestive heart failure. *Journal of the American Medical Association, 275,* 1557–1562.

Lichtenstein, A. H., & Russell, R. M. (2005). Essential nutrients: Food or supplements? Where should the emphasis be? *Journal of the American Medical Association, 294,* 351–358.

Liu, L., Bopp, M. M., Roberson, P. K., & Sullivan, D. H. (2002). Undernutrition and risk of mortality in elderly patients within 1 year of hospital discharge. *Journals of Gerontology, Series A: Biological Sciences and Medical Sciences, 57M,* 741–746.

Mantovani, G., Maccio, A., Bianchi, A., Curreli, L., Ghiani, M., Santona, M. C., et al. (1995). Megestrol acetate in neoplastic anorexia/cachexia: Clinical evaluation and comparison with cytokine levels in patients with head and neck carcinoma treated with neoadjuvant chemotherapy. *International Journal of Clinical and Laboratory Research, 25,* 135–141.

Martinez, M., Arnalich, F., & Hernanz, A. (1993). Alterations of anorectic cytokine levels from plasma and cerebrospinal fluid in idiopathic senile anorexia. *Mechanisms of Ageing and Development, 72,* 145–153.

McCay, C. M., Crowell, M. F., & Maynard, L. A. (1935). The effect of retarded growth upon the length of life span and upon the ultimate body size. *Journal of Nutrition, 10,* 63–79.

Millen, B. E., Ohls, J. C., Ponza, M., & McCool, A. C. (2002). The Elderly Nutrition Program: An effective national framework for preventative nutrition interventions. *Journal of the American Dietetics Association, 102,* 234–240.

Mokdad, A. H., Bowman, B. A., Ford, E. S., Vinivor, F., Marks, J. S., & Koplan, J. P. (2001). The continuing epidemics of obesity and diabetes in the United States. *Journal of the American Medical Association, 286,* 1195–2000.

Morley, J. E. (1997). Anorexia of aging: Physiologic and pathologic. *American Journal of Clinical Nutrition, 66,* 760–773.

Morley, J. E. (1998). The elderly type 2 diabetic patient: Special considerations. *Diabetic Medicine, 115,* S41–S46.

Morley, J. E., Baumgartner, R. N., Roubenoff, R., Mayer, J., & Nair, K. S. (2001). Sarcopenia. *Journal of Laboratory and Clinical Medicine, 137,* 231–243.

National Institute of Arthritis and Musculoskeletal and Skin Diseases. (2002). *Handout on health: Osteoarthritis.* Retrieved January 10, 2006, from http://www.niams.nih.gov/hi/topics/arthritis/oahandout.htm

National Institutes of Health. (1998). *Clinical guidelines on the identification, evaluation and treatment of overweight obesity in adults: The evidence report.* Rockville, MD: National Institutes of Health, National Institute of Heart, Lung and Blood Institute.

Newman, A. B., Yanez, D., Harris, T., Duxbury, A., Enright, P. L., & Fried, L. P. (2001). Weight change in old age and its association with mortality. *Journal of the American Geriatrics Society, 49,* 1309–1318.

Nieves, J. W. (2002). Nutrition and osteoporosis. In S. Cummmings, F. Cosman, & S. Jamal (Eds.), *Osteoporosis: An evidence based approach to the prevention and management* (pp. 85–108). Philadelphia: American College of Physicians.

Nieves, J. W. (2003). Calcium, vitamin D, and nutrition in elderly adults. *Clinics in Geriatric Medicine, 19,* 321–335.

Nieves, J. W. (2005). Osteoporosis: The role of micronutrients. *American Journal of Clinical Nutrition, 8,* 1232S–1239S.

Nutrition Screening Initiative. (1991). *Nutrition screening manual for professionals caring for older Americans.* Washington, DC: Author.

Piers, L. S., Soares, M. J., McCormack, L. M., & O'Dea, K. (1998). Is there evidence for an age-related reduction in metabolic rate? *Journal of Applied Physiology, 85,* 2196–2204.

Pitts, D. G. (1982). The effects of aging on selected visual function: Dark adaptation, visual acuity, stereopsis and brightness contrast. In R. Seduler, D. W. Kline, & K. Dismukes (Eds.), *Aging and human visual function* (Vol. 2, pp. 131–159). New York: A. R. Liss.

Ponza, M., Ohls, J. C., & Millen, B. E. (1996). *Serving elders at risk.* Princeton, NJ: Mathematica Policy Research.

Radimer, K. L., Olson, C. M., Greene, J. C., Campbell, C. C., & Habicht, J. P. (1992). Understanding hunger and developing indicators to assess it in women and children. *Journal of Nutrition Education, 14,* 36S–45S.

Reed, M. J., Penn, P. E., Li, Y., Birnbaum, R., Vernon, R. B., Johnson, T. S., et al. (1996). Enhanced cell proliferation and biosynthesis mediate improved wound repair in refed, caloric-restricted mice. *Mechanisms of Aging and Development, 890,* 21–43.

Rosenberg, I. H. (1989). Epidemiologic and methodologic problems in determining nutritional status of older persons. *American Journal of Clinical Nutrition, 50* (suppl.), 1231–1233.

Roth, G. S., Lane, M. A., Ingram, D. K., Mattison, J. A., Elahi, D., Tobin, J. D., et al. (2002). Biomarkers of caloric restriction may predict longevity in humans. *Science, 297,* 811.

Roubenoff, R. (2001). Origins and clinical relevance of sarcopenia. *Canadian Journal of Applied Physiology, 26,* 78–89.

Russell, R. M. (2000). The aging process as a modifier of metabolism. *American Journal of Clinical Nutrition, 72,* 529S–532S.

Schiffman, S. S., & Warwick, Z. E. (1992). Effect of flavor enhancement of foods for the elderly on nutritional status: Food intake, biochemical indices and anthropomorphic measures. *Physiology and Behavior, 53,* 395–402.

Semba, R. D., Garrett, E., Johnson, B. A., Guralnik, J. M., & Fried, L. P. (2000). Vitamin D deficiency among older women with and without disability. *American Journal of Clinical Nutrition, 72,* 1529–1534

Short, K. R., & Nair, K. S. (2000). The effect of age on protein metabolism: Current opinion. *Current Opinion in Clinical Nutrition and Metabolic Care, 3,* 39–44.

Sturm, K., Parker, B., Wishart, J., Feinle-Bisset, C., Jones, K, L., Chapman, I., et al. (2004). Energy intake and appetite are related to antral area in healthy young and older subjects. *American Journal of Clinical Nutrition, 80,* 2656–2667.

Thomas, D. R., Ashmen, W., Morley, J. E., Evans, W. J., & Council for Nutritional Strategies in Long-Term Care. (2000). Nutritional management in long-term care: Development of a clinical guideline. *Journals of Gerontology, Series A: Biological Sciences and Medical Sciences, 55A,* M725–M734.

Thomas, D. R., Zdrowski, C. D., Wilson, M. M., Conright, K. C., Lewis, C., Tariq, S., et al. (2002). Malnutrition in subacute care. *American Journal of Clinical Nutrition, 75,* 308–313.

Thomas, J. A., & Burns, R. A. (1998). Important drug-nutrient interactions in the elderly. *Drugs Aging, 13,* 199–209.

Thompson, J. S., Robbins, J., & Cooper, J. K. (1987). Nutritional and immune function in the geriatric population. *Clinics in Geriatric Medicine, 3,* 309.

U.S. Department of Agriculture. (2005). *MyPyramid.* Retrieved May 25, 2006, from http://mypyramid.gov

U.S. Department of Health and Human Services. (2005). *The Administration on Aging's (AoA) American Indian, Alaskan Native, and Native Hawaiian Program—Title VI of the Older Americans Act* (OAA). Retrieved January 10, 2006, from http://www.aoa.gov/prof/aoaprog/natives/native.asp

Vellas, B. J., Hunt, W. C., Romero, L. J., Koehler, K. M., Baumgartner, R. N., & Garry, P. J. (1996). Changes in nutritional status and patterns of morbidity among free-living elderly: A 10-year longitudinal study. *Nutrition, 13,* 515–519.

Wakimoto, P., & Block, G. (2001). Dietary intake, dietary patterns and changes with age: An epidemiological perspective. *Journal of Gerontology, 56A,* 65–80.

Walston, J., & Fried, L. P. (1999). Frailty and the older man. *Medical Clinics of North America, 83,* 1173–1194.

Weindruch, R., & Sohal, R. S. (1997). Caloric intake and aging. *New England Journal of Medicine, 337,* 986–994.

Weindruch, R., & Walford, R. L. (1988). *The retardation of aging and disease by dietary restriction.* Springfield, IL: Charles C. Thomas.

Wilson, M. M. G., & Morley, J. E. (2003). Physiology of aging, invited review: Aging and energy balance. *Journal of Applied Physiology, 95,* 1728–1736.

Wilson, P. W., & Kannel, W. B. (2000). Obesity, diabetes and risk of cardiovascular disease in the elderly. *American Journal of Geriatric Cardiology, 11,* 119–123.

Wolfe, W. S., Olson, C. M., Kendall, A., & Frongillo, E. A. (1996). Understanding food insecurity in the elderly: A conceptual framework. *Journal of Nutrition Education, 28,* 92–100.

Yeh, S. S., Wu, S. Y., Lee, T. P., Olson, J. S., Stevens, M. R., Dixon, T., et al. (2000). Improvement in quality-of-life measures and stimulation of weight gain after treatment with megestrol acetate oral suspension in geriatric cachexia: Results of a double-blind, placebo-controlled study. *Journal of the American Geriatrics Society, 48,* 485–492.

Yeh, S. S., Wu, S. Y., Levine, D. M., Parker, T. S., Olson, J. S., Stevens, M. R., et al. (2001). The correlation of cytokine levels with body weight after megestrol acetate treatment in geriatric patients. *Journals of Gerontology, Series A: Biological Sciences and Medical Sciences, 56A,* M48–M54.

Yim, P. K. (2002). Treating diabetes with diet. *Geriatric Nursing, 23,* 175–176.

Young, K. W., & Greenwood, C. E. (2001). Shift in diurnal feeding patterns in nursing home residents with Alzheimer's disease. *Journals of Gerontology, Series A: Biological Sciences and Medical Sciences, 56A,* M700–M706.

Young, W. H., Greenwood, C. E., van Reekum, R., & Binns, M. A. (2004). Providing nutrition supplements to institutionalized seniors with probably Alzheimer's disease is least beneficial to those with low body weight status. *Journal of the American Geriatrics Society, 52,* 1305–1312.

Young, K. W., Binns, M. A., & Greenwood, C. E. (2001). Meal delivery practices do not meet needs of Alzheimer patients with increased cognitive and behavioral difficulties in a long-term care facility. *Journals of Gerontology, Series A: Biological Sciences and Medical Sciences, 56A,* M656–M661.

CHAPTER 8

Exercise and Aging

Michael G. Flynn

In the previous edition of this book, Ferraro (1997) encouraged us to develop our "gerontological imagination." Among the seven key tenets of this new awareness, we are reminded that aging does not cause all age-related phenomena, that aging is associated with heterogeneity, and that there are substantial individual differences in the rate of decline with aging. People working in the exercise field are fortunate to find frequent instances of individual differences in the rate of decline and cases of older adults functioning at exceptionally high levels. Exercise scientists are employing their developing gerontological imaginations to understand what is possible later in life when a person remains or becomes physically active or becomes more physically active.

There are astonishing examples of physical prowess in older people who have performed fitness activities throughout their lifetime. Their performance capacity is likely a combination of a lifelong dedication to fitness activities and to good genes. We cannot do anything about the gene set we inherit, but the former can have a remarkable effect on late-life functional capacity, health, and well-being. We now know that significant exercise adaptations occur in individuals over 100 years of age, but are just starting to scratch the surface of exercise's potential to mitigate biological changes associated with aging. Despite what we know about the potential for exercise to influence health and chronic disease, a significant number of older adults have no regular physical activity (U.S. Department of Health and Human Services, 2000).

In general, exercise has a potent influence on maintenance or restoration of physical function. The extreme cases of, for example, octogenarians completing marathons or competing as bodybuilders generally garner the news headlines, but the stories of everyday people who have invested in physical fitness activities throughout their life or become exercise enthusiasts in later life are equally impressive. These stories are also more applicable to the average person concerned about the potential impact of physical activity on the aging process.

Research in the area of exercise and aging has a relatively short, but rather robust, history. There has been a dramatic development and expansion of exercise and aging research over the past two decades. The completed research has contributed significantly to the field of gerontology in a short time frame. Among other things, researchers have provided evidence of potential low-cost alternatives to medical therapies for the treatment and prevention of disease, and potential for improving quality of life and overall health and vitality. This chapter reviews the rapidly growing body of literature on exercise and aging. The chapter topic is broad and far reaching. While several topics of interest have been selected, it is inevitable that several interesting subtopics will remain unexplored.

EXERCISE GERONTOLOGY AND GERONTOLOGICAL INQUIRY

The exercise scientist's approach to gerontological inquiry can best be summed up using a single term: *multidisciplinary*. Exercise science researchers pursue questions in gerontological research with a wide array of research tools and techniques that cover a broad span of academic inquiry. For example, researchers in exercise physiology, the main emphasis of this chapter, examine the influence of exercise or physical activity on selected physiological systems (e.g., cardiovascular, muscular, endocrine, immune, skeletal) or may examine how exercise alters nutritional needs, the risk of illness, or rehabilitative processes.

In Chapter 1, Ferraro and Wilmoth use a fountain analogy to describe the process of gerontological discovery. The jets at the perimeter of the fountain propel water toward a central fountain, the height of which is dependent on the water from the surrounding jets. Exercise scientists "shoot water" toward the central fountain from both the physical aspects of aging (exercise physiology, biomechanics, motor control and development) and social aspects of aging (e.g., sport and exercise psychology) areas, using a wide array of techniques and research tools to answer their specialized research questions. For example, biomechanists use physical science to determine the influence of exercise on balance, risk of falls, and ability to perform activities of daily living. Sport and exercise psychologists study motivation, cognitive function, self-perception, and mental health as they relate to sports participation, increased physical activity, or regular exercise participation. An exercise physiologist's approach is, by definition, different from the parent discipline of physiology, because exercise, physical activity, or sport participation is always included as a confounding variable.

Over the past two decades, the exercise variable has been employed with increasing frequency by researchers of aging not previously considered to fall under the exercise science umbrella. This is good news for exercise scientists and for gerontological inquiry in general because of the enormous potential that exercise has for prevention or remediation of chronic illnesses and disabilities. Some of these illnesses and disabilities were previously attributed to old age but are now often linked to physical inactivity. A renowned exercise scientist, A. H. Ismail, was fond of saying, "Exercise is nature's medicine." This is a potent concept, which sometimes creates the awkward stance in our field that exercise is good for everything and everyone. Biomedical and behavioral researchers are gradually uncovering layer by positive layer of the exercise story—with regular missteps to remind us that we do not live in a one-(exerc)size-fits-all world.

SARCOPENIA

Sarcopenia, literally "flesh poverty," is the age-associated loss in skeletal muscle mass (Evans, 1996). Sarcopenia is likely the result of several different causes, including reduced anabolic stimuli or increased catabolic stimuli, as may be present with chronic low-grade inflammation (Roubenoff, 2003) (see Figure 8.1). Sarcopenia has been defined as muscle mass of 2 or more standard deviations below the mean for young, healthy volunteers (Roubenoff, 2003). According to Morley, Baumgartner, Roubenoff, Mayer, and Nair (2001), the prevalence of sarcopenia increases from about 11% in persons aged 70 to 74 to 17% at 75 to 79 and to 22% over the age of 80 years. Some researchers have reported substantially higher sarcopenia prevalence (30% for those over 60 years of age) (Doherty, 2003). The differences in reported prevalence may be dependent on the methods used to estimate sarcopenia. Furthermore, some researchers suggest that sarcopenia is grossly underreported in obese individuals (Janssen, Heymsfield, & Ross, 2002; Newman, Kupelian, et al., 2003). Regardless of the debate over prevalence, sarcopenia is associated with significant functional deficits and increased dependence on medical care (Janssen, Shepard, Katzmarzyk, & Roubenoff, 2004). For example, over $18 billion in medical costs was directly attributed to sarcopenia in the year 2000 (Janssen et al., 2004).

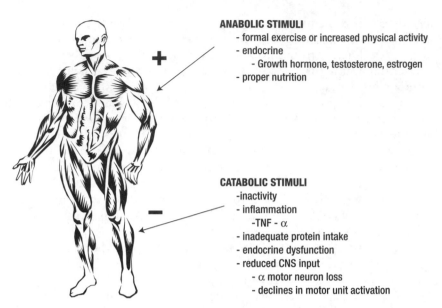

ANABOLIC STIMULI
- formal exercise or increased physical activity
- endocrine
    - Growth hormone, testosterone, estrogen
- proper nutrition

CATABOLIC STIMULI
- inactivity
- inflammation
    - TNF - α
- inadequate protein intake
- endocrine dysfunction
- reduced CNS input
    - α motor neuron loss
    - declines in motor unit activation

FIGURE 8.1 Factors that stimulate (anabolic) or inhibit (catabolic) the growth and maintenance of skeletal muscle.

The loss in muscle mass that occurs with age is, by itself, highly significant, but there may also be a loss in muscle quality with increasing age (Kehayias, Fiatarone, Zhuang, & Roubenoff, 1997; Newman, Haggerty, et al., 2003; Yarasheski, 2003). For example, a strong relationship was reported between body fatness and declines in muscle strength, suggesting that a higher intracellular fat content in muscle, concomitant with increased body fat, contributes to reduced muscular force (Newman, Haggerty et al., 2003). There are also reports of a decline in muscle protein synthesis, decline in intracellular mass, and a selective decline in type II muscle fibers (the power fibers) with aging (Grimby, 1995; Hortobagyi et al., 1995; Kehayias et al., 1997; Yarasheski, 2003). Some of these changes may be ameliorated with resistive training and proper nutrition (Singh et al., 1999; Yarasheski, 2003). For example, resistive exercise stimulated muscle protein synthesis rates in those over the age of 75 (Yarasheski, 2003). Furthermore, Singh et al. (1999) reported substantial increases in muscular strength and muscle fiber area when octogenarians participated in resistive exercise training and ingested a nutritional supplement (360 kilocalories, 35% of the recommended daily allowance of essential vitamins and minerals). Resistive training without nutritional supplements increased strength but did not increase fiber area. Thus, nutritional needs should be addressed when trying to reverse sarcopenia, especially in old-old subjects. Proper nutrition is a significant concern for this age group. A substantial proportion of persons over age 75 get insufficient amounts of the key nutrients required to increase lean tissue mass during an exercise program (Cid-Ruzafa, Caulfield, Barron, & West, 1999; Singh et al., 1999).

Sarcopenia is associated with increased rates of physical disability, particularly among obese sarcopenic persons (Morley et al., 2001; Zoico et al., 2004). When compared to subjects of normal muscle mass, sarcopenic men and women had roughly three to four times the risk of disability and increased requirements for using a cane or walker or having a greater prevalence of falls (Baumgartner et al., 1998). Treatment for sarcopenia would appear to be quite simple—exercise and eat right—but the multifactorial nature of the disease (Figure 8.1) makes treatment choices less than obvious. For example, the number of α-motor neurons innervating skeletal muscle cells has been shown to decline with age (Brown, Strong, & Snow, 1988; Faulkner, Brooks, & Zerba, 1995; Brown & Chan, 1997), possibly from activity-induced damage or injury. Neuronal repair is known to be quite sluggish, and even an aggressive determined combination of resistive exercise training and improved nutrition would not influence the decline in function attributable to denervated fibers.

RESISTIVE AND ENDURANCE EXERCISE IN OLDER ADULTS

Resistive Exercise and Strength Development

The potential benefits of increased physical activity have long been recognized by the scientific and medical communities, but exercise research on older individuals was slow to develop. As late as 1984, researchers were asking questions about whether resistive exercise training was beneficial for pensioners (Aniansson, Ljungberg, Rundgren, & Wetterqvist, 1984). Over the next several years, researchers found that resistive training programs increased muscle strength and size and improved functional capacity in older adults (Aniansson et al., 1984; Frontera, Meredith, O'Reilly, Knuttgen, & Evans, 1988; Fiatarone et al., 1990; Grimby et al., 1992). A now-classic study from Tufts University in 1990 documented the ability of frail nonagenarians to increase muscular strength and size following resistive training (Fiatarone et al., 1990). What made this study so shocking at the time it was published was that these researchers employed high-intensity resistive training. That is, these subjects were trained using conventional resistive-exercise machines and at a relative intensity similar to what would be used for a college-aged population. This

study stimulated a dramatic increase in interest in strength-related research for older adults.

Muscular strength declines at a rate of approximately 7 to 8% per
decade after age 30. Some argue that the declines in muscular strength are
more precipitous at roughly 50 years of age and of even greater magnitude after age 70. Nevertheless, the loss of muscular strength with aging
is indisputable (Danneskiold-Samsoe et al., 1984). Nearly 25 years ago,
the Framingham data showed that a significant proportion of individuals
over age 65 could not lift a weight greater than 4.5 kilograms (10 pounds)
(Jette & Branch, 1981). In fact, only about 40% of women and 60% of
men responding to the survey were able to perform this task.

It would be easy to attribute the declines in muscular strength to age-
related phenomena alone, but physically active people do not experience
the same degree of muscular dysfunction as those who remain sedentary.
A considerable portion of the decline in muscular strength that occurs
with aging is likely related to inactivity and not to the aging process per
se. In addition, resistive training stimulates muscular strength and hypertrophy in any age group tested, even in persons over the age of 90 (Evans,
1996). Thus, much of the decline in muscular strength can be prevented
or reversed with resistive exercise training.

Declines in muscular strength that occur concomitant with increased
chronological age, regardless of cause, can have a significant impact on
mobility, ability to perform activities of daily living (ADLs), and length of
independent functioning, overall health, and health care costs (Schneider
& Guralnik, 1990; Potter, Evans, & Duncan, 1995; Janssen et al., 2004).
For example, muscular strength has been correlated with gait speed, and
gait speed is strongly related to the ability to perform ADLs (Potter et al.,
1995). It follows that resistive exercise training could be used to prevent
the declines in muscular strength, improve the ability of older individuals
to care for themselves, and increase the length of independent functioning.

Skeletal muscle is quite responsive to resistive training. The literature
contains consistent evidence of improvements in muscular strength when
an older person completes a resistive exercise training program. These improvements in muscular strength are associated with modest improvements in physical functioning (Latham, Bennett, Stretton, & Anderson,
2004) and a reduced risk of falls (Lord et al., 2003; Chang et al., 2004).

It is interesting to note that the strength training programs employed
by most researchers are quite similar to those employed to develop
strength in a college-aged population. That is, older adults respond fa-
vorably to resistance exercise performed at a similar relative intensity as
younger adults. Frequent testing of muscular strength using the greatest
weight that can be lifted (one repetition maximum, 1RM) may, however,
increase the risk of injury in older subjects (Pollock et al., 1991). There is

evidence that one set of an exercise performed to volitional fatigue with a weight that allows 7 to 10 repetitions (7–10 RM testing) provides a reasonable proxy measurement for strength (Braith, Graves, Leggett, & Pollock, 1993). With these basic principles in mind, Figure 8.2 shows two options that might be employed to develop strength in an older population.

Many resistance exercise machines were not designed with older exercisers in mind. Among the problems are starting weights that are too high, especially for some upper-extremity exercises, or weight increments that are too large to allow older users to progress smoothly during the early stages of training. Some resistive exercise training machines can be modified to address these concerns. For example, smaller clip-on or magnetic weights can be purchased or fabricated to allow a lower starting weight and smaller progressions after strength improvements. There are

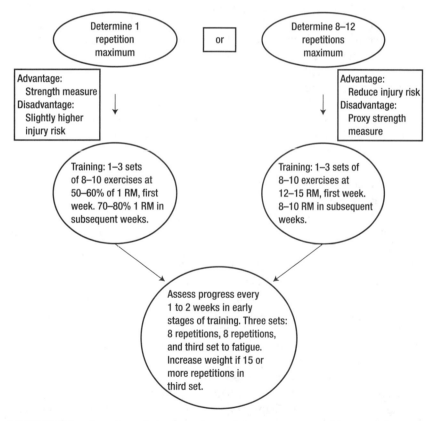

FIGURE 8.2   Sample resistive exercise training program used in research on older men and women for the development of muscular strength and hypertrophy.

also pneumatic machines that allow near-zero starting weights and small increments (0.45 kilograms) in resistance.

Resistive exercise machines are an appealing choice for training because they offer ease of use and relative safety. Nevertheless, the muscular and nervous systems do not "know" how they are being overloaded; rather, they adapt to any suitable overload by increasing muscular strength and, eventually, muscle size. Training with free weights, flexible bands, socks filled with sand, or progressively larger soup cans could provide an appropriate stimulus to elicit muscular development. In addition, a range of appropriate physical activities that overload the neuromusculoskeletal system (e.g., gardening, stair climbing) can help to maintain or develop muscular strength.

Endurance, Exercise, and Aging

Strength training research has been a central focus among exercise gerontology researchers. The emphasis on strength could be related to the argument that frail elderly often do not possess the physical strength required to perform dynamic activities (e.g., walking) that will stimulate cardiorespiratory development. Even the frail elderly person can perform resistive exercise, and resistive exercise training can improve ambulatory capacity (Fiatarone et al., 1990).

There are other arguments in favor of resistive training. A portion of the decline in endurance capacity with aging has been attributed to loss of fat-free mass (FFM) (Fleg & Lakatta, 1988; Rosen, Sorkin, Goldberg, Hagberg, & Katzel, 1998). FFM could be maintained or improved by resistive exercise. Recent research also shows that resistive training stimulates adaptations similar to those normally associated with endurance training. Nevertheless, endurance exercise is usually recommended over resistive training for, among other things, reducing cardiovascular risk, stimulating improvements in oxygen consumption, cardiovascular development, and eliciting blood pressure changes (Mazzeo et al., 1998; Talbot, Morrell, Metter, & Fleg, 2002; Pescatello et al., 2004).

Maximal oxygen consumption ($VO_{2\,max}$) tests allow us to measure a person's capacity for the exchange (lungs), delivery (heart and blood), and use (tissue mitochondria) of oxygen during maximal exercise. These measurements are made in the last few minutes of a dynamic exercise test (e.g., treadmill walking) of gradually increasing intensity. $VO_{2\,max}$ is an effective indicator of cardiorespiratory fitness, and there is a strong relationship between maximal oxygen consumption and physical functioning. Thus, it is surprising that research to determine whether endurance exercise improves maximal aerobic capacity ($VO_{2\,max}$) in older adults has such a short history. Questions about training-induced improvements in $VO_{2\,max}$ of younger persons were answered decades earlier. Nevertheless, there are now several studies to support the contention that aerobic capacity can be improved at any age by endurance training (Denis et al., 1986; Kohrt et al., 1991; Puggaard, Larsen, Stovring, & Jeune, 2000). It was 1986 before we learned that training-induced improvements in $VO_{2\,max}$ were similar between older and younger men (Denis et al., 1986). Likewise, Kohrt et al. (1991) reported similar relative (percentage) improvements in maximal oxygen consumption between younger and older persons.

It has been clearly demonstrated there are progressive declines in $VO_{2\,max}$ of 8 to 10% per decade (Tanaka et al., 1997; Rosen et al., 1998; Pimentel, Gentile, Tanaka, Seals, & Gates, 2003). However, $VO_{2\,max}$ is always higher in trained than in untrained subjects of similar age. It is also known that there is a critical level of aerobic capacity ($15–18$ ml $\cdot$ kg^{-1} $\cdot$ min^{-1}) required for older adults to maintain independence (Paterson, Cunningham, Koval, & St. Croix, 1999). Thus, activity-elicited maintenance of $VO_{2\,max}$ has the potential to maintain the length of independent functioning.

Generally, relative improvements in $VO_{2\,max}$ following endurance exercise training are similar, ranging from 10 to 30 percent in younger and older subjects (Denis et al., 1986; Kohrt et al., 1991). Nevertheless, there are several subtle differences in the mechanisms for adaptation to endurance training between younger and older subjects (Lawrenson, Hoff, & Richardson, 2004). For example, aging is associated with a decrease in arterial elasticity, but this difference did not offset the improvements in $VO_{2\,max}$ that occurred after older subjects completed exercise training (Lawrenson et al., 2004). It is also known that the multitude of potential benefits from endurance training—lower blood pressure, improved insulin sensitivity, increased high-density lipoprotein (HDL) cholesterol, improved mitochondrial function, strengthened myocardium, and others—can all be realized by older persons who complete an endurance exercise training program (Hughes et al., 1993; Ryan, Pratley, Elahi, & Goldberg, 1995; Clevenger, Parker Jones, Tanaka, Seals, & DeSouza, 2002; Yoshiga, Higuchi, & Oka, 2002; Maeda et al., 2003; Rimbert et al., 2004). That is, older adults may rely on a slightly different mechanism for adaptation to endurance exercise, but the benefits of regular exercise training are not a special privilege of the young exerciser.

In the general population, declines in $VO_{2\,max}$ with age appear to be strongly related to the loss of lean body mass (Rosen et al., 1998). Thus, physical inactivity reduces the stimulus for maintenance of aerobic capacity and also reduces the anabolic stimulus for maintenance of lean tissue. When $VO_{2\,max}$ reaches a critically low level, older individuals are less able to perform tasks for themselves, and this *enforced inactivity* results in continued losses in muscle mass, contributing to the further decline in $VO_{2\,max}$.

In summary, there are several benefits associated with endurance exercise training and it is clear that older adults can garner these benefits. There is no apparent age cut-off for endurance-training-induced adaptations.

Endurance Versus Resistive Training for Older Persons

Lack of time has been identified as a potential barrier to exercise participation (Clark, 1999). Even after an individual commits to starting an exercise program, time constraints could force him or her to choose between endurance or resistive training. Thus, the difficult question is, "Which is the best type of exercise for older adults?" The short answer is that there is no one best type of exercise, but increased physical activity of any kind can be beneficial. There are, however, some interesting considerations for those working with an older population.

Endurance exercise, long considered the benchmark for those wishing to reduce body fat or improve cardiorespiratory function, blood lipid profile, insulin sensitivity, or blood pressure, is getting competition from resistive exercise. Resistive exercise has been shown, in fewer studies, to have many of the same effects as endurance exercise (Ryan, Pratley, Goldberg, & Elahi, 1996; Mazzeo et al., 1998; Ryan, Treuth, Hunter, & Elahi, 1998; Ryan et al., 2001; Pimentel et al., 2003). In addition, the decline in muscular strength and loss of physical function in some older populations may make traditional endurance exercise difficult. For example, a frail older man may not have sufficient muscular strength to start a walking program, but would likely be able to reap the benefits of a resistive exercise training program. Resistive exercise training could restore his ability to walk or perform other previously difficult tasks and allow a generalized increase in physical activity.

Another area where resistive exercise training is gaining ground is in the area of weight loss or, more precisely, fat loss. As recently as 10 years ago, an exercise prescription for weight or fat loss would have included predominantly endurance activities. This prescription would have followed the logic that continuous, dynamic exercises such as walking, bicycling, or jogging expend many more calories per minute than intermittent, high-intensity resistive exercise. The caloric argument during exercise has not changed. Researchers have revealed, however, that older subjects with low lean body mass levels (lower amount of metabolically active tissue) have difficulty with weight or fat loss. Thus, it has been argued that increased muscle mass from resistive training increases the amount of metabolically active tissue. Having more metabolically active tissue increases the odds of reducing body fat stores (Ryan et al., 1995; Bryner et al., 1999). Researchers have also shown that resistive training can offset the reduction in metabolic rate that is often observed when individuals go on low-calorie diets (Ryan et al., 1995).

When combined with calorie restriction, endurance exercise is less effective than resistive exercise for preserving lean tissue (Bryner et al., 1999). For example, when an 800 kilocalorie diet was combined with endurance training, subjects lost 4 kilograms of lean body mass. When the same diet was combined with resistive training, subjects maintained their prestudy lean body mass (Bryner et al., 1999).

In the past, some feared resistive training would build large muscles that were aesthetically unpleasing or cause excessive weight gain. However, researchers and the popular media have effectively communicated the benefits of resistive exercise for older adults and helped potential exercisers to understand that stronger muscles do not have to be substantially larger muscles. Furthermore, far greater numbers of seniors suffer from sarcopenia and associated dysfunction than from too much muscle. Thus, public concerns about building bulky muscles appear to have diminished, but additional education is required to dispel some of the myths associated with resistive exercise training.

We now know that resistive training provides many of the benefits of endurance training and added benefits to seniors that are not derived from endurance training. In addition, resistive exercise may have synergistic effects when combined with endurance training (Ferrara, McCrone, Brendle, Ryan, & Goldberg, 2004). Collectively, these factors have made it easier to convince seniors of the potential benefits of resistive exercise.

BENEFITS OF EXERCISE TRAINING

Exercise Training and the Risk of Falling

The loss of muscle mass and concomitant loss of muscular strength that occurs with aging likely leads to increased disability and increased risk of falls. Fall risk is multifactorial, such that poor muscular strength is only one factor that might lead to an increased risk of falls (McMurdo, Millar, & Daly, 2000; Chang et al., 2004). Programs that focus on several potential contributing factors, such as sensory acuity, environmental hazards, balance and gait, and drug interactions, are more likely to reduce fall risk (Chang et al., 2004).

The multifactorial nature of falls may help to explain the lack of an effect on falling or fall risk in some strengthening studies (McMurdo et al., 2000). It is also likely that balance and fall risk are easier to change in persons with substantial deficits or in those who have already fallen. That is, it is more difficult to measure an effect of exercise on fall risk and balance when healthy, ambulatory older persons are the research subjects. However, when subject health and ambulatory ability were controlled for, some researchers still did not observe an influence of regular exercise on fall risk (McMurdo et al., 2000). In contrast, several researchers reported improvements in balance and reduced risk of falls following an exercise intervention (Buchner et al., 1997; LaStayo, Ewy, Pierotti, Johns, & Lindstedt, 2003). Nevertheless, programs that address a number of fall factors along with endurance or resistive exercise are most effective in the prevention of falls (Chang et al., 2004).

Combining balance training with resistive training might produce a more effective fall risk reduction. For example, researchers employing tai chi, a combination of movement and meditation, as an exercise intervention reported significant reductions in both fear of falling and the risk of falls (Wolf et al., 2003). In addition, simple walking exercise, without concomitant strength training, has also been shown to improve selected aspects of balance (Buchner et al., 1997). Walking provides older subjects with balance training, but does not significantly improve muscular strength. Therefore, improving muscular strength without some means of balance training reduces the chance of improving balance and reducing fall risk.

Exercise and Insulin Sensitivity

There has been a shocking increase in the number of children and adults who are classified as overweight and obese in the United States and around the world. Obesity has been linked to the development of type II diabetes and several associated complications, including cardiovascular disease (Haffner & Cassells, 2003). While there has been a disturbing increase in the occurrence of type II diabetes in adolescents, the prevalence of type II diabetes also increases as we age. It has been known for some time that exercise ameliorates insulin resistance. It also requires surprisingly little exercise to exert these effects (Rogers, 1989; Kishimoto et al., 2002).

A substantial portion of the exercise effect on insulin resistance is exerted by increasing the movement of glucose transporter proteins from the cell cytoplasm to the cell membrane, where they can do the job of moving glucose into the cell (Reynolds, Brozinick, Rogers, & Cushman, 1997). Both insulin and exercise activate glucose transporters, but exciting new research shows that exercise exerts its effect through a different pathway from insulin. The insulin receptor and associated parts of the insulin signaling pathway appear to be faulty in persons with type II diabetes. The alternative (exercise) pathway—AMP-kinase—is without defect in diabetics (Musi & Goodyear, 2003; Musi, Yu, & Goodyear, 2003). Exercise researchers have recently shown that exercise exerts an insulin-like effect by working through contraction-stimulated activation of the alternative pathway (Musi et al., 2003). In short, exercise allows the diabetic to work around his or her insulin sensitivity defect and enhance cellular glucose uptake. This alternative pathway provides a new avenue for exercise and diabetes research.

Endurance exercise training will elicit significant improvements in insulin resistance. In fact, a single endurance exercise session elicits significant improvements in whole-body sensitivity to insulin. Endurance exercise has long been known to be effective for the prevention or treatment of type II diabetes. New evidence is emerging to show that there are similar benefits from resistive exercise training (Singh et al., 1999; Willey & Singh, 2003). A recent review by Willey and Singh (2003) suggested that resistive training be considered for management and prevention of type II diabetes. These authors acknowledged, however, that both treatment and prevention data are scarce for resistive exercise. Nevertheless, emerging evidence that resistive exercise improves glycemic control in diabetic persons is suggestive that resistive exercise is another low-cost, positive side-effect treatment for type II diabetes (Ryan et al., 1996; Ryan, 2000).

Exercise and the Aging Immune System

As we age, there is an increase in the incidence of infection and autoimmune disease and a higher rate of cancer (Shephard & Shek, 1995). Our immune system, designed to protect against diseases and pathogens, is weakened with increasing chronological age. The term *immunosenescence* has been coined to describe the age-related decline in immune function. As described above, regular exercise exerts a positive influence on many physiological systems. Thus, it would be logical to assume that exercise training would positively influence the immune system of older adults, particularly those with compromised immune systems. Unfortunately, the evidence to support this assumption is weak.

Before examining possible exercise-induced improvements in the immune system of older adults following exercise training, it is important to consider that certain aspects of cellular immunity are reduced following strenuous or prolonged activity in young subjects (Nieman, Simandle, et al., 1995; Pedersen et al., 1999). This postexercise suppression of immune function, typically observed 1 to 6 hours after exercise (Nieman, Johanssen, Lee, & Arabatzis, 1990; Nieman, Armandle, et al., 1995; Pedersen et al., 1999), is known as the open window hypothesis (Nieman, Buckley, et al., 1995; Pedersen et al., 1999). That is, strenuous exercise provides a window of opportunity during which athletes are deemed more susceptible to infections. Indeed, the incidence of upper respiratory tract infection (URTI) is increased following marathon and ultramarathon running competitions (Peters & Bateman, 1983; Nieman et al., 1990). Furthermore, URTI frequency doubled when runners trained more than 100 minutes per week (Heath et al., 1991).

A more optimistic view is one that allows the possibility that regular exercise training strengthens immunity. Indeed, there is some evidence to suggest that exercise training could have beneficial effects on the immune system. For example, selected indexes of immunity were reported to be higher in well-trained athletes compared with untrained persons. Additionally, exercise-trained persons, who are not overtraining, have a lower incidence of URTI (Nieman, 1995). When the older exerciser is considered, the findings from studies conducted on younger subjects lead to two obvious questions. Is infection risk increased in older adults during the early stages of exercise programs designed to achieve physical fitness? Does long-term exercise training improve immune system function in older persons? The answers to these questions are "probably not" and "possibly," respectively.

First, few researchers have examined whether acute exercise can induce an open window effect in older subjects. Prolonged or strenuous exercise was required to induce an open window effect in studies on younger subjects, but these studies have not been done using older subjects. Fitness activities are rarely performed at an intensity or duration sufficient to have a negative effect on immune function. Even a novel activity, such as a single bout of the high-intensity resistive exercise described in Figure 8.2, did not adversely effect indexes of immune function in older subjects (Flynn et al., 1999). Thus, there is no evidence that a visit to the gym or a walk in the park induces the transient immune suppression observed after prolonged or strenuous exercise in younger people.

The second question, regarding the ability of exercise training to improve immunity, remains surprisingly difficult to answer. A major problem lies in the complexity of the immune system. That is, it is time-consuming and expensive to make measurements that can assess the many redundant layers of protection provided by the immune system (Cannon, 1993). For example, measurements of natural killer cell function after exercise do not provide insight into the responses of other arms of the immune system. Thus, one arm of the immune system, the one you measured, could be up-regulated following exercise and the backup system you did not measure, could be suppressed.

Despite these shortcomings, several promising studies provide evidence of a positive influence of exercise training on host defense in older subjects (Nieman et al., 1993; Woods et al., 1999; Kostka, Berthouze,

Lacour, & Bonnefoy, 2000; Yan et al., 2001). However, the few existing studies often use very small subject numbers, which makes it difficult to make a definitive statement about the benefits of regular exercise on host defense. A conservative interpretation of the available literature would be to suggest that larger, long-term studies are required to get a definitive answer regarding the protective effects of exercise (Woods, Lowder, & Keylock, 2002). Collectively however, the paucity of studies showing negative effects of exercise on the aging immune system and the other benefits associated with regular exercise leads to the suggestion to "just do it."

Aging and Inflammation: Can Exercise Help Put the Fire Out?

Inflammation refers to the local buildup of fluid, leukocytes, and blood proteins that occurs in response to tissue injury, invading pathogens, or a local immune response (Janeway, Travers, Walport, & Shlomchik, 2001). Hippocrates was among the first to recognize that inflammation is an important part of the healing process (Ley, 2001). The classic signs of inflammation—dolor, color, rubor, tumor (pain, heat, redness and swelling)—were identified nearly 2,000 years ago, with the fifth sign of inflammation, impaired function, identified roughly 100 years later (Ley, 2001).

Immunologists are now working to distinguish between good inflammation and bad inflammation. *Good inflammation* is transient, resulting from an appropriate innate immune response to infection or injury and facilitates recovery. *Bad inflammation* is chronic, resulting from autoimmune disease or dysregulated immunity (Brod, 2000), which might persist for several weeks, months, or indefinitely. Inflammation can facilitate the development of, exacerbate, or even cause chronic diseases, such as heart disease, diabetes, sarcopenia, cachexia, or other wasting diseases (Yeh & Schuster, 1999; Pradhan, Manson, Rifai, Buring, & Ridker, 2001; Roubenoff, 2003; Schulze et al., 2004).

Inflammation and its potential contribution to chronic diseases has become a vibrant area of biomedical research over the past decade from a standpoint of the volume of published research and the significance of recent research findings. Cardiovascular disease, type II diabetes, osteoporosis, geriatric cachexia (a form of wasting disease), Alzheimer's disease, and several other diseases frequently associated with aging or physical inactivity have been shown to have an inflammatory etiology (Yeh & Schuster, 1999; Brod, 2000; Pradhan et al., 2001; Sutherland et al., 2003). For example, cardiovascular disease, long considered to be primarily a disease of lipids, is now believed to get a strong assist from the inflammatory process.

There is substantial evidence that inflammatory proteins (cytokines) are increased in age-advanced humans and animals (Ershler & Keller, 2000; Rosas, Zieman, Donabedian, Vandegaer, & Hare, 2001). It has been argued that elevated inflammatory cytokines in older persons are a result of uncontrolled disease and not a normal consequence of aging (Beharka et al., 2001). Thus, it may remain unresolved whether elevated inflammatory cytokines are the cause of disease or are caused by disease, but elevated cytokines or increased cytokine production in elderly subjects is well documented (Clark & Peterson, 1994; Riancho, Zarrabeitia, Amado, Olmos, & Gonzales-Macias, 1994; Roubenoff et al., 1998).

High levels of inflammatory cytokines are known to be associated with increased risk of morbidity and mortality (Ershler & Keller, 2000; Schumacher et al., 2002). For example, Schumaker et al. (2002) found that IL-6 and TNF-α were strong predictors of various stages of cardiovascular disease and were significantly elevated in coronary heart disease patients versus controls. Others have found IL-6 and CRP to be independent predictors of all-cause mortality. These findings lead to the suggestion that low-cost interventions to reduce systemic inflammation would provide significant benefits to the older population (Harris et al., 1999; Volpato et al., 2001).

Several researchers have observed anti-inflammatory effects of exercise training (Smith et al., 1999; Greiwe, Cheng, Rubin, Yarasheski, & Semenkovich, 2001; Flynn et al., 2003). Greiwe et al. (2001) for example, found that resistive training reduced skeletal muscle production of the inflammatory protein TNF-α in older subjects. Inflammatory cytokines like TNF-α have a wide range of metabolic, systemic, and endocrine-like effects, but a simple example of a TNF-α effect is its ability to inhibit insulin receptor function. Simply stated, high TNF-α is linked to insulin insensitivity (Rosenzweig et al., 2002). Work from our lab and the work of other investigators shows that exercise training reduced the ability of blood monocytes to produce inflammatory proteins such as TNF-α (Smith et al., 1999; Flynn et al., 2003). These studies await confirmation by larger studies but provide promise of a low-cost, readily available, positive-side-effect-intervention against chronic inflammation and inflammatory disease.

What is lacking is a mechanism for the anti-inflammatory effects of exercise. For example, exercise is commonly found to improve the course of rheumatoid arthritis, but no mechanism for the exercise-induced improvements has been proposed. We hypothesize that exercise blunts inflammatory cytokine production by down-regulating cytokine-signaling proteins and have found that exercise decreases the expression of a key receptor in cytokine signaling (toll-like receptor) (Flynn et al., 2003; Stewart et al., 2005). However, much work needs to be done in these nascent areas of exercise research before concrete conclusions can be drawn.

PRACTICAL CONSIDERATIONS FOR EXERCISE AMONG OLDER ADULTS

Barriers to Exercise

Physical inactivity and poor diet are among the leading causes of death in American adults (Mokdad, Marks, Stroup, & Gerberding, 2004). Despite this and the fact that older adults appear to acknowledge the value of remaining physically active, physical activity levels decrease with advancing age (U.S. Department of Health and Human Services, 1996; Marcus et al., 2000; U.S. Department of Health and Human Services, 2000; Van der Bij, Laurant, & Wensing, 2002). According to *Healthy People 2010* (U.S. Department of Health and Human Services, 2000), approximately 50% of women and 35% of men engage in no regular physical activity after the age of 75. The prospects are even bleaker for those of low socioeconomic status and for minorities.

Unfortunately, getting people started in a formal exercise program may not be as effective as expected over the long term. For example, an exercise program that improved muscular strength and motor function in older subjects did not lead to an increase in spontaneous activity in the months after the formal exercise program ended. Additionally, the trained subjects quickly became indistinguishable from their sedentary counterparts (Hauer, Pfisterer, Schuler, Bartsch, & Oster, 2003). Therefore, programs that endeavor to increase the amount of physical activity in the daily routine of the participants could be more effective over the long term.

There are potential barriers to staying physically active for persons of all age groups, but several factors could provide more imposing barriers for seniors. There may be concerns about safety, fear of injury, pain, poor health, lack of knowledge, motivational barriers such as lack of time, and environmental barriers including no sidewalks, crime, or bad weather (Clark, 1999). In short, there are many variables that might prevent or limit exercise participation. Clark (1999) argued that several barriers likely coalesce to reduce the likelihood of exercise participation in a particular individual. Additionally, barriers may differ by gender or by racial/ethnic groups.

A complete discussion of behavioral issues that lead to more compliant older exercisers falls outside the scope of this chapter; however, it is important to discuss the barrier to exercise participation in later life created by fear of injury or illness. These issues are clearly addressed in *Exercise: A Guide from the National Institute on Aging* (U.S. Department of Health and Human Services, 2001). The guide tells us that there are few medical conditions that should keep older adults from increasing their physical activity. The position is summed up by the statement, "Older people become sick or disabled more often from not exercising than from exercising." Thus, the general recommendation is that exercise is considered safe for persons whose diseases are under control. Nevertheless, there are some conditions for which vigorous exercise can be dangerous (e.g., aortic aneurysm, aortic stenosis, unstable chronic heart failure), and a physician should be consulted if there is uncertainty. The authors of the National Institute on Aging guide remind us that no one is too old for exercise and no one should be deemed too frail to exercise.

A recommendation from a physician to incorporate more exercise or physical activity might be an effective way to increase an older person's motivation to exercise. Researchers tell us, however, that relatively few physicians are making these types of recommendations (Damush, Stewart, Mills, King, & Ritter, 1999; Honda, 2004). Damush et al. (1999) for example, surveyed over 800 older men and women found that fewer than half had ever received advice from a physician to exercise. On a more positive note, recommendations from physicians to exercise were increased to those with the greatest need (e.g., high BMI or more sedentary).

Supervised Versus Home-Based Exercise: Does It Matter Where?

Older individuals who seek an exercise facility or fitness center will frequently encounter facilities designed to appeal to a different market of exercisers. Indeed, an older adult who enters a fitness facility filled with glistening, grunting, and muscular young exercisers may experience apprehension or "acrylophobia" (fear of spandex). The latter is an amusing means of describing the trepidation experienced by older exercisers entering a fitness facility. Several serious issues, however, need to be addressed if we are to increase exercise participation among seniors.

Some seniors might be motivated by a pleasant place to exercise or a pleasant person to exercise with; others might be motivated by the fact that exercise can be done in the privacy of their homes. Home-based exercise programs are as effective as supervised exercise programs for promoting participation, but the ability of home-based programs to elicit equivalent physiological improvements or influence health outcomes remains to be determined (Van der Bij et al., 2002). When previously hospitalized persons were randomly assigned to group training or home-based exercise groups, the group-training subjects had significantly better knee-extensor strength, walking velocity, and balance than the home-based exercise group (Timonen et al., 2002). There are other studies in which marginal success of home-based exercise programs has been reported (Capodaglio et al., 2002). This could be due to a lack of supervision or motivation provided by an exercise leader; however, the total number of subjects enrolled in home-based versus group exercise studies is small. Thus, the weight of available studies is insufficient to make definitive recommendations.

CONCLUDING THOUGHTS

Accumulated exercise gerontology research leads to the conclusion that exercise can have a significant impact on physical functioning, disease prevention, and overall health as we age. The exercise gerontology literature also shows that there are no apparent age cut-offs for the benefits of and adaptations to endurance or resistive exercise training. Increased physical activity or formal exercise training appears to have positive effects throughout the life span. In addition, many physical or biological changes commonly associated with advancing age can be attributed instead to physical inactivity. Sarcopenia, for example, while multifactorial in nature, is known to result from reduced anabolic stimulus during periods of inactivity, and sarcopenia is known to be prevented by or reversed with resistive training.

Exercise gerontology researchers have made significant strides in other areas as well, showing how strength development may reduce disability, increase ability to perform ADLs, and reduce risk of falls. Endurance training, long considered the benchmark for reducing cardiovascular risk and improving insulin sensitivity, is getting welcome competition from resistive exercise training. Resistive training may provide the added benefit of conserving lean tissue and increased muscular strength, making it a prudent choice for those with limited time for an exercise program. Finally, we now know that exercise training may influence our susceptibility to infection and to chronic diseases. The ability of strenuous or prolonged exercise to negatively influence immune function in young subjects is a surprising finding, yet to be confirmed in older exercisers. On the positive side, exercise to improve fitness level has not been shown to be immunosuppressive, even in younger subjects. Additionally, long-term exercise training is believed to have a beneficial influence on host defense in younger and older persons, but the research, especially on older subjects, is inconclusive. Exercise training may also alleviate some of the aberrant inflammatory responses as we age, which could help explain the positive effects of exercise on chronic diseases such as heart disease, diabetes, and rheumatoid arthritis. Thus, the anti-inflammatory effects of exercise might influence the course of several chronic diseases, many of them linked to aging or physical inactivity.

Collectively, the work completed by exercise gerontologists is quite promising and shows the potential for exercise to mitigate changes associated with biological aging. The exercise gerontology field is growing rapidly, and new advances and applications for exercise interventions are emerging with increasing regularity. Exercise is low cost, has mainly positive side effects, is available to most older people, and can have a tremendous influence on those who choose to take a regular dose.

REFERENCES

Aniansson, A., Ljungberg, P., Rundgren, A., & Wetterqvist, H. (1984). Effect of a training programme for pensioners on condition and muscular strength. *Archives of Gerontology and Geriatrics, 3,* 229–341.

Baumgartner, R. N., Koehler, K. M., Gallagher, D., Romero, L., Heymsfield, S. B., Ross, et al. (1998). Epidemiology of sarcopenia among the elderly in New Mexico. [erratum appears in Am J Epidemiol 1999 Jun 15;149(12): 1161]. *American Journal of Epidemiology, 147,* 755–763.

Beharka, A. A., Meydani, M., Wu, D., Leka, L. S., Meydani, A., & Meydani, S. N. (2001). Interleukin-6 production does not increase with age. *Journal of Gerontology: Biological Sciences, 56,* B81–B88.

Braith, R. W., Graves, J. E., Leggett, S. H., & Pollock, M. L. (1993). Effect of training on the relationship between maximal and submaximal strength. *Medicine and Science in Sports and Exercise, 25,* 132–138.

Brod, S. A. (2000). Unregulated inflammation shortens human functional longevity. *Inflammation Research, 49,* 561–570.

Brown, W. F., & Chan, K. M. (1997). Quantitative methods for estimating the number of motor units in human muscles. *Muscle and Nerve Supplement, 5,* S70–S73.

Brown, W. F., Strong, M. J., & Snow, R. (1988). Methods for estimating numbers of motor units in biceps-brachialis muscles and losses of motor units with aging. *Muscle and Nerve, 11,* 423–432.

Bryner, R. W., Ullrich, I. H., Sauers, J., Donley, D., Hornsby, G., Kolar, M., et al. (1999). Effects of resistance vs. aerobic training combined with an 800 calorie liquid diet on lean body mass and resting metabolic rate. *Journal of the American College of Nutrition, 18,* 115–121.

Buchner, D. M., Cress, M. E., de Lateur, B. J., Esselman, P. C., Margherita, A. J., Price, R., et al. (1997). A comparison of the effects of three types of endurance training on balance and other fall risk factors in older adults. *Aging—Clinical and Experimental Research, 9,* 112–119.

Cannon, J. G. (1993). Exercise and resistance to infection. *Journal of Applied Physiology, 74,* 973–981.

Capodaglio, P., Facioli, M., Burroni, E., Giordano, A., Ferri, A., & Scaglioni, G. (2002). Effectiveness of a home-based strengthening program for elderly males in Italy. A preliminary study. *Aging—Clinical and Experimental Research, 14,* 28–34.

Chang, J. T., Morton, S. C., Rubenstein, L. Z., Mojica, W. A., Maglione, M., Suttorp, et al. (2004). Interventions for the prevention of falls in older adults: Systematic review and meta-analysis of randomised clinical trials. [see comment]. *British Medical Journal, 328,* 680.

Cid-Ruzafa, J., Caulfield, L. E., Barron, Y., & West, S. K. (1999). Nutrient intakes and adequacy among an older population on the eastern shore of Maryland: The Salisbury Eye Evaluation. *Journal of the American Dietetic Association, 99,* 564–571.

Clark, D. O. (1999). Physical activity and its correlates among urban primary care patients aged 55 years or older. *Journals of Gerontology, Series B: Psychological Sciences and Social Sciences, 54,* S41–S48.

Clark, J. A., & Peterson, T. C. (1994). Cytokine production and aging: Overproduction of IL-8 in elderly males in response to lipopolysaccharide. *Mechanisms of Aging and Development, 77,* 127–139.

Clevenger, C. M., Parker Jones, P., Tanaka, H., Seals, D. R., & DeSouza, C. A. (2002). Decline in insulin action with age in endurance-trained humans. *Journal of Applied Physiology, 93,* 2105–2111.

Damush, T. M., Stewart, A. L., Mills, K. M., King, A. C., & Ritter, P. L. (1999). Prevalence and correlates of physician recommendations to exercise among older adults. *Journals of Gerontology, Series A: Biological Sciences and Medical Sciences, 54,* M423–M427.

Danneskiold-Samsoe, B., Kofod, V., Munter, J., Grimby, G., Schnohr, P., & Jensen, G. (1984). Muscle strength and functional capacity in 78–81-year-old men and women. *European Journal of Applied Physiology and Occupational Physiology, 52,* 310–314.

Denis, C., Chatard, J. C., Dormois, D., Linossier, M. T., Geyssant, A., & Lacour, J. R. (1986). Effects of endurance training on capillary supply of human skeletal muscle on two age groups (20 and 60 years). *Journal of Physiology (Paris), 81,* 379–383.

Doherty, T. J. (2003). Invited review: Aging and sarcopenia. *Journal of Applied Physiology, 95,* 1717–1727.

Ershler, W. B., & Keller, E. T. (2000). Age-associated increased interleukin-6 gene expression, late-life diseases, and frailty. *Annual Review of Medicine, 51,* 245–270.

Evans, W. J. (1996). Reversing sarcopenia: How weight training can build strength and vitality. *Geriatrics, 51,* 46–47.

Faulkner, J. A., Brooks, S. V., & Zerba, E. (1995). Muscle atrophy and weakness with aging: Contraction-induced injury as an underlying mechanism. *Journals of Gerontology, Series A: Biological Sciences and Medical Sciences, 50*(Spec No.), 124–129.

Ferrara, C. M., McCrone, S. H., Brendle, D., Ryan, A. S., & Goldberg, A. P. (2004). Metabolic effects of the addition of resistive to aerobic exercise in older men. *International Journal of Sports Nutrition and Exercise Metabolism, 14,* 73–80.

Ferraro, K. F. (1997). The gerontological imagination. In K. F. Ferraro (Ed.), *Gerontology: Perspectives and issues* (2nd ed.). New York: Springer Publishing.

Fiatarone, M. A., Marks, E. C., Ryan, N. D., Meredith, C. N., Lipsitz, L. A., & Evans, W. J. (1990). High-intensity strength training in nonagenarians: Effects on skeletal muscle. *Journal of the American Medical Association, 263,* 3029–3034.

Fleg, J. L., & Lakatta, E. G. (1988). Role of muscle loss in the age-associated reduction in $VO_{2\ max}$. [see comment]. *Journal of Applied Physiology, 65,* 1147–1151.

Flynn, M. G., Fahlman, M., Braun, W. A., Lambert, C. P., Bouillon, L. E., Brolinson, P. G., et al. (1999). Effects of resistance training on selected indexes of immune function in elderly women. *Journal of Applied Physiology, 86,* 1905–1913.

Flynn, M. G., McFarlin, B. K., Phillips, M. D., Stewart, L. K., & Timmerman, K. L. (2003). Toll-like receptor 4 and CD14 mRNA expression are lower in resistive exercise-trained elderly women. *Journal of Applied Physiology, 95,* 1833–1842.

Frontera, W. R., Meredith, C. N., O'Reilly, K. P., Knuttgen, H. G., & Evans, W. J. (1988). Strength conditioning in older men: Skeletal muscle hypertrophy and improved function. *Journal of Applied Physiology, 64,* 1038–1044.

Greiwe, J. S., Cheng, B., Rubin, D. C., Yarasheski, K. E., & Semenkovich, C. F. (2001). Resistance exercise decreases skeletal muscle tumor necrosis factor alpha in frail elderly humans. *Faseb Journal, 15,* 475–482.

Grimby, G. (1995). Muscle performance and structure in the elderly as studied cross-sectionally and longitudinally. *Journals of Gerontology, Series A: Biological Sciences and Medical Sciences, 50*(Spec No.), 17–22.

Grimby, G., Aniansson, A., Hedberg, M., Henning, G. B., Grangard, U., & Kvist, H. (1992). Training can improve muscle strength and endurance in 78- to 84-yr-old men. *Journal of Applied Physiology, 73,* 2517–2523.

Haffner, S. J., & Cassells, H. (2003). Hyperglycemia as a cardiovascular risk factor. *American Journal of Medicine, 115*(Suppl. 8A), 6S–11S.

Harris, T. B., Ferrucci, L., Tracy, R. P., Corti, M. C., Wacholder, S., Ettinger, Jr., W. H., et al. (1999). Associations of elevated interleukin-6 and C-reactive protein levels with mortality in the elderly. *American Journal of Medicine, 106,* 506–512.

Hauer, K., Pfisterer, M., Schuler, M., Bartsch, P., & Oster, P. (2003). Two years later: A prospective long-term follow-up of a training intervention in geriatric patients with a history of severe falls. *Archives of Physical Medicine and Rehabilitation, 84,* 1426–1432.

Heath, G. W., Ford, E. S., Craven, T. E., Macera, C. A., Jackson, K. L., & Pate, R. R. (1991). Exercise and the incidence of upper respiratory tract infections. *Medicine and Science in Sports and Exercise, 23,* 152–157.

Honda, K. (2004). Factors underlying variation in receipt of physician advice on diet and exercise: Applications of the behavioral model of health care utilization. *American Journal of Health Promotion, 18,* 370–377.

Hortobagyi, T., Zheng, D., Weidner, M., Lambert, N. J., Westbrook, S., & Houmard, J. A. (1995). The influence of aging on muscle strength and muscle fiber characteristics with special reference to eccentric strength. *Journals of Gerontology, Series A: Biological Sciences and Medical Sciences, 50,* B399–B406.

Hughes, V. A., Fiatarone, M. A., Fielding, R. A., Kahn, B. B., Ferrara, C. M., Shepherd, P., et al. (1993). Exercise increases muscle GLUT-4 levels and insulin action in subjects with impaired glucose tolerance. *American Journal of Physiology, 264*(6 Pt. 1), E855–E862.

Janeway, C. A., Travers, P., Walport, M., & Shlomchik, M. (2001). *Immunobiology: The immune system in health and disease.* New York: Garland Publishing.

Janssen, I., Heymsfield, S. B., & Ross, R. (2002). Low relative skeletal muscle mass (sarcopenia) in older persons is associated with functional impairment and physical disability. *Journal of the American Geriatrics Society, 50,* 889–896.

Janssen, I., Shepard, D. S., Katzmarzyk, P. T., & Roubenoff, R. (2004). The healthcare costs of sarcopenia in the United States. *Journal of the American Geriatrics Society, 52,* 80–85.

Jette, A. M., & Branch, L. G. (1981). The Framingham Disability Study: II. Physical disability among the aging. *American Journal of Public Health, 71,* 1211–1216.

Kehayias, J. J., Fiatarone, M. A., Zhuang, H., & Roubenoff, R. (1997). Total body potassium and body fat: Relevance to aging. *American Journal of Clinical Nutrition, 66,* 904–910.

Kishimoto, H., Taniguchi, A., Fukushima, M., Sakai, M., Tokuyama, K., Oguma, T., et al. (2002). Effect of short-term low-intensity exercise on insulin sensitivity, insulin secretion, and glucose and lipid metabolism in non-obese Japanese type 2 diabetic patients. *Hormone and Metabolic Research, 34,* 27–31.

Kohrt, W. M., Malley, M. T., Coggan, A. R., Spina, R. J., Ogawa, T., Ehsani, A. A., et al. (1991). Effects of gender, age, and fitness level on response of $VO_{2\ max}$ to training in 60–71 yr olds. *Journal of Applied Physiology, 71,* 2004–2011.

Kostka, T., Berthouze, S. E., Lacour, J., & Bonnefoy, M. (2000). The symptomatology of upper respiratory tract infections and exercise in elderly people. *Medicine and Science in Sports and Exercise, 32,* 46–51.

LaStayo, P. C., Ewy, G. A., Pierotti, D. D., Johns, R. K., & Lindstedt, S. (2003). The positive effects of negative work: Increased muscle strength and decreased fall risk in a frail elderly population. [see comment]. *Journals of Gerontology, Series A: Biological Sciences and Medical Sciences, 58,* M419–M424.

Latham, N. K., Bennett, D. A., Stretton, C. M., & Anderson, C. S. (2004). Systematic review of progressive resistance strength training in older adults. *Journals of Gerontology, Series A: Biological Sciences and Medical Sciences, 59,* 48–61.

Lawrenson, L., Hoff, J., & Richardson, R. S. (2004). Aging attenuates vascular and metabolic plasticity but does not limit improvement in muscle $VO_{(2)\ max}$. *American Journal of Physiology—Heart and Circulatory Physiology, 286,* H1565–H1572.

Ley, K. (Ed.). (2001). *Physiology of inflammation*. New York: Oxford University Press.

Lord, S. R., Castell, S., Corcoran, J., Dayhew, J., Matters, B., Shan, A., et al. (2003). The effect of group exercise on physical functioning and falls in frail older people living in retirement villages: A randomized, controlled trial. *Journal of the American Geriatrics Society, 51,* 1685–1692.

Maeda, S., Tanabe, T., Miyauchi, T., Otsuki, T., Sugawara, J., Iemitsu, M., et al. (2003). Aerobic exercise training reduces plasma endothelin-1 concentration in older women. *Journal of Applied Physiology, 95,* 336–341.

Marcus, B. H., Dubbert, P. M., Forsyth, L. H., McKenzie, T. L., Stone, E. J., Dunn, A. L., et al. (2000). Physical activity behavior change: Issues in adoption and maintenance. *Health Psychology, 19*(1 Suppl.), 32–41.

Mazzeo, R., Cavanagh, P., Evans, W., Fiatarone, M., Hagberg, J., McAuley, E., et al. (1998). American College of Sports Medicine position stand: Exercise and physical activity for older adults. *Medicine and Science in Sports and Exercise, 30,* 992–1008.

McMurdo, M. E., Millar, A. M., & Daly, F. (2000). A randomized controlled trial of fall prevention strategies in old peoples' homes. *Gerontology, 46,* 83–87.

Mokdad, A. H., Marks, J. S., Stroup, D. F., & Gerberding, J. L. (2004). Actual causes of death in the United States, 2000. [see comment]. *Journal of the American Medical Association, 291,* 1238–1245.

Morley, J. E., Baumgartner, R. N., Roubenoff, R., Mayer, J., & Nair, K. S. (2001). Sarcopenia. *Journal of Laboratory and Clinical Medicine, 137,* 231–243.

Musi, N., & Goodyear, L. J. (2003). AMP-activated protein kinase and muscle glucose uptake. *Acta Physiologica Scandinavica, 178,* 337–345.

Musi, N., Yu, H., & Goodyear, L. J. (2003). AMP-activated protein kinase regulation and action in skeletal muscle during exercise. *Biochemical Society Transactions, 31*(Pt. 1), 191–195.

Newman, A. B., Haggerty, C. L., Goodpaster, B., Harris, T., Kritchevsky, S., Nevitt, M., et al. (2003). Strength and muscle quality in a well-functioning cohort of older adults: The Health, Aging and Body Composition Study. *Journal of the American Geriatrics Society, 51,* 323–330.

Newman, A. B., Kupelian, V., Visser, M., Simonsick, E., Goodpaster, B., Nevitt, M., et al. (2003). Sarcopenia: Alternative definitions and associations with lower extremity function. *Journal of the American Geriatrics Society, 51,* 1602–1609.

Nieman, D. C. (1995). Upper respiratory tract infections and exercise. *Thorax, 50,* 1229–1231.

Nieman, D. C., Buckley, K. S., Henson, D. A., Warren, B. J., Suttles, J., Ahle, J. C., Simandle, S., Fagoaga, O. R., & Nehlsen-Cannarella, S. L. (1995). Immune function in marathon runners versus sedentary controls. *Medicine and Science in Sports and Exercise, 27,* 986–992.

Nieman, D. C., Henson, D. A., Gusewitch, G., Warren, B. J., Dotson, R. C., Butterworth, D. E., et al. (1993). Physical activity and immune function in elderly women. *Medicine and Science in Sports and Exercise, 25,* 823–831.

Nieman, D. C., Johanssen, L. M., Lee, J. W., & Arabatzis, K. (1990). Infectious episodes in runners before and after the Los Angeles Marathon. *Journal of Sports Medicine and Physical Fitness, 30,* 316–328.

Nieman, D. C., Simandle, S., Henson, D. A., Warren, B. J., Suttles, J., Davis, J. M., et al. (1995). Lymphocyte proliferative response to 2.5 hours of running. *International Journal of Sports Medicine, 16,* 404–409.

Paterson, D. H., Cunningham, D. A., Koval, J. J., & St. Croix, C. M. (1999). Aerobic fitness in a population of independently living men and women aged 55–86 years. *Medicine and Science in Sports and Exercise, 31,* 1813–1820.

Pedersen, B. K., Bruunsgaard, H., Jensen, M., Toft, A. D., Hansen, H., & Ostrowski, K. (1999). Exercise and the immune system—influence of nutrition and ageing. *Journal of Science and Medicine in Sports, 2,* 234–252.

Pescatello, L. S., Franklin, B. A., Fagard, R., Farquhar, W. B., Kelley, G. A., & Ray, C. A. (2004). American College of Sports Medicine position stand: Exercise and hypertension. *Medicine and Science in Sports and Exercise, 36,* 533–553.

Peters, E. M., & Bateman, E. D. (1983). Ultramarathon running and upper respiratory tract infections: An epidemiological survey. *South African Medical Journal, 64,* 582–584.

Pimentel, A. E., Gentile, C. L., Tanaka, H., Seals, D. R., & Gates, P. E. (2003). Greater rate of decline in maximal aerobic capacity with age in endurance-trained than in sedentary men. *Journal of Applied Physiology, 94,* 2406–2413.

Pollock, M. L., Carroll, J. F., Graves, J. E., Leggett, S. H., Braith, R. W., Limacher, M., et al. (1991). Injuries and adherence to walk/jog and resistance training programs in the elderly. *Medicine and Science in Sports and Exercise, 23,* 1194–1200.

Potter, J. M., Evans, A. L., & Duncan, G. (1995). Gait speed and activities of daily living function in geriatric patients. *Archives of Physical Medicine and Rehabilitation, 76,* 997–999.

Pradhan, A. D., Manson, J. E., Rifai, N., Buring, J. E., & Ridker, P. M. (2001). C-reactive protein, interleukin 6, and risk of developing type 2 diabetes mellitus. *Journal of the American Medical Association, 286,* 327–334.

Puggaard, L., Larsen, J. B., Stovring, H., & Jeune, B. (2000). Maximal oxygen uptake, muscle strength and walking speed in 85-year-old women: Effects of increased physical activity. *Aging (Milano), 12,* 180–189.

Reynolds, T. H. T., Brozinick, Jr., J. T., Rogers, M. A., & Cushman, S. W. (1997). Effects of exercise training on glucose transport and cell surface GLUT-4 in isolated rat epitrochlearis muscle. *American Journal of Physiology, 272*(2 Pt. 1), E320–E325.

Riancho, J. A., Zarrabeitia, M. T., Amado, J. A., Olmos, J. M., & Gonzalez-Macias, J. (1994). Age-related differences in cytokine secretion. *Gerontology, 40,* 8–12.

Rimbert, V., Boirie, Y., Bedu, M., Hocquette, J-F., Ritz, P., & Morio, B. (2004). Muscle fat oxidative capacity is not impaired by age but by physical activity: Association with insulin sensitivity. *FASEB Journal, 18,* 737–739.

Rogers, M. A. (1989). Acute effects of exercise on glucose tolerance in non-insulin-dependent diabetes. *Medicine and Science in Sports and Exercise, 21,* 362–368.

Rosas, G. O., Zieman, S. J., Donabedian, M., Vandegaer, K., & Hare, J. M. (2001). Augmented age-associated innate immune responses contribute to negative inotropic and lusitropic effects of lipopolysaccharide and interferon gamma. *Journal of Molecular and Cellular Cardiology, 33,* 1849–1859.

Rosen, M. J., Sorkin, J. D., Goldberg, A. P., Hagberg, J. M., & Katzel, L. I. (1998). Predictors of age-associated decline in maximal aerobic capacity: A comparison of four statistical models. *Journal of Applied Physiology, 84,* 2163–2170.

Rosenzweig, T., Braiman, L., Bak, A., Alt, A., Kuroki, T., & Sampson, S. R. (2002). Differential effects of tumor necrosis factor-alpha on protein kinase C isoforms alpha and delta mediate inhibition of insulin receptor signaling. *Diabetes, 51,* 1921–1930.

Roubenoff, R. (2003). Sarcopenia: Effects on body composition and function. *Journals of Gerontology, Series A: Biological Sciences and Medical Sciences, 58,* 1012–1017.

Roubenoff, R., Harris, T. B., Abad, L. W., Wilson, P. W., Dallal, G. E., & Dinarello, C. A. (1998). Monocyte cytokine production in an elderly population: Effect of age and inflammation. *Journal of Gerontology: Medical Sciences, 53,* M20–M26.

Ryan, A. S., Hurlbut, D. E., Lott, M. E., Ivey, F. M., Fleg, J., Hurley, B. F., et al. (2001). Insulin action after resistive training in insulin resistant older men and women. *Journal of the American Geriatrics Society, 49,* 247–253.

Ryan, A. S., Pratley, R. E., Elahi, D., & Goldberg, A. P. (1995). Resistive training increases fat-free mass and maintains RMR despite weight loss in postmenopausal women. *Journal of Applied Physiology, 79,* 818–823.

Ryan, A. S., Pratley, R. E., Elahi, D., & Goldberg, A. P. (2000). Changes in plasma leptin and insulin action with resistive training in postmenopausal women. *International Journal of Obesity and Related Metabolic Disorders: Journal of the International Association for the Study of Obesity, 24,* 27–32.

Ryan, A. S., Pratley, R. E., Goldberg, A. P., & Elahi, D. (1996). Resistive training increases insulin action in postmenopausal women. *Journals of Gerontology, Series A: Biological Sciences and Medical Sciences, 51,* M199–M205.

Ryan, A. S., Treuth, M. S., Hunter, G. R., & Elahi, D. (1998). Resistive training maintains bone mineral density in postmenopausal women. *Calcified Tissue International, 62,* 295–299.

Schneider, E. L., & Guralnik, J. M. (1990). The aging of America: Impact on health care costs. [see comment]. *Journal of the American Medical Association, 263,* 2335–2340.

Schulze, M. B., Rimm, E. B., Li, T., Rifai, N., Stampfer, M. J., & Hu, F. B. (2004). C-reactive protein and incident cardiovascular events among men with diabetes. *Diabetes Care, 27,* 889–894.

Schumacher, A., Seljeflot, I., Sommervoll, L., Christensen, B., Otterstad, J. E., & Arnesen, H. (2002). Increased levels of markers of vascular inflammation in patients with coronary heart disease. *Scandinavian Journal of Clinical Laboratory Investigation, 62,* 59–68.

Shephard, R. J., & Shek, P. N. (1995). Exercise, aging and immune function. *International Journal of Sports Medicine, 16*(1), 1–6.

Singh, M. A., Ding, W., Manfredi, T. J., Solares, G. S., O'Neill, E. F., Clements, K. M., et al. (1999). Insulin-like growth factor I in skeletal muscle after weight-lifting exercise in frail elders. *American Journal of Physiology, 277*(1 Pt. 1), E135–E143.

Smith, J. K., Dykes, R., Douglas, J. E., Krishnaswamy, G., & Berk, S. (1999). Long-term exercise and atherogenic activity of blood mononuclear cells in persons at risk of developing ischemic heart disease. *Journal of the American Medical Association, 281,* 1722–1727.

Stewart, L. K., Flynn, M. G., Campbell, W. W., Craig, B. A., Robinson, J. P., McFarlin, B. K., et al. (2005). Influence of exercise training and age on CD14+ cell-surface expression of toll-like receptor 2 and 4. *Brain, Behavior, and Immunity, 19,* 389–397.

Sutherland, M. S., Lipps, S. G., Patnaik, N., Gayo-Fung, L. M., Khammungkune, S., Xie, W., et al. (2003). SP500263, a novel SERM, blocks osteoclastogenesis in a human bone cell model: Role of IL-6 and GM-CSF. *Cytokine, 23,* 1–14.

Talbot, L. A., Morrell, C. H., Metter, E. J., & Fleg, J. L. (2002). Comparison of cardiorespiratory fitness versus leisure time physical activity as predictors of coronary events in men aged < or = 65 years and > 65 years. *American Journal of Cardiology, 89,* 1187–1192.

Tanaka, H., Desouza, C. A., Jones, P. P., Stevenson, E. T., Davy, K. P., & Seals, D. R. (1997). Greater rate of decline in maximal aerobic capacity with age in physically active vs. sedentary healthy women. *Journal of Applied Physiology, 83,* 1947–1953.

Timonen, L., Rantanen, T., Ryynanen, O. P., Taimela, S., Timonen, T. E., & Sulkava, R. (2002). A randomized controlled trial of rehabilitation after hospitalization in frail older women: Effects on strength, balance and mobility. *Scandinavian Journal of Medicine and Science in Sports, 12,* 186–192.

U.S. Department of Health and Human Services. (1996). *Physical activity and health: A report of the surgeon general.* Atlanta, GA: U.S. Department of Health and Human Services, Centers for Disease Control and Prevention, National Center for Chronic Disease Prevention and Health Promotion.

U.S. Department of Health and Human Services. (2000). *Healthy people 2010: Understanding and improving health.* Washington, DC: Government Printing Office.

U.S. Department of Health and Human Services. (2001). *Exercise: A guide from the National Institute on Aging.* Washington, DC: National Institutes on Aging.

Van der Bij, A. K., Laurant, M. G., & Wensing, M. (2002). Effectiveness of physical activity interventions for older adults: A review. *American Journal of Preventative Medicine 22,* 120–133.

Volpato, S., Guralnik, J. M., Ferrucci, L., Balfour, J., Chaves, P., Fried, L. P., et al. (2001). Cardiovascular disease, interleukin-6, and risk of mortality in older women: The Women's Health and Aging Study. *Circulation, 103,* 947–953.

Willey, K. A., & Singh, M. A. (2003). Battling insulin resistance in elderly obese people with type 2 diabetes: Bring on the heavy weights. *Diabetes Care, 26,* 1580–1588.

Wolf, S. L., Barnhart, H. X., Kutner, N. G., McNeely, E., Coogler, C., Xu, T., et al. (2003). Selected as the best paper in the 1990s: Reducing frailty and falls in older persons: An investigation of tai chi and computerized balance training. *Journal of the American Geriatrics Society, 51,* 1794–1803.

Woods, J. A., Ceddia, M. A., Wolters, B. W., Evans, J. K., Lu, Q., & McAuley, E. (1999). Effects of 6 months of moderate aerobic exercise training on immune function in the elderly. *Mechanisms of Ageing and Development, 109*(1), 1–19.

Woods, J. A., Lowder, T. W., & Keylock, K. T. (2002). Can exercise training improve immune function in the aged? *Annals of the New York Academy of Sciences, 959,* 117–127.

Yan, H., Kuroiwa, A., Tanaka, H., Shindo, M., Kiyonaga, A., & Nagayama, A. (2001). Effect of moderate exercise on immune senescence in men. *European Journal of Applied Physiology, 86,* 105–111.

Yarasheski, K. E. (2003). Exercise, aging, and muscle protein metabolism. *Journals of Gerontology, Series A: Biological Sciences and Medical Sciences, 58*(10), M918–M922.

Yeh, S. S., & Schuster, M. W. (1999). Geriatric cachexia: The role of cytokines. *American Journal of Clinical Nutrition, 70,* 183–197.

Yoshiga, C. C., Higuchi, M., & Oka, J. (2002). Serum lipoprotein cholesterols in older oarsmen. *European Journal of Applied Physiology, 87,* 228–232.

Zoico, E., Di Francesco, V., Guralnik, J. M., Mazzali, G., Bortolani, A., Guariento, S., et al. (2004). Physical disability and muscular strength in relation to obesity and different body composition indexes in a sample of healthy elderly women. *International Journal of Obesity and Related Metabolic Disorders: Journal of the International Association for the Study of Obesity, 28,* 234–241.

PART III

Social Aspects
of Aging

CHAPTER 9

Socioemotional Aspects of Aging

Karen L. Fingerman
Brooke N. Baker

Scholarly interest in the social and emotional arena of late life arose as a reaction to American fascination with the nuclear family. Prior to the 20th century, extended families dominated an agrarian American economy with family farms. Around World War II, social scientists became increasingly interested in family structure involving couples raising children. In 1943, Talcott Parsons published a widely cited treatise suggesting that as the nuclear family became the dominant norm, older adults were being relegated to distant kin rather than central members of the family. Researchers in the field of aging became interested in whether older adults were lonely or whether they were, in fact, still well embedded among families and friends. Social science on the whole has since refuted the premise that families have cast off older members (Coontz, 2000). In the process of examining these issues, the field has accumulated an understanding of the complex social and emotional world of late life.

Indeed, research has documented the positive emotions and relationships that characterize older adults' lives. Most older adults are not lonely; older adults describe their relationships as rewarding (Carstensen, Isaacowitz, & Charles, 1999). Individuals often experience their greatest anxieties and unhappiness in early adulthood, when the world is filled with opportunities, rather than in old age, when they are losing social roles and the future is short.

Furthermore, there is considerable variability in the way people react to social circumstances of late life. Social relationships vary in structure, processes, and outcomes throughout the life span (Fingerman & Lang, 2004). To examine these issues, researchers study the number of social partners that adults of different ages have, who those social partners are (e.g., spouse, friend, grandchild), how social partners interact with one another, and the benefits or costs of those relationships to individuals of different ages. These phenomena form a core of socioemotional gerontology.

MULTIDISCIPLINARY PERSPECTIVES ON SOCIAL AND EMOTIONAL AGING

Initially, sociologists conducted much of the research examining adults' relationships in old age (Rosow, 1970; Shanas & Streib, 1965). In the early and mid-20th century, psychologists who were interested in aging focused on cognitive changes, and few researchers of any sort studied emotions in late life. By the early 21st century, however, scholars from a variety of disciplines investigated social and emotional aspects of aging. Much research on this topic is still sociological or psychological in nature, but anthropologists, social workers, nurses, public health specialists, and scholars in the humanities also make contributions. It is notable, however, that researchers in different fields tend to focus on distinct aspects of social and emotional aging.

Sociologists examine how older adults' relationships vary as a function of ascribed characteristics (e.g., gender, race, and social class), achieved characteristics (e.g., education and occupation), social institutions (e.g., economy, family), cohort membership (e.g., the baby boomers), and historical time period. Such sociological research is described elsewhere in this book (e.g., chapters 10 and 11). With regard to social ties, sociologists bring attention to the ways in which social contexts influence qualities of relationships and behaviors within those relationships. For example, while maternal grandparents are dominant in the United States (Fingerman, 2004), sociologists have considered patrilineal ties between grandparents and grandchildren in the context of the changing rural farm economy in the U.S. Midwest (e.g., King & Elder, 1995).

Anthropologists have considered cultural aspects of relationships and emotional experiences by examining older adults in other countries and considering ethnic differences within the United States (Becker, Beyene, Newsom, & Mayen, 2003; Johnson & Barer, 1997). For example, Johnson and Barer provided detailed descriptions of African American and European American adults over the age of 80 and their social networks. The qualitative techniques anthropologists employ are particularly useful with certain populations, where use of forced-choice items or standard procedures might alienate participants.

Psychologists tend to focus on micro factors embedded within the individual, such as developmental stage, motivation, social cognition, personality, interpersonal interactions, and emotions. Psychologists have considered how older adults benefit from their relationships with other people and how their emotional processes may differ from those of younger adults. For example, psychologists have examined individuals' motivation to maintain different types of relationships (e.g., Carstensen, Fung, & Charles, 2003), whether close friends and family members provide different types of support to adults of different ages (e.g., Antonucci et al., 2002), and how positive and negative emotions vary across adulthood (Charles, Reynolds, & Gatz, 2001). Recently psychologists have examined physiological indicators such as heart rate (Labouvie-Vief, Lumley, Jain, & Heinze, 2003) or images of the brain captured through functional magnetic resonance imaging (Mather et al., 2004) to assess physical underpinnings of emotional reactions or social interactions.

We focus in this chapter on the psychological components of relationships from our own research. We examine behavioral and emotional processes that allow adults of different ages to regulate negative emotions in ways that favor positive feelings in relationships. At the same time, we draw extensively on research that our colleagues in sociology, anthropology, social work, and other fields have conducted with regard to adults' social relationships. For example, sociologists have found that relationships between parents and offspring vary as a function of gender; mothers and daughters have both closer and more problematic ties than do fathers and sons (Rossi & Rossi, 1990). Our work has considered social cognitions, behaviors, and emotions underlying these patterns (e.g., Fingerman, 1996, 2003). Therefore, we cover a range of disciplines in this chapter, but acknowledge that our implicit view of socioemotional aging is colored by a psychological, micro-level perspective.

Elsewhere in this volume (chapter 5), psychologists describe cognitive and physiological aspects of the aging process. Here, we describe questions that gerontologists from a variety of disciplines have asked about social and emotional processes in old age and the answers they have found. Surprisingly, although scholars from many different fields are interested in social and emotional aspects of aging, they rarely collaborate on the same study. There are few examples of truly interdisciplinary research in this field. Instead, we consider what the multidisciplinary perspectives in this field can tell us about the social and emotional world of older adults.

Understanding Social Ties in Late Life

Gerontological interest in social contexts arose from the recognition that old age is a period when individuals seem to experience a series of losses in the social world. Their spouse may die, their friends may become infirm, they retire and no longer participate in work roles, their parenting obligations are behind them, and societal recognition for their contributions may be minimal. Yet, in general, older adults do not seem depressed. It is easy to think of examples of adults who have aged well. These individuals in their 70s or early 80s continue to travel, do volunteer work, tend beautiful gardens, and have interesting things to say when engaged in conversations. Researchers from a variety of disciplines have examined individuals of this type under the broader heading of "successful" or "optimal" aging (Baltes & Baltes, 1990; Kahn & Rowe, 1998).

Sociologists and public health scholars look at how social structures, contexts, and health contribute to relationship patterns in these situations. For example, sociologists might demonstrate that older individuals with better health or more resources show better adaptation on a variety of measures of physical or emotional functioning. Sociologists who study social ties also focus on contexts and structures, such as the number of social partners an older adult has or the distance this person lives from his or her children. This research suggests that many social structures that appear to be difficult for older adults do not actually affect their satisfaction with their relationships. For example, older people who live far from their grown children still report feeling close to those children and report that their children assist them in different ways (Litwak, 1965; Moss, Moss, & Moles, 1985). This type of research suggests that older adults find ways to get around structural barriers, such as geographic distance from a close relative, that might upset younger adults. Older adults may be able to enjoy the positive feelings about the relationship, rather than focus on their inability to visit with the family member in person.

Similarly, psychologists are interested in micro-level processes explaining why some older adults show such adaptation and other older adults do not, even when they have the same amount of money or similar health status. Psychologists have examined the actions or behaviors older people use to maximize functioning and benefits in old age, regardless of what appear to be unfavorable objective circumstances. For example, Paul Baltes's (1987; Baltes & Smith, 2003) model of successful aging has been widely applied in studies examining this type of successful adaptation. His theory of successful aging introduced the idea that individuals must engage in three subprocesses to produce beneficial outcomes: selection, optimization, and compensation. Individuals who engage in these processes to maximize gains over losses (or desirable states over undesirable states) are more likely to age successfully. In a similar vein, Heckhausen and Schulz (1995) described adaptive shifts in sense of control that might contribute to well-being in late life. In this model, older adults may stop trying to alter the environment or situation and instead, focus on their own perspective and emotions.

Of course, not all gerontologists believe that the aging process is simply a matter of making the right choices and engaging in behaviors to overcome a given situation. Research also has focused on situations in which older adults encounter insurmountable difficulties, such as cognitive declines associated with dementia or frailty associated with strokes. Indeed, Baltes's more recent work has suggested that successful aging can extend only until individuals are in their mid-80s, at which point physical declines may accumulate to such an extent that individual efforts are not sufficient to surmount the problems of aging (Baltes & Smith, 2003). In these situations, scholars interested in socioemotional aging have considered not only the functional status of the older adult suffering health problems, but the friends and family members who provide support to this individual. For example, the stresses caregivers encounter in providing care to an older adult may have more to do with their own subjective sense of burden than with objective indicators of the older adult's health status (e.g., Zarit, Reever, & Bach-Peterson, 1980). Chapter 14 in this book describes caregiving and caregivers' attributions in greater detail. Here, we focus on successful aging.

We note here, however, that initial studies of socioemotional aging often provided a dichotomous view of older adults: those who were successfully aging in good health with friends and close family and those who were declining into dementia or frailty and serving as a source of stress to friends and family. More recent research has sought to differentiate complexities in the aging process, including social and emotional development. For example, close friends and family members can also serve as sources of irritation or annoyance (e.g., Fingerman, Hay, & Birditt, 2004), and caregivers can derive deep satisfaction from their work (Walker & Pratt, 1995). More recent studies have considered such complexities involved in aging.

Social Support

Older adults tend to have fewer social partners than younger adults. Early theories attributed the smaller networks to older adults' desire to disengage from their worldly connections as they approached the end of life. Cumming and Henry (1961) portrayed this disengagement as a means of dealing with inevitable losses. Yet disengagement theory did not account for findings indicating that older adults are more satisfied with their personal relationships than are younger adults.

This situation is not the paradox it appears to be. Older adults may lose some social ties, but they appear to retain relationships with their closest social partners. Antonucci and her colleagues have repeatedly shown that adults of all ages report having 5 to 10 close social partners (e.g., Antonucci & Akiyama, 1987; Antonucci et al., 2002). Antonucci and colleagues (2002) used a standard measure of social support to examine age differences in social and emotional patterns in the United States, Japan, France, and Germany. Across nations, in comparison to younger adults, older adults listed fewer social partners overall, but those social partners tended to be close relatives and friends.

Further, older adults may derive pleasure from social contacts with whom they have infrequent contact, such as holiday card exchanges and encounters at family reunions with their cousins, former roommates, and college chums. Older adults might not list these contacts as social partners in their social network, but they derive meaning from these exchanges. For example, in our prior work, we looked at adults' reactions to the holiday cards they receive in December to understand how and why individuals might retain contact with people whom they have not seen in 40 or 50 years (e.g., Fingerman & Griffiths, 1999). Individuals who received a great number of holiday cards felt socially embedded and connected to their personal past, even if those cards were from distant social partners. In sum, although older adults have fewer social partners than do younger adults, they have as many close social partners as do younger adults and also derive satisfaction from ties that are distant in nature.

Carstensen and her colleagues developed Socioemotional Selectivity Theory to explain how and why older adults have only their few close social partners in their social networks (Carstensen et al., 1999). According to this theory, adults selectively cull their social networks in late life to maximize rewards from their remaining social partners. They let go of ties to unrewarding social partners and acquaintances, which allows them to focus greater effort and attention on relationships with close friends and family. More broadly, motivations for social contact appear to vary as a function of time perspective. When people perceive the future as expansive and open, as in young adulthood, they are motivated by information-seeking goals and attempt to generate new liaisons. When individuals foresee the future as short and foreclosed, as in old age, they seek emotional rewards and attempt to maximize their positive experiences with social partners.

Socioemotional selectivity theory articulates the old cliché that on their deathbed, people wish for more time with friends and family rather than more time at the office. A plethora of data support Carstensen's theory. An early study found that older individuals had little desire to get to know a novel social partner, whereas younger participants were eager to meet their favorite author or a potentially exciting acquaintance (Frederickson & Carstensen, 1990). Carstensen and colleagues also examined situations in which they could differentiate age from time perspective. For example, a study examining older adults and young men who were symptomatic for AIDS found that both groups placed greater weight on emotional qualities of social partners than on informational qualities of social partners because they viewed their time as limited. Likewise, middle-aged adults and young adults who were HIV positive but not symptomatic responded similarly, with a moderate desire for close social contacts and a somewhat limited desire to establish new social ties (Carstensen & Frederickson, 1998).

Support for socioemotional selectivity theory is also derived from a series of studies conducted in and around the transition of Hong Kong to Chinese sovereignty in 1997 (Fung, Carstensen, & Lutz, 1999). Hong Kong was a British colony for 150 years prior to 1997. The researchers hypothesized that sociopolitical anxiety over the shift to Chinese sovereignty would generate a curtailed sense of time across the population during the period immediately preceding the shift. Their research revealed that one year prior to the handover and one year after the handover, older Hong Kong residents expressed a preference for familiar social partners, but younger Hong Kong residents expressed a preference for novel social partners. Two months before the handover, however, both younger and older Hong Kong residents showed a preference for familiar social partners. Other studies have found similar patterns (Lang & Carstensen, 2002; Lansford, Sherman, & Antonucci, 1998). In sum, evidence indicates that older adults have fewer social partners because they want to spend time with the people they care about most.

Problematic Aspects of Relationships

Of course, social partners are not solely a beneficial resource. Friends and family members can also ask favors, criticize, proffer unsolicited advice, and show up later for dinner than expected. Yet older adults consistently report few interpersonal problems with their social partners (e.g., Akiyama, Antonucci, Takahashi, & Langfahl, 2003; Fingerman & Birditt, 2003; Rook, 1984). These findings are evident in relationships between parents and children (Fingerman, 1996; Umberson, 1989), grandparents and grandchildren (Fingerman, 1998), and siblings (Bedford, 1989); even difficult marriages appear to be less conflicted in later life (Levenson, Carstensen, & Gottman, 1993).

Older adults might have fewer difficulties with their relatives for several reasons: (1) as they grow older, adults may better regulate their own emotions and the emotional qualities of their relationships (Birditt & Fingerman, 2003; Carstensen, et al., 1999); (2) older adults' social partners may be better behaved than younger adults' social partners; (3) older adults might encounter fewer annoying people on a daily basis than do younger adults; and (4) older adults may behave in ways that prevent annoyances in relationships. We discuss emotion regulation in the next section and consider the other three issues in this section.

In most studies, age of social partner and age of participant are highly correlated; older people have older friends and family members than do younger people (e.g., Antonucci et al., 2002; Fingerman, 1998). If older people are better able to regulate their emotions and behaviors, it follows that they make better social partners than do younger people. Our research pertaining to mothers and daughters provides examples of this phenomenon. An in-depth study of mothers (mean age 76) and their adult daughters (mean age 44) revealed that middle-aged women often act in ways that enhance their mothers' sense that the relationship is strong and positive (Fingerman, 1996, 2003). When they were interviewed alone, each daughter had at least one complaint about her mother. Later, when mother and daughter completed interviews together, daughters acted in positive ways and denied that they were ever upset with their mothers (Fingerman, 1998; Lefkowitz & Fingerman, 2003). Some of these daughters further explained that they wanted to protect their mothers from unpleasant interactions, given that their mothers were elderly and would not live forever.

Older adults are also less likely to find themselves in contexts in which there is opportunity to get annoyed with other people. Akiyama and colleagues (2003) studied individuals aged 13 to 99 in Japan and in the United States. They found that reports of interpersonal problems were strongly associated with shared residences in both countries. Many older adults in the United States are widowed and live alone. Thus, they may have fewer opportunities to get upset with other people than do younger people. Our research also supports this premise (Fingerman, Hay, et al., 2004). Individuals listed social partners whom they consider close and positive and social partners whom they consider problematic. Problematic social partners disproportionately included acquaintances: coworkers, teachers, members of a club, or neighbors. Older adults may have greater latitude than younger adults in avoiding such social partners.

Finally, research suggests older adults behave in ways that allow them to avoid difficulties with their social partners. In a national daily diary study, participants completed telephone interviews every evening for eight evenings in a row. They reported the daily stresses they had encountered and what they did about those stressors. Older adults were more likely to try to avoid getting upset about interpersonal stressors than were younger adults; older adults reported doing nothing or trying to keep calm, whereas younger adults reported arguing or confronting the other person (Birditt et al., 2004). Similarly, Blanchard-Fields, Jahnke, and Camp (1995) asked younger and older adults to complete story vignettes involving personal problems that were either easy to solve or were highly emotionally charged. There were few age differences in solutions participants proposed when problems were easy to solve. When problems were emotionally salient age, differences emerged: older adults were more likely to try to avoid getting upset or to avoid the situations altogether than were younger adults.

Ambivalence in Relationships

In conjunction with increased attention to problematic aspects of social ties, family science researchers have recently begun to examine ambivalence in relationships. Ambivalence toward social partners may present unique challenges to individuals (e.g., Rook, 1984; Uchino, Holt-Lunstad, Uno, & Flinders, 2001). For example, loving family members who offer unwanted advice or interfere in a stressful situation can exacerbate stressors (Morgan, 1989; Rook, 2003). A burgeoning literature addresses ambivalence in intergenerational ties in late life (e.g., Lüscher & Pillemer, 1998; Pillemer & Suitor, 2002; Willson, Shuey, & Elder, 2003), but researchers have also examined ambivalence in the broader social network (e.g., Fingerman, Hay, et al., 2004; Uchino et al., 2001).

Theorists differentiate between ambivalence involving mixed feelings (i.e., positive and negative feelings) and feeling torn toward a given person (e.g., wanting to be close but respecting autonomy). Patterns of age differences may vary depending on the type of assessment. Pillemer and Suitor (2002) examined what is called direct ambivalence by asking older mothers if they feel torn in their relationships with their offspring. Over half of the mothers endorsed at least one statement suggesting that they felt torn. These findings suggest that problematic relationships are not synonymous with ambivalent relationships. Older adults report fewer problems but may nonetheless feel torn.

When ambivalence is assessed indirectly, however, the findings appear more consistent with age difference in problematic ties. In our study of close and problematic social networks, we considered ambivalent ties. Individuals of all ages reported their greatest ambivalence toward family members. Yet older adults reported less ambivalence toward their family members, and a greater likelihood of viewing these ties as solely positive, than did younger adults (Fingerman, Hay, et al., 2004).

Summary of Positive, Negative, and Ambivalent Ties

In sum, relationships provide benefits to younger and older adults. Older adults tend to have smaller social networks than younger adults, but they enjoy those social partners a great deal. Older adults also report fewer problems with their social partners than do younger adults. Older adults report ambivalent feelings in the sense of being torn rather than in feeling negative, as well as positive emotions. On the whole, relationships appear to improve in old age. One consideration that has not been addressed, however, is the possibility that older adults who encounter social problems refuse to participate in the research. Although we might expect this to be equally true of younger adults, variability in health may contribute to age differences in the likelihood of socially problematic people participating in studies. Older adults who suffer health problems may encounter more difficulties with their social partners than older adults in good health. Older adults in poor health are generally absent from studies of interpersonal relationships.

Finally, from a psychological perspective, features of relationships do not solely reflect interpersonal processes or contexts. Rather, a variety of studies suggest that older adults regulate their emotions in ways that enhance their feelings about their relationships (e.g., Birditt & Fingerman, 2003; Carstensen et al., 2003). In late life, individuals may not experience as much anger and irritation with friends and family as they did earlier in life. We consider these processes in the next section.

Emotional Development

Research pertaining to older adults' relationships reveals that emotions serve important functions in the aging process and in social relationships. Charles and Mavandadi (2004) proposed that emotions are the primary mechanism through which personal relationships affect health in old age. They posit that (1) emotion regulation is the central mechanism linking social relationships with health; (2) emotion regulation includes physiological, cognitive, and behavioral processes, all of which influence health; and (3) socioemotional processes affect health throughout the life span but are most evident at the very beginning and end of the life cycle, when people are most physically vulnerable. Based on this view of emotions, individuals experience events, interpret those events, and have emotional reactions to the events. It is the emotional reactions that affect their health and well-being.

Social partners evoke strong emotional reactions throughout life. A majority of daily stressors involve a romantic partner, roommate, parent, sibling, or child (Birditt et al., 2004). Social partners can generate negative feelings such as sadness, anger, irritation, and frustration through confrontations or disagreements. Older adults may also experience distress over a social partner's personal problems, such as when a grown offspring is going through a divorce or a grandchild is ill. Even in social interactions that appear to be benign, older adults may experience distressful emotional reactions. For example, Smith and Goodnow (1999) found that older adults were not pleased with help they did not request or did not want and sometimes found such help upsetting.

Yet, most studies document positive changes in emotions as adults grow older. For example, Charles et al. (2001) conducted a secondary data analysis using a study of 2,804 individuals representing four generations of family members interviewed from 1971 to 1994. The survey included questions about emotions at each wave of data collection. Adults reported fewer negative emotions as they grew older, but their feelings of happiness remained fairly stable. These findings held true regardless of cohort. Individuals born during the 1940s did not show greater happiness than individuals born in the 1960s; individuals generally reported stability of happiness regardless of the period when they were born. Similarly, Mroczek (2001) examined two large studies of adults aged 20 to 100 and found that positive feelings increased slightly and negative emotions decreased from midlife until individuals were in their mid-70s.

Researchers have investigated many explanations for these findings, including better ability to regulate emotions, proactive efforts to circumvent situations in which negative emotions might arise, better coping abilities, decreased sensitivity to negative stimuli, decreasing processing ability to deal with negative emotions, merging of positive and negative emotions, and physiological changes that reduce negative emotional experiences. For example, a recent study using functional magnetic resonance imaging of the brain examined age differences in activation in the amygdala (the part of the brain associated with emotions). Younger (aged 18 to 29) and older (aged 70 to 90) adults viewed pictures that were positive, negative, or neutral in emotional tone. Older adults showed increased activation in the amygdala when they saw positive pictures compared to when they saw negative pictures; this difference was not evident for younger adults (Mather et al., 2004).

Older adults' more extensive experiences and practice with negative events may also contribute to these differences. Knight, Gatz, Heller, and Bengtson (2000) studied age differences in response to stressors by interviewing younger and older adults regarding a 1994 earthquake in Los Angeles, California. Older adults fared better than younger adults on emotional distress outcome measures (e.g., depression) because older adults had been previously exposed to natural disasters. More specifically, the older adults showed better psychological adjustment and tended not to reflect on the disaster, whereas younger adults had more difficulty adjusting because they were more inclined to ruminate about the disaster.

Of course, adults' emotional reactions are not simply a matter of age; individuals who have been temperamental or difficult do not become vivacious in late life. Rather, personality plays a role in emotional experiences. Individuals who score higher on measures of neuroticism (e.g., who have a negative outlook in general) tend to show less of a decrease in negative emotions as they age. Similarly, individuals who score higher on measures of extraversion (e.g., who enjoy people and social events) tend to show more positive feelings as they age (Charles et al., 2001). It is possible that studies that find older adults report more positive emotional experiences than younger adults have somehow excluded the less introverted and more neurotic older adults. Yet research in the field of personality suggests this is not the case. A review of cross-sectional and cross-cohort longitudinal research suggests that personality changes across adulthood, with people scoring higher on conscientiousness, agreeableness, and norm adherence with age (Helson, Kwan, John, & Jones, 2002). These personality changes parallel the changes noted in emotional experience, providing additional validation for those studies and negating the idea that temperamental older adults did not participate in the research.

Finally, theorists have noted that emotions are not solely positive or negative in old age (e.g., Carstensen, Pasupathi, Mayr, & Nesselroade, 2000; Ong & Bergmann, 2004). Age differences exist not only in the dimensions of emotions (e.g., positive versus negative), but in the mixture of emotions individuals experience. As individuals grow older, negative emotions may encroach on events that are primarily positive in tenor. For example, an elderly woman attending a grandchild's wedding may feel both joy at the celebration and a sense of loss in recognition that she may not live long enough to see great-grandchildren. Other theorists suggest that older adults may experience fewer complexities in their emotions in old age. Labouvie-Vief (2003) argued that studies find older adults report more positive feelings than younger adults because older adults lose cognitive capacity to integrate complex positive and negative emotional experiences, and instead turn to denial of the negative experience. Recent work by Ong and colleagues has also considered emotional complexities, but from an intraindividual perspective. They looked at 34 widows' emotional experiences over a three-month period following bereavement. On days when the widows experienced more positive emotions, they reported fewer feelings of depression (Ong, Bergeman, & Bisconti, 2004). Thus, complexities in emotional experiences can alleviate stresses of late life. Indeed, complexities in emotional experiences, coupled with increased positive and decreased negative feelings, appear to contribute to the processes of successful or satisfactory old age.

The Oldest Old

Thus far, our discussion has focused on the ways in which older adults surmount what appear to be insurmountable odds from a young person's perspective. In actuality, the pace of physical and cognitive decline begins to accelerate when adults are in their 80s. Gerontologists have referred to adults over age 60 who remain fit and active as the young old, whereas adults over age 85 are referred to as the oldest old (e.g., Baltes & Smith, 2003; Femia, Zarit, & Johansson, 2001; Johnson & Barer, 1997). It is notable that fifteen years ago, gerontologists often referred to adults over age 75 or over age 80 as the oldest old. The shift to age 85 reflects the increased health, well-being, and functional status of many adults in their late 70s.

Oldest-old adults often fit stereotypical views of the downside of old age: they have lost their spouse, friends, often even their children. Nearly all adults over the age of 85 have at least one chronic illness, and many suffer multiple impairments (Fingerman, Nussbaum, & Birditt, 2004; National Center for Health Statistics, 2001). Rates of Alzheimer's disease and dementia increase dramatically after the age of 80 (Suthers, Kim, & Crimmins, 2003). Given these health declines, improvements in positive and negative emotions described in the prior section may not hold true for this age group. In old-old age, happiness may decrease slightly, and negative emotions may increase slightly (Charles et al., 2001).

From a social perspective, Johnson and Barer (1997) suggested that the oldest old are "survivors:" they have often outlived their spouses, friends, and family members. This survivorship affects their feelings of connections to the broader social world. They have lost the people they would have relied on for companionship, support, and affection throughout their lives. Yet many oldest-old adults do not seem as bereft as their situation might suggest. Studies suggest that many demonstrate an ability to regulate qualities of their relationships in ways that enhance these ties.

For example, in a qualitative study, Ingersoll-Dayton and Talbott (1992) interviewed 31 oldest-old adults about their exchanges with their social partners. They found many infirm elderly adults had ways of reframing their situation to make themselves feel better. For example, an elderly minister who recently had a stroke never mentioned the help his wife provided to him when asked about social support. Other participants pointed out how much they had given when they were younger, and emphasized that it was only because of their age that they did not give more now.

Nonetheless, we do not mean to imply old age is a journey toward continually better rewards. Obviously, physical detriments generate tensions and difficulties for many aging individuals, particularly as frailties accrue. Physical problems may generate problems in daily functioning. Social integration can help mitigate difficult circumstances, but cannot delay physical declines indefinitely (Femia et al., 2001).

In sum, despite losses of social partners, physical functioning, cognitive abilities, and social roles, old age can also be a period of gains and rewards. The ability to engage in relationships with other people, improvements in emotion regulation, and decreases in negative interactions can lead older adults to a sense of increased well-being. At the very end of life, detriments may accumulate and feelings of well-being deteriorate. Nonetheless, even oldest-old adults may use coping behaviors to retain integrity.

A MODEL FOR FUTURE RESEARCH ON SOCIOEMOTIONAL AGING

Different disciplines provide insights into distinct facets of social and emotional aging. Yet an integrated interdisciplinary understanding of older adults' social worlds remains to be explored. For example, sociologists have shown that the overall emotional quality of intergenerational ties is not diminished by geographic distance (Litwak, 1965; Moss et al., 1985). Yet psychologists have not investigated whether geographic distance affects more micro-level features of the relationship, such as the ability to share memories or feelings of intimacy. Psychologists have studied social cognitive phenomena, such as how people of different ages think they should respond to interpersonal problems of different types (Blanchard-Fields et al., 1995), but sociologists have not looked at whether these responses vary by social contexts, such as education level or ethnicity. Research conducted by scholars from multiple disciplines, working in an interdisciplinary fashion, might move the field of gerontology even further in understanding socioemotional aging.

To accomplish this goal of more integrative research, researchers might consider a broader model including social contexts, psychological features of the individual, and input from the social partner. We have developed the Social Input Model of Socioemotional aging (SIMS), which focuses on understanding the effects of social relationships on individuals of different ages. The model incorporates existing research to expand an understanding of how and why individuals react to their interpersonal relationships as they do.

This model addresses the experiences older adults evoke from their social world by considering age variability in the types of relationships people have, what they bring to their relationships, and the behaviors they evoke from their social partners. Structural factors expose older and younger adults to different types of social partners. For example, compared to younger adults, older adults are more likely to live alone, less likely to be engaged in a paid work setting, and more likely to encounter health care personnel. These differences in social contacts render responses to the social world distinct. In comparison to younger adults, older adults also tend to have older social partners, embedded in longer-enduring relationships. Relationships that have endured for years may weather problems and irritations better than newly forming relationships. Furthermore, age-associated differences in emotion regulation and behaviors allow older adults to perceive their relationships in ways that are generally beneficial. Because older adults are less likely to get upset in general, they are also less likely to be angry or irritated with social partners (Birditt & Fingerman, 2003).

In addition, older adults may evoke specific types of social input, such as positive reactions from friends and family. In a feedback loop, older adults bring greater investment and equanimity to their relationships, and their partners may respond in kind. Relationships involve dynamics between social partners, including the way they perceive and treat one another (Fingerman & Lang, 2004; Hinde, 1997). As such, adults' socioemotional reactions may reflect social input they receive. Social input involves stimuli to which adults are exposed, such as the way social partners treat them and the reactions they evoke from those partners. Research presented in this chapter suggests that older adults tend to view their social ties in a favorable manner, and their social world often supports positive views of relationships.

A fundamental issue in future research involves examining the interface between individual and environmental influences on positive and negative reactions to relationships. Researchers have rarely considered how social input contributes to age differences in positive aspects of relationships, however. Researchers have demonstrated that social partners may encourage deficits and declines among older adults residing in nursing homes (Baltes, 1996), but input from the social world may also foster positive socioemotional reactions in late life (Fingerman, 2003).

Research applying the SIMS model cannot encompass all possible variables; such research risks descending into a list of variables and associations rather than theoretically meaningful data. To apply this model to meaningful research questions, specific components of the model need to be defined at each level. For example, investigators might consider the experiences of older adults as they make the transition into retirement. Our prior work suggests that the workplace may be a venue for problematic social encounters (e.g., Fingerman, Hay, et al., 2004).

A first level of analysis might involve examination of the macro- and microstructural components of social networks, examining how the configuration of the social network changes pre- and postretirement. Associated with these shifts may come changes in individuals' psychological reactions to relationships, including investment in family, motivation for close ties, and emotional rewards in those ties.

Researchers might also assess social partners' reactions to the retiring individual. Research in the field of child development often includes teachers' reports or parental assessments in studies of children's adaptations on a variety of measures. Surprisingly few studies attempt to assess such perspectives in the adult development literature. In the hypothetical study proposed here, the preretirement assessment might measure stress in the workplace. If the stress level in the workplace is high, the older adult may become more relaxed and thus evoke more positive reactions from close family and friends following retirement.

Researchers might consider similar approaches to investigate a variety of other topics: the effects of health impairments on older adults' relationships, variability in older widows' social integration a year after bereavement, and age differences in young-old and oldest-old adults' perceptions of assistance, for example. The possibilities allow for further integration of disparate disciplines examining socioemotional aging across a range of issues.

In sum, human experience includes emotional and social experiences from the beginning of life. Humans are an inherently social species with an emotional activation system that functions to regulate interactions with the world around them. As individuals grow older and accumulate experiences, their abilities to regulate socioemotional experiences seem to improve. The fiery, argumentative conflicts of adolescence give way to mellow, golden-hued emotional rewards of late life. Few other areas of aging allow for such a positive assessment, but with regard to socioemotional aging, most individuals can believe that the best is yet to come.

REFERENCES

Akiyama, H., Antonucci, T., Takahashi, K., & Langfahl, E. S. (2003). Negative interactions in close relationships across the lifespan. *Journal of Gerontology: Psychological Sciences, 58B,* P70–P79.

Antonucci, T. C., & Akiyama, H. (1987). Social networks in adult life and a preliminary examination of the convoy model. *Journals of Gerontology, 42,* P519–P527.

Antonucci, T. C., Lansford, J. E., Akiyama, H., Smith, J., Baltes, M. M. Takahashi, K., et al. (2002). Differences between men and women in social relations, resource deficits, and depressive symptomatology during later life in four nations. *Journal of Social Issues, 58,* 767–783.

Baltes, M. M. (1996). *The many faces of dependency in old age.* New York: Cambridge University Press.

Baltes, P. B. (1987). Theoretical propositions of life-span developmental psychology: On the dynamics between growth and decline. *Developmental Psychology, 23,* 611–626.

Baltes, P. B., & Baltes, M. M. (1990). *Successful aging: Perspectives from the social sciences.* New York: Cambridge University Press.

Baltes, P. B., & Smith, J. (2003). New frontiers in the future of aging: From successful aging of the young old to the dilemmas of the fourth age. *Gerontology, 49,* 123–135.

Becker, G., Beyene, Y., Newsom, E., & Mayen, N. (2003). Creating continuity through mutual assistance: Intergenerational reciprocity in four ethnic groups. *Journal of Gerontology: Social Sciences, 58B,* S151–S159.

Bedford, V. H. (1989). Understanding the value of siblings in old age: A proposed model. *American Behavioral Scientist, 33,* 33–44.

Birditt, K. S., & Fingerman, K. L. (2003). Age and gender differences in adults' emotional reactions to interpersonal tensions. *Journal of Gerontology: Psychological Sciences, 58B,* P237–P245.

Birditt, K. S., Fingerman, K. L., & Almeida, D. (2005). Age and gender differences in reported reactions to interpersonal tensions: A daily diary study. *Psychology; Aging, 20,* 330–340.

Blanchard-Fields, F., Jahnke, H. C., & Camp, C. (1995). Age differences in problem-solving style: The role of emotional salience. *Psychology and Aging, 10,* 173–180.

Carstensen, L. L., & Frederickson, B. L. (1998). Influence of HIV status and age on cognitive representations of others. *Health Psychology, 17,* 494–503.

Carstensen, L. L., Fung, H. H., & Charles, S. T. (2003). Socioemotional selectivity theory and the regulation of emotion in the second half of life. *Motivation and Emotion, 27,* 103–124.

Carstensen, L. L., Isaacowitz, D. M., & Charles, S. T. (1999). Taking time seriously: A theory of socioemotional selectivity. *American Psychologist, 54,* 165–181.

Carstensen, L. L., Pasupathi, M., Mayr, U., & Nesselroade, J. R. (2000). Emotional experience in everyday life across the adult life span. *Journal of Personality and Social Psychology, 79,* 644–655.

Charles, S. T., & Mavandadi, S. (2004). Social support and physical health across the life span: Socioemotional influences. In F. Lang & K. L. Fingerman (Eds.), *Growing together: Personal relationships across the life span* (pp. 240–267). New York: Cambridge University Press.

Charles, S. T., Reynolds, C. A., & Gatz, M. A. (2001). Age related differences and change in positive and negative affect over 23 years. *Journal of Personality and Social Psychology, 80,* 136–151.

Coontz, S. (2000). Historical perspectives on family studies. *Journal of Marriage and the Family, 62,* 283–297.

Cumming, E., & Henry, W. (1961). *Growing old: The process of disengagement.* New York: Basic Books.

Femia, E. E., Zarit, S. H., & Johansson, B. (2001). The disablement process in very late life: A study of oldest-old in Sweden. *Journals of Gerontology: Psychological Sciences, 56B,* P12–P23.

Fingerman, K. L. (1996). Sources of tension in the aging mother and adult daughter relationship. *Psychology and Aging, 11,* 591–606.

Fingerman, K. L. (1998). The good, the bad, and the worrisome: Complexities in grandparents' relationships with individual grandchildren. *Family Relations, 47,* 403–414.

Fingerman, K. L. (2003). *Mothers and their adult daughters: Mixed emotions, enduring bonds.* Amherst, NY: Prometheus Books.

Fingerman, K. L. (2004). The role of offspring and children-in-law in grandparents' ties to their grandchildren. *Journal of Family Issues, 25(B),* 1026–1049.

Fingerman, K. L., & Birditt, K. S. (2003). Do age differences in close and problematic social ties reflect the pool of available relatives? *Journal of Gerontology: Psychological Sciences, 58B,* P80–P87.

Fingerman, K. L., & Griffiths, P. C. (1999). Season's greetings: Adults' social contact at the holiday season. *Psychology and Aging, 14,* 192–205.

Fingerman, K. L., Hay, E. L., & Birditt, K. S. (2004). The best of ties, the worst of ties: Close, problematic, and ambivalent relationships across the lifespan. *Journal of Marriage and Family, 66,* 792–808.

Fingerman, K. L., & Lang, F. (2004). Coming together: A lifespan perspective on personal relationships. In F. Lang & K. L. Fingerman (Eds.), *Growing together: Personal relationships across the life span* (pp. 1–23). New York: Cambridge University Press.

Fingerman, K. L., Nussbaum, J., & Birditt, K. S. (2004). Keeping all five balls in the air: Juggling family communication at midlife. In A. L. Vangelisti (Ed.), *Handbook of family communication* (pp. 135–152). Hillsdale, NJ: Erlbaum.

Frederickson, B., & Carstensen, L. L. (1990). Choosing social partners: How old age and potential endings make people more selective. *Psychology and Aging, 5,* 335–347.

Fung, H. H., Carstensen, L., & Lutz, A.M. (1999). Influence of time on social preferences: Implications for life-span development. *Psychology and Aging, 14,* 595–604.

Heckhausen, J., & Schulz, R. (1995). A life-span theory of control. *Psychological Review, 102,* 284–304.

Helson, R., Kwan, V. S. Y., John, O. P., & Jones, C. (2002). The growing evidence for personality change in adulthood: Findings from research with personality inventories. *Journal of Research in Personality, 36,* 287–306.

Hinde, R. A. (1997). *Relationships. A dialectical perspective.* Hove, East Sussex, Great Britain: Psychology Press.

Ingersoll-Dayton, B., & Talbott, M. M. (1992). Assessments of social support exchanges: Cognitions of the old-old. *International Journal of Aging and Human Development, 35,* 125–143.

Johnson, C., & Barer, B. (1997). *Life beyond 85 years: The aura of survivorship.* New York: Springer Publishing.

Kahn, R. L., & Rowe, J. W. (1998). *Successful aging.* New York: Random House.

King, V., & Elder, G. H. (1995). American children view their grandparents: Linked lives across three rural generations. *Journal of Marriage and the Family, 57,* 165–178.

Knight, B. G., Gatz, M., Heller, K., & Bengtson, V. L. (2000). Age and emotional response to the Northridge earthquake: A longitudinal analysis. *Psychology and Aging, 15,* 627–634.

Labouvie-Vief, G. (2003). Dynamic integration: Affect, cognition, and the self in adulthood. *Current Directions in Psychological Science, 12,* 201–206.

Labouvie-Vief, G., Lumley, M. A., Jain, E., & Heinze, H. (2003). Age and gender differences in cardiac reactivity and subjective emotion responses to emotional autobiographical memories. *Emotion, 3,* 115–126.

Lang, F. R., & Carstensen, L. L. (2002). Time counts: Future time perspective, goals, and social relationships. *Psychology and Aging, 17,* 125–139.

Lansford, J. E., Sherman, A. M., & Antonucci, T. C. (1998). Satisfaction with social networks: An examination of socioemotional selectivity theory across cohorts. *Psychology and Aging, 13,* 544–563.

Lefkowitz, E. S., & Fingerman, K. L. (2003). Positive and negative emotional feelings and behaviors in mother-daughter ties in late life. *Journal of Family Psychology, 17,* 607–617.

Levenson, R. W, Carstensen, L. L., & Gottman, J. M. (1993). Long-term marriage: Age, gender, and satisfaction. *Psychology and Aging, 8,* 301–313.

Litwak, E. (1965). Extended kin relations in an industrialized democracy. In E. Shanas & G. F. Streib (Eds.), *Social structure and family: Generational relations.* Englewood Cliffs, NJ: Prentice Hall.

Lüscher, K., & Pillemer, K. (1998). Intergenerational ambivalence: A new approach to the study of parent-child relations in later life. *Journal of Marriage and the Family, 60,* 413–425.

Mather, M., Canli, T., English, T., Whitfield, S., Wais, P., Ochsner, K., et al. (2004). Amygdala responses to emotionally valenced stimuli in older and younger adults. *Psychological Science, 15,* 259–263.

Morgan, D. L. (1989). Adjusting to widowhood. *Gerontologist, 29,* 101–107.

Moss, M. S., Moss, S. Z., & Moles, E. L. (1985). The quality of relationships between elderly parents and their out-of-town children. *Gerontologist, 25,* 134–140.

Mroczek, D. K. (2001). Age and emotion in adulthood. *Current Directions in Psychological Science, 10,* 87–89.

National Center for Health Statistics. (2001). *Health, United States.* Retrieved March 1, 2002, from http://www.cdc.gov/nchs/products/pubs/pubd/hus/tables/2001/01hus057.pdf

Ong, A. D., & Bergman, C. S. (2004). The complexity of emotions in late life. *Journals of Gerontology: Psychological Sciences, 59B,* P117–P122.

Ong, A. D., Bergman, C. S., & Bisconti, T. L. (2004). The role of daily positive emotions during conjugal bereavement. *Journals of Gerontology: Psychological Sciences, 59B,* P168–P177.

Parsons, T. (1943). The kinship system of the contemporary United States. *American Anthropologist, 45,* 22–28.

Pillemer, K., & Suitor, J. J. (2002). Explaining mothers' ambivalence toward their adult children. *Journal of Marriage and Family, 64,* 602–613.

Rook, K. S. (1984). The negative side of social interaction: Impact on psychological well-being. *Journal of Personality and Social Psychology, 46,* 1097–1108.

Rook, K. S. (2003). Exposure and reactivity to negative social exchanges: A preliminary investigation using daily diary data. *Journals of Gerontology, Series B: Psychological Sciences and Social Sciences, 58B,* P100–P111.

Rossi, A. S., & Rossi, P. H. (1990). *Of human bonding: Parent-child relations across the life course.* New York: Aldine de Gruyter.

Rosow, I. (1970). Older people: Their friends and neighbors. *American Behavioral Scientist, 14,* 59–69.

Shanas, E., & Streib G. F. (Eds.). (1965). *Social structure and family: Generational relation.* Englewood Cliffs, NJ: Prentice Hall.

Smith, J., & Goodnow, J. J. (1999). Unasked-for support and unsolicited advice: Age and quality of social experience. *Psychology and Aging, 14,* 108–121.

Suthers, K., Kim, J. K., & Crimmins, E. (2003). Life expectancy with cognitive impairment in the older population of the United States. *Journal of Gerontology: Social Sciences, 58B,* S179–S186.

Uchino, B. N., Holt-Lunstad, J., Uno, D., & Flinders, J. B. (2001). Heterogeneity in the social networks of young and older adults: Prediction of mental health and cardiovascular reactivity during acute stress. *Journal of Behavioral Medicine, 24,* 361–382.

Umberson, D. (1989). Relationships with children: Explaining parents' psychological well-being. *Journal of Marriage and the Family, 51,* 999–1012.

Walker, A. J., & Pratt, C. C. (1995). Informal caregiving to aging family members: A critical review. *Family Relations, 44,* 402–412.

Willson, A. E., Shuey, K. M., & Elder, G. H. (2003). Ambivalence in the relationship of adult children to aging parents and in-laws. *Journal of Marriage and Family, 65,* 1055–1072.

Zarit, S., Reever, K., & Bach-Peterson, J. (1980). Relatives of the impaired elderly: Correlates of feelings of burden. *Gerontologist, 20,* 649–655.

CHAPTER 10

Age Structures, Aging, and the Life Course

Linda K. George

Among sociologists, the terms *gerontology* and *social gerontology* are evolving. The term *aging* remains a key concept, defined as multilevel processes that unfold over time, especially processes that are consistently observed across place and historical time. But the term *life course* has become the dominant concept for thinking about and understanding the social significance of age and aging. What are we to make of this change in vocabulary? Is the term *life course* simply a professional fad, similar, for example, to the recent trend in which disadvantaged subgroups are labeled "challenged" rather than "handicapped" or "disabled"? Or does this change in vocabulary signal something more fundamental, profound, and distinctive about the way we think about and study human lives?

In this chapter, I argue that life course perspectives represent a fundamental change in our understanding of human lives. I seek to demonstrate that life course perspectives offer a richer, more dynamic view of human lives than other research strategies. Even more important, I hope to provide convincing evidence that life course perspectives better highlight the roles of social structure and social context in aging than other research designs are able to do. This chapter is organized in four sections. In the first, core principles of life course research are described. The second section reviews three research topics that constitute milestones in life course sociology—research that sets the stage for future efforts and continues to influence life course research. The third section focuses on the intersections between life course research and mainstream sociology, with primary focus on the ways in which life course research contributes to issues confronting social science more broadly. The final section highlights some of the challenges that investigators confront in life course research.

Although the major focus of this chapter is on the strengths of life course research, other important research questions about aging remain. That is, life course perspectives will not and should not totally replace research that is restricted to contemporaneous and short-term longitudinal studies of older adults. Indeed, life course perspectives are either unnecessary or inappropriate for many research questions. Three examples are illustrative of a larger set of research questions for which life course perspectives and methods are not needed. First, when the goal of research is to understand heterogeneity among older adults and it is not important to know the long-term determinants of that heterogeneity (which is often the case for policy research, for example), longitudinal studies covering long periods of time are not needed. Second, some phenomena are exclusively or nearly exclusively relevant to late life. Efforts to understand these phenomena are likely to ignore earlier segments of the life course, with few, if any, negative repercussions. If, for example, we wish to identify the predictors of institutionalization or hospice care in late life, it is likely that the strongest predictors can be identified in the absence of data about study participants' childhoods and early adult years. Third, research intended to evaluate the effects of interventions designed to promote well-being among older adults can generate compelling evidence in the absence of life course data.

Let me also note from the outset my recognition that past is prologue to the future in personal biography as well as in the evolution of science. There is no definitive line between gerontology and life course sociology. Moreover, life course research builds on gerontology as well as other sociological traditions—and, in turn, is enriching and changing gerontological research. I am not creating an artificial dichotomy, but rather illustrating how our understanding of aging has evolved.

LIFE COURSE PERSPECTIVES: CORE PRINCIPLES

Let us consider what life course perspectives bring to the sociological table that traditional gerontological research and other sociological traditions do not. It is important to recognize that there is no unified life course theory—nor, I would argue, should there be. Rather, life course perspectives rest on a set of core principles. There is probably dissensus in the field about all of the core characteristics of life course perspectives, but four principles are consistently viewed as central to them (Elder, George, & Shanahan, 1996). Each will be briefly described.

First, however, a note on semantics is in order. Most authors use the term *the life course perspective*. In contrast, I use the plural term: *life course perspectives*. I use the plural phrase for two reasons. First there is no unified theory of the life course and, to me, *the life course perspective* conveys a level of consensus and integration that is misleading. Second, investigations need not include all four core principles to qualify as life course research. Attention to temporality is undoubtedly a universal characteristic of life course research. The other three principles are not universal in life course research, although they are commonly addressed in it. Again, it seems to me that *life course perspectives* is a more realistic descriptor of the loose coupling of concepts that characterizes the field.

Emphasis on Temporality in the Long Term

The most basic and most obvious principle in life course research is that human lives unfold over long periods of time and that experiences and conditions early in the life course set processes in motion that have long-term consequences. One cannot understand late life, for example, without taking into account individuals' earlier lives. This basic principle has been understood by gerontological investigators for decades. Indeed, the first Duke Longitudinal Study of Aging began in 1955 with a sample of adults age 65 and older. But the investigators of this classic study soon were convinced that they needed to begin their observations earlier in life, and the Second Longitudinal Study of Aging was initiated in 1968 with a cohort of adults age 45 to 64. Despite early recognition of the potential importance of long-term longitudinal data, the availability and use of data covering large segments of the life course is very recent.

Conceptually, life course scholars think about long-term patterns of stability and change as trajectories or pathways. Consequently, in life course research, there is a dual emphasis on intraindividual change and interindividual differences. At the intraindividual level, investigators focus on the linkages between early events and experiences and their long-term outcomes; at the interindividual level, the emphasis is on comparisons of groups whose trajectories differ in origin, shape, or rate of change—or all of these. When examining trajectories, *origin* refers to differences in beginning states (at baseline), *shape* refers to the form of the trajectory (e.g., linear increase, U-shaped curve), and *rate of change* is observed in the steepness of the curve (the steeper the curve, the more rapid the rate of change).

Emphasis on the Intersection of Personal Biography and Social Change

A second principle of life course research focuses on the fact that the individual life course is historically embedded and reflects, to a significant degree, the conditions, constraints, and opportunities of the historical context. Life course research based on this principle often focuses on the ways that major historical events, such as the Great Depression (Elder, 1974) or participation in World War II (Hastings, 1991; Hautamaeki & Coleman, 2001; Hunt & Robbins, 2001; Major, 2003), impinge on the lives of individuals and the persisting effects of those historical events. There is clear evidence, for example, that cohorts who were children and adolescents during the Great Depression differ in many ways—ranging from political attitudes to occupational careers to marital stability—from cohorts who preceded and succeeded them. Public policies, such as the introduction of the GI bill at the end of World War II, also can drastically alter the opportunities available to individuals (Elder, 1986; Sampson & Laub, 1996). Again, the dual emphasis on intraindividual change and interindividual differences is important. At the interindividual level, social change is likely to differentiate cohorts who experience the change from those who precede and follow them. At the intraindividual level, however, the effects of social change can differ substantially (e.g., life course consequences of the Great Depression differed depending on the level of deprivation experienced).

Explicit recognition of the links between social change and personal biography serves another important function: highlighting the ways in which and mechanisms by which social structure penetrates individual lives. Explicating macro-micro links has been an important goal of the social sciences for decades, but securing compelling evidence has proven to be difficult. Tracing the contemporaneous and persisting effects of social change on individuals' lives over time has proved to be an effective strategy for documenting how social structure affects personal biography.

Emphasis on Linked Lives

A third principle of life course perspectives is the notion of linked lives: the recognition that humans are linked to others in complex ways and that these connections are powerful forces in personal biography. Several implications of this principle merit mention. First, attention to linked lives increases the ability to explain interindividual differences in many life course outcomes. For example, controlling on a myriad of other variables, the effects of employment on women's health are contingent on marital status and the presence of minor children in the home (Ali & Avison, 1997; Wethington & Kessler, 1989). Second, as implied by this example, social bonds frequently have spillover effects (Stets, 1995), affecting not just the obvious domains of family and friends, but also less closely linked domains such as work and community involvement. In this sense, the principle of linked lives alerts us to the fact that central topics in social science theories (e.g., occupational careers) will be incompletely understood without taking into account other domains of life experience. In short, attention to linked lives more accurately describes the context within which decisions are made and life is experienced than an overly narrow view of individuals as independent actors.

Emphasis on Human Agency

The final principle of life course research is a focus on the power of human agency and, conversely, rejection of an oversocialized view of human lives (Wrong, 1961). At the same time that life course perspectives highlight the opportunities and constraints imposed by social structure, they also focus attention on individual decisions and the long-term consequences of those decisions. As a historical example, consider the GI bill enacted at the end of World War II. Many veterans eligible for the GI bill used it to obtain higher levels of education than would otherwise have been available to them; most, however, did not. Tracing the socioeconomic achievements of those who did and did not use the GI bill enables us to understand the full economic consequences of this decision. An especially attractive aspect of focusing on human agency is the ability to identify the conditions under which individual decisions literally become turning points in the life course—times at which some individuals sharply increase the rewards or resources available to them, as well as decisions that result in deprivation. Identification of individual decisions that yield improvements in life quality, as variously defined, provides information that can be used to target interventions and encourage productive decisions.

MILESTONES IN LIFE COURSE SOCIOLOGY

The importance of life course principles for understanding human lives can best be appreciated by seeing them in action. In this section, I review three major early life course contributions that were critical in establishing the utility of life course perspectives and that remain key contributions to life course sociology: age stratification theory, social change and personal biography, and the social construction of the life course.

Age Stratification Theory

Social stratification is a core—arguably *the* core—sociological concept. It refers to the allocation of goods and resources to societal members. In addition, stratification systems define the conditions under which and the extent to which individuals are able to move up and down the status hierarchy. In American sociology, economic status has been the primary focus of stratification theory and research. Thousands of articles and hundreds of books have addressed the distribution of income, power, and privilege in U.S. society and the extent to which upward mobility is possible and achieved.

Despite the results of comparative research in anthropology, which has long documented stratification systems other than those based on economics (e.g., Simmons, 1945), only recently have multiple and competing stratification systems in the United States been taken seriously. Sociologists now recognize that age, race, and gender are all powerful forms of stratification.

It was the seminal work of Matilda White Riley that provided a rich conceptualization of age stratification and its life course implications. Riley's conceptualization and elaboration of age stratification theory span several decades (e.g., Riley, Johnson, & Foner, 1972; Riley, 1976; Riley, Foner, & Riley, 1999). Age stratification theory rests on three premises: (1) there are identifiable age strata that are formally and informally institutionalized, (2) age strata differ in the value placed on them, and (3) rights and responsibilities are differentially allocated across age strata. Riley posits three primary age groups in U.S. society: early life, middle age, and old age. In terms of societal value, middle-aged adults, who occupy key positions in the social structure, are valued most and are allocated greater power and privilege than other age strata. In contrast, old age is the least-valued age stratum, and its members enjoy less power and fewer privileges than their younger peers.

One of the differences between socioeconomic status (SES) and other stratification systems relates to the possibility of mobility up and down the hierarchy. At one end of the continuum are stratification systems based on ascribed, unchangeable statuses such as gender and race. Stratification based on ascribed statuses precludes mobility, although cultural change can alter the distance between strata, as many would argue has happened for race and gender as a result of the civil rights and women's movements. At the other end of the continuum are stratification systems based on achieved status, which permit upward and downward mobility. SES is clearly the primary example of stratification based on achieved status, although all societal members do not enter the contest for high SES with the same resources. Age stratification has a different dynamic. Age itself is an ascribed status, but the aging process ensures that every societal member who lives to old age traverses all the age strata. Such movement is very different from upward and downward mobility in the SES hierarchy.

As Riley and her colleagues note, two fundamental dynamics underlie age stratification. At the individual level, one traverses the life course as one ages. But the unfolding of personal lives is embedded in social and cultural change as well. This dual dynamic highlights the importance of cohorts: each cohort traverses its life course in a specific historical context. There is now overwhelming evidence that growing older differs substantially depending on the social, cultural, and historical contexts within which it is experienced.

In her later writings, Riley linked age stratification theory to the concept of age integration (Riley & Riley, 1994). She points out that what is now viewed as the natural or normal life course—in which early adulthood is devoted to the acquisition of human capital, middle age is dominated by labor force participation, and old age is a time for leisure—rests on social convention rather than biological necessity. She argues forcefully for concurrent rather than separate age-graded pursuit of these domains. Specifically, she posits that education, paid work, and leisure should be pursued in tandem across adulthood. A compelling case is made that integration of the major tasks of adulthood would both generate higher-quality lives for societal members and better use the talents of societal members for societal goals. Another rationale for age integration is the strain that the current system of age segmentation places on families. Riley also argues that the dynamism between cohorts and social change is reciprocal: social change shapes cohort's life experiences, but cohorts change social structure through collective action. In addition, age integration would largely eliminate age stratification, bringing an end to one form of institutionalized inequality.

Age stratification theory has a rather unique role in life course sociology. On the one hand, little, if any, research directly tests its central propositions. On the other hand, a large proportion of life course research, in which other theories are the basis of specific hypotheses, is compatible with age stratification theory. Indeed, I am not aware of a single study that is discrepant with age stratification theory. Some have argued that age stratification theory is not really a theory in the sense of leading to specific and testable hypotheses, suggesting that it is better viewed as an orienting conceptual framework. Whether it meets the technical criteria of constituting a theory, the age stratification perspective incorporates life course principles of temporality, the intersection of social change and personal biography, linked lives, and human agency. Perhaps the greatest contribution of age stratification theory is that it linked aging and the life course to mainstream sociology. Aging will never again be viewed as marginal to the core concerns of the sociological enterprise.

Social Change and Personal Biography

Although there were earlier studies examining lives from childhood through adulthood, Glen Elder's *Children of the Great Depression* (1974) laid the foundation for the sociological study of the life course for the past quarter-century. The title of the book describes its content. Elder creatively used data from the 1930s through the mid-1960s to trace the lives of cohorts who were children and adolescents during the Great Depression. The book's subtitle, *Social Change in Life Experience*, highlights the sociological underpinnings of the research: tracing the effects of the childhood economic disruptions on long-term achievements.

My goal is not to review the complex and intriguing findings of Elder's work, but rather to describe the ways that this early work set the stage for what is now known as life course sociology. First, the major focus of this work is temporality—identifying the short- and long-term effects of the economic deprivation generated by the Great Depression. Elder examines a variety of outcomes. Short-term outcomes include family dynamics during the depression, children's self-concepts, and academic achievements. Adult outcomes include occupational status, attitudes toward work, marital relationships and quality, parenthood, and personality (primarily self-concept). The recognition that a historical event can affect multiple domains of life experience has become a key characteristic of life course perspectives.

Another facet of the focus on temporality is identifying the processes by which early events and experiences do and do not have long-term effects. Elder observed substantial heterogeneity in the short- and long-term effects of the depression. Some of the sample exhibited patterns of sustained deprivation; others overcame conditions of early poverty and family disruption to achieve high levels of occupational success and family stability. Elder demonstrates that acquiring human and social capital during early adulthood was critical in the ability to overcome early deprivation, but so too was human agency. Indeed, individuals differed widely in the extent to which they persevered in efforts to obtain the human and social capital needed for success.

One of the most important contributions of this seminal work is the recognition that social change does not affect all cohort members in the same ways or to the same degree. A critical factor was the amount of economic disruption experienced by children's families during the depression. Some families suffered severe decreases in income; others experienced relatively little deprivation. Moreover, the amount of economic deprivation caused by the depression interacted with previous SES. One of the most fascinating findings of Elder's research is the fact that high SES prior to the depression, combined with severe economic loss during the depression, was associated with high levels of success during adulthood, providing empirical support (but only under specific conditions) for the adage that adversity builds character.

Personal characteristics also interacted with the effects of the depression in complex ways. Adaptation to the immediate effects of the depression took different forms for fathers and mothers, boys and girls. The long-term effects of the depression also differed substantially by gender, with men exhibiting unusually strong attachments to the labor market and women overwhelmingly forgoing paid work for full-time homemaking.

Finally, the principle of linked lives is prominently observed in Elder's study. During the depression, children's lives were intertwined with those of their parents and siblings, with boys often required to contribute to family finances through part-time or intermittent work. Mothers' and fathers' lives were contingent as well, with mothers frequently working outside the home when their husbands were unable to secure employment. These altered family roles changed the distribution of power and privilege in the family.

Children of the Great Depression quickly and deservedly became a classic. Gerontological investigators, who were already proponents of longitudinal research and had long grappled with separating the effects of age and cohort, quickly embraced life course perspectives, especially for research questions concerning the origins of heterogeneity in late life. But this book also impressed the broader sociological community. For this broader audience, it was the ability to link personal experience with social change that caught the sociological imagination. The body of life course research has grown immensely since 1974, but it was Elder's creative and compelling work that set the stage for prominently placing personal biography, with all its complexities, on the sociological map.

Social Construction of the Life Course

With its strong attention to history and social change, it is not surprising that scholars rather quickly asked themselves about the history of the life course itself. In fact, family historians had addressed this issue to some degree, pointing out that throughout human history, some people have lived to advanced old ages (e.g., Demos, 1978). However, it was not until the twentieth century that old age became part of the typical life course. Part of the explanation for the emergence of the life course as it has been defined and studied rests on simple survivorship. It was not until the majority of adults lived to late life that old age became a predictable segment of the life course (Hagestad, 1990; Uhlenberg, 1980).

But there is more to the emergence of the life course than increased life expectancy. In a now classic study, Mayer and Muller (1986) documented the strong links between social structure, in the form of the state, and the modern view of the life course. They argue that the institutionalization of age norms (e.g., required schooling, elimination of child labor, and, later, age at eligibility for state-supported retirement benefits) and the rise of the various forms of the welfare state played critical roles in the social and cultural construction of the life course. At the same time, Meyer (1986) identified the links between the social construction of the life course and the modern sense of the self. The institutionalized life course encouraged what Meyer calls an individualized and "temporalized" view of self—individualized because the rules and regulations of the welfare state are tied to individual rights and responsibilities; temporalized by the sequence of age requirements for political and economic participation as well as for receipt of welfare state resources. Scholars who have studied the emergence of the life course agree that the advent of the welfare state catalyzed processes that had been playing out for centuries, especially the shift from the family as a unit of economic production to a unit of consumption and the related movement of education and jobs from households to social institutions (Esping-Andersen, 1997).

The historical, archival, and comparative research that documented the emergence and social construction of the life course differs from other life course research, which traces individuals over long periods of time. Nonetheless, this research tradition also attends to the core principles of life course research. The attention paid to temporality and the intersection of social structure and personal biography are obvious. Although this brief review has not focused on the role of human agency, that principle is not neglected in this research tradition. Indeed, the social construction of personal agency is a key component of Meyer's explication of the links between the emergence of the life course and the modern sense of self. The principle of linked lives also has not been neglected. For example, substantial attention has been paid to the effects of the modern life course on household-based division of labor (Heath, Ciscel, & Sharp, 1998; Stolzenberg, 2001), length of time spent in family roles (Gee, 1986; Watkins, Menken, & Bongaarts, 1987), and the characteristics and quality of both intragenerational and intergenerational relationships (Imhoff, 1986; Silverstein & Bengtson, 1997).

KEY CONTRIBUTIONS TO MAINSTREAM SOCIOLOGY

Thus far, I have outlined the core principles of life course sociology and briefly reviewed three classic contributions that are cornerstones of life course research and illustrate life course principles in action. In this section, I focus on more recent and broader themes of life course research that constitute key contributions to mainstream sociology. Because of space limitations, this section is restricted to three research themes.

Social Selection and Social Causation

The distinction between social selection and social causation has long been a central concern in social science research. Social causation hypotheses posit that a specific social factor has a deterministic, causal effect on an outcome of interest. Social selection hypotheses posit the reverse causal order: that the outcome is in fact the determinant of the social factor under consideration. This debate can be found in many sociological research traditions, but is probably most prominent in the study of social factors and health where, for example, scholars debate whether SES has a causal impact on health (social causation) or poor health leads to downward social mobility (social selection) (e.g., Smith, 1999). Another example is the relationship between social support and depressive symptoms. Does lack of social support increase the risk of depression (social causation), or are depressed individuals unable to develop and sustain high-quality social relationships (social selection) (e.g., Johnson, 1991)?

It has long been recognized that one cannot begin to unravel the direction of causality without longitudinal data. A study in which, for example, social support at baseline is observed to predict changes in depression between baseline and a later measurement point provides much stronger evidence of social causation than is possible with cross-sectional data. Nonetheless, even these kinds of longitudinal analyses cannot rule out selection effects because the investigator cannot know that social support at baseline does not result in part from depressive symptoms earlier in the life course.

Thus, selection effects are a methodological threat to inferences of social causation. It seems safe to assume that investigators typically are not substantively interested in selection processes; rather, they wish to eliminate or control selection effects in order to obtain unbiased estimates of hypothesized causal agents. And, indeed, the most sophisticated studies attempt to statistically control or estimate selection effects. One method of accomplishing this is to perform analyses both ways by examining variable X's effect on Y and estimating variable Y's effect on X, then to assume social causation if variable X's effect on Y is stronger than the reverse (see Murray, 2000, and Ross & Mirowsky, 1995 for empirical examples). Another strategy is to use statistical adjustments (e.g., the Heckman procedure [1979]) to estimate selection effects in a first step and then estimate social causation effects in a second step with selection effects statistically controlled.

An important contribution of life course perspectives has been to transform the distinction between social selection and social causation from statistical conundrum to recognition that examining long-term patterns of change and stability subsumes both social selection and social causation. On logical grounds, the distinction between social selection and social causation is less meaningful than it appears. Let us assume that I am interested in the effects of employment on women's health. From the traditional social selection/causation framework, I want to demonstrate that the direction of causality is from employment to health rather than the reverse. My concern is that healthier women are selected into employment. Let us also assume that I have a colleague who is interested in identifying the determinants of labor force participation among women. If my colleague finds that health is a significant predictor of women's employment, he will have to worry about the extent to which employment affects health rather than the reverse. Clearly, the selection and causation effects about which investigators must be concerned are a function of the research question.

Life course perspectives, with their emphasis on long-term patterns of stability and change, focus on the interrelationships of variables over time. Complex patterns of both one-way and bidirectional change are anticipated and investigated using a variety of concepts seldom encountered in debates about selection and causation. These concepts include sequencing (pinpointing the order of changes), duration dependence (estimating change as a function of time spent in a given state), and timing (whether changes vary as a result of when they occur in the life course). Life course perspectives focus on the unfolding of individual lives without engaging in arguments about causation and selection.

Rate of Change: An Understudied Indicator of Social Processes

A necessary prerequisite for the flourishing of life course sociology is statistical techniques capable of testing the models implied by life course perspectives. A veritable statistical revolution has taken place over the past-quarter century—a revolution without which life course sociology would remain largely conceptual rather than empirical. I will briefly note three such analytical techniques and their implications for life course research.

Event history or survival models permit a straightforward analysis of time. For example, although logistic regression analysis can be used to predict the occurrence of an event, event history models predict "time 'til" an event (e.g., time until retirement) (Allison, 1984; Mayer & Tuma, 1990). When there are three or more waves of data, latent growth curve analysis (LGCA) allows the investigator to model and analyze trajectories of independent or dependent variables (Bryk & Roudenbush, 1992; McCardle & Hamagami, 1992). If, for example, an investigator is interested in trajectories of disability in later life, LGCA can be used to predict these trajectories. The coefficients for the independent variables are interpreted as the rate of growth in the disability trajectories (e.g., high levels of education may negatively predict rate of growth in disability over time, whereas the onset of chronic conditions positively predicts rate of growth). Finally, latent class analysis can be used to predict a set of trajectories that take distinct forms (e.g., a trajectory of linear growth over time versus a trajectory of linear decline over time or a J-shaped curve trajectory) (Vermunt & Magidson, 2000). The common element in these statistical methods is the attempt to model rates of change or growth, not simply the level of an outcome at the end of a period of observation.

The difference between predicting the occurrence of an event and the timing of that event can be substantial. For example, the strongest predictors of a transition may be very different from those that best predict time until the transition. Consider the relationship between teenage pregnancy and educational attainment. It is well known that teen births often disrupt the mothers' education. But are we more interested in determining if teen fertility predicts school dropout or whether it increases the time until education is completed? This is not an either-or choice, of course, because they are different research questions. Furstenberg and colleagues' longitudinal study of teenage mothers (Furstenberg, Brooks-Gunn, & Morgan, 1987) demonstrates that answers to these questions also are quite different. Their research documented immediate disruptions in teenage mothers' educations compared to their peers without children. By the middle of early adulthood, however, educational attainment was unrelated to teenage pregnancy, which disrupted but apparently did not truncate educational achievement. It is only recently that researchers have begun to seriously distinguish between predicting the occurrence of an event and predicting its timing.

Thinking in terms of rate of change is very different from thinking in terms of an outcome measured at one point in time—even if it is measured at the end of a longitudinal study. For example, various studies document that negative events reported at one point in time are associated with subsequent increases in depression. This research demonstrates that a static measure of stress predicts changes in depression between times of observation. More recently, we (George & Lynch, 2003; Lynch & George, 2000) used LGCA to demonstrate that rate of growth of loss-related events predicted rate of growth in depressive symptoms among older adults. The implications of these growth models extend beyond the empirical findings. Traditional debates about the explanatory power of stress exposure versus vulnerability to stress need to be reconceptualized to encompass dynamic processes of rate of growth of both stress and its outcomes. Thus, studying rate of change not only yields new empirical findings; it also forces us to confront the atemporal assumptions of the discipline's core theories.

Highlighting Social Context

Life course perspectives cannot take credit for the surge of interest in social context during the past two decades, but life course research has played a significant role in documenting the importance of embedding human action in social and historical context. Life course research to date has been especially vigilant in attending to the historical context during which cohorts traverse the life course. In some cases, historical context is a key element of the research question, such as studies that focus on the effects of the Great Depression (e.g., Elder, 1974), World War II (e.g., Hastings, 1991), and the civil rights movement (e.g., McAdam, 1989) on the life course. In addition, investigators whose research questions do not directly concern historical conditions increasingly provide information about the social context at the time data were collected (e.g., general economic conditions). One sequela of this is an increased proportion of mixed-mode research, involving both quantitative and qualitative methods.

Life course research also highlights social context through its emphases on the whole person and on linked lives. For example, life course researchers are unlikely to study patterns of labor force participation without also taking into account family composition and responsibilities. Although the language used in creating empirically complex models of human lives is not always that of social context, the effects of social context are in fact what are revealed.

CONTINUING CHALLENGES IN LIFE COURSE RESEARCH

Although life course research has made impressive strides, much more remains to be done. Many relevant topics have not yet been examined using life course perspectives, and only beginning efforts have been made for others. In addition, there are conceptual and methodological issues that challenge life course sociology. Three of these issues are reviewed briefly.

Is the "Value-Added" Approach the Appropriate Goal of Life Course Research?

One strategy for evaluating life course research is to determine whether it offers explanatory power over and above that generated by other approaches. For example, abundant cross-sectional evidence shows that married individuals enjoy better health than their unmarried peers (Gove, Style, & Hughes, 1990; Lillard & Waite, 1995; Waite & Gallagher, 2000). Recently, life course scholars have explored the possibility that marital history explains more variation in health outcomes than current marital status. In essence, marital history decomposes sources of heterogeneity masked by marital status (e.g., some of the currently married have been married once, others two or more times). Research to date suggests that marital history is a more powerful predictor of mental health than marital status (Barrett, 2000; Peters & Liefbroer, 1997).

A broader issue is the degree to which the utility of life course perspectives rests on their "value-added" explanatory power. I believe that an overemphasis on the value-added potential of life course research neglects many of its other contributions. The primary goal of life course research is to understand long-term patterns of stability and change as they unfold in social and historical context. Even in studies in which the effects of distal factors are totally "explained by" more proximal predictors, inclusion of distal factors elaborates our understanding of human lives. It is important for the field to develop informal norms concerning the conditions under which, and research questions for which, life course perspectives are and are not required

Aggregate Versus Disaggregated Trajectories

In studies that trace patterns across multiple time points, investigators face the decision of whether to use aggregate or disaggregated trajectories. Consider, for example, the situation in which a researcher wants to trace the effects of stress on health over time. There are two methods for constructing health trajectories. One option is to estimate the average health trajectory for the sample as a whole and determine the extent to which varying levels of stress explain variability around the average trajectory. LGCA does exactly that. A second option is to develop a set of decision rules that generate discrete and distinct trajectories, such as improving health over time, declining health over time, stable good health, and stable poor health. Latent class analysis then can be used to determine the extent to which stress is associated with these discrete trajectories. Statistically, both approaches are defensible, although LGCA has been used much more frequently in research to date.

Life course research will advance, I believe, if investigators develop informal norms for the choice of trajectory construction. Some of the criteria for those norms might include the following. First, and foremost, the choice of a trajectory analysis method should be determined primarily by the research question. To the extent that the investigator wishes to compare and contrast trajectories that take different forms, disaggregated trajectories estimated using latent class analysis would be the best choice. In contrast, if the investigator's goal is to determine the trajectory that best describes a population of interest, an aggregate trajectory estimated by LGCA would be sufficient and more parsimonious.

Empirical constraints also should be considered in selecting a method of trajectory analysis. Disaggregated trajectories are feasible only if the sample size is large, yielding sufficient observations for each trajectory to permit stable estimation. It also is valuable to examine variability around an average trajectory. Extreme variability around a trajectory, based on the sample as a whole, suggests that there are multiple, distinct patterns of change within the sample. In general, additional work is needed to compare the relative advantages of aggregated versus disaggregated trajectories and to understand the conditions under which and research questions for which each is best suited.

Is the Life Course Becoming Deinstitutionalized?

An important theme of life course research has been tracing the emergence and institutionalization of the modern life course. Life course scholars are increasingly grappling with the idea that the predictable, patterned life course is eroding as both a normative ideal and an empirical reality. The major evidence supporting the so-called deinstitutionalization of the life course is the immense heterogeneity observed in life course patterns, even over a relatively short segment of the life course. A study by Rindfuss, Swicegood, and Rosenfeld (1987) illustrates this point dramatically. Using data from the National Longitudinal Survey of the High School Class of 1972, the authors coded participants' sequences of five roles—work, education, homemaking, military, and a residual "other" category—for 8 years after high school graduation. They report that 1,100 sequences were required to describe the 6,700 men in the sample, and 1,800 sequences were needed for the 7,000 women. Clearly, this level of heterogeneity challenges the notion of a predictable transition to adulthood.

Deinstitutionalization of the life course also can be argued on more social structural grounds. During the past two to three decades, formal and informal age norms seem to have been eroding. In the United States, mandatory retirement is now illegal. In contrast to eligibility for social security retirement benefits, pension eligibility now usually rests on years of work rather than age. More informally, it is now common to observe older and middle-aged adults seeking formal education or changing careers. Along these lines, I would argue that the emergence of the individualized and temporal self that Meyer (1986) argues convincingly was both a product and producer of the institutionalized life course also is a prerequisite for the deinstitutionalized life course. The modern self works aggressively to base life course decisions on personal needs and preferences rather than on conventional timetables.

Debates about the extent to which the life course is institutionalized will undoubtedly continue for some time. Although many argue in favor of deinstitutionalization among recent cohorts, other researchers are uncovering evidence of new life course markers. Pettit and Western (2004), for example, argue that incarceration during young adulthood has become so prevalent among young African American men with low levels of education that it constitutes a predictable life course marker.

It is important to note that the future of life course research does not rest on the presence or absence of a predictable life course. The major challenge posed by the deinstitutionalized life course is heterogeneity in life course patterns. Basic life course principles concerning temporality, social and historical context, linked lives, and human agency remain key elements in our understanding of how individuals negotiate opportunities and constraints to construct their personal biographies.

In summary, life course perspectives offer a rich array of core principles, justification for collecting data from individuals for decades rather than shorter intervals, and statistical techniques that allow us to disentangle intraindividual change from interindividual differences. The increasing volume of life course research speaks to its value. It has the potential to permit us to identify pathways of deprivation and resilience in ways that previously were not possible. At their core, however, life course principles and life course research focus on lives unfolding over time, reflecting the consequences of proactive behavior, structural opportunities, and structural constraints. A number of years ago while I was interviewing an older woman for one of our research projects, she laughed and said, "You'll probably think this is funny, but sometimes I just like to sit on the porch and think back to what brought me here." It is a lovely thought and expresses the heart of life course research.

REFERENCES

Ali, J., & Avison, W. R. (1997). Employment transitions and psychological distress: The contrasting experiences of single and married mothers. *Journal of Health and Social Behavior, 38*, 345–362.

Allison, P. D. (1984). *Event history analysis: Regression for longitudinal event data*. Beverly Hills, CA: Sage.

Barrett, A. E. (2000). Marital trajectories and mental health. *Journal of Health and Social Behavior, 41*, 451–464.

Bryk, A. S., & Roudenbush, S. W. (1992). *Hierarchical linear models: Applications and data analysis methods*. Beverly Hills, CA: Sage.

Demos, J. (1978). Old age in early New England. *American Journal of Sociology, 84*(suppl.), S248–S287.

Elder, G. H., Jr. (1974). *Children of the Great Depression*. Chicago: University of Chicago Press.

Elder, G. H., Jr. (1986). Military times and turning points in men's lives. *Developmental Psychology, 22*, 233–245.

Elder, G. H., Jr., George, L. K., & Shanahan, M. J. (1996). Psychosocial stress over the life course. In H. B. Kaplan (Ed.), *Psychosocial stress: Perspectives on structure, theory, life course, and methods* (pp. 247–291). Orlando, FL: Academic Press.

Esping-Andersen, G. (1997). Welfare states at the end of the century: The impact of market, family, and demographic change. In P. Hennesy & M. Peersen (Eds.), *Family, market, and community: Equity and efficiency in social policy* (pp. 63–76). Paris: OECD.

Furstenberg, F. F., Jr., Brooks-Gunn, J., & Morgan, S. P. (1987). *Adolescent mothers in later life*. New York: Cambridge University Press.

Gee, E. M. (1986). The life course of Canadian women: A historical and demographic analysis. *Social Indicators Research, 18*, 263–283.

George, L. K., & Lynch, S. M. (2003). Race differences in depressive symptoms: A dynamic perspective on stress exposure and vulnerability. *Journal of Health and Social Behavior, 44*, 353–369.

Gove, W. R., Style, C. B., & Hughes, M. (1990). The effect of marriage on the well-being of adults. *Journal of Family Issues, 11*, 4–35.

Hagestad, G. O. (1990). Social perspectives on the life course. In R. H. Binstock & L. K. George (Eds.), *Handbook of aging and the social sciences* (3rd ed., pp. 151–168). San Diego: Academic Press.

Hastings, T. J. (1991). The Stanford-Terman study revisited: Postwar emotional health of World War II veterans. *Psychology, 3*, 201–214.

Hautamaeki, A., & Coleman, P. G. (2001). Explanation for low prevalence of PTSD among older Finnish war victims: Social solidarity and continued significance given to wartime sufferings. *Aging and Mental Health, 5*, 165–174.

Heath, J., Ciscel, D., & Sharp, D. (1998). The work of families: The provision of market and household labor and the role of public policy. *Review of Social Economy, 56*, 501–521.

Heckman, J. (1979). Sample selection bias as a specification error. *Econometrica, 47*, 153–161.

Hunt, N., & Robbins, J. (2001). The long-term consequences of war: The experience of World War II. *Aging and Mental Health, 5*, 183–190.

Imhoff, A. E. (1986). Life course patterns of women and their husbands. In A. B. Sorensen, F. E. Weinert, & L. R. Sherrod (Eds.), *Human development and the life course: Multidisciplinary perspectives* (pp. 247–270). Hillsdale, NJ: Erlbaum.

Johnson, T. P. (1991). Mental health, social relationships, and social selection: A longitudinal analysis. *Journal of Health and Social Behavior, 32*, 408–423.

Lillard, L. A., & Waite, L. J. (1995). Till death do us part: Marital disruption and mortality. *American Journal of Sociology, 100*, 1131–1156.

Lynch, S. M., & George, L. K. (2000). Interlocking trajectories of loss-related events and depressive symptoms among elders. *Journal of Gerontology: Social Sciences, 57B*, S117–S125.

Major, E. F. (2003). Health effects of war stress on Norwegian World War II resistance groups: A comparative study. *Journal of Traumatic Stress, 16*, 595–599.

Mayer, K. U., & Muller, W. (1986). The state and the structure of the life course. In A. B. Sorensen, F. E. Weinert, & L. R. Sherrod (Eds.), *Human development and the life course: Multidisciplinary perspectives* (pp. 217–245). Hillsdale, NJ: Erlbaum.

Mayer, K. U., & Tuma, N. B. (1990). Life course research and event history analysis: An overview. In K. U. Mayer & N. B. Tuma (Eds.), *Event history analysis in life course research* (pp. 3–20). New York: Springer Publishing.

McAdam, D. (1989). The biographical consequences of activism. *American Sociological Review, 54,* 744–760.

McCardle, J. J., & Hamagami, F. (1992). Modeling incomplete longitudinal and cross-sectional curves using latent growth structural models. *Experimental Aging Research, 18,* 145–166.

Meyer, J. W. (1986). The institutionalization of the life course and its effects on the self. In A. B. Sorensen, F. E. Weinert, & L. R. Sherrod (Eds.), *Human development and the life course: Multidisciplinary perspectives* (pp. 199–216). Hillsdale, NJ: Erlbaum.

Murray, J. E. (2000). Marital protection and marital selection: Evidence from a historical-prospective sample of American men. *Demography, 37,* 511–521.

Peters, A., & Liefbroer, A. C. (1997). Beyond marital status: Partner history and well-being in old age. *Journal of Marriage and the Family, 59,* 687–699.

Pettit, B., & Western, B. (2004). Mass imprisonment and the life course: Race and class inequality in U.S. incarceration. *American Sociological Review, 69,* 151–169.

Riley, M. W. (1976). Age strata in social systems. In R. H. Binstock & E. Shanas (Eds.), *Handbook of aging and the social sciences* (pp. 189–217). New York: Van Nostrand Reinhold.

Riley, M. W., Foner, A., & Riley, J. W., Jr. (1999). The aging and society paradigm. In V. L. Bengtson & K. W. Schaie (Eds.), *Handbook of theories of aging* (pp. 327–343). New York: Springer Publishing.

Riley, M. W., Johnson, M., & Foner, A. (1972). *Aging and society, Volume 3: A sociology of age stratification.* New York: Russell Sage Foundation.

Riley, M. W., & Riley, J. W., Jr. (1994). Structural lag: Past and future. In M. W. Riley, R. L. Kahn, & A. Foner (Eds.), *Age and structural lag: Society's failure to provide meaningful opportunities in work, family, and leisure* (pp. 15–36). New York: Wiley.

Rindfuss, R. R., Swicegood, C. G., & Rosenfeld, R. A. (1987). Disorder in the life course: How common and does it matter? *American Sociological Association, 52,* 785–801.

Ross, C. E., & Mirowsky, J. (1995). Does employment affect health? *Journal of Health and Social Behavior, 36,* 230–243.

Sampson, R. J., & Laub, J. H. (1996). Socioeconomic achievement in the life course of disadvantaged men: Military service as a turning point. *American Sociological Review, 61,* 347–367.

Silverstein, M., & Bengtson, V. L. (1997). Intergenerational solidarity and the structure of adult child–parent relationships in American families. *American Journal of Sociology, 103,* 429–460.

Simmons, L. W. (1945). *The role of the aged in primitive society.* New Haven, CT: Yale University Press.

Smith, J. P. (1999). Healthy bodies and thick wallets: The dual relation between health and economic status. *Journal of Economic Perspectives, 13,* 145–166.

Stets, J. E. (1995). Job autonomy and control over one's spouse: A compensatory process. *Journal of Health and Social Behavior, 36,* 244–258.

Stolzenberg, R. M. (2001). It's about time and gender: Spousal employment and health. *American Journal of Sociology, 107,* 61–100.

Uhlenberg, P. (1980). Death and the family. *Journal of Family History, 5,* 313–320.

Vermunt, J. K., & Magidson, J. (2000). *Latent gold user's guide.* Belmont, MA: Statistical Innovations.

Waite, L J., & Gallagher, M. (2000). *The case for marriage: Why married people are happier, healthier, and better off financially.* New York: Broadway Books.

Watkins, S. C., Menken, J. A., & Bongaarts, J. (1987). Demographic foundations of family change. *American Sociological Review, 52,* 346–358.

Wethington, E., & Kessler, R. C. (1989). Employment, parental responsibility, and psychological distress: A longitudinal study of married women. *Journal of Family Issues, 10,* 527–546.

Wrong, D. H. (1961). The oversocialized conception of man in modern sociology. *American Sociological Review, 26,* 183–193.

CHAPTER 11

Social Forces, Life Course Consequences

Cumulative Disadvantage and "Getting Alzheimer's"

Kathryn Z. Douthit
Dale Dannefer

The field of life course studies encompasses several theoretical perspectives and includes a wide range of problems to be explained. What is the study of the life course about? Dannefer and Uhlenberg (1999) identified three classes of phenomena that are of interest to life-course scholars: *individual* (individual life course outcomes), *collective* (cohort-based life course outcomes), and *symbolic* (life course as an idea or set of ideas that may take on normative power). Unlike the first two types, this third, symbolic type does not refer to the phenomena of actual individual life course patterns at all. The term *symbolic* denotes the realm of knowledge and ideas. Thus, it refers to concepts or constructs that come to be accepted as normal, natural, or true in a given situation. Such objectified and taken-for-granted symbolic constructions include adolescence and retirement. These ideas define a typical stage of the life course but are actually not inherent properties of individuals. Instead they represent taken-for-granted practices and institutions that impose on experience a socially constructed set of instructions for how one's biography should be organized.

Issues related to the first of these three types, *individual outcomes*, characterize much of the research on the life course in the United States. In Chapter 10, Linda George provides an authoritative and innovative treatment of the life course from this individual-level perspective. In this chapter, we take up the latter two types of problems: life course as a feature of *cohorts* and life course as an *idea*, that is, a feature of culture (of the images and values that are part of our basic understanding of society and the world). In both cases, understanding the individual life course requires, perhaps paradoxically, analysis beyond the individual level (Hagestad & Dannefer, 2001). As we will see, some of its most central features are irreducibly structural and cultural.

To illustrate the importance and utility of these generically socio-dynamic processes, we focus on a problem that has received increasing attention in the study of age and the life course over the past decade: the phenomenon of cumulative advantage and disadvantage. We examine how this plays out as both a collective phenomenon (as a feature of cohorts that is regulated by social processes) and a cultural phenomenon (related to ideologies of the individual life course, medicine, and health).

CUMULATIVE ADVANTAGE/DISADVANTAGE AS A COLLECTIVE PHENOMENON AND COHORT-BASED PROCESS

The concept of cumulative advantage/disadvantage (CAD) resonates with popular folk sayings like "success breeds success" (e.g., Huber, 1998) and "the rich get richer, the poor get poorer" (Entwisle, Alexander, & Olson, 2001). Thus, it refers to a set of social dynamics that operate on a population, not on individuals. Although it refers to social system processes acting on populations or other collectivities, the impact of CAD is unavoidably reflected in the lives and life chances of individuals.

The concept of cumulative advantage has its origins in studies of how scientists get credit for their scientific work and was introduced to sociology by venerated social theorist Robert Merton in a classic essay, "The Matthew Effect in Science" (1968). CAD can be defined as the systemic tendency for interindividual divergence in a given characteristic (e.g., money, health, status) with the passage of time (Dannefer, 2003). When speaking of quantifiable or ranked characteristics such as wealth or health status, *interindividual divergence* is another way of saying "increasing inequality." An important point to note about both divergence and inequality is that they are not features of individuals. Rather, they are terms that necessarily imply comparison of multiple individuals along some meaningful dimension. In this case, the properties of interest are typically social, economic, and personal resources, as well as social opportunities. Income and other such measures are considered important, and not only because they reflect consumer buying power. Much more important, epidemiologists and others have consistently found that the social class differences reflected in income measures are the most powerful and robust predictors of personal health. Thus, CAD suggests that everyday social life entails participation in stratified routines, resulting in both differential opportunities and differential consequences for individual health and well-being, morbidity, and longevity. Individual health and aging outcomes are thus bound up with these dynamics.

Scholars began to see the connection of CAD to aging and the life course when it was linked to the observation that intracohort income inequality tends to increase as the cohort members age and is thus at its highest point when the cohort reaches later life. The pattern of increasing inequality with increasing age is apparently quite robust, at least in the United States. This has been observed in multiple cohorts by several researchers using a variety of data sources (Crystal & Shea, 1990; Dannefer & Sell, 1988; O'Rand, 1995). These researchers agree in interpreting these findings as reflecting CAD processes.

At the same time, social tendencies toward CAD are not unavoidable and inevitable. They appear to fluctuate from time to time and from cohort to cohort based on social and economic conditions, state tax and pension policies, and many other factors. Such fluctuations may either attenuate or exacerbate inherent intracohort tendencies toward the development of CAD (Dannefer & Sell, 1988). Indeed, policy initiatives, such as the implementation of public and private pension programs, may have led to a trend of reduction in old-age poverty and inequality in the 20th century (Pampel, 1981; Vincent, 1995). Recent initiatives that counter these long-term trends are also at work in some countries and may reverberate across the life course. In the United States, for example, to the extent that recent trends toward privatizing risk and reducing health benefits mean that greater inequality exists among young cohorts than in the past, these inequalities may, *ceteris paribus*, tend to increase even more with the passage of time.

Many kinds of social dynamics contribute to the overall process of CAD. These include work-related factors—not only income and job benefits (e.g., health care) but also job characteristics, such as the extent to which one's work is physically damaging or psychically energizing. A key principle of CAD is the recognition that jobs are stratified with regard to such characteristics. Similar dynamics also operate earlier in the life course, for example, in tracking and selection processes operating in schools and, before that, to the long-term consequences of early childhood and prenatal health. Whatever the process or outcome in question, the point that distinguishes a *structural* approach to the life course, such as CAD, is that these factors are seen not just as the outworking of individual practices and trajectories, but as operating on the entire population at the cohort level through opportunity structures that involve systemic mechanisms of resource allocation and other forces that regulate distribution of rewards and access of opportunities.

In a rather straightforward extrapolation of the strong connection between social class and health, several scholars have begun to extend this finding along CAD trajectories using both aggregate data and large samples of individuals derived from survey data (Crystal & Shea, 2003). Others have begun the task of tracing the highly intricate interplay of social-structural and individual factors with regard to physical and mental health (Falletta & Dannefer, 2005; Farkas, 2003; Ferraro & Kelly-Moore, 2001; Ross & Mirowsky, 1999). In this chapter, we examine the life course connections of such processes more concretely, tracing the effects of specific material circumstances, injurious social conditions, and other life experiences that shape the risk of affliction by one specific disease process: Alzheimer's disease.

Recently great attention has been given to the neurophysiological and genetic mechanisms that operate to produce dementia of the Alzheimer's type (DAT). Although the relationship between DAT and various social factors, including social class, has received some attention, clinical research agendas and intervention strategies generally focus on the biological underpinnings of the disorder. By building on what is known about the biology of Alzheimer's disease and its reciprocal relationship with various social practices, we show how the cognitive and social incapacities of DAT are related across the life course to conditions of accumulating social disadvantage.

DEMENTIA OF THE ALZHEIMER'S TYPE: DEFINITION AND ETIOLOGY

Definition

DAT, a devastating manifestation of Alzheimer's disease, is characterized by a progressive decline in various aspects of cognitive functioning. The array of cognitive impairments that typify DAT is common to other forms of dementia, which have similar phenomenological outcomes but contrasting etiologies. The work of defining dementia and classifying its subtypes has been the purview of psychiatry and is detailed in the American Psychiatric Association's *Diagnostic and Statistical Manual of Men-*

tal Disorders (DSM-IV-TR). In describing the common thread running through the range of dementias, the DSM-IV-TR states that:

> The essential feature of a dementia is the development of multiple cognitive deficits that include memory impairment and at least one of the following cognitive disturbances: aphasia, apraxia, agnosia, or a disturbance in executive functioning. The cognitive deficits must be sufficiently severe to cause impairment in occupational or social functioning and must represent a decline from a previously higher level of functioning. (2000, p. 147)

Etiology and Prevention

The symptoms of dementia are shared by a long list of dementia disorders including DAT, vascular dementia, substance-induced persisting dementia, and dementia due to HIV, Huntington's disease, head trauma, Parkinson's disease, and Creutzfeldt-Jakob disease. The etiology of these disorders ranges from Huntington's disease, which has clearly defined genetic origins and is known to carry the specter of a tragic inevitability, to Creutzfeld-Jakob disease, a variant of "mad cow disease," is contracted through exposure to an infectious agent.

The etiology of DAT is less well understood than many of the other dementia-related disorders. Although some evidence suggests that certain genes increase the risk that an individual will display the symptoms of DAT, the risk seems to be more robust for early-onset Alzheimer's disease (before the age of 60–65 years) than the more common form of DAT arising later in life. For the more prevalent later-life form of DAT, there is an increasingly recognized interaction between genetic and environmental factors in the production of the characteristic beta-amyloid plaques and neurofibrillary tangles that are present in the brain tissue of DAT patients (Edwardsons & Morris, 1998; Selkoe, 2001).

In the following section, we review evidence that supports the proposition that the risk of being diagnosed with DAT is correlated with the accumulation of individual-level effects of social processes acting across the life course. We suggest how social processes, beginning in the prenatal period, may influence and shape opportunities and experiences that alter individuals' life chances and opportunity structures and, hence, in a cumulative manner, alter the likelihood of DAT in the future. We further hypothesize that such risk trajectories are unequally but systematically distributed in a population at any point in time and that their distribution reflects CAD processes. What are the specific factors that underlie such risks and outcomes? In the next sections, we look at two of these in some detail: cardiovascular health and the obesity-related triad of poor nutrition, stress, and sedentary lifestyle. We also briefly consider the possible effects of life course literacy practices on DAT outcomes.

Cumulative Advantage/ Disadvantage and Cardiovascular Health

To understand the interaction of available social and economic resources, cardiovascular health, and the development of DAT requires following a chain of events woven through the life course. Two basic empirical realities underlie this socioeconomic-cardiovascular-DAT dialectic. First, throughout the life course, economic position has a significant bearing on the general health of the cardiovascular system, including the condition of the arteries that supply blood to the brain (Marmot & Wilkerson, 1999). The relationship between economics and cardiovascular health is mediated through factors such as metabolic syndrome, stress, and exercise, all of which are considered below. Second, poor cardiovascular health in later life, particularly in relation to the arterial blood supply to the brain, is correlated with a greater preponderance of DAT symptoms (Bowler, 2004; Breteler, 2000; Iadecola & Gorelick, 2003; Tzourio et al., 2003).

The impact of poor cerebrovascular health on DAT is vividly illustrated in the now-famous Nun Study (Snowdon et al., 1997), which clearly shows that having one or more strokes in combination with Alzheimer's neuropathology (plaques and tangles present on autopsy) is much more powerfully predictive of DAT symptoms than either stroke or Alzheimer's neuropathology alone. The association of vascular health and DAT is also demonstrated in the work of Honig, Kukull, and Mayeux (2005), who show a significant increase in the presence of neuritic plaques in subjects with large-vessel cerebrovascular disease. Beginning with adulthood and working backward in time to the prenatal period, the role of poverty-related social and economic forces in producing these empirical realities will be elaborated.

Cardiovascular Health in Adulthood: Dietary Links

The notion that a health crisis related to cardiovascular problems exists among American adults, particularly of low-income status, has captured the attention of the American public. Many poor adults live in communities where there are geographic and economic barriers to obtaining high-quality, low-fat food sources rich in vitamins, phytochemicals, and fiber. Particularly for those living in conditions of urban poverty, fresh produce and low-fat sources of protein are often unavailable in local neighborhood grocery stores (Horowitz, Colson, Herbert, & Lancaster, 2004; Johnson, Wilson, Fulp, Schuetz, & Orton, 2005; Shaffer, 2002). Inexpensive processed foods that are high in saturated fat, refined carbohydrates, and sodium and low in fiber, phytochemicals, and naturally oc-curring vitamins become dietary staples (Drewnowski & Specter, 2004), forming the foundation for epidemic levels of obesity, hypertension, and poor cardiovascular health (Marmot & Elliot, 1992; Marmot & Wilker-son, 1999).

The inaccessibility of grocery stores with high-quality food products is exacerbated in low-income environments by the ready availability of fast food restaurants serving products that are low in nutritional value and high in fat and cholesterol. In many urban neighborhoods, fast food chains are virtually omnipresent and contribute to the epidemic levels of cardiovascular disease (Drewnowski & Specter, 2004; Dwyer, 2005). Moreover, such neighborhoods may be deliberately targeted by corporate marketing strategies of the fast food industry (Maxwell & Jacobsen, 1989; Schlosser, 2002).

Although the link between cardiovascular disease and high-fat, sodium, and refined carbohydrate diets has become widely recognized, another component of a healthy diet has more recently begun to attract public awareness. Antioxidants, found in intensely colored fruits and veg-etables (e.g., blueberries, strawberries, blackberries, grapes, kale, toma-toes), have been implicated in the prevention of a host of diseases, including DAT. Although the results of clinical trials have yielded con-tradictory results, this has become an active area of research. Vitamins C and E and the plant substances called carotenes all have antioxidant ef-fects that have suggested some promise in preventing DAT (Englehart et al., 2002; Martin, 2003). Additionally, by promoting cardiovascular health, antioxidants may also ward off the DAT-exacerbating effects of stroke (Adams, Wermuth, & McBride, 1999).

In any case, having high-quality produce available for purchase, and having the requisite economic resources to secure those nutrient-rich whole food substances, may have a significant bearing on prevention of DAT. Conversely, not having the knowledge or economic resources to ac-quire healthy dietary alternatives, lacking transportation needed to access such alternatives, and the availability of low-cost foods that are high in saturated fat, sodium, white flour, and refined sugar, are problems asso-ciated with poverty that potentially subvert DAT prevention.

Cardiovascular Disease in Adulthood: The Stress Link

Of course, the unavailability of high-quality food sources is only one factor contributing to cardiovascular pathology in low-income populations. En-vironmental stress is itself a precursor to cardiovascular disease (Heming-way & Marmot, 1999; Marmot & Elliot, 1992). As endocrinologists have long known, conditions of stress cause release of the stress hormone corti-sol (Henry, 1988). Cortisol provides chemical energy for emergency or

high-stress situations by increasing the secretion of insulin and the metabolism of fats and carbohydrates. As a result, appetite increases, and when
cortisol is persistently elevated by prolonged stress, weight gain occurs.

While all excessive weight gain threatens cardiovascular health, the
type of weight gain resulting from persistent stress is particularly toxic
(Samaras et al., 2000). Fat formed in response to elevated cortisol tends to
be deposited in the abdomen (Epel et al., 2000). Abdominal fat (unlike fat
in the hips and thighs) is strongly correlated with cardiovascular disease,
including heart attack and stroke (Lamarche, 1998). Thus, for adults living under the stressful conditions of poverty, including violence exposure,
deteriorating housing, poorly functioning schools, rampant drug-related
crime, inadequate health care, and absence of community resources, the
predictable levels of stress-related obesity, added to the obesity related to
accessibility and affordability of high-quality food sources, create conditions that readily explain the relatively high levels of DAT in low-income
populations.

Exercise in Adulthood: Cardiovascular Health and DAT Prevention

The relationship between DAT prevention and exercise has been substantiated by a number of clinical studies (Abbott et al., 2004; Weuve et
al., 2004). It is likely that the benefits of exercise on late-life brain health,
and in particular on curbing the symptoms of DAT, are derived from at
least three different types of benefits incurred by an exercise regime. First,
the most obvious benefit of regular exercise is its positive effect on weight
control and, hence, cardiovascular disease. The relationship between obesity and cardiovascular disease is a part of common lay understanding of
health and well-being and is helpful in control of DAT symptoms in late
life. Second, exercise has an ameliorative impact on the toxic stress response (Landers, 1997). Exercise has repeatedly been shown to reduce
anxiety triggered by environmental stress (Fox, 1999) and may consequently play a role in preventing deposition of toxic abdominal fat de-
posits and hypertension that place strain on the cardiovascular system
(Youngstedt, O'Connor, Crabbe, & Dishman, 1998). A third benefit of
regular exercise relates to nutrient metabolism by brain cells. It appears
that increased oxygen perfusion of brain cells during exercise permits
brain cells to more efficiently capture the energy contained in foods and
is ultimately beneficial to overall brain health (Colcombe et al., 2003).

But how is adult exercise related to CAD? To maintain an exercise regimen requires that adults have a safe place to engage in an exercise program
and that they are able to carve out a regular time to exercise. The urban
poor may not have access to safe, adequate exercise facilities, and those already suffering from obesity and cardiovascular disease may not have the
guidance of athletic trainers who provide safe and manageable exercise

routines. Additionally, stress and fatigue from demanding and often repetitive physical labor leave little energy for health-building exercise.

It is noteworthy that the protective factors that have been discussed in this section on exercise operate through multiple channels, of which obesity-related cardiovascular disease is one, but only one. Exercise also affects health and mental functioning by reducing cortisol-inducing stress and increasing oxygen perfusion in the brain. Thus, cumulative and cascading effects can be readily seen even within the constantly ongoing and interacting physiological processes within the adult body.

Childhood and Adolescence: Laying the Groundwork for Cardiovascular Disease

Nutrition in Childhood and Adolescence

Nutritional practices established in childhood and adolescence have implications for adult health. Obesity in childhood portends obesity and cardiovascular disease in adulthood, with major recognition currently being given to the development of metabolic syndrome in children and adolescents (Cruz & Goran, 2004). Metabolic syndrome (also known as insulin resistance syndrome) is a reliable predictor of cardiovascular disease in adults. It consists of four metabolic markers: impaired glucose tolerance, high triglyceride and low high-density lipoprotein (HDL) cholesterol levels, hypertension, and obesity (Minehira & Tappy, 2002). Metabolic syndrome carries a very high risk for adult cardiovascular disease, particularly when paired with other injurious practices such as smoking and a sedentary lifestyle. It typically arises in adulthood, but it is also present in approximately 50 percent of severely obese children and adolescents (Weiss et al., 2004).

The numerous sociostructural factors that contribute to weight gain among low-income adults also apply to low-income children and adolescents (Drewnowski & Specter, 2004; Maxwell & Jacobsen, 1989; Shaffer, 2002). The steady rise in preadult obesity and preadult metabolic syndrome (Keller & Lemberg, 2003; Weiss et al., 2004) suggests one mechanism through which large-scale trends of growing inequality may translate into stronger patterns of CAD in the future, as increased inequalities in childhood accelerate CAD processes operating through the life course.

Childhood Exercise: The Foundation for a Healthy Adulthood

Early life commitment to an exercise regimen may also prove to be helpful in later prevention of DAT symptoms. The benefits of exercise, including weight control and oxygen perfusion, promote brain development that is resistant to the later-life manifestations of DAT (Dik, Deeg, Visser, & Jonker, 2003). Regular participation of youth in an exercise program requires that, minimally, children and adolescents have safe, accessible community facilities with needed equipment and adequate supervision. Unfortunately, the deteriorating infrastructure associated with low-income residential areas, threats of violence in public playgrounds, lack of community resources to produce safe and accessible green spaces, and strained education budgets that do not support sports activities are all factors that discourage regular physical activity by youth and potentially reduce possibilities for protective brain development. Such lack of opportunity, when considered in concert with the liabilities incurred through limited dietary options, portends greater possibilities for adult cardiovascular disease, hypertension, and vascular dementia, as well as DAT. These considerations lead to the concern that when there are increases in hardship for disadvantaged families and when resources for public education and health care are reduced, the foundation is laid in childhood to increase the divergence of inequality over the life course.

Prenatal and Early Postnatal Care, Cardiovascular Health, and CAD

Retrospective studies linking poor prenatal nutrition with later-life obesity (Kuzawa, 2004; McGill & McMahan, 2003) point again to the impact of early dietary practices on later-life cardiovascular health. Either nutritional deficits or nutritional surpluses during the prenatal period establish characteristic metabolic patterns of energy utilization that favor childhood obesity (Cruz & Goran, 2004; Oken & Gillman, 2003). Thus, if poor women's dietary practices reflect the availability of low-cost, high-calorie, nutrient-poor foods, they are more likely to give birth to children who will endure a subsequent weight problem and adult cardiovascular disease. Likewise, the risk for childhood obesity, and ultimately adult obesity, is increased if prenatal development is marked by the kind of calorie deficiency accompanying addiction problems, severe mental illness, substandard health care, or other overwhelming life circumstances. In either case, prenatal development may be compromised.

Thus, the interactions of cardiovascular health and social position present a compelling illustration of the potential for CAD in the development of DAT symptoms. The principles of political economy impose formidable barriers to the brain health of low-income citizens that begin at conception and reverberate expansively over the life course. While the story of cardiovascular CAD and DAT is one that commands attention, it is hardly the end of the CAD–DAT story. A number of other factors associated with economic hardship also contribute to the manifestation of Alzheimer's disease. To illustrate the diversity of such factors, we turn to one that operates at quite a different level from cardiovascular health: literacy skills.

Literacy as Cumulative Advantage in the Prevention of DAT

The renowned Nun Study, an extensive DAT research project launched by David Snowdon (2002), suggests other dimensions through which CAD processes operate. In addition to confirming much of the research linking cardiovascular health and DAT, Snowdon et al. (1996) illuminated a possible association between early childhood literacy practices and acquisition of Alzheimer's disease in later life. Using autopsy data to confirm the presence of Alzheimer's disease, they devised a retrospective study to explore the links between DAT and early linguistic ability. A strong connection was found between linguistic ability in early life and cognitive function and Alzheimer's disease in late life. Early-age linguistic ability was measured by the density of ideas found in autobiographical narratives produced by study participants more than half a century earlier, when the women were in their early twenties. Moreover, low linguistic ability in young adult life was found to be positively associated with the presence, on autopsy, of the neurofibrillary tangles and beta-amyloid plaques of Alzheimer's disease and with low-level cognitive functioning. Snowden (2002) speculates that these data may underscore the importance of childhood literacy practices in maintaining cognitive function in later life. If, as numerous studies suggest (e.g., Bailey, Bruer, Symons, & Lichtman, 2001), the quality and quantity of childhood exposure to written and spoken language result in a more complex handling of text later in adult life, Snowdon's conjecture concerning the importance of early childhood literacy practices may indeed become one of the tenets of DAT prevention.

Although further research in the area of childhood literacy is needed to definitively link DAT prevention to early verbal training, other evidence supports this hypothesis. For example, Letenneur et al. (1999) found that for both men and women, the risk of being diagnosed with Alzheimer's disease is associated with lower educational attainment. Also, in a retrospective study of Alzheimer's disease subjects, Moceri et al. (2001) found that the children born to unskilled manual laborers harbor a greater risk of developing DAT than randomly chosen subjects and that the children of fathers employed in manual labor are at a greater risk for Alzheimer's disease regardless of the presence of a strong genetic risk factor: the apolipoprotein epsilon-4 allele (APOE-4).

Such studies lend support to Snowdon's hypothesis regarding early childhood literacy practices. It follows that parents whose occupational success is not contingent on utilization and honing of verbal skills would be less likely than parents engaged in occupations requiring verbal sophistication to expose children to complex language utilization skills. Hence, there is a strong suggestion that low-income households are less likely than high-income households to be routinely engaged in utilization of complex language practices and that the disparity in exposure to complex language in low- versus high-income home environments is another plausible example of the CAD mechanism's shaping DAT outcomes.

Extrapolating these patterns to the neurological level, they are pertinent to the closely related hypothesis that childhood exposure to verbally stimulating environments increases the quantity and quality of synaptic connections established early and that the resultant neural networks may impart protection against the destructive effects of Alzheimer's disease in late life (Barnes, Tager, Satariano, & Yaffe, 2004; Mortimer, Borenstein, Gosche, & Snowdon, 2005). Moreover, acquisition of complex verbal skills in youth and adolescence provides advantage in the societal opportunity structure, increasing the chances of finding an advantaged position in the labor market and being engaged in mentally stimulating work. Thus, the conditions that serve to bolster formation of complex neural pathways—conditions that for a variety of reasons are correlated with conditions of privilege—provide a compelling exemplar of the impact of CAD on the prevention of DAT. Conversely, conditions that compromise the construction of these complex pathways, particularly conditions in which cognitive development is overshadowed by struggles for basic survival needs, poignantly illustrate how mechanisms of cognitive disadvantage favor the manifestations of DAT.

The potential preventive value of promoting cognitive development, not only in childhood but throughout the life course, is underscored by a subject in the Nun Study (Snowdon, 2002). The case of Sister Mary, an exceptionally vital 101 year old, demonstrated that even in the presence of a profusion of beta-amyloid plaques and neurofibrillary tangles, the debilitating cognitive and behavioral manifestations of DAT can be averted. Despite the abundance of neuropathological markers and her extreme age, she displayed unimpaired levels of cognitive facility by routinely engaging in complex cognitive activity and a vigorous exercise regimen. Although not conclusive, the suggestions that emerge from Snowdon's work with Sister Mary may prove to be germane to Alzheimer's prevention efforts. These include the possibility that a rich set of synaptic connections developed earlier in life and maintained through the life course may compensate for later destruction of neurological pathways and that exercise is an important tool for dealing with cardiovascular health, stress management, and oxygen perfusion of brain tissue, is important in prevention of DAT symptoms.

Summary: CAD and DAT Across the Life Course

In this section, we have identified interconnections among resources, experience, and DAT by focusing on examples related to cardiovascular health and literacy. Although these examples are compelling, they are simply two illustrative cases among many. Other direct and indirect links among resources, lifestyle, and DAT risk have also been observed. One important mediator of such links is depression, which is predicted by many of the risk factors addressed here. Depression may increases DAT risk by acting on the hippocampus, a brain structure involved in memory (Bremner et al., 2000; Sapolsky, 2000). In any case, we have attempted to show that DAT, a disorder that has received considerable attention for its biological foundations, may be inextricably intertwined with structures of opportunity and the life experiences they impose.

DAT AND THE LIFE COURSE AS A CULTURAL CONSTRUCT: NATURALIZING DEMENTIA AND CAD

Analysis of the life course as a cultural construct entails understanding the life course as a set of social practices that become objectified in social institutions and taken for granted as normative and as "real." Recognition of the importance of such analysis dates back to Matilda Riley's classic insight that age must be recognized not just as a feature of individuals but also as a feature of social structure (Riley, Johnson, & Foner, 1972; Riley, Kahn, & Foner, 1994). Taking seriously the power of such objectifications is a crucially important precondition for gaining a full understanding of the life course. This may seem paradoxical at first, since what is being studied is not primarily the lives of individuals at all, but rather the construction of a set of institutionalized structures that define roles in a culturally sanctioned, age-graded sequence—from prekindergarten educational programs all the way to the structured sequence of care levels found within many large nursing homes. As individuals' role occupancy, and transition timing and sequencing, have come increasingly into conformity with such generalized ideas of age appropriateness and age-graded developmental needs, sociologists have come to speak of the "institutionalization of the life course" (Kohli, 1986). Many aspects of the institutionalized life course—from schooling to special care units in nursing homes designed for end-of-life care for Alzheimer's patients—have become *social facts* in the Durkheimian sense. Thus, although they are themselves features of social structures and not individual biographies, they have come to exert powerful influence over the lives of individuals by defining in authoritative terms what is "normal" or "good" for individuals at various points in the life course (Dannefer, 1984, 1988).

The institutionalization of the life course has been a specific aspect of the broader processes of modernization, which involves an expansion of rationality in the form of professional expertise and bureaucratic organization into more and more cracks and crevices of human experience. Recently, debates over postmodernity and evidence of the dismantling of the welfare state have led to arguments and claims that deinstitutionalization may be occurring in numerous societal spheres. There has been considerable speculation about the deinstitutionalization of the life course (e.g., Dannefer, 2000; Kohli, 1986; Quadagno, 2005; Settersten, 1999; Uhlenberg & Dannefer, 2006) in the spheres of both work and family (Dannefer & Patterson, in press; Hughes & Waite, in press) Whether such trends are in motion does not change the principle under discussion here but illustrates one of its dynamics: the greater the institutionalization, the greater the normative force of age norms, life course "stages," "transitions," and so forth.

In this section, we focus on a specific concomitant of the institutionalized life course, the process of *medicalization*, especially as it applies to the later life. The medical model of the life course is one that defines reality in the terms asserted by the medical profession. Medical knowledge relies heavily on statistical age norms and age thresholds as predictors of health problems and medical needs. For example, physicians are trained to regard age 50 as a critical benchmark; by age 65 everyone begins to experience brain cell death; by age 85 nearly everyone has some dementia.

Several scholars have shown how medicalization tends to encourage a view of the aged as needy, incompetent, passive consumers and best cared for by insisting on compliance with pharmacological regimes and dietary proscriptions. Such an approach represents *ageism* when viewed from the standpoint of geriatrics—a specialty that recognizes the diversity of health in aged individuals and that emphasizes exercise, nutrition, and meaningful activities as routes to health gains and positive psychological growth in later life. Geriatrics is a recently developed medical specialization, however. Thus, in the context of the medical profession and the overall contemporary practice of medicine, the geriatricians who advocate such an approach are a muted minority.

Medicalization is thus an aspect of the institutionalization of the later stages of life. It supports the popular view that old age is an unappealing stage of life in which people are useless, costly, out-of-date, and unattractive and are thought of primarily in terms of health and medical problems. There is sometimes a preemptive expectation among health care professionals of deterioration, cascading problems, and unavoidable, inevitable decline among aged patients. Diagnoses can thus outrun symptoms, and management of pathologies and pain replaces ideas of prevention, cure, or gaining strength.

Thus, the medicalization of later life is part of the cultural construction of the life course that has meant a general devaluation and stigmatization of elderhood that cuts across all socioeconomic strata. However, this generalized impact of a socially constructed negativity about age intersects with CAD processes to produce an added, *multiple jeopardy* situation for socioeconomically disadvantaged elders. This subpopulation is at risk for disadvantage on a diverse array of health-related social forces, including access to needed health care, drugs, and medical information.

We have already reviewed how those who are disadvantaged early are put at greater risk for DAT by events occurring throughout the life course. Focusing on the medicalization of old age suggests a completely different dynamic by which disadvantaged elders may be further adversely affected by an aggressive and somewhat arbitrary diagnostic process. Authoritative diagnosis of DAT is still possible only postmortem, which can reveal diagnostic errors. At the same time, diagnosis can be analyzed as a social practice with its own sociodynamic and social-interactional force (Gubrium, 1986; Lyman, 1989). Moreover, the diagnostic process is itself stratified, applied across socioeconomic levels (Husaini et al., 2003; Lindsey & Paul, 1989). To the extent that DAT is improperly diagnosed based on limited and selective attention to symptoms, poor elders may be especially vulnerable to such questionable diagnosis and to the concomitant loss of freedom and, possibly, unneeded and disabling medications.

CONCLUSION

This chapter has shown that a full understanding of the life course requires not only paying attention to the biographical dynamics of individual lives in context, but also to two other important sets of social forces: the social-structural dynamics that are at work in populations, and more specifically in cohorts, and the objectification of social practices in the normative and other symbolic constructs of life course institutionalization. We have suggested the importance of both kinds of processes by focusing on the social process of CAD and the disease processes of DAT.

DAT is only one of many disease processes in which CAD processes can be shown to operate, through both social-structural dynamics and the diagnosis-constructing processes that are part of the institutionalized life course. This chapter might have focused on heart disease or certain cancer risks to illustrate similar processes at work. In the case of DAT as in other processes of disease and debility, those already disadvantaged are at risk for additional disadvantage, by the risk of both developing DAT as an actual disease process and being improperly diagnosed or treated for DAT, outcomes that produce added disadvantage.

The insidious nature of CAD processes is evident in a wide array of examples ranging from educational and occupational achievement to health concerns such as cardiovascular disease, depression, anxiety disorders, cancer, developmental disabilities, addiction, diabetes, and various forms of dementia. DAT, because it is specific to later life, illustrates the life course trajectory of CAD processes. A host of variables related to economic disadvantage form a complex web of interrelated phenomena that together impose serious risk on the brain health of older individuals. Ironically, those same individuals, if stricken with DAT, will continue to experience cumulative disadvantage in the form of compromised dementia care. Families living in poverty will have fewer resources available for the remediative or palliative care that might ease the painful regressive journey that characterizes Alzheimer's disease. The stress-filled existence of these families will be further strained, limited resources will be further stretched, and the inability of overtaxed community clinical resources to respond to the needs of patients will be particularly painful for families and their ailing elders.

Especially in a strongly individualized society such as the United States, there is a predisposition toward *microfication* (Hagestad & Dannefer, 2001)—analyzing health and other topics either as issues of individuals or as issues to be apprehended at the level of primary relations, giving primacy to themes such as family, microinteraction, choice, and decision making. A sociological analysis must also recognize how the microworlds of everyday experience and interaction are located within, and partially regulated by, larger social-structural dynamics such as CAD processes. In addition, broader cultural dynamics impose specific normative assumptions on everyday processes of defining self and others in old age, as well as on diagnostic, legal, and other processes by which individual competencies and potentials are decreed. Without such a serious interrogation of the role of social processes, we will continue to underestimate the power of social forces and misattribute the result of specific social practices and processes to genetic, volitional, and other individual-level processes.

REFERENCES

Abbott, R. D., White, L. R., Ross, G. W., Masaki, K. H., Curb, J. D., & Petrovitch, H. (2004). Walking and dementia in physically capable elderly men. *Journal of the American Medical Association, 292,* 1447–1453.

Adams, A. K., Wermuth, E. O, & McBride, P. E. (1999, September 1). Antioxidant vitamins and the prevention of coronary heart disease. *American Family Physician*. Retrieved July 17, 2006, from http://www.aafp.org/afp/990901ap/895.html

American Psychiatric Association. (2000). *Diagnostic and statistical manual of mental disorders* (4th ed., text revision). Washington, DC: Author.

Bailey, D. B., Bruer, J. T., Symons, F. J., & Lichtman, M. D. (Eds.). (2001). *Critical thinking about critical periods*. Baltimore, MD: Paul H. Brookes.

Barnes, D. E., Tager, I. B., Satariano, W. A., & Yaffe, K. (2004). The relationship between literacy and cognition in well-educated elders. *Journals of Gerontology, Series A: Biological Sciences and Medical Sciences, 59*, M390–M395.

Bowler, J. V. (Ed.). (2004). *Vascular cognitive impairment: Preventable dementia*. New York: Oxford University Press.

Bremner, J. D., Narayan, M., Anderson, E. R., Staib, L. H., Miller, H. L., & Charney, D. S. (2000). Hippocampal volume reduction in major depression. *American Journal of Psychiatry, 157*, 115–118.

Breteler, M. M. B. (2000). Vascular risk factors for Alzheimer's disease: An epidemiologic perspective. *Neurobiological Aging, 21*, 153–160.

Colcombe, S. J., Erickson, K. I., Raz, N., Webb, A. G., Cohen, N. J., McAuley, E., et al. (2003). Aerobic fitness reduces brain tissue loss in aging humans. *Journals of Gerontology, Series A: Biological and Medical Sciences, 58*, M176–M180.

Cruz, M. L., & Goran, M. L. (2004). The metabolic syndrome in children and adolescents. *Current Diabetes Reports, 4*, 53–62.

Crystal, S., & Shea, D. (1990). Cumulative advantage, cumulative disadvantage, and inequality among elderly people. *Gerontologist, 30*, 437–443.

Crystal, S. & Shea, D. (2003). Introduction: Cumulative advantage, public policy, and inequality in later life. In S. Crystal & D. Shea (Eds.), *The annual review of gerontology and geriatrics, 22* (pp. 1–14). New York: Springer Publishing.

Dannefer, D. (1984). Adult development and social theory. *American Sociological Review 49*, 100–116.

Dannefer, D. (1988). What's in a name? An account of the neglect of variability in the study of aging. In J. E. Birren & V. L. Bengtson (Eds.), *Emergent theories of aging* (pp. 356–384). New York: Springer Publishing.

Dannefer, D. (2000). Paradox of opportunity: Work and age integration in the U.S. and Germany. *Gerontologist, 40*, 282–286.

Dannefer, D. (2003). Cumulative advantage/disadvantage and the life course: Cross-fertilizing age and social science theory. *Journals of Gerontology, Series B: Psychological Sciences and Social Sciences, 58*, S327–S337.

Dannefer, D., & Patterson, R. S. (in press). Aging families and the aging of the institutionalized life course in the 21st century. In P. Uhlenberg & K. W. Schaie (Eds.), *The impact of demographic changes on the well-being of the older persons*. New York: Springer Publishing.

Dannefer, D., & Sell, R. (1988). Age structure, the life course and "aged heterogeneity": Prospects for research and theory. *Comprehensive Gerontology, 2*, 1–10.

Dannefer, D., & Uhlenberg, P. (1999). Paths of the life course: A typology. In V. L. Bengtson & K. W. Schaie (Eds.), *Handbook of theories of aging* (pp. 306–326). New York: Springer Publishing.

Dik, M. G., Deeg, D. J. H., Visser, M., & Jonker, C. (2003). Early life physical activity and cognition in old age. *Journal of Clinical and Experimental Neuropsychology, 25,* 643–653.

Drewnowski, A., & Specter, S. E. (2004). Poverty and obesity: The role of energy density and energy costs. *American Journal of Clinical Nutrition, 79,* 6–16.

Dwyer, J. C. (2005). *Hunger and obesity in East Harlem: Environmental influences on urban food access.* Retrieved November 30, 2005, from http://www.nyccah.org//media/eastharlem.doc

Edwardson, J., & Morris C. (1998). The genetics of Alzheimer's disease—The number of genetic risk factors associated with this disorder is increasing steadily. *British Medical Journal, 317,* 361–362.

Englehart, M. J., Geerlings, M. I., Ruitenberg, A., van Sweiten, J. C., Hofman, A., Witterman, J. C. M., et al. (2002). Dietary intake of antioxidants and risk of Alzheimer disease. *Journal of the American Medical Association, 287,* 3223–3229.

Entwisle, D. R., Alexander, K. L., & Olson, L. S. (2001). Keep the faucet flowing: Summer learning and home environment. *American Educator,* Fall, 10–15, 47.

Epel, E. S., McEwen, B., Seeman, T., Matthews, K., Castellazzo, G., Brownell, K. D., et al. (2000). Stress and body shape: Stress-induced cortisol secretion is consistently greater among women with central fat. *Psychosomatic Medicine, 62,* 623–632.

Falletta, L., & Dannefer, D. (2005, November). *Does cumulative advantage occur early in the life course?* Paper presented at the Annual Meeting of the Gerontological Society of America, Orlando, FL.

Farkas, G. (2003). Human capital and the long-term effects of education on late-life inequality. In S. Crystal & D. Shea (Eds.), *Annual review of gerontology and geriatrics 22,* 138–154. New York: Springer Publishing.

Ferraro, K. F., & Kelley-Moore J. A. (2001). Self-rated health and mortality among black and white adults: Examining the dynamic evaluation thesis. *Journals of Gerontology, Series B: Psychological Sciences and Social Sciences, 56,* S195–S205.

Fox, K. R. (1999). The influence of physical activity on mental well-being. *Public Health Nutrition, 2,* 411–418.

Gubrium, J. (1986). *Oldtimers and Alzheimer's: The descriptive organization of senility.* Greenwich, CT: JAI Press.

Hagestad, G. O., & Dannefer, D. (2001). Concepts and theories of aging: Beyond microfication in social science approaches. In R. H. Binstock & L. K. George (Eds.), *Handbook of aging and the social sciences* (pp. 3–19). New York: Academic Press.

Hemingway, H., & Marmot, M. (1999). Psychosocial factors in the aetiology and prognosis of coronary heart disease: A systematic review of prospective cohort studies. *British Medical Journal, 318,* 1460–1467.

Henry, J. (1988). The archetypes of power and intimacy. In J. E. Birren & V. L. Bengtson (Eds.), *Emergent theories of aging* (pp. 269–298). New York: Springer Publishing.

Honig, L. S., Kukull, W., & Mayeux, R. (2005). Atherosclerosis and AD: Analysis of data from the U.S. National Alzheimer's Coordinating Center. *Neurology, 64,* 494–500.

Horowitz, C. R., Colson, K. A., Herbert, P. L., & Lancaster, K. (2004). Barriers to buying healthy foods for people with diabetes: Evidence of environmental disparities. *American Journal of Public Health, 94,* 1549–1554.

Huber, J. C. (1998). Cumulative advantage and success-breeds-success: The value of time pattern analysis. *Journal of the American Society for Information Science, 49,* 471–76.

Hughes, M. E., & Waite, L. J. (in press). The aging of the second demographic transition. In P. Uhlenberg & K. W. Schaie (Eds.), *The impact of demographic changes on the well-being of the older persons.* New York: Springer Publishing.

Husaini, B. A., Sherkat, D. E., Moonis, M., Levine, R., Holzer, C., & Cain, V. A. (2003). Racial differences in the diagnosis of dementia and in its effects on the use and costs of health care services. *Psychiatric Services, 54,* 92–96.

Iadecola, C., & P. B. Gorelick. (2003). Converging pathogenic mechanisms in vascular and neurodegenerative dementia. *Stroke, 34,* 335–337.

Johnson, P., Wilson, R., Fulp, R., Schuetz, B., Orton, P. (2005). *The healthy heart initiative: Barriers to eating a heart healthy diet in a low income African American community.* Retrieved November 30, 2005, from http://www.brighamandwomens.org/ConnorsCenter/

Karp, A., Kåreholt, I., Qui, C., Bellander, T., Winblad, B., & Fratiglioni, L. (2004). Relation of education and occupation-based socionomic status to incident Alzheimer's disease. *American Journal of Epidemiology, 159,* 175–183.

Keller, K. B., & Lemberg, L. (2003). Obesity and metabolic syndrome. *American Journal of Critical Care, 12,* 167–170.

Kohli, M. (1986). Social organization and the subjective construction of the life course. In A. B. Sorensen, F. E. Weinert, & L. R. Sherrod (Eds.), *Human development and the life course* (pp. 271–293). Hillsdale, NJ: Erlbaum.

Kuzawa, C. W. (2004). Modeling fetal adaptation to nutrient restriction: Testing the fetal origins hypothesis with a supply-demand model. *Journal of Nutrition, 134,* 194–200.

Lamarche, B. (1998). Abdominal obesity and its metabolic complications: Implications for the risk of ischaemic heart disease. *Coronary Artery Disease, 9,* 473–481.

Landers, D. M. (1997). The influence of exercise on mental health. *The President's Council on physical fitness and sports,* series 2, number 12 (Dec.).

Letenneur, L., Gilleron, V., Commenges, D., Helmer, C., Orgogozo, J. M., & Dartigues, J. F. (1999). Are sex and educational level independent predictors of dementia and Alzheimer's disease? Incidence data from the PAQUID project. *Journal of Neurology, Neurosurgery, and Psychiatry, 66,* 177–183.

Lindsey, K. P., & Paul, G. L. (1989). Involuntary commitments to public mental institutions: Issues involving the overrepresentation of Blacks and assessment of relevant functioning. *Psychological Bulletin, 106,* 171–183.

Lyman, K. A. (1989). Bringing the social back in: A critique of the biomedicalization of dementia. *Gerontologist, 29,* 597–605.

Marmot, M., & Elliot, P. (1992). *Coronary heart disease: From etiology to public health.* New York: Oxford University Press.

Marmot, M., & Wilkerson, R. (1999). *Social determinants of health.* New York: Oxford University Press.

Martin, A. (2003). Antioxidant vitamins E and C and risk of Alzheimer's disease. *Nutrition Reviews, 61,* 69–73.

Maxwell, B., & Jacobson, M. (1989). *Marketing disease to Hispanics.* Washington, DC: Center for Science in the Public Interest.

McGill, H. C., & McMahan, C. A. (2003). Starting earlier to prevent heart disease. [editorial] *Journal of the American Medical Association, 290,* 2320–2322.

Merton, R. K. (1968). The Matthew effect in science. *Science, 159,* 56–63.

Minehira, K., & Tappy, L. (2002). Dietary and lifestyle interventions in the management of the metabolic syndrome: Present status and future perspective. *European Journal of Clinical Nutrition, 56,* 1264–1269.

Moceri, V. M., Kukull, W. A., Emanual, I., van Belle, G., Starr, J. R., Schellenberg, G. D., et al. (2001). Using census data and birth certificates to reconstruct the early-life socioeconomic environment and the relation to the development of Alzheimer's disease. *Epidemiology, 12,* 383–389.

Mortimer, J. A., Borenstein, A. R., Gosche, K. M., & Snowdon, D. A. (2005). Very early detection of Alzheimer neuropathology and the role of brain reserve in modifying its clinical expression. *Journal of Geriatric Psychiatry and Neurology, 18,* 218–223.

Oken, E., & Gillman, M. W. (2003). Fetal origins of obesity. *Obesity Research, 11,* 496–506.

O'Rand, A. (1995). The cumulative stratification of the life course. In R. H. Binstock, L. K. George, & Associates (Eds.), *Handbook of aging and the social sciences* (4th ed., pp. 188–207). San Diego: Academic Press.

Pampel, F. (1981). *Social change and the aged: Recent trends in the United States.* Lexington, MA: Lexington Books.

Quadagno, J. (2005). *Aging and the life course: An introduction to social gerontology.* New York: McGraw-Hill.

Riley, M. W., Kahn, R. L., & Foner, A. (Eds.). (1994). *Age and structural lag.* New York: Wiley.

Riley, M. W., Johnson, M., & Foner, A. (Eds.). (1972). *Aging and society, Vol. 3: A sociology of age stratification.* New York: Russell Sage Foundation.

Ross, C. E., & Mirowsky, J. (2005). Refining the association between education and health: The effects of quantity, credential and selectivity. *Demography 36,* 445–460.

Samaras, K., Nguyen, T. V., Jenkins, A. B., Eisman, J. A., Howard, G. M., Kelly, P. J., et al. (2000). Clustering of insulin resistance, total and central abdominal fat: Same genes or same environment? *Twin Research, 2,* 218–225.

Sapolsky, R. M. (2000). The possibility of neurotoxicity in the hippocampus in major depression: A primer on neuron death. *Biological Psychiatry, 48,* 755–765.

Schlosser, E. (2002). *Fast food nation: The dark side of the American meal.* New York: Perennial.

Selkoe, D. J. (2001). Alzheimer's disease: Genes, proteins, and therapy. *Neurology, 81,* 742–766.

Settersten, R. (1999). *Lives in time and place.* Amityville, NY: Baywood.

Shaffer, A. (2002, May). *The persistence of L.A.'s grocery gap: The need for a new food policy and approach to market development.* Los Angeles: Center for Food and Justice, Urban and Environmental Policy Institute, Occidental College.

Snowdon, D. (2002). *Aging with grace: What the Nun Study teaches us about leading longer, healthier, and more meaningful lives.* New York: Bantam Dell Publishing Group.

Snowdon, D. A., Greiner, L. H., Mortimer, J. A., Riley, K. P., Greiner, P. A., & Markesbery, W. R. (1997). Brain infarction and the clinical expression of Alzheimer disease: The Nun Study. *Journal of the American Medical Association, 277,* 813–817.

Snowdon, D., Kemper, S., Mortimer, J., Greiner, L., Wekstein, D., & Markesbery, W. (1996). Linguistic ability in early life and cognitive function and Alzheimer's disease in late life: Findings from the Nun Study. *Journal of the American Medical Association, 275,* 528–532.

Tzourio, C., Anderson, C., Chapman, N., Woodward, M., Neal, B., MacMahon, S., et al. (2003). Effects of blood pressure lowering with perindopril and indapamide therapy on dementia and cognitive decline in patients with cerebrovascular disease. *Archives of Internal Medicine, 63,* 1069–1075.

Uhlenberg, P., & Dannefer, D. (2006) Age stratification. In J. E. Birren (Ed.), *Encyclopedia of gerontology.* New York: Elsevier.

Vincent, J. (1995). *Inequality and old age.* London: Taylor & Francis.

Weiss, R., Dziura, J., Burgert, T. S., Tamborlane, W. V., Taksali, S. E., Yeckel, C. W., et al. (2004). Obesity and the metabolic syndrome in children and adolescents. *New England Journal of Medicine, 350,* 2362–2374.

Weuve, J., Kang, J. H., Manson, J. E., Breteler, M. M. B., Ware, J. H., & Grodstein, F. (2004). Physical activity, including walking, and cognitive function in older women. *Journal of the American Medical Association, 292,* 1454–1461.

Youngstedt, S. D., O'Connor, P. J., Crabbe, J. B., & Dishman, R. K. (1998). Acute exercise reduces caffeine-induced anxiogenesis. *Medicine and Science in Sports and Exercise, 30,* 740–745.

CHAPTER 12

Humanistic Gerontology and the Meaning(s) of Aging

Thomas R. Cole

Michelle Sierpina

Gerontology as a formal field of inquiry is a creature of the 20th century. One might date its origins as late as 1945—when the Gerontological Society of America (GSA) was founded—or as early as 1908, when Metchnikoff coined the term *gerontology* (Achenbaum, 1995). In either case, early researchers and scholars deliberately distanced themselves from older forms of authoritative knowledge, which had allowed permeable borders between religion and science, faith and insight, reason and revelation (Cohen, 1985).

The formative literature of gerontology and geriatrics was written between 1890 and 1930 (Cole, 1992). During this era, scientists understood that they were purposely closing the borders, narrowing the range of questions and the type of knowledge that would be considered legitimate. As Claude Bernard, the father of modern experimental medicine, wrote, "We know absolutely nothing about the essence . . . of life; but we shall nevertheless regulate vital phenomena as soon as we know enough of their necessary conditions" (cited in Cole, 1992, p. 191). Alexis Carrel, famous for cultivating "immortal" cells outside the body, spoke for many when he proclaimed that spiritual questions had been removed to the dustbin of history: "Scientific civilization has destroyed the world of the soul. But the realm of matter is widely opened to man. He must, then, keep intact the vigor of his body and his intelligence. Only the strength of youth gives the power to satisfy physiological appetites and to conquer the outer world" (cited in Cole, 1992, p. 191).

This embrace of modernist science helps explain why gerontologists historically stayed away from questions of meaning and value, of ethics, metaphysics, and spirituality. When these questions became more urgent in the last quarter of the 20th century, gerontologists tended to answer them from within the paradigm of modernist science. They wrote authoritative books like *Successful Aging* (Rowe & Kahn, 1998) and *How and Why We Age* (Hayflick, 1996) without acknowledging that the answers to certain questions require scholarship from disciplines such as philosophy, history, theology, ethics, and literature. Beginning in the 1970s, professionally trained humanists and humanistically oriented scientists began grappling with moral and spiritual questions in a more intellectually rigorous way.

The 1970s witnessed political and social movements aimed at constructing a "new" old age or an "ageless society." As the attack on ageism swung into high gear, academic gerontologists, humanists, health professionals, social workers, organized elders, and others attempted to eliminate negative stereotypes of and prejudice toward older people. The social meanings of aging and old age were in great flux. In this context, many people became aware that something important was missing in gerontology: urgent existential, moral, and spiritual issues had no place on the map of gerontological knowledge. The basic question of humanistic gerontology—What does it mean to grow old?—had not been raised.

This question, of course, has no single or universal answer—at least not one that finite historical beings can provide. The answers depend on a culture's background understanding of what underlies human dignity, what makes life worth living. Indeed, the question itself is abstracted from other innumerable questions that arise in historically and culturally specific forms—for example, What is a good old age? Is there anything important to be done after children are raised and careers completed? Is old age the fulfillment of life or a second childhood? What are the possibilities of flourishing in old age? How do we bear decline of body and mind? What kind of elders do we want to be? What are the paths to wisdom? What are the vices and virtues of elderly people? What kind of support and care does society owe its frail and broken elders? What are the obligations of the old?

Of course, thoughtful people have always pondered such questions, but modern scientific methodology, which is technical, instrumental, avowedly objective, and value neutral, had obscured or denied them as legitimate academic subjects. The scientific method is designed to break down questions into their smallest measurable units in order to analyze and explain. Reproducible results are then deployed through technology, clinical care, social services, and public policy to improve the health and well-being of older people. Trouble arises when the methods of science are taken to be the only method of knowing. Then scientism replaces science; thus, gerontology fails to distinguish between aging as a problem to be solved and aging as an experience to be lived meaningfully and fully.

Oversimplifying, we might say that while science breaks things down into smaller units to create mathematically reproducible, decontextualized knowledge, the humanities look at things holistically and contextually in order to interpret their meaning. The humanities disciplines (languages and literature, history, philosophy, jurisprudence, religious studies, and the interpretive social sciences) may include scientific method as part of their inquiry, but their primary tools are interpreting, contextualizing, valuing, and self-knowing. The humanities aim at understanding (rather than explaining) human experience through the disciplined development of insight, perspective, critical understanding, discernment, and creativity. Ideally, gerontological knowledge uses both styles of inquiry in collaboration, each compensating for the other's limits.

If we try to locate the beginning of humanistic gerontology, I suggest the year 1975, when historian David Van Tassel launched a two-year Human Values and Aging project, supported by the National Endowment for the Humanities. (For earlier work, see Grmek, 1958; Gruman, 1966.) At the time, a framework of human values had already been successfully developed by the Society for Health and Human Values, established in 1965 to challenge dehumanization in medicine and health care (Fox, 1985). Using the rhetoric of human values, Van Tassel brought together senior and junior scholars in two interdisciplinary conferences to look at aging from various humanities disciplines. (I, Cole, was a graduate student at the time and thrilled to attend as an onlooker.) The best papers from these conferences were collected and edited in the first two volumes of humanistic gerontology (Spicker, Woodward, & Van Tassel, 1978; Van Tassel, 1979; Moss, 1976).

Van Tassel was also a founding member of the GSA's Humanities and Arts Committee, created in 1976 at the request of former GSA president Joseph Freeman, a humanistically oriented physician and scholar. Van Tassel's efforts opened up a steady stream of scholarship in the humanities and aging. By the mid-1980s, when the Humanities and Arts Committee commissioned an annotated bibliography, more than 1,100 books and articles had been written (Polisar, Wygant, Cole & Perdomo, 1988). In 1992, Cole, Van Tassel, and Kastenbaum edited the first *Handbook of the Humanities and Aging*, which mapped the field's temporary boundaries, introduced readers to state-of-the-art research, established intellectual standards, and suggested new lines of research.

Meanwhile, humanists, along with their social science colleagues in Britain and America, were creating a "critical gerontology"—concerned with removing forms of domination and with identifying possibilities for emancipatory social change (Phillipson & Walker, 1987; Minkler & Estes, 1991; Cole, Achenbaum, Jakobi, & Kastenbaum, 1993). In 2000, publication of the second edition of the *Handbook of the Aging and Humanities* (Cole, Kastenbaum & Ray, 2000) revealed the maturation of humanistic gerontology—summarizing its scholarly accomplishments, its linkages with the social sciences and health professions, along with new efforts in spirituality, cultural studies, film studies, and performance studies.

DISCIPLINARY PERSPECTIVES: HISTORY, LITERATURE, PHILOSOPHY, AND RELIGIOUS STUDIES

American historians were the first humanistic disciplinary group to ply their trade in the field of aging. Before the 1970s, the history of aging was written by sociologists and anthropologists (Haber, 2000). Working from large-scale models of social change (e.g., modernization theory), social scientists told a story of declining prestige, power, and income. According to this grand narrative, older people enjoyed power and prestige before the coming of urban industrial society. They presided over three-generational patriarchal households, and their experience, knowledge, and control over property guaranteed a high social status. In the 19th century, as more people moved into cities and began working in factories, older people were separated from their families, forced out of the labor market, and relegated to the scrap heap of industrial society.

Historical research done by David Hackett Fischer (1978), W. Andrew Achenbaum (1978), Carole Haber (1983), Brian Gratton (1986), and Thomas Cole (1992), among others, revealed that this decline narrative was defective in several ways. Historians of colonial New England, for example, found that three-generational households were the exception rather than the norm. Most aging couples lived in two-generational households and were still responsible for the care of their adolescent children. When one spouse died or became incapacitated, the other spouse often moved into the household of a grown child. Whatever power they possessed came from control over resources or legal arrangements made in advance. Unlike immigrants from southern and eastern Europe, immigrants from northwestern Europe brought with them an ideal of independent households, which they pursued whenever resources allowed.

American historians also critiqued the large-scale quantitative generalizations sought by social science theories of modernization. They explored diaries, letters, and publications of the old. They probed the values and individual differences of older people rather than treating them as a unified category. Rather than seeing old people as passive recipients of large-scale social forces, historians wanted to know how older people actually felt, what part they played in shaping their own history, what views they had on the nature of a good old age.

As Pat Thane has pointed out, it is very difficult to generalize about the history of aging in the West (Thane, 2000). Historians of old age in Britain have written primarily about demography and the material conditions of older people: "the numbers of old people, their geographical distribution, their living arrangements; . . . household structures and family relationships: . . . welfare arrangements, medical provisions, property transactions, work and retirement" (Thane, 2000, p. 3). French historians have given attention to demography and welfare, but also to the history of medicine and representations of old age. Work on old age in Germany, Canada, Australia, and New Zealand is fragmentary and still developing. Differences between social groups, different time periods, places, and national cultures create a patchwork of snapshots that defy generalizations.

In Europe, as in America, the long-standing belief that the status of older people is always declining is unsupportable. Ironically, the history of old age in the 20th century becomes less diverse and more uniform across national, cultural, and social boundaries, as the institutionalized life course and the welfare state become primary social institutions. Historians and social scientists have produced essential work for understanding the rise of the welfare state and American exceptionalism (Achenbaum, 1983; Myles, 1984).

Literature followed history as the next discipline in the humanities to explore aging in a serious way. Throughout the late 1970s and 1980s, Kathleen Woodward was the most prolific writer and editor of work on aging, literature, and culture (Woodward, 1978, 1991; Woodward & Schwartz, 1986). Literary critics faced two basic tasks: to demonstrate literature's contribution to understanding aging and the impact of aging on the life and work of creative writers. Although scholars argued convincingly that aging is an essential but missing element of literary criticism, they attracted little interest in English departments or at the Modern Language Association. In traditional humanities departments, as in the culture at large, aging and old age are not welcome topics.

In her survey of literary gerontology in 1992, Anne Wyatt Brown, herself an important contributor to this field, divided the scholarship into five categories: (1) analyses of literary attitudes toward aging; (2) humanistic approaches to literature and aging; (3) psychoanalytic explorations of literary works and their authors; (4) applications of the gerontological theories about autobiography, life review, and midlife transitions; and (5) psychoanalytically informed studies of the creative process.

One fascinating discovery of the 1980s was that older people began appearing as heroes and heroines in contemporary novels and short stories. In 1972, Simone de Beauvoir had confidently declared that an old person could not be a good hero for a novel; older people were "finished, set, with no hope, no developments to be looked for . . . nothing that can happen . . . that's of any importance" (de Beauvoir, 1972). Fifteen years later however, Margaret Gullette analyzed a new genre she called "midlife progress novels" (Gullette, 1988). Shortly thereafter Constance Rooke identified the genre of *vollendungsroman* (story of completion)— "novels presenting the struggle for affirmation in old age, offering a new paradigm of hope in contemporary fiction" (Rooke, 1992, p. 241).

Throughout the 1990s and beyond, literary studies of aging led the way in humanistic gerontology, influenced by the cultural studies movement, the growth of narrative studies, as well as the proliferation of guided autobiography and life story programs for elders (Birren & Cochran, 2001; Ray, 2000). Margaret Gullette emerged as the primary theorist and practitioner of what she called "age studies"—modeled after studies of race, class, and gender (Gullette, 2000, Gullette, 2004). During the same time period, Anne Basting and others were developing the field of performance studies and aging, which included both the theory and practice of theatrical work with elders (Basting, 1998).

Philosophy as a professional discipline has actually contributed relatively little to our knowledge of aging—with the exception of bioethics, which we treat separately below. As noted above, physiological, clinical, and behavioral criteria of successful aging have overshadowed philosophical inquiry into the meanings and purposes of old age, the rights and obligations of older people, and other topics. In 1982, Patrick McKee edited the first contemporary collection of ancient and modern philosophers on aging (McKee, 1982). In 2000, Ronald Manheimer divided the field into four basic topics: (1) philosophers' depictions of the possibilities and limitations of later life, (2) ethical questions of meaning and purpose in old age, (3) the study of wisdom, and (4) the current relationship of academic philosophy to the study of aging (Manheimer, 2000).

The history of philosophy yields no single path as the way to a good old age or the appropriate role of older citizens. Plato, Aristotle, Cicero, Montaigne, Schopenhauer—and more recently de Beauvoir, Norton, Moody, and Manheimer—all present ideals of old age that acknowledge its harsh reality and seek forms of adaptation, transformation, resignation, or engagement (Manheimer, 1999, 2000; de Beauvoir, 1972; Norton, 1976; Moody, 1988). Margaret Urban Walker's recent edited volume, *Mother Time*, is the first contemporary philosophical volume of feminist thought on aging, focusing primarily on ethical issues (Walker,

2000). Feminists remind us that questions about the meaning of aging are inseparable from race, gender, and class, as well as from the cultural, historical, and personal circumstances in which they arise.

Many traditional philosophical issues (such as the nature of time, identity of the self, wisdom, memory, and mortality) have been eagerly taken up by scholars in the fields of the social sciences and humanities (Birren & Clayton, 1980; Labouvie-Vief, 1990; Kaufman, 1986; Tornstram, 1997). Social and clinical gerontologists—adopting methods of critical theory, phenomenology, and hermeneutics—are making seminal qualitative and quantitative contributions. Perhaps the central limiting factor in the discipline of philosophy is that few philosophers have made an effort to become knowledgeable in gerontology, and few gerontologists are philosophically trained.

The new discipline of religious studies, which is barely 35 years old, has yet to investigate aging in a sustained way (Stoneking, 2003; Sapp, 2003; Bianchi, 1982). While the study of aging in various religious traditions (Isenberg, 2000; Moody, 2003; Thursby, 2000; Kimble, 2000) is still in an early phase, it will likely grow more quickly in the next decade. Like philosophy, very few scholars in religious studies have made an effort to become knowledgeable in gerontology. To date, the majority of the work in the study of religion and aging has come largely from Christian seminaries and pastoral care programs, clinical gerontologists, and social scientists. Melvin Kimble (an emeritus professor of pastoral care) and Susan McFadden (a psychologist with deep religious and spiritual commitments) have provided primary leadership in the cross-disciplinary field of religion and aging (Kimble & McFadden, 1995, 2003). We hope they will be joined by as yet unknown religious studies scholars who become fascinated with and committed to gerontology.

INTERDISCIPLINARY METHODS

Humanistic gerontology was born during a period of sweeping social and intellectual upheaval, just as the wave of postmodernism reached American shores (Harvey, 1989). It is important to remember that the term *postmodern* refers not only to a range of cultural and intellectual perspectives but also to a temporal watershed marking a new historical era. Observers like Anthony Giddens use the label *late modern* rather than *postmodern*, but no serious observer of contemporary culture doubts that the world has passed into a qualitatively new period of historical time (Giddens, 1991). Think of the forces at play: the computer and the digital revolution, which created an explosion of information and the speed-up of almost everything, including the production of new scientific knowledge; the saturation of the self with images generated by all kinds of electronic media spurred by consumer culture; globalization; identity confusion; intensified status anxiety; and the rapid growth of immigration from Asia, the Middle East, Latin America, and, to a lesser extent, Africa. These forces burst old moral, intellectual, religious, and cultural boundaries; they have placed us in a period of the most extensive, daunting, and creative confusion since the Renaissance.

Under these historical conditions, previously accepted disciplinary boundaries and unifying ideas gave way to *blurred genres*—forms of knowledge that accept (rather than erase) the inevitable contradiction, paradox, irony, and uncertainty in any explanation of human activity (Geertz, 1980). In 1998, the sociobiologist Edward Wilson predicted that the natural sciences and the humanities would continue as the "two great branches of learning in the 21st century"; the social sciences, he thought, would divide—"with one part folding into or becoming continuous with biology, and the other fusing with the humanities" (Manheimer, 2000, p. 89).

Gerontology seems to be following this pattern, with the majority of social scientists leaning toward the natural sciences, especially biology. An important minority, however, are pursuing qualitative methods, often under the rubric of the human sciences (Thomas, 1988). The recent resurgence of the human sciences (Rabinow & Sullivan, 1987; Polkinghorne, 1988; Marcus, 1994) is fundamentally based on reappropriation of classic humanistic forms of knowing—in particular interpretation, rhetoric, and narrative.

Interpretive inquiry, as Steven Weiland points out, acknowledges the perspective of the researcher while attempting "to reveal the meanings of human experience from the perspective of individuals, groups, institutions, and organizations being studied" (Weiland, 2000, p. 240). It marks a radical departure from the hypothesis-driven, quantitative methods of modern science. When Bernice Neugarten, one of the founders of contemporary gerontology, embraced "the interpretive turn," she put it this way:

> There are no immutable laws; no reductionist models that are securely based in logical self evidence; no "received" truths; and surely no value free social science. Change is fundamental; change is dialectical; meanings are multiple and inexhaustible. The aim is understanding, within the limits of our cultural and historical present. (Weiland, 2000, p. 241)

The human (or interpretive) sciences insist that no knowledge of human beings is complete unless it does justice to the thoughts, feelings, and expressions of the people being studied (Taylor, 1979). In gerontology, the sociologist Jaber Gubrium has criticized the positivist methodology of his colleagues for neglecting subjectivity—that is, the lived experience of aging as expressed in the words, speech, stories, and writings of older people (Gubrium, 1993a; Gubrium & Holstein, 1997). Gubrium's work on the experiences of nursing home residents involves extensive collection and interpretation of their spoken narratives (Gubrium, 1993b).

Contemporary philosophy of interpretation (hermeneutics) has made clear that every act of interpretation is itself a historically situated event. Understanding a story, a poem, painting, or an action does not take place outside time but within it. Even the best interpretation is circumscribed by the interpreter's historical, social, and personal situation. Among psychologists of aging, Harry Berman effectively adopts this perspective in his work on autobiographical narratives of older writers, in particular, journals of the poet May Sarton (Berman, 1994). Among anthropologists of aging, the work of Barbara Myerhoff and Sharon Kaufman relies heavily on humanistic concepts of interpretation and narrative (Myerhoff & Kaminsky, 1992; Kaufman, 1986).

Rediscovery of narrative as an essential form of seeking and representing knowledge has profoundly shaped gerontology's understanding of the search for meaning and identity. Narrative's influence is pervasive—from psychiatrist Robert Butler's original formulation of the life review (Butler, 1963), to the revaluation of reminiscence in clinical work with the elderly (Kaminsky, 1984; Sherman 1991), to narrative study of development (Cohler, 1982), to the articulation of narrative gerontology (Kenyon, Clark, & De Vries, 2001), to the explosion of life story writing among elders (Kenyon & Randall, 1997; Birren & Cochran, 2001), to name a few important areas.

Along with interpretation and narrative, rhetoric has also emerged as a tool of gerontological study. As a style of inquiry, rhetoric attempts to understand how human beings use language to develop and sustain their social practices. As Stephen Weiland puts it, "Rhetoric of Inquiry focuses on science, scholarship, and the professions as social institutions with distinctive habits of communication" (Weiland, 2000, p. 242). It explores, to quote Clifford Geertz, how a disciplinary discourse "gets its effects and what those are" (Weiland, 2000, p. 241). Stephen Katz's *Disciplining Old Age: The Formation of Gerontological Knowledge* is an especially effective example of a rhetoric of inquiry in gerontology (Katz, 1996). Influenced by Foucault's emphasis on the link between power and knowledge, Katz alerts readers that gerontological knowledge can be used to discipline and manage older people.

PRACTICING THE HUMANITIES:
BIOETHICS AND CREATIVITY

Humanistic gerontology has enticed some academic humanists to "com-
mute," so to speak, between theory and practice—between the library/
classroom and the hospital, the nursing home, the congregation, and the
community. The opportunity to practice the humanities—either directly
with older people themselves or indirectly with health care professionals—has borne special fruit in the areas of bioethics, spirituality, and creativity. As in other gerontological arenas, formally trained academic
humanists are few in number compared to formally trained social scientists and health professionals. Such work is done at interstices of various
disciplines, with all the excitement, messiness, and uncertainty that accompany new ventures.

Bioethics emerged in the early 1970s as a field of study and practice
in the health care professions. As noted above, medical progress generated its own set of problems: the very technology that allows people to
live longer lives also gives rise to ethical dilemmas in death and dying.
When is it permissible to terminate treatment or withdraw nutritional support? Who is authorized to make such decisions and on what grounds?
Although these problems can arise among patients of all ages, they occur
disproportionately with elderly patients, since more than two-thirds of all
deaths occur at age 65 and over (Moody, 2001; Klatz, 2001).

By the late 1980s, a significant literature on bioethics and aging had
appeared. Scholars and researchers identified ethical problems distinctive
to care of the elderly. Diminished mental capacity, for example, due to
Alzheimer's disease or other forms of dementia, raised thorny questions
about informed consent, autonomy, and proxy decision making. Other
prominent issues included vulnerability to elder abuse, ethical problems
in long-term care, and the just allocation of scarce medical resources
(Thornton, 1987; Spicker, Ingram, & Lawson, 1987; Callahan, 1987).

Bioethics is itself a strikingly interdisciplinary field, drawing on the
disciplines of philosophy, religious studies, law, qualitative and quantitative social sciences, as well as the basic and clinical sciences of the health
care professions. Considered as a subfield of bioethics, McCollough
(2000) argues that "aging and bioethics"

> undertakes the disciplined study of what morality ought to be for
> healthcare professionals responsible for the care of elderly patients
> and clients, for family members who participate in the care of elders
> in decisions about that care, for health institutions (broadly under-
> stood) responsible for the care of elderly patients and clients, and
> for society or guiding healthcare services for the elderly and their
> families. (p. 94)

Aging poses special problems for American bioethics, which has come to place so much emphasis on the principle of autonomy—which demands that competent individuals have the right to make their own decisions about health care. Increasing disability due to progressive chronic disease gradually reduces an elderly individual's capacity for self-determination. Geriatricians have noted the phenomenon of "fluctuating competence," which challenges the traditional assumption that one is either autonomous or not. Advance directives (e.g., the Living Will and Durable Power of Attorney for Healthcare) have attempted to extend the autonomy of patients beyond the point where they become incapacitated. Studies have shown, however, that patients rarely make use of these legal mechanisms; when they do so, physicians often ignore them (The SUPPORT Investigators, 1996).

As Harry R. Moody has shown (Moody, 1992) the principle of autonomy was developed and well suited to the acute care and hospital setting, where a decision about treatment led to the course of action, followed by discharge. In the long-term care setting, however, decisions rarely take the form of either-or but tend to revolve around smaller but no less important decisions of everyday life—where to spend time, how to decorate one's room, when to eat, freedom to move around versus considerations of safety. Hence, a great deal of nursing home reform is based on attention to the personal daily needs of residents in contrast to the bureaucratic needs of the nursing home (Thomas, 1999).

Ethical issues in health care policy for the elderly have occupied considerable attention since the 1980s. People over age 65 enjoy excellent health care entitlements in the United States, and the growing cost of this care has generated a heated debate under the rubric of "justice between generations." Prominent philosophers have argued for restraining the growth of life-extending interventions among the very old in order to allocate health care resources more equitably to the young (Callahan, 1987; Daniels, 1988). Others have argued that such policies would constitute age discrimination; just as society spends more money on education for children, it is only logical to spend more money on health care with the elderly (Barry & Bradley, 1991; Homer & Holstein, 1990). These issues are likely to be decided by political negotiation rather than moral deliberation. But the problem of funding long-term care of the baby boom generation may well prove the most intractable health care policy issue of all.

In addition to bioethics' contributions to patient care and public policy, creativity is a rapidly growing area of humanistic practice in gerontology. "Creativity," says George Vaillant, "can turn an old person into a young person." He believes that "creativity produces awe" and "provides a means of containing wonder" (Vaillant, 2002, p. 235). Perhaps Vaillant's observation helps account for the continuing productivity of

great artists from Michelangelo to Picasso. But recent work in creativity
and aging suggests that great artists may be exceptional only in the caliber
of the work they produced. One can make a strong case that all people of
all ages are creative to a greater or lesser degree. What is unique now
about the intersection of aging and creativity is what Ronald J. Manheimer calls today's "amazingly rich cultural milieu" that fosters opportunity for self-expression (Manheimer, Snodgrass, & Moskow-McKenzie,
1995): "Today, in the United States and other countries, many seniors
have joined a class of mature citizens with unprecedented leisure time for
pursuing recreation, entertainment, travel, knowledge of the arts and humanities, fellowship, civic duty, and physical fitness" (p. xv). This creative urge has more outlet for expression and more opportunities for
acceptance in today's societal context than perhaps at any other time in
recent history

At about the time humanistic gerontology was taking root, pioneers
like Susan Perlstein and Bonnie L. Vorenberg were birthing their own approach to gerontology services. "In 1979, I founded Elders Share the Arts
(ESTA) which focuses on living-history arts," says Perlstein, "a way of
synthesizing oral history and the creative arts." She continues, "In contrast to the apathy I encountered a quarter century ago, the recent growth
of the field of creative aging thrills me" (Perlstein, 2004, p. 2). Two
decades after the formation of ESTA, Perlstein partnered with the American Society on Aging to develop the National Center for Creative Aging
(NCCA), dedicated to supporting creative aging, by maintaining a data-
base of resources such as "professional training, replication of best practices, email newsletter, clearinghouse for information exchange, and
supports research, policy and advocacy" (Perlstein, 2004, p. 2).

Founded in 1978, Arts for Elders—Vorenberg's arts academy and
senior theater touring company—has provided leadership for others
around the country, according to colleagues at the University of Nevada,
Las Vegas, and has received funding from the National Endowment for
the Arts (Senior Theater, 2004). Vorenberg's *Senior Theater Connections*
is a compendium of resources, performing groups, and more, demon-
strating how widespread this creative outlet for elders has become.
(Vorenberg, 1999). Another leader in the field of creativity for elders,
Anne Davis Basting, Director of the Center on Age and Community at the
University of Wisconsin, Milwaukee, writes about "the lack of recognition of aging in cross-disciplinary explorations of cultural difference and
social practice over the last decade. Theories of social practice, including
groundbreaking work of scholars such as historian Michel de Certeau
and philosopher Judith Butler, tended to overlook physical and psychological changes inherent in the aging process" (Basting, 1998, p. 2). Basting developed the Time*Slips*© method of storytelling for patients with
dementia, including professional theater productions and a nationwide

training network, and she has expanded her research far beyond the examination of senior performance (Basting, 2001, 2002).

No less creative are the countless lifestory writers nationwide who express themselves by writing and sharing their lifestories. Pioneers in this field include James Birren and Kathryn Cochran, James Pennebaker, Ronald Manheimer, Ruth Ray and others (Birren & Cochran, 2001; Pennebaker, 1990; Manheimer, 1999; Ray, 2000). Cole and colleagues have brought this process to national attention through the PBS film *Life Stories* (Cole, 2001). Research continues to mount that writing about life experiences has positive therapeutic effect (Smyth, Stone, Hurewitz, & Kaell, 1999; Spiegel, 1999; Pennebaker & Seagal, 1999). Humanistic gerontologists at the University of Texas Medical Branch have developed training materials to assist others in implementing lifestory groups (Sierpina & Cole, 2004). Theorizing that "no lifestory can be studied apart from the joint construction of teller and listener," Cohler and Cole suggest ". . . there can be no lifestory apart from the particular collaboration between narrator and listener, or reader and text, apart from the matrix of their shared telling and listening" (Cohler & Cole, 1996, pp. 61, 67). Thorsheim and Roberts, researchers at St. Olaf College, may be taking the theory even further as they examine health outcomes such as blood pressure of story listeners. Their work "strongly suggests that when people listen to 'remember when' stories that are meaningful, their systolic blood pressure and heart rate are lowered significantly below resting baseline levels" (Thorsheim & Roberts, 2004).

Creativity among elders is a healthy practice. Research points to positive health outcomes for those who practice even basic activities that exercise the mind. Studies mount in support of this concept. Scientists in Chicago saw that cognitive activity across the life span had positive effects (Wilson, Barnes, & Bennett, 2003). Not only quality of life, but length of life is expanded for those who exercise creativity. Such activities have been found to enhance survival in all causes of mortality (Glass, de Leon, Marotolli, & Berkman, 1999). Recently, physicians at Albert Einstein College of Medicine in New York discovered that even reading, playing board games, or doing word games forestalled dementias in subjects age 75 and older (Verghese et al., 2003).

Geriatrician Gene Cohen believes that "what is considerably under-appreciated—even denied—is the opportunity for and frequency of creative growth and expression among the aged" (Cohen, 2000). We are encouraged by the signs that the situation is changing. Robert Kastenbaum suggests that creativity is an essential ingredient for a healthy and meaningful old age. As he writes,

> Those whose concerns center on mental health and illness might find valuable clues by exploring antecedents and consequences

of thwarted creativity. People who do not have the opportunity to develop and express their sparks of creativity are apt to become deeply frustrated. This is a more stressful situation than is commonly realized, contributing to impaired relationships and deteriorated health. Viewed in this light, creativity is a central rather than a peripheral element in living a meaningful life through a great many years. (Kastenbaum, 2000 pp. 398–399)

CONCLUSION

As this chapter has demonstrated, humanistic gerontology is now a flourishing subfield containing three basic clusters: disciplinary scholarship (history, philosophy, literature, religious studies), interdisciplinary research (especially the overlap and combination of humanistic and social science methods), and practicing the humanities (e.g., bioethics and creativity), which involves cross-disciplinary research and practice. The leading edges of humanistic gerontology now appear to be in research and practice related to narrative and creativity, as well as in feminist perspectives, age studies, and performance studies. Exciting things are happening at the collaborative intersections of humanities, social science, and clinical care. At the same time, pure humanities scholarship continues to evolve slowly but surely in various disciplines. The stage is set for more sustained and creative collaboration between humanists in gerontology and mainstream gerontologists. All of these developments bode well for gerontological inquiry.

REFERENCES

Achenbaum, W. A. (1978). *Old age in the new land.* Baltimore: Johns Hopkins University Press.

Achenbaum, W. A. (1983). *Shades of gray.* Boston: Little, Brown.

Achenbaum, W. A. (1995). *Crossing frontiers.* New York: Cambridge University Press.

Barry, R. L., & Bradley, G. V. (Eds.). (1991). *Set no limits: A rebuttal to Daniel Callahan's proposal to limit health care for the elderly.* Urbana: University of Illinois Press.

Basting, A. (1998). *The stages of age: Performing age in contemporary American culture.* Ann Arbor: University of Michigan Press.

Basting, A. (2001). It's 1924 and somewhere in Texas, two nuns are driving a backwards Volkswagen: Storytelling with people with dementia. In S. McFadden & R. Atchley (Eds.), *Aging and the meaning of time* (pp. 131–149). New York: Springer Publishing.

Basting, A. (2002). Time*Slips*© *educational guide.* Milwaukee: University of Wisconsin Press.

Berman, H. (1994). *Interpreting the aging self: Personal journals of later life*. New York: Springer Publishing.

Bianchi, E. C. (1982). *Aging as a spiritual journey*. New York: Crossroad.

Birren, J., & Clayton, V. (1980). The development of wisdom across the lifespan: A reexamination of ancient topic. In P. Baltes & O. Brim Jr. (Eds.), *Lifespan development and behavior* (Vol. 3, pp. 103–135). New York: Academic Press.

Birren, J. E., & Cochran, K. N. (2001). *The stories of life through guided autobiography groups*. Baltimore: John Hopkins University Press.

Brown, A. W. (1992). *Literary gerontology comes of age: Handbook of the humanities and aging*. New York: Springer Publishing.

Butler, R. (1963). The life review: An interpretation of reminiscence in the aged. *Psychiatry, 26,* 65–76.

Callahan, D. (1987). *Setting limits: Medical goals in an aging society*. New York: Simon & Schuster.

Cohen, G. (2000). *The creative age*. New York: Avon Books.

Cohen, I. B. (1985). *Revolution in science*. Cambridge, MA: Belknap Press of Harvard University Press.

Cohler, B. (1982). Personal narrative and life-course. In P. Baltes & O. Brim, Jr. (Eds.), *Lifespan development and behavior* (Vol. 4, pp. 205–241). New York: Academic Press.

Cohler, B., & Cole, T. (1996). Studying older lives: Reciprocal acts of telling and listening. In J. Birren, G. Kenyon, J. Ruth, J. Schroots, & T. Svensson (Eds.), *Aging and biography: Explorations in adult development*. New York: Springer Publishing.

Cole, T. R. (1992). *The journey of life: A cultural history of aging in America*. New York: Cambridge University Press.

Cole, T. (Producer). (2001). *Life stories*. [PBS video]. (Available from New River, Media, 1219 Connecticut Ave., NW, Suite 200, Washington, DC 20036.)

Cole, T. R., Achenbaum, W. A., Jakobi, P. L., & Kastenbaum, R. (Eds.). (1993). *Voices and visions of aging: Toward a critical gerontology*. New York: Springer Publishing.

Cole, T. R., Kastenbaum, R., & Ray, R. (Eds.). (2000). *Handbook of the humanities and aging* (2nd ed.). New York: Springer Publishing.

Cole, T. R., Van Tassel, D. D., & Kastenbaum, R. (Eds.). (1992). *Handbook of the humanities and aging*. New York: Springer Publishing.

Daniels, N. (1988). *Am I my parent's keeper? An essay on justice between the young and the old*. New York: Oxford University Press.

de Beauvoir, S. (1972). *The coming-of-age* (P. O'Brien, Trans.). New York: Norton.

Fischer, D. H. (1978). *Growing old in America* (2nd ed.). New York: Oxford University Press.

Fox, D. M. (1985). Who we are: The political origins of the medical humanities. *Theoretical Medicine, 6,* 327–341.

Geertz C. (1980). Blurred genres: The refiguration of social thought. *American Scholar, 49,* 165–179.

Giddens, A. (1991). *Modernity and self-identity*. Stanford: Stanford University Press.

Glass, T. A., de Leon, C. M., Marotolli, R. A., & Berkman, L. F. (1999). Population based study of social and productive activities as predictors of survival among elderly Americans. *British Medical Journal, 319*, 478–483.

Gratton, B. (1986). *Urban elders: Family, work and welfare in Boston, 1890–1950.* Philadelphia: Temple University Press.

Grmek, M. D. (1958). On ageing and old age; Basic problems and historic aspects of gerontology and geriatrics. *Monographia Biologicae, 5*, 57–162.

Gruman, G. J. (1966). A history of ideas about the prolongation of life. *Transactions of the American Philosophical Society, 56*, 3–102.

Gubrium, J. (1993a). *Gerontology and the construction of old age: A study in discourse analysis.* New York: Aldine de Gruyter.

Gubrium, J. (1993b). *Speaking of life: Horizons of meaning for nursing home residents.* New York: Aldine de Gruyter.

Gubrium, J., & Holstein, J. (1997). *The new language of qualitative methods.* New York: Oxford University Press.

Gullette, M. M. (1988). *Safe at last in the middle years: The invention of the midlife progress novel.* Berkeley: University of California Press.

Gullette, M. M. (2000). Age studies as cultural studies. In T. Cole, R. Kastenbaum, & R. Ray (Eds.), *Handbook of humanities and aging* (2nd ed., pp. 214–234). New York: Springer Publishing.

Gullette, M. M. (2004). *Aged by culture.* Chicago: University of Chicago Press.

Haber, C. (1983). *Beyond sixty-five.* New York: Cambridge University Press.

Haber, C. (2000). Historians' approach to aging in America. In T. Cole, R. Kastenbaum, & R. Ray (Eds.), *Handbook of humanities and aging* (2nd ed., pp. 25–40). New York: Springer Publishing.

Harvey, D. (1989). *The condition of postmodernity.* Cambridge, MA: Blackwell.

Hayflick, L. (1996). *How and why we age.* New York: Ballantine Books.

Homer, P., & Holstein, M. (Eds.). (1990). *A good old age? The paradox of setting limits.* New York: Simon & Schuster.

Isenberg, S. (2000). Aging in Judaism: "Crown of Glory" and "Days of Sorrow." In T. Cole, R. Kastenbaum, & R. Ray (Eds.), *Handbook of humanities and aging* (2nd ed., pp. 114–141). New York: Springer Publishing.

Kaminsky, M. (Ed.). (1984). *The uses of reminiscence.* New York: Haworth.

Kastenbaum, R. (2000). Creativity and the arts. In T. Cole, R. Kastenbaum, & R. Ray (Eds.), *Handbook of humanities and aging* (2nd ed., pp. 381–401). New York: Springer Publishing.

Katz, S. (1996). *Disciplining old age: The formation of gerontological knowledge.* Charlottesville: University Press of Virginia.

Kaufman, S. (1986). *The ageless self: Sources of meaning in late life.* Madison: University of Wisconsin Press.

Kenyon, G. M., Clark, P. G., & De Vries, B. (2001). *Narrative gerontology: Theory, research, and practice.* New York: Springer Publishing.

Kenyon, G. M., & Randall, W. (1997). *Restorying our lives: Personal growth through autobiographical reflections.* Westport, CT: Praeger.

Kimble, M. (2000). Aging in the Christian tradition. In T. Cole, R. Kastenbaum, & R. Ray (Eds.), *Handbook of humanities and aging* (2nd ed., pp. 142–154). New York: Springer Publishing.

Kimble, M., & McFadden, S. (Eds.). (1995). *Aging, spirituality, and religion: A handbook*. Minneapolis: Fortress Press.

Kimble, M., & McFadden, S. (Eds.). (2003). *Aging, spirituality, and religion: A handbook*. Minneapolis: Fortress Press.

Klatz, R. (2001). Anti-aging medicine: Resounding, independent support for expansion of an innovative medical specialty. *Generations, 21,* 59–62.

Labouvie-Vief, G. (1990). Adaptive dimensions of adult cognition. In N. Datan & N. Logman (Eds.), *Transitions of aging* (pp. 3–26). New York: Academic Press.

Manheimer, R. J. (1999). *A map to the end of time: Wayfarings with friends and philosophers*. New York: Norton.

Manheimer, R. J. (2000). Aging in the mirror of philosophy. In T. Cole, R. Kastenbaum, & R. Ray (Eds.), *Handbook of humanities and aging* (2nd ed., pp. 77–92). New York: Springer Publishing.

Manheimer, R., Snodgrass, D., & Moskow-McKenzie, D. (1995). *Older adult education: A guide to research, programs, policies*. Westport, CT: Greenwood Press.

Marcus, G. (1994). On ideologies of reflexivity in contemporary efforts to remake the human sciences. *Poetics Today, 15,* 383–404.

McCullough, L. B. (2000). Bioethics and aging. In T. Cole, R. Kastenbaum, & R. Ray (Eds.), *Handbook of humanities and aging* (2nd ed., pp. 93–113). New York: Springer Publishing.

McKee, P. (Ed.). (1982). *Philosophical foundations of gerontology*. New York: Human Sciences Press.

Minkler, M., & Estes, C. (Eds.). (1991). *Critical perspectives on aging: Perspectives from political and moral economy*. New York: Baywood.

Moody, H. R. (1988). *Abundance of life: Human development policies for an aging society*. New York: Columbia University Press.

Moody, H. R. (1992). *Ethics and aging*. Baltimore: Johns Hopkins University Press.

Moody, H. R. (2001). Who's afraid of life extension? *Generations, 25,* 33–37.

Moody, H. R. (2003). Conscious aging: The future of religion in later life. In M. Kimble & S. McFadden (Eds.), *Aging, spirituality, and religion: A handbook* (Vol. 2, pp. 422–433). Minneapolis: Fortress Press.

Moss, W. (1976). *Humanistic perspectives on aging: An annotated bibliography and essay*. Ann Arbor: Institute of Gerontology, University of Michigan and Wayne State University.

Myerhoff, B., & Kaminsky, M. (Eds.). (1992). *Remembered lives: The work of ritual, storytelling, and growing older*. Ann Arbor: University of Michigan Press

Myles, J. (1984). *Old age in the welfare state*. Boston: Little, Brown.

Norton, D. L. (1976). *Personal destinies: A philosophy of ethical individualism*. Princeton, NJ: Princeton University Press.

Pennebaker, J. (1990). *Opening up: The healing power of expressing emotions*. New York: Guilford Press.

Pennebaker, J., & Seagal, J. (1999). Forming a story: The health benefits of narrative. *Journal of Clinical Psychology, 55,* 1243–1254.

Perlstein, S. (2004, November–December). Elder arts programs are thriving from California to the N.Y. Island. *Aging Today, 25,* 2. Retrieved July 8, 2004, from www.asaging.org/at/at-236/IF_elder_arts.cfm

Phillipson, C., & Walker, A. (1987). The case for critical gerontology. In S. Gregorio (Ed.), *Social gerontology: New directions* (pp. 1–15). London: Croom Helm.

Polisar, D., Wygant, L., Cole, T., & Perdomo, C. (1988). *Where do we come from? What are we? Where are we going? An annotated bibliography of aging and the humanities.* Washington, DC: Gerontological Society of America.

Polkinghorne, D. (1988). *Narrative knowing and the human sciences.* Albany, NY: SUNY Press.

Rabinow, P., & Sullivan, W. (Eds.). (1987). *Interpretive social science: A second look.* Berkeley: University of California Press.

Ray, R. (2000). *Beyond nostalgia: Aging and life story writing.* Charlottesville: University of Virginia Press.

Rooke, C. (1992). Old age in contemporary fiction: A new paradigm of hope. In T. Cole, D. D. Van Tassel, & R. Kastenbaum (Eds.), *Handbook of humanities and aging* (pp. 241–257). New York: Springer Publishing.

Rowe, L. W., & Kahn, R. L. (1998). *Successful aging.* New York: Patheon Books.

Sapp, S. (2003). Ethics and dementia: Dilemmas encountered by clergy and chaplains. In M. Kimble & S. McFadden (Eds.), *Aging, spirituality, and religion: A handbook* (Vol. 2, pp. 355–367). Minneapolis: Fortress Press.

Senior Theater Resource Center. (2004). Retrieved July 9, 2004, from http://seniortheater.com

Sherman, E. (1991). *Reminiscence and self in old age.* New York: Springer Publishing.

Sierpina, M. & Cole, T. R. co-producers. (2004). Bringing stories to life: Lifestory group facilitator training video. (Available from UTMB Osher Lifelong Learning Institute, 301 University Blvd., Galveston, Texas, 77555-0972.)

Smyth, J. M., Stone, A. A., Hurewitz, A., & Kaell, A. (1999). Effects of writing about stressful experiences on symptom reduction in patients with asthma or rheumatoid arthritis. *Journal of the American Medical Association, 281,* 1304–1309.

Spicker, S. F., Ingman, S. R., & Lawson, I. (Eds.). (1987). *Ethical dimensions of geriatric care.* Norwell, MA: Reidel.

Spicker, S., Woodward, K., & Van Tassel, D. (1978). *Aging and the elderly: Humanistic perspectives in gerontology.* New York: Academic Press.

Spiegel, D. (1999). Healing words: Emotional expression and disease outcome. *Journal of the American Medical Association, 281,* 1328–1329.

Stoneking, C. (2003). Postliberal, postmodern theological views of longevity. In M. Kimble & S. McFadden (Eds.), *Aging, spirituality, and religion: A handbook* (Vol. 2, pp. 303–315). Minneapolis: Fortress Press.

SUPPORT Investigators. (1996). A controlled trial to improve care for the seriously ill hospitalized patients. *Journal of the American Medical Association, 274,* 1591–1598.

Taylor, C. (1979). Interpretation and the sciences of man. In R. Rabinow & W. Sullivan (Eds.), *Interpretive social science* (pp. 27–51). Berkeley: University of California Press.

Teno, J. M., Licks, S., Lynn, J., Wenger, N., Connors, A. F. Jr., Phillips, R. S., et al. (1997, April). *Journal of the American Geriatrics Society, 45,* 508–512.

Thane, P. (2000). The history of aging in the West. In T. Cole, R. Kastenbaum, & R. Ray (Eds.), *Handbook of humanities and aging* (2nd ed., pp. 3–24). New York: Springer Publishing.

Thomas, L. E. (Ed.). (1988). *Research on adulthood and aging: The human sciences approach.* Albany, NY: SUNY Press.

Thomas, W. H. (1999). *The Eden alternative handbook: The art of building human habitats.* Sherburne, NY: Summer Hill.

Thornton, J. (Ed.). (1987). *Ethics and aging.* Vancouver: University of British Columbia Press.

Thorsheim, H., & Roberts, B. (2004). *Reminiscing, social support, and well-being.* Retrieved May 16, 2004, from www.stolaf.edu/people/thorshm/reminiscing-well-being.htm

Thursby, E. (2000). Aging in Eastern religious traditions. In T. Cole, R. Kastenbaum, & R. Ray (Eds.), *Handbook of humanities and aging* (2nd ed., pp. 235–257). New York: Springer Publishing.

Tornstram, L. (1997). Gerotranscendence: A theory about maturing into old age. *Journal of Aging and Identity, 2,* 37–50.

Vaillant, G. (2002). *Aging well: Surprising guideposts to a happier life from the landmark Harvard Study of Adult Development.* Boston: Little, Brown.

Van Tassel, D. D. (Ed.). (1979). *Aging, death, and the completion of being.* Philadelphia: University of Pennsylvania Press.

Verghese, J., Lipton, R., Katz, M., Hall, C., Derby, C., Kuslansky, G., et al. (2003). Leisure activities and the risk of dementia in the elderly. *New England Journal of Medicine, 25,* 2508–2516.

Vorenberg, B. (1999). *Senior theater connections: The first directory of senior theater performing groups, professionals, and resources.* Portland, OR: ArtAge Publications.

Walker, M. U. (Ed.). (2000). *Mother time.* Lanham, MD: Rowman & Littlefield.

Weiland, S. (2000). Social sciences towards the humanities. In T. Cole, R. Kastenbaum, & R. Ray (Eds.), *Handbook of humanities and aging* (2nd ed., pp. 235–257). New York: Springer Publishing.

Wilson, R., Barnes, L., & Bennett, D. (2003). Assessment of lifetime participation in cognitively stimulating activities. *Journal of Clinical Experimental Neuropsychology, 25,* 634–642.

Woodward, K. (1978). *At last, the real distinguished thing: The late poems of Eliot, Pound, Stevens, and Williams.* Columbus: Ohio State Press.

Woodward, K. (1991). *Aging and its discontents: Freud and other fictions.* Bloomington: Indiana University Press.

Woodward, K., & Schwartz, M. M. (Eds.). (1986). *Memory and desire: Aging—literature—psychoanalysis.* Bloomington: Indiana University Press.

PART IV

Public Policy

CHAPTER 13

Retirement and Financial Security

An Economist Thinks Out Loud

Timothy M. Smeeding

At its heart, this chapter is about how economists think about the process of aging and retirement at both an individual and a societal level. I begin with some of the substantive topics and policy arenas where economists have been writing and researching lately—especially those best suited for a broad audience, and the places (online) to find the most objective continuing research on these topics. Then I move to a discussion of economics, including economic models and their strengths and limitations for analyzing the aging processes. The overall goal is to provide some of the tools and insights that economists bring to the analysis of individual and population aging. The role of the government in providing financial security is addressed in the final part of the chapter. I conclude with some of the cutting-edge research topics that will need to be considered as we continue to address the economics of an aging society.

The reader should know that I am but one economist, and many others might view retirement security slightly differently than I do. But most will agree with how I go about setting up the questions that must be addressed by almost any type of retirement security policy.

CUTTING-EDGE TOPICS IN THE ECONOMICS OF AGING AND RELATED POLICY ARENAS

Old-fashioned economists begin with the notion that aging and security are purely an economic or financial issue. Of course, most readers of this book understand that while economics per se is important for an understanding of well-being in old age, demography, family structure, health status, and policy toward each of these are also important. Indeed the best empirical work demands databases that include each of these aspects of life. And so the best analyses of retirement and financial security are those that combine economic status (income, consumption, wealth) with health and family status. The *Health and Retirement Study* at the University of Michigan (http://hrsonline.isr.umich.edu) is a good place to begin to find these elements. Another self-serving suggestion is my recent textbook, *The Economics of an Aging Society* (Clark, Burkhauser, Moon, Quinn, & Smeeding, 2004), where we address each of these aging topics as well as health care finance. The Congressional Budget Office (CBO; see www.cbo.gov) and the National Academy of Social Insurance (NASI; see www.nasi.org) are good general and reliable sources for analyses of topics related to aging society, especially those involving social security reform, private pension insurance, and Medicare.

Increasingly the United States shares the issues related to older societies with other rich countries, and so cross-national comparative research will yield insights into the ways that different societies provide economic security and assistance for aging members. Thus, resources such as the Luxembourg Income Study (LIS; www.lisproject.org) and the Organization for Economic Cooperation and Development (OECD; www.oecd.org), especially the Social Affairs Division (OECD, 2006), will allow one to compare aging issues and their policy solutions across countries.

Over the next few years, a number of topics are going to be important, such as increased labor force participation and more market work at older ages (in my opinion, the best way to increase security in advanced old age); the security of retirement assets; the willingness of the population to save; long-term care finance; and employer pension participation and portfolio choice. Tomorrow's elders will also be different from today's in good ways (e.g., more highly educated elders, more women with work-related benefits and good earnings histories, and increasingly beneficial health care procedures and products) and not-so-good ones (e.g., rising health care costs, longer life expectancy in old age with the potential for increased disability, and asset insecurity). Growing wealth inequality will increasingly be a topic of study, along with the continuing impoverishment of very elderly women and minorities. Finally, the rising budgetary and personal costs of health care and who will bear these costs is also a continuing priority. The field of economics provides a number of constructs that will help us understand the challenges that aging individuals and aging societies face.

BASIC ECONOMICS AND RETIREMENT SAVING ECONOMICS

All societies and the individuals in those societies face the same basic economic question of what goods and services to produce, how to produce them, and for whom (Haveman & Knopf, 1981). All societies make choices in answering these questions by means of a market-based socioeconomic system in which the basic decisions are made by individual producers and consumers. These producers and consumers are all striving to achieve their own personal retirement and financial security goals, and in so doing, they respond as best they can to the incentives that penalize or reward their activities. In a market system, the primary incentives are expressed in prices that are generated in markets. These prices guide human behavior, as households and individuals decide how much of their services to sell in the labor market to producers and how to use the proceeds of this labor (their incomes) to consume, save, and provide for their old age.

When people save, they postpone consumption today in return for greater consumption tomorrow. Compensation for this postponement is called *interest* (or *investment*) *income*. Of course, everyone must consume some amount of goods and services from their incomes to survive. The amount consumed today versus tomorrow is also determined by both prices and individual preferences. These prices include both the dollar amounts spent to consume goods and services today, and the return to saving, which is also a price. Economists call this price the *interest rate*. Preferences relate to an individual's desire to consume now or wait until later. If the interest rate is high enough or if individuals believe they will need more income later to support future consumption (e.g., in retirement), they may postpone current consumption now to have more later, or they may decide to keep working to supplement their retirement savings.

These private retirement plans must also take into account public sector provision of the same needs for economic security in old age. So while I ignore public policy initially, I return later to consider social versus own provision of incomes, consumption, and key goods like health insurance (for acute health care and for chronic or long-term care).

Stocks and Flows: Income and Net Worth

Economic status is measured by both stocks and flows. *Flows* are amounts received (amounts earned by or transferred to a household or person) and amounts paid for expenditures or for services received over a given period. The earnings of a household plus its return on investments, including pensions, are called its *market income* (MI). MI is used to pay for consumed goods and services (C) and to either save (S) if consumption is less than income, or to borrow (B), if we consume more than we earn over a given period. Thus:

$$C + S = MI \text{ if } C < MI$$
$$C - B = MI \text{ if } C > MI$$

Market income is also used to pay taxes (T) to governments. These taxes may be on income earnings (e.g., payroll taxes), property (e.g., homes), or expenditures (e.g., sales taxes). Some taxes paid by citizens are returned to them in the form of government transfers (R), which I discuss in a later section. *Transfers* are payments received as entitlements or in discretionary benefits from other individuals or from governments. For instance, social security benefits are transfers, as are some parts of Medicare, as well as transfers targeted on those least able to care for themselves: Medicaid, SSI, and food stamps. A household's *disposable*, or *spendable, income* (DI) is its market income, net of taxes, after adding back transfers received. Thus:

$$DI = MI - T + R$$

Each of these items is a flow. Flows are always defined over a period such as a year, month or week.

Stocks are defined as an amount available at a point in time. Persons hold assets such as savings, investments, homes, other buildings, businesses, and vehicles. These assets are defined as a person's (or household's) *wealth* (W). At any point in time, persons may also have a set of liabilities that are owed to other persons, such as home mortgages, car loans, credit card debt, or school loans. These are called *debts* (D). A person's *net worth* (NW) is defined as wealth minus debts at any point in time:

$$NW = W - D$$

Stocks change from one period to another. The change in a stock is a flow. People who are net savers during a given period add to their net worth by either increasing wealth (W) or paying off debts (D); if they draw down their assets, they reduce net worth by decreasing W or increasing D. For instance, the idea of taking a second mortgage on an existing home and spending the money on a trip to Europe or to help grandchildren pay for college will reduce W and increase D. A *reverse annuity mortgage* will transfer the ownership of a stock (i.e., a house) to a financial institution such as a bank, in return for a steady flow of income over a given period. Thus, one can convert stocks to flows.

Those looking forward to enjoying retirement can add to their net worth by saving some of their income. Over time, the process of reducing consumption and adding to savings builds up a stock of wealth that can be used to sustain consumption in retirement or when disabled or out of work. Persons may add to retirement savings through savings plans, pension funds, or other financial vehicles. They may also build up equity in their homes. Persons may also dissave (or reduce net worth) by cashing in pension funds in emergencies or running down their wealth by consuming more than they are earning.

Law of Compound Interest

Why is it that financial planners especially urge young people to save for retirement? How much difference does it make if we start saving for retirement when we are young instead of when we are older? A short foray into financial home economics will underscore the power of compound interest and the importance of starting early and then maintaining savings for retirement.

Let us assume you are going to retire at age 65 and want to know the value of saving $1,000 for retirement (until age 65) in any given year. Next, assume there are two types of investments: one yielding a "safe" 5%, the other a "risky" 10%. Usually riskier investments have higher interest rates as a reward for those who take these risks (noting that they can lose as well as gain), but for now I will abstract from these risks. Suppose you invested $1,000 at age 45 and left it for 20 years. During that period, the initial value (IV) of the investment grows according to the law of compound interest. The future value (FV) will equal $(1 + i)$ where i is the interest rate, compounded over the n years of the investment. Thus:

$$FV = IV (1 + i)^n$$

At the end of one year with an initial investment (IV) of $1,000 and an interest rate of 5% ($i = .05$), the (FV) of the asset rises to $1,050 since $50 in interest is added to the initial investment. If $i = .1$, the value rises to $1,100, and $100 of it will be interest. The power of compound interest takes hold if the amount left at the end of the first period, the $1,050 (or $1,100), stays invested at the same interest rate over a long number of years. This process is called *compounding* because not only does the initial $1,000 grow, but also the interest each year is added to savings, and eventually earns interest as well. If a person aged 45 puts aside $1,000 for 20 years at 5%, it will be worth $2,653 at age 65. If the interest rate were 10%, the amount would $6,727.

Age 45 is, unfortunately, when many people begin to save for retirement. But instead of starting at age 45, what if one put away $1,000 for retirement at age 25 and left it there for 40 years? Even at 5%, the $1,000 would be worth $7,040 at age 65. If the return were a riskier 10%, the $1,000 would grow to $45,259. Thus, beginning to save for retirement at age 25 yields a substantially larger amount than waiting until age 45 to save. Table 13.1 presents a larger series of returns on an initial investment with constant returns of 5% and 10% over a number of years. Consistent annual investments, even if small, mount up substantially over time.

Risky Investments and Postponing Retirement

Of course, people would prefer a constant and safe 10% return instead of a more modest 5% return. Unfortunately, this is not the way that investment works. Few investments can guarantee a constant 10% return, especially over a 40-year period. However, over a long period of time, a

TABLE 13.1 Future Value and Compound Interest for $1000 Invested Once and Left to Grow in an Interest-Bearing Account

Years	Age	FV at $i = .05$	FV at $i = .10$
1	65	$1,050 = 1,000 (1 + .05)^1$	$1,100 = 1,000 (1 + .10)^1$
10	55	$1,629 = 1,000 (1 + .05)^{10}$	$2,593 = 1,000 (1 + .10)^{10}$
20	45	$2,653 = 1,000 (1 + .05)^{20}$	$6,727 = 1,000 (1 + .10)^{20}$
30	35	$4,322 = 1,000 (1 + .05)^{30}$	$17,449 = 1,000 (1 + .10)^{30}$
40	25	$7,040 = 1,000 (1 + .05)^{40}$	$45,259 = 1,000 (1 + .10)^{40}$

Notes:
$$FV = IV (1 + i)n$$
where:
FV = future value of investment, assuming money is not withdrawn until age 65.
IV = initial value of investment made in a given year.
n = number of years for investment.
i = interest rate on investment.
Age = age at which you begin to invest for retirement, assuming money is not withdrawn until age 65.

risky investment, even with ups and downs at any point over the period, usually produces a higher return than a safe, fixed investment. For instance, longer-term certificates of deposit or government bonds may yield a safe 3 to 5% return. One can even buy inflation-protected bonds that pay a small return of 1 to 2% but also are adjusted for inflation so the value of the investment is protected against price changes. Corporate stocks and bonds are much riskier because they vary with the profitability of the company and the general health of the economy. They sometimes pay 10%, but other times more, and sometimes less. Over the past 50 years, however, stocks and bonds have averaged about a 7% return. Assuming that the $1,000 is invested for 40 years at 7%, this investment will yield $12,974, nearly twice the $7,040 return on the 5% investment (and any change in prices experienced over the period may be subtracted from both investments, thus making the 7 and 5% returns more like a 4 and a 2% real return with long-term inflation at 3%). While it may take a strong stomach to withstand the ups and downs of the stock market over a 40-year period, history has shown that those who do so are likely to be rewarded for taking such risks—not at a peak return in all periods, but at a higher return than the low-risk investments.

The final basic point to be made is that with investments like these, there is a reward to delaying retirement (or withdrawal of funds). In the example on the final line of Table 13.1, the hypothetical individual has saved a single one-time investment of $1,000 for 40 years, depositing the initial amount at age 25 and realizing his investment at age 65, and has $7,040 for his efforts. Now suppose this person decided to work another five years, until age 70, and to leave his retirement savings intact for the five years at the assumed rate of interest. The reward for waiting is an extra $1,945. At a 10% interest rate; the difference is $17,631. Thus, postponing retirement by five years may pay handsome dividends to those who hold their accumulated savings and instead choose to work to support their consumption over this period. Of course, compound interest works the other way as well. Stopping work and retiring early at age 60 reduces the value of the $1,000 put away at age 25 to $28,102 at the 10% interest rate, $17,157 less than if it were left until age 65.

Finally, risky investments at older ages may not always be the best choice. The 10% return over 45 years yields $45,259 at age 65, but if the stock market loses 5% per year over the next five years, this $45,259 will fall to only $35,021. Putting the $45,259 at age 65 into a safer 5% investment still yields $57,763 at age 70. This is a lesson that many investors on the verge of retirement in 2001 and 2002 learned the hard way. As most people grow older and retirement is drawing near, switching to a safe asset reduces the risks inherent in the stock market and provides added financial security. Indeed, most savvy investors split their savings by investing larger amounts in safer financial vehicles and putting smaller amounts in riskier investments as they draw closer to retirement. This process is called *portfolio diversification*. In all cases, economists recommend that retirement investment portfolios include many types of assets—foreign, domestic, financial assets (e.g., stocks, bonds, and mutual funds—which are just specific combinations of stocks and bonds), and nonfinancial assets (e.g., owner-occupied housing). Most readers will also note that work-related old age benefits, like employment pensions and retiree health insurance, and public sector assets, like social security and Medicare, should also be figured into a retirement portfolio. The issue will then be how secure and safe these nontraditional assets are compared to others that one might control more directly. Indeed the issue of saving to pay long-term care costs or out-of-pocket medical costs is directly affected by changes in both employer and public sector benefits.

Opportunity Costs: Other Behaviors

Most of economics is really not about risk and reward in financial markets. Rather, it is about behavior—how people make decisions or "choices" about work, schooling, consumption, and in other areas. While financial behavior is important, there are many other types of behavior that are also of economic importance. One of the most important principles that economists use to describe basic choices is called *opportunity cost*. All actions have consequences. We must choose between doing one socioeconomic activity (e.g., eating, sleeping, working, consuming, saving) versus another (e.g., spending, borrowing, lending). The decision to consume more today means having less saved for tomorrow's consumption, given a fixed level of income. But income, the return for providing labor to employers or from investing in stocks or bonds, can also vary, as we have seen above. This is because we can decide, within limits, how much to invest in various types of accounts and because, within limits, we can postpone or speed up retirement from work.

Indeed, the decision of how much to work (versus enjoy leisure) is made every day by all working-age persons. Both the number of hours worked within any one year and the number of total years worked over a lifetime are subject to our discretion. As illustrated above, choosing to stop work (retire) at age 60 versus age 70 may produce more leisure and less work, but it may also have high opportunity costs for investment income, just as choosing risky versus safe investments may have opportunity costs as well. Retirement also means lower—or even zero—income from wages and the often daunting prospect of stopping what we have done for a long time: work for pay. Indeed as people continue to add to their education and find more satisfaction in their work lives, there will be continued interest in combining work with retirement during the transition into old age.

LIFE CYCLE MODEL

The economic choices people make are governed by prices, preferences, and constraints. Economists describe the process of making these choices *models*. Models are simplifications of reality. They are judged by their ability to predict or explain reality. Most economic models rely on the role of prices to influence behavior and help explain the choices that people make as individuals and as societies.

Choices are affected by tastes and preferences, and by constraints. Tastes and preferences are what you would like to do; constraints are limits on these choices. For example, we might prefer to never work, or only to work at a very interesting job that paid a high salary in return for little effort. But ultimately, the best-paying jobs require lots of skill, training, and experience, and a great deal of effort as well. Ultimately, the choices we make early in life or even in middle age will determine what opportunities and choices we have later in life. Constraints may also arise because of factors beyond our control, such as discrimination by race or gender or even age. Here we formalize these choices in a simple economic model of the life span.

The process of aging, from birth until death, can be presented as a model of the economic life cycle. At each stage of the life cycle, an individual makes many important choices: schooling, taking a job, marriage, parenthood, location of residence, job tenure with a given employer, saving and investing (or borrowing and repaying). While most of these choices are made before old age, they nonetheless have a large and cumulative effect on economic decisions such as retirement, living arrangements at older ages, and provisions for long-term care as health status declines. Each person will make these choices, either implicitly or explicitly, while moving through his or her own life cycle.

Of course, not all of these choices will be unconstrained. Most choices made at earlier ages pose both opportunities and constraints for later choices. And unforeseen events of good luck (e.g., good employment, health, and steady high incomes) or bad luck (e.g., unemployment, disability, and low or erratic incomes) can greatly affect the choices an individual can make.

The simplest model of the life cycle is usually attributed to Albert Ando and Franco Modigliani (1963). In the model, an individual is assumed to begin economic life with no inheritances (money given to them from another generation—e.g., from parents, grandparents) and to end it leaving behind no bequests (e.g., money left to another generation). These features of the model can be added onto the basic structure, but only complicate the simple points I want to make here. The individual in this model lives in a world of perfect foresight, borrows when young, earns enough during the working years to both repay these loans and save for retirement, and saves exactly enough so that when work is terminated, he or she can spend a certain known period of retirement, living off savings until he or she conveniently dies exactly at the same time that the saved money runs out.

This model is depicted in Figure 13.1, where income rises and then falls and where one finds a flatter line of total lifetime consumption. During younger ages and at older ages, consumption (measured in dollars per year) exceeds income (areas I and III). In the middle period, income exceeds consumption (area II). In the simple model, lifetime consumption equals lifetime income, and so areas I + III = II.

Even when complications are added, this model can still be very powerful. And to be more realistic, a number of other factors need to be

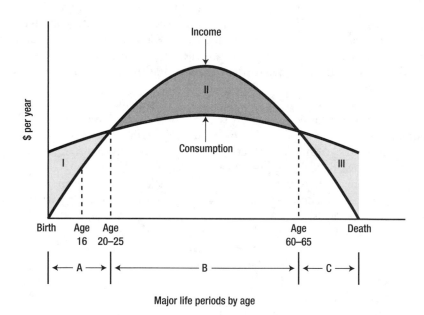

Note: Major Life Periods
  A. "Youth": Period when consumption exceeds income (up to age 20–25).
  B. "Working Life": Period where income exceeds consumption (20–25 to 60–65).
  C. "Retirement": Period where consumption exceeds income (60–65 and beyond).

FIGURE 13.1   Stages of the simple economic life cycle.

added to the model. For example, most of us are cared for by our parents when we are young. Thus, much of the consumption in period A is financed by parents. Then we may borrow to pay for additional years of schooling (or that education may also be financed by parents). Most people choose to marry (for at least some period) and have children. Complicated decisions arise about work and family life since both partners must choose whether to work in the labor market and how to balance the benefits of marriage and parenthood against such possibilities as divorce or chronic illness of self, child, or spouse. As we grow older and contemplate retiring from the labor force, we are constrained by imperfect information about how long we will live and how our health will change at older ages. We may well have motives to leave some of our accumulated wealth to our children, either at death through bequests or during our lifetime. But even with these complications, the basic life cycle choices and predictions remain the same: consume from the income of others when young (e.g., parents or borrowing); attend school (and therefore, beyond age 14 or so, give up some market earnings until say age 25) (Area I); work for an extended period after school and accumulate assets (e.g., house, car, savings for retirement) while also paying off debts (Area II); at some point (say age 60–65) retire from the labor force (often gradually), live in retirement off savings (Area III); and then die. Thus, the life cycle model, however it may be complicated, still typifies the economic lives and the stages of economic life that almost everyone will experience.

Choices Made in a Life Cycle Context

Now let us return to the basic choices made in the original one-period model and extend the model to many periods. In so doing, the following individual key choices are made, abstracting, for now, from societal trends and from government actions.

Schooling Choice

A key choice is to decide how much *human capital* to accumulate when young and then through the rest of the life course. Human capital reflects the skills and knowledge of an individual. The notion of treating a human body and mind as a piece of capital—a stock that produces a flow of value—is attributed to Gary Becker (1964, 1993) and Jacob Mincer (1958). The model has also been applied to health status as well as productive skills (e.g., Grossman, 1972). One can add to human capital by formal education, by job training, and through experience. Most people add to human capital by staying in school beyond the compulsory age and sometimes earning a college or university degree. Some go on further to professional school for law, medicine, or business, for example. Of course, the added years of schooling have both a money cost (e.g., tuition) and an opportunity cost (e.g., loss of wages while in school). However, for most persons, the investment in more education produces higher levels of skill and abilities (i.e., human capital). As these skills are added, the worker becomes more productive and therefore earns more. The higher earnings for college and professional degrees more than compensate for the initial tuition and opportunity cost of schooling, even if the individual has to obtain school loans to make this investment. Several authors have pointed to the fact that the better educated not only earn more, but make better decisions as consumers, parents, and in terms of their own health (e.g., Haveman & Wolfe, 1984; Wolfe & Haveman, 2001; Wolfe & Zuvekas, 1997). And finally the better-educated elderly are more likely to be able to find work in retirement on their own terms compared to lesser educated retirees.

Saving Choices: General

All individuals can decide to save or consume their market incomes. Borrowing early in life (section A of Figure 13.1) means repaying those loans later in life (section B). But then once school loans are paid off, the individual makes additional savings or consumption choices. Most persons have some amount of savings that they have made in case of emergency or unexpected losses. This so-called precautionary savings takes place all the time. Indeed President Bush has proposed a whole new set of tax-favored health savings accounts that can be used to finance out-of-pocket health care outlays should the participant be willing to accept an insurance policy with a high-deductible feature.

Once precaution is accounted for, a whole set of new savings choices can be made. Most people save for a down payment on the purchase of a home, and then take out a mortgage to finance the rest of the purchase. Indeed once the home is paid off, it becomes the most important asset that older adults enjoy (Fisher, Johnson, Marchand, Smeeding, & Boyle, 2006). Many people who have children save for their education so the children do not have to be indebted early in their work lives (thereby minimizing the area I for their children, in Figure 13.1). And these too are offered favorable income tax status in certain cases.

Saving for Retirement

The decision to save for retirement competes with other reasons for saving—for example: education, new cars, better homes, and expensive vacations. And all of these reasons for saving compete with the needs for current consumption and instant gratification: meals, wines, expensive suits, swimming pools, and more. One of the major problems with retirement saving is that its benefits are so far away and the return is unsure due, in part, to mortality. As we have seen in our exploration of financial economics, compound interest is a mighty tool for accumulated savings. Yet to a 25-year-old, a new iPod or computer system, a week in the Bahamas, or a fancier car offer a much more tangible and satisfying return than does the $1,000 of retirement savings.

Most people in fact do not voluntarily choose to begin to make long-term retirement savings decisions at early ages. But many people who would not choose to increase savings by themselves will subject themselves to savings through regular deductions from their current salaries. Both employers and government may further help employees to make retirement savings decisions by matching these retirement savings (employers) or by granting tax-favored status to retirement asset buildup (governments).

Changes in employer and government polices will also affect private retirement savings. For instance, addressing the current budgetary shortfalls in social security and Medicare will entail either lower benefits or higher taxes to maintain current benefits. And employers are fast changing their commitments to guaranteed pensions and retiree health insurance that supplements Medicare. Changes in these components of retirement income security will necessitate changes in one's own savings to compensate.

Retirement Choice

When people approach older age and begin to consider retirement, the fortunate ones will have saved some amount to add to their retirement incomes. These dollars will at least partially offset lost wage income from retirement. In terms of Figure 13.1, people presumably look at the amount accumulated in area II (net of borrowing in I that they have repaid) and estimate the amount they will need in period C to maintain consumption at close to their preretirement level. The retirement decision is a complex one. Each year of postponed retirement in the simple model yields one more year of earned income and one more year of compound interest (as we have seen above). But each additional year of work means one less year of being able to visit grandchildren, travel, or enjoy the pleasure of longer life while still in relatively good health.

Long-Term Care Insurance

There is an additional risk that as we age, our health will decline and we will no longer be able to care for ourselves. In retirement, as in all of life, one needs a place to live; one will also experience the need for acute medical care (doctor and hospital visits) with increasing frequency for most of us as we age. On top of this, we may need a different type of care: assistance with carrying out daily tasks of living.

Being old, frail, and dependent on others for basic care and daily needs is worrisome for most of us. It is possible that we may suddenly die from a heart attack or other quick action and not need such care. But at age 65, there is a 20% chance that a woman will need 2 years (or more) of nursing home care, while a man has a 7% chance of such needs (Murtaugh, Kemper, & Spillman, 1995). Later periods, changing health circumstances, and other factors might influence these results. The fraction of women using long-term care in nursing homes is higher than men because most men receive long-term care in old age from their wives. Since most women live longer than men in old age, and younger women often marry older men, older women in poor health are more likely than men to need formal long-term care services.

If we receive the assistance we need in our own homes, then home care may be less expensive and less savings are needed. But we may also have to use another facility—a nursing home, intermediate-care facility, or similar long-term care setting—should our needs become too great to be dealt with safely and continuously at home. Since good nursing home care can cost $70,000 or more per year, the need for nursing home care in old age poses a significant financial risk for most people. The private market offers a few alternative ways to account for this risk. Some individuals might be able to self-insure, for example, by saving an extra $120,000 or more for such an event. Some might use their home equity to finance such a need. Others might find it useful to buy private insurance against such risk. Again price matters, but so does age. As people become older, the chances of needing long-term care increase, as do the premiums for long-term care insurance policies. Most people are reluctant to purchase long-term care insurance at younger ages, when there is some chance they will not use it and when it is relatively cheap. However, as they become older and recognize that they might well need such coverage, it becomes very expensive. Again, individuals face a number of trade-offs that affect both their current and future economic well-being.

Summary

In each of the examples given here, private market decisions about human capital, saving for retirement, retirement security, and long-term care insurance are being made by individuals in a dynamic context. Government also plays an active and vital role in most areas in the economics of aging. I now turn to this role, beginning with the economic rationale for government action in aging policy.

ROLE OF THE PUBLIC SECTOR

All modern economies rely to some extent on the public sector to influence economic choice. At the very least, the government plays a role in making private markets work better by guaranteeing people's property rights and facilitating the exchange of market information. But governments in every modern economy do much more than that.

The traditional reason for public sector involvement in a market economy is market failure. When markets do not work at all, the government substitutes for the market by collecting taxes and providing public goods, which are available to all without exclusion. National defense is one example of a good that is provided by the public sector because it is impossible or inefficient for the private sector to do so. But how and why does government become involved in the economics of aging? Government intervention is needed to establish property rights guarantees, subsidize savings, and provide both social insurance and minimum income protection. Rather than present a complex model of the government's multiple economic roles in the economy, I illustrate their current and potential roles through a number of examples germane to the economics of aging.

Government as Insurer of Property Rights

Self-provision of retirement income is an important goal for individuals. Employers also effectively act as intermediaries for workers in arranging retirement savings in employer-sponsored pensions. In this area, government's role has been to protect workers' rights to pension promises made by employers. The Employee Retirement Income Security Act (ERISA) of 1974 assures workers that promised employer-based occupational pensions will be provided. These are called *occupational pensions* since they are established by both companies and unions for both public and private sector workers. Government requires private institutions to meet certain standards if they offer a pension. For example, ERISA guards against pension funds' running too low to meet obligations and forbids discrimination across various types of workers who are eligible for company pensions. Government also makes separate provision for self-employed workers to set up their own pension funds. Of course, if a company goes bankrupt without having paid off its pension promises, the liability for pension costs is transferred to the Pension Benefit Guaranty Corporation (PBGC), forcing pension insurance premiums to rise. In recent years, major airlines have joined steel companies in transferring liabilities to the government insurer and increasing its liabilities (Congressional Budget Office, 2005).

Subsidies to Increase Savings by Individuals

Because greater provision of occupational pensions offers the general public some assurance that they will not have to directly support older adults as taxpayers, the U.S. government encourages pension plan contributions by granting tax exclusions for qualified contributions and allowing accumulated pension earnings to grow tax free until they are used as retirement income. Both convey large advantages to employees who invest in pension plans. Without these subsidies, savings would likely be lower.

For instance, as shown in Table 13.1, a pension plan that pays a compound interest rate of 10% turns an initial $1,000 into $45,259 over a 40-year period. Suppose, however, that all contributions to the pension plan were taxed at 30% and, further, that all earnings from this plan were also taxed at 30%. In effect, this would reduce the compound interest rate on that $1,000 from 10% to 7% and the 40-year accumulation would fall from $45,259 to $14,974. These tax provisions (income tax deductibility and postponement of income tax on pension earnings until plan realization) make a huge difference for pension accumulation. In 1998 alone, pension plan contributions in the United States allowed citizens to avoid over $53 billion in taxes that would otherwise be collected (U.S. Congress, 2000). This is but one way that governments encourage particular forms of behavior through the tax system. Tax breaks for home mortgages and employer-sponsored health insurance are two additional ways that tax deductibility encourages particular forms of behavior by changing effective prices through tax subsidies. Of course, recent changes in the income tax law have affected the citizens who benefit from these deductions. In 2003, 85% of all federal income tax liabilities were paid by the top 40% of tax filers by income category, 50% to the top 10%. The bottom half of the tax-paying population does not benefit at all from these provisions, as they pay low or zero taxes (Congressional Budget Office, 2005b).

In a similar vein, governments encourage human capital accumulation by offering tuition-free, tax-financed elementary and secondary school education to young children and their families. Moreover, governments reduce the borrowing costs for attending college by subsidizing college loans, offering partial tuition grants, and charging heavily discounted tuition at public universities and colleges. Thus, governments also heavily subsidize schooling decisions as well as pension accumulations; they just do it in a different way.

Social Insurance and Welfare

The costs of insurance in old age can be very high, not only for long-term care insurance but also for health insurance. A market economy in general may treat harshly those who cannot compete because of disability, sickness, or unemployment in old age. While private insurance may fill some of these gaps, it does not cover them all. Even given strong tax incentives, many people do not save adequately for retirement.

One way to overcome inadequate private insurance is to provide public insurance against both seen and unforeseen events. Social insurance is a compulsory risk-sharing scheme whereby workers are forced to contribute tax dollars to a public trust fund and become entitled to certain benefits from that fund after having met qualifying requirements. Such programs are called *entitlements*. Social insurance also provides protection against risks that the private sector cannot do, bolstering retirement incomes for those with low earnings or gaps in earnings, for example.

Our social security system, formally known as the Old Age, Survivors Disability and Health Insurance (OASDHI) system, is one such social insurance program. Both employers and employees contribute to the fund (through Federal Insurance Contributions Act—FICA taxes), and after contributing a minimal amount for a certain period (e.g., 40 quarters or 10 years of employment before retirement), a worker is eligible for various benefits. The largest of these is Old Age Insurance, which offers a level of benefits determined by a formula based on contributions and age at retirement. This system also qualifies workers for Disability Insurance benefits should they become permanently unable to work before age 62. Further, if the insured worker dies, the spouse and younger children are guaranteed some level of income through the Survivors Insurance benefit. Finally, on reaching age 65 (or having been on social security disability for 2 years), qualified individuals are entitled to Medicare health insurance benefits. While this chapter does not go into the details of social security and Medicare, it is important to know that almost every modern nation has some form of OASDHI system. Further, most have a completely nationalized (government-run) health care system for all persons, regardless of age.

In the United States, Old Age benefits are related to previous contributions, but also reflect other adjustments. The United States provides higher benefits to low-wage contributors than they would have received had benefits been strictly tied to contributions. We accomplish this end by giving a higher replacement rate to low-income contributors. Many Western European nations have a much higher "first-tier" social retirement benefit that guarantees a nonpoor income level to all who are entitled to benefits, and then a "second-tier" benefit that is more closely related to the worker's lifetime contributions to the trust fund. In the United States there is not such a distinction within the social security program. Instead, the U.S. system relies on a separate means-tested program known as Supplemental Security Income (SSI). The SSI system guarantees a certain level

of benefits to those over age 65 whose earnings, savings, and other benefits are less than about $600 per month. In order to qualify for SSI, a per-
son must submit to a thorough income and assets test (financial assets less
than $2,000 for a single person) that proves that they cannot support
themselves. Once a person qualifies for SSI, they must repeatedly reapply
to show they are still needy. SSI also covers the permanently disabled,
often limited to those who do not qualify for the Social Security Disability Insurance program. Federal benefit levels in the means-tested SSI program are below the poverty line in the United States and do not provide
enough by themselves to bring the recipient out of poverty (although
some states modestly supplement the basic SSI levels).

In contrast to health insurance and old age insurance, the OASDHI
program meets the needs of most retirees, the United States does not have
a contributory social insurance program for long-term care. While workers contributing to private long-term care insurance are provided a tax
subsidy, the only other direct government support for long-term care
needs comes from the income- and means-tested Medicaid program. In effect, those without adequate private long-term care insurance and those
without adequate savings for long-term care and nursing home expenses
can qualify for Medicaid benefits once they have depleted their assets.
And after that, they still must devote most of their incomes to pay for
long-term care each year before Medicaid steps in. Many Western nations,
notably Canada, Germany, and Austria, plus Japan, have a contributory
social insurance scheme for long-term care. The United States has not developed such a system.

Currently the most contentious element of the retirement security
system is Medicare, the health insurance program for the elderly. Due
mainly to a proliferation of new treatments and new drugs that help older
people cope with declining health, Medicare program outlays are growing much faster than its revenues. Part D was added to Medicare to provide some coverage for prescription drugs beginning in January 2006.
While initially the program was designed to mostly pay for itself, it is now
clear that the Medicare prescription drug benefit will add significantly to
the costs of Medicare in coming years (Social Security and Medicare
Board of Trustees, 2005).

Pay-As-You-Go Versus Self-Funded Social Retirement Schemes: The Role of Population Aging

The U.S. OASDI system and most European social retirement systems are
run on what is called a *pay-as-you-go basis*. This means that younger generations of workers pay taxes into trust funds, but those funds are used
to support older generations of workers in the same period. In terms of

Figure 13.1, taxes are paid by workers in life cycle periods A and especially in B, and older adults in life cycle period C collect these taxes as benefits in the same period. Funds contributed by workers are paid directly to the next generation, with any excess going into a trust fund. Such systems are fundamentally stable and can pay high benefits to older generations as long as populations grow smoothly and other programmatic and demographic features (such as age of receipt of initial benefit and life expectancy in old age) do not dramatically change. However, most rich nations' social retirement schemes are already coming under pressure as the baby boom population ages. The large cohort of persons born between 1946 and 1964, dubbed the baby boom generation, will reach retirement ages between 2011 and 2029. But even after then, the numbers of people over age 65 will remain high because of longer life expectancies. Moreover, in recent years, people have tended to retire before age 65 in many nations. Together these influences put pressure on entitlement schemes funded on a pay-as-you-go basis. To meet the promises of these social retirement systems, either taxes must rise or benefits must be trimmed, or, more likely, both actions will be needed in a large number of Western nations, including the United States.

In contrast, many developing nations, notably Australia, Chile, and other emerging Asian nations, have begun self-funded social retirement systems. Here intergenerational transfers from younger taxpayers to older beneficiaries are far fewer. Instead, when younger workers contribute to their retirement systems, these contributions are invested in public or private enterprises and held there until retirement. Benefits are much more directly tied to contributions, and younger workers' contributions do not directly support other retirees. For developing nations just starting social retirement schemes, these self-funded systems provide vehicles for forced savings, and a source of domestic private investment in each nation, as workers' funds grow. Once workers retire, governments must make sure that the returns on these investments accrue to the contributors according to plan rules. But since each generation funds only its own retirement, population aging has no direct effect on taxes or benefits as with pay-as-you-go systems.

The dilemma faced by richer Western nations such as the United States, but to a much greater degree by Italy, France, and Germany, is that converting from a pay-as-you-go to a self-funded system generates a number of problems. One generation is caught in the transition because taxes to support the older generation must still be paid while at the same time a self-funded system is begun. It is particularly awkward to do this at a time when the size of the retiring generation is very large. Countries like Chile, where retirement systems were largely nonexistent, have an easier time establishing a funded program because they do not have obligations to those currently in retirement. The United Kingdom is the only modern nation to have at least partially made such a transition, and it has faced a number of problems. It may be much easier for governments to limit the growth of pay-as-you-go systems and to add a second or third tier of self-funded contributory pensions on top of existing pay-as-you-go systems, than to make a wholesale change over from one system to another (for more on this issue, see Schieber & Shoven, 1999; Aaron & Reischauer, 1998). Indeed President Bush's attempt to privatize OASI (social security) in 2005 failed miserably for these and other reasons.

PROGRAM INTERACTIONS, SOCIETAL AGING, AND THE LIMITS OF PUBLIC VERSUS PRIVATE RESPONSIBILITY

Both private pensions and social insurance help support older people when they reach retirement age. Part-time work beyond retirement, later retirement more generally, and other nonpension savings also provide income support in old age. Ideally older workers will have many sources of support in old age, including some earnings, OASI, private pensions, and other savings. However, the mix of support varies by both income level and by age. Younger and better-off retirees are likely to have all these types of support. Older women living alone (e.g., those 80 and over) are much more likely to rely on OASI alone (Smeeding, 1999). Moreover, some analysts worry that generous provision of public sector support may discourage efforts by individuals to make provisions for their own support.

Another important issue arises from the fact that as the U.S. population ages, it puts enormous pressure on younger taxpayers to support retirees. Some policy changes will be necessary. For example, OASDI taxes will have to rise by about 26 percent to ensure full OASDI benefits under current rules for the next 75 years (Social Security and Medicare Board of Trustees, 2005). And this ignores the even larger future gap between revenues and outlays for elder health benefits under Medicare, now including prescription drugs as well as hospital and physician benefits.

Benefit reductions or greater self-finance of retirement income, health insurance, and long-term care would reduce the amount of taxes that need to be paid to support future generations of older adults. While economic growth can soften the impacts of either lower benefits or higher taxes, they cannot forestall the need to significantly raise taxes or cut benefits in order to restore solvency to the system (Social Security and Medicare Board of Trustees, 2005). If workers' productivity rises even modestly, the share of their incomes devoted to FICA taxes might need to go up only modestly, leaving them with substantially higher incomes than today's workers. Alternatively, if retirees' incomes also rise from private sources, they will be better able to absorb cuts in guaranteed benefits. Thus, much of the debate about social security reform in America revolves around two questions: Who will pay for an increasingly older society, and what is the proper level of collective (government, social insurance, and safety net) retirement income support versus individual and private sector support for income and insurance in old age?

Economists alone cannot answer these final questions. Indeed, while we can provide perspective and insight, economists alone should not decide questions like these. It takes all of society to reach consensus on how to proceed.

SUMMARY

There is ever more interest in retirement and financial security in our aging nation. Economists can use their tools to show how we arrived at our current situation and the sometimes difficult choices that we must make to lessen the social burden of our aging society. The commonsense economics of retirement and the life cycle economic model briefly laid out in this chapter provide a framework in which we can consider changes in retirement income policy and retiree health care policy. They allow us to bring consideration of both economic efficiency and equity to retirement income and health care policy choices. But they do not help us to make difficult tax and benefit choices, only to weigh the costs and benefits of such actions once taken.

Future research on the economics of aging will focus on several important areas: the need to promote longer work lives in aging societies in which some workers are more able to work into old age than others; the need to be more cost-efficient in delivering health care and drug benefits in aging societies; and coping with how to provide for long-term care needs in a more judicious fashion. Virtually all economists agree that we need to deal with the issue facing us now—the OASDI deficit—so that we can then tackle the more difficult issues related to health care in old age. Everyone will have an opinion, but the more we understand the economics of an aging society, the easier it will be to find good solutions to the blessings of longer healthier lives.

REFERENCES

Aaron, H. J., & Reischauer, R. D. (1998). *Countdown to reform: The great social security debate.* New York: Century Foundation Press.

Ando, A., & Modigliani, F. (1963). The life cycle hypothesis of saving. *American Economic Review, 53,* 55–84.

Becker, G. S. (1964). *Human capital.* New York: Columbia University Press.

Becker, G. S. (1993). *Human capital: A theoretical and empirical analysis, with special reference to education* (3rd ed.). Chicago: University of Chicago Press.

Clark, R. L., Burkhauser, R. V., Moon, M., Quinn, J. R., & Smeeding, T. M. (2004). *The economics of an aging society.* Oxford: Blackwell.

Congressional Budget Office. (2005a, September). *The risk exposure of the Pension Benefit Guaranty Corporation.* Washington, DC: U.S. Congress.

Congressional Budget Office. (2005b, December). *Historical effective federal tax rates: 1979 to 2003.* Washington, DC: U. S. Government Printing Office.

Fisher, J. D., Johnson, D. S., Marchand, J. T., Smeeding, T. S., & Boyle Torrey, B. (2006). *Aging housing flows: The importance of housing consumption and assets.* Unpublished manuscript.

Grossman, M. (1972). *The demand for health: A theoretical and empirical investigation.* New York: Columbia University Press.

Haveman, R. H., & Knopf, K. A. (1981). *The market system: An introduction to microeconomics* (4th ed.). New York: Wiley.

Haveman, R. H., & Wolfe, B. L. (1984). Schooling and economic well-being: The role of nonmarket effects. *Journal of Human Resources, 19,* 377–407.

Mincer, J. (1958). Investment in human capital and personal income distribution. *Journal of Political Economy, 66,* 281.

Murtaugh, C. M., Kemper, P., & Spillman, B. C. (1995). Risky business: Long-term care insurance underwriting. *Inquiry, 32,* 271–284.

Organization for Economic Co-operation and Development. (2006). *Ageing and employment policies—live longer, work longer.* Paris: Organization for Economic Co-operation and Development.

Schieber, S. J., & Shoven, J. B. (1999). *The real deal: The history and future of social security.* New Haven, CT: Yale University Press.

Smeeding, T. M. (1999). *Social security reform: Improving benefit adequacy and economic security for women.* Syracuse, NY: Syracuse University.

Social Security and Medicare Boards of Trustees. (2005). *Status of the social security and medicare programs: A summary of the 2005 annual reports.* http://www.ssa.gov/OACT/TRSUM/trsummary.html

U.S. Congress. (2000). *2000 green book: Background material and data on programs within the jurisdiction of the Committee on Ways and Means.* Washington, DC: U.S. Government Printing Office.

Wolfe, B., & Haveman, R. (2001). Accounting for the social and non-market benefits of education. In J. F. Helliwell with A. Bonikowska (Eds.), *The contribution of human and social capital to sustained economic growth and well-being: International symposium report* (pp. 221–250). Hull, Quebec: Human Resources Development Canada.

Wolfe, B. L., & Zuvekas, S. (1997). Nonmarket outcomes of schooling. *International Journal of Educational Research, 27,* 491–502.

CHAPTER 14

Social Lives in Later Life

Christine L. Himes
Ying Fang

Where we live and with whom we share our time form integral parts of our social life. Sociologists studying the lives of older adults are interested in both the macro-level structures that shape experiences and the micro-level interactions of day-to-day life. Structures of political units, neighborhoods, and social and political institutions shape the social world in which individuals operate, but the intimate and interpersonal relationships of everyday life color our experiences. In later life, both macro- and micro-level processes influence our social roles and needs. The choices we have for social interaction, meeting care needs, and living arrangements vary based on the social welfare policies of the nation and state, resources available in neighborhoods, and cultural norms influencing the social roles of all ages. Our decisions, however, also depend on our relationships with spouses, partners, children and friends, individual preferences, and economic resources.

Sociologists interested in aging are increasingly focused on studying the roles that older adults play in society. Rather than viewing aging as primarily a time of decline and detachment from society, researchers are interested in the ways in which older adults contribute to families, the workplace, and society. This focus has led, for instance, to recognition of the role of grandparents in raising grandchildren, the increase in postretirement employment, and the levels of volunteering by older adults. Including these experiences extends the picture of aging from one based on decline to a richer portrayal of the diversity in the aging experience.

The increasing interest of sociologists in life course perspectives has guided much of the recent research on the social lives of older adults. Rather than viewing later life in isolation, lives in old age are seen as extensions and consequences of earlier life conditions and decisions. Economic security, health, and family relationships are all viewed as part of a life-long process. The connection between social structures and individual lives is an important concept in the life course perspective. Viewing the movement of individuals through age strata, with unique roles and statuses, is a central part of the age stratification framework developed by Riley, Foner, and Waring (1988), which has guided many sociologists.

However, despite improvements in health and economic status, later life can still be a time when individuals need care and assistance. Unlike the more general interest in the social roles of later life, the emphasis of research on living arrangements is a reflection of our interests in the care needs of older adults and how those needs are met, bringing us back to a view of aging as a time of decline and deficit. Across the life course, sociological interest in care is motivated by similar concerns, forming what Cherlin (2004) has called the public family, that is, the extent to which the family is functioning as a provider of a "public good" by raising children and caring for the frail, sick, or disabled. When sociologists examine whether children live with one or two parents, with grandparents, or in some other family household, their interest is in how well that group is meeting the needs of the children. In our examination of the living arrangements of older adults, we are similarly interested in how the family is meeting the needs of the vulnerable members of the older adult population.

Implicit, if not always explicit, in these examinations is a comparison of what would happen to children, the frail, or sick if families were not available. We have an underlying assumption that those who are living with others can have their needs cared for by those with whom they are coresiding. Of course, this is not the only paradigm for an interest in living arrangements that we could choose. For instance, some might be more interested in the quality of the housing stock or the implications of aging for home construction. Although some researchers have examined the housing stock and housing options available to older adults (Clark & Dieleman, 1996; Golant, 1992; Mutchler & Burr, 2003), it has not been the focus of the majority of aging research by sociologists. Other social scientists have interests in the living and care arrangements of older adults. Psychologists might focus on the emotional aspects of sharing housing, the personal relationships that form and change with age, or the role of cognitive functioning on independent living. Health care researchers are more interested in the types of services needed by the frail older adult population, their access to and use of health care services, and the financing of health care costs. Similarly, economists often address the availability and use of public and private health insurance, intergenerational transfers of resources, or changes in wealth and net worth with age.

Since families are such an important factor in studying the lives of older individuals, we will first describe the important demographic changes affecting families. Then we will focus on three particular social roles that older individuals occupy—grandparent, worker, and volunteer—and how these roles affect later life. A discussion of the care needs of older adults, and especially the role that families play in meeting those needs, is followed by the related discussion of where and with whom older adults live. Finally, we discuss some of the broad macro-level influences on these areas and where future research may be needed.

FAMILIES

Families are at the center of most social life. Families are created by simple demographic processes—the union formation (and union dissolution), fertility, and mortality of individuals. These demographic processes play out on both the macro- and micro-levels, and these simple processes interact in complex ways to create a variety of family forms. Changes in the age structure of a country resulting from changes in mortality and fertility affect the ability of the public sphere to finance the care of frail older adults. In the United States, concerns about the rising costs of Medicare and Medicaid are based on a combination of increases in health care costs, increases in the size of the eligible population, and decreases in the size of the working-age population who finance these public programs. In addition, the availability of family members to provide care influences the policy discussions of how, where, and by whom care is provided.

At the individual level, however, changes in fertility, mortality, and union formation influence the personal resources available in terms of the number of family members, their health, and their willingness to provide care. American families consist of single mothers or fathers raising children, married couples and cohabitors with or without children, grandparents raising grandchildren, siblings living together, and partners of the same sex who may or may not have children. This variety in family forms means that the resources available to an individual in terms of economic, physical, and emotional support will vary considerably.

Mortality patterns affect the length of life, the survival of children, and the stability of marriages. As adult life expectancy increases, the odds of becoming a grandparent increase, and the odds of children having living grandparents increase. This demographic change leads to a necessary redefinition of the role of a grandparent in a family and in the kin available to help older grandparents. Improved infant survival means that fewer families experience the death of a child and most parents have at least one child surviving into adulthood. The presence of living adult children is one of the most important indicators of the provision of informal support to the older individuals. Mortality rates are higher for men than women, meaning that women are much more likely to outlive their husbands and to be caring for their spouse before his death.

While mortality rates have steadily declined, fertility patterns over the past 75 years have fluctuated dramatically. During the Great Depression, many women remained childless or had few children. Many of these mothers, born at the beginning of the 20th century, reached the end of their lives over the past decade, and their needs for care fell on a few adult children. The issues faced by these children raised concerns about families' ability to be the primary source of care and put increasing burdens on older caregivers. In contrast, the children of the depression era were the parents of the baby boom generation. These women had relatively larger families and were less likely to remain childless. This cohort of men and women is more likely than those before or after them to have adult children available to provide care (Himes, 1992). As this group reaches their later years, the number of children available to provide care is greater, but new concerns arise about the ability and willingness of those children to provide the support needed.

Union (and its dissolution) is the third process involved in the creation and structure of families. Among Whites, marriage continues to be a normative experience. About 80% of teenagers expect to marry (Thornton & Young-DeMarco, 2001), and it is expected that nearly 90% will (Goldstein & Kenney, 2001). The rates of marriage are much lower for other racial and ethnic groups. Recent estimates show that nearly half of African American women will not marry (Harrington Meyer, Wolf, & Himes, 2006). For all groups, marriage is occurring later in life and often includes children already present in the relationship from one or the other partner. In addition, nonmarital cohabitation is becoming increasingly common (U.S. Census Bureau, 2001), although there are few studies that explicitly examine older cohabitors (Brown, Bulanda, & Lee, 2005).

Not all unions endure into later life. Some end due to the death of a spouse or partner, and some dissolve due to divorce. Although divorce among older adults is relatively rare, many older persons, particularly women, will reach age 65 unmarried due to an earlier divorce (Harrington Meyer, Wolf, & Himes, 2005). Remarriage of older adults, and the divorce and remarriage of their adult children, has implications for later-life care. Older adults living alone have less support in times of illness, and parents of children who have divorced may lose contact or access to their assistance.

The combination of mortality, fertility, union formation, and dissolution creates families of a variety of shapes and sizes, and broad differences exist between older and younger generations and race and ethnic subgroups. These demographic changes and differences underlie many of the others factors affecting social roles, as well as living and care arrangements, in later life.

SOCIAL ROLES

The social roles of later life differ little in name from those of early adulthood. Individuals are parents, spouses, partners, employees, volunteers, and students. The nature of these roles, however, and their meaning in society, may change significantly over the life course. The range and variety of the roles that older adults play in society form the foundation for Riley and Riley's (1994a) concept of *age integration*. They argue that we increasingly need to think of the life course not as one divided by age norms into distinct categories (e.g., education, employment, and leisure) but as one in which individuals may follow a variety of paths based on their needs and interests rather than age. Increasingly, older adults are working part time after retiring from career employment, sometimes in the same career or occupation but often in an unrelated field. The age norms for educational attainment are weakening with increasing numbers of middle-age adults returning to school, to gain or update market skills, complete education interrupted earlier in life, or pursue personal interests. These changes make old ideas of a linear progression through life obsolete. However, our societal structures can be slow to adapt to such individual-level changes, a phenomenon Riley and Riley (1994b) refer to as *structural lag*. Colleges are still primarily geared to people in their early 20s, the age for receiving full social security retirement benefits is increasing, despite a trend toward earlier retirement, and some employers are reluctant to hire older workers.

One of the most common roles associated with later life is becoming a grandparent. National survey data show that among adults with children aged 40 or older, nearly 95% are grandparents (Szinovacz, 1998). In addition, the longer life expectancy of older generations means that most children will have at least one, and more commonly several, living grandparents (Silverstein & Marenco, 2001). Grandparenthood occurs relatively early in the life course for most adults, on average before age 50, and grandparents are more likely than not to have a child still at home when their first grandchild is born. In addition, grandparents are to a large extent still participating in the formal labor market. Forty-two percent of all grandfathers and 30% of all grandmothers are working 30 or more hours per week. Many grandparents, about one-third, still have a living parent and are part of four-generation families (Szinovacz, 1998).

A role that is often unexpected by older adults is that of surrogate parents to their grandchildren. Grandparents usually take on these parenting roles due to economic or social problems of their adult children, including incarceration, substance abuse, death, or illness. Many households with grandparents contain three generations, but the most rapid growth has occurred in households containing grandchildren and grandparents only (Bryson & Casper, 1999). Many of these households consist of only a woman and her grandchildren and are more likely than not to live below the poverty line. Among the grandmother-only families, poor health is common as well; 51% of the grandmothers report their health as fair or poor, while only 9% report their health as excellent (Bryson & Casper, 1999).

Volunteering is another important role for some older adults. The Administration on Aging (2002) estimates that about 15 million older persons are involved in volunteer activities. Older Americans are seen as a resource with both time and expertise that can benefit communities. Several organized efforts have evolved to tap into the desire of older persons to contribute their time and efforts to community work. Groups like Senior Corps, which includes the Foster Grandparent Program, the Senior Companion program, the Retired and Senior Volunteer Program, the Service Corps of Retired Executives, and the National Park Service Volunteers in Parks program, all provide ways for older adults to be involved through mentoring, advocacy, teaching, and leadership. In addition, local community agencies and nonprofit organizations recognize the importance of the time and talents of older adults.

Work is a primary organizing feature of adulthood. Comparisons of labor force participation rates over time show changes in the importance of work and retirement for groups of the population. Among men age 62 to 64, fewer than half are in the labor force compared to nearly 90% of men age 45 to 54 (U.S. Bureau of Labor Statistics, 2005). In addition, male labor force participation has declined at all ages over time, but particularly for those in their early 60s. At the same time, labor force participation rates for older women have increased. At a time when large numbers of men were leaving the labor force due to retirement or disability, more women than ever before were becoming active participants in the paid labor force.

Participation in paid work is still uncommon after age 65. In 1950, the median age of retirement for men in the United States was 67, by 1980, it had dropped to 63, and by 2000, the median age of retirement for men was estimated to be 62 (Gendell & Siegel, 1992). Those who continue to work are often professionals or self-employed individuals who continue to work through either economic necessity or personal preference. Self-employed workers may lack pension and retirement benefits, while professional workers tend to stay in the labor force longer due to greater job satisfaction and the cost of leaving work (Quinn, Burkhauser, Cahill, & Weathers, 1998). But the definition of retirement is becoming more difficult as increasing numbers of workers leave one profession or job, and receive retirement income, while continuing to work in a new profession or job. Others continue to work part-time to supplement pension and social security income.

The roles of grandparent, volunteer, and worker are just a few examples of how later-life roles have changed over time. The demographic and social changes that have led to the increased role of grandparents in raising children are not likely to reverse soon. The role of grandparent is likely to become increasingly important as mothers enter and stay in the labor force, the number of single parents increases, and social welfare safety nets disappear. Volunteerism by the older population is also likely to increase. Traditionally, civic, religious, and educational organizations relied on women, many of them highly educated and not employed in paid work, to provide services. As this typical base of volunteers shrinks due to women's labor force participation, these organizations are recognizing how to reach the group of willing and able older adults who can fill their needs. As life expectancy increases and the age of retirement decreases, there are more years of later life for leisure, return to formal education, or volunteering. However, the economic necessities of longer life may require that individuals continue to work, even if part time, to support themselves and their families. How the roles of later life evolve, and how societal structures adapt to accommodate or hinder those roles, will continue to be a fruitful area of investigation for sociologists in the years to come.

LIVING ARRANGEMENTS

Independent living, either alone or with a spouse, is the preference of the majority of older adults. In general, we have accepted the premise that older adults prefer to live independently based partly on evidence from attitudinal surveys, but also on the increased prevalence of living alone over time (Fields, 2004; Treas & Torrecilha 1995; Wister & Burch, 1987). The proportion of the older population living alone has increased over time, not due to a change in underlying attitudes but because of the greater economic stability of the older population. Older adults are increasingly able to afford to act on their long-standing preferences for independent living arrangements. This desire, called by some *aging in place*, means that most older persons want to stay in familiar surroundings, regardless of the condition of their housing unit, the nature of the neighborhood, or their own changing personal needs. While the quality of homes owned by most older adults is good, older people often live in homes that are big, costly to maintain, and expensive to heat and cool. The past several decades have seen an increase in the types of housing available for older Americans. In 2000, about 80% of those age 65 and older owned a home, compared to 76% in 1990 (U.S. Bureau of the Census, 2004). Most older adults live alone or with their spouse. About 40% of women over the age of 65 live alone, compared to 19% of older men, and only 11% of women and 8% of men live with someone other than their spouse (Fields, 2004).

Changes in living arrangements of older adults are not only the result of changes in preferences on the part of the older individual. For instance, we know that adult children may move into their parents' home temporarily or for longer periods of time, and grandparents may take on the care and rearing of grandchildren. Government policies to increase or restrict subsidized housing may result in a forced housing change, as would changes in zoning, urban renewal, or new home construction. Unfortunately, data rarely allow us to test the motivations for the shared household.

Another question sociologists ask is to what extent the ideal of independent living is at odds with a system of health care that is based on efficiency and effectiveness. Our national system of health care promotes efficiency through centralized services and the use of largely unpaid family care. This reinforces a focus on maintaining independent living, coupled with family care. The effectiveness of families to provide that care then becomes a central concern and the structure of families an important area of study.

Decision making regarding living and care arrangements can be conceptualized as a rational process in which the older adults and their families evaluate available resources and opportunities and come to the most beneficial or the least detrimental solution (Soldo, Wolf, & Agree, 1990; Spitze, Logan, & Robinson, 1992). Wolf and Soldo (1988) categorized the factors influencing the living arrangement outcomes into four types of indicators: opportunities, resources, needs, and preferences. The opportunities category includes the characteristics of the older adults' family structures, particularly the kin availability. The resources category consists of the external factors that facilitate or hinder particular types of living arrangements, such as economic resources. The needs category refers to those internal factors leading to a change in living arrangements, such as illness, disability, and widowhood. Preference is a subjective indicator of living arrangement choice, as well as a reflection of the cultural and societal norms to some extent (Soldo et al., 1990; Wolf & Soldo, 1988). While the terminology used may vary somewhat among researchers, at the operational level, these models capture the fundamental variables that influence the living arrangements, such as kin structure, economic resources, health status, demographic characteristics, and preference. These determinants are also shared by care arrangement choice, as co-residing family members and close kin are expected to be the primary caregivers for older people.

There is a strong relationship between living arrangements and health. Declining health and increasing disability decrease the likelihood that an older adult will live alone and increase the likelihood of co-residence or of being institutionalized (De Jong, Wilmoth, Angel, & Cornwell, 1995; Spitze et al., 1992; Wilmoth, 1998). This relationship does not disappear when controlling for age, gender, race, and martial status. Older adults who have difficulties in performing basic activities of daily living (ADLs) such as bathing, dressing, eating, toileting, and getting around the house necessitate assistance from others on a frequent basis.

Empirical studies in the United States generally show that older parents with lower income and those who do not own homes are more likely to live with children, and those with higher income and those who own their own home are more likely to live independently (Soldo et al., 1990; Wolf & Soldo, 1988). The increasing financial resources of the older population provides them the means and opportunity to purchase their preferred living environment and services (e.g., health care, housing, and leisure) to maintain independent living (Wilmoth, 2000). Controlling for disability and kin availability, older adults with sufficient resources are more likely to live independently. Similarly, high education generally leads to a good occupation with high income, which enables the elders to afford the cost of independent living (Avery, Speare, & Lawton, 1989; De Jong et al., 1995). Moreover, higher education also brings more awareness of personal privacy and independence, which subtly influences the living arrangement preferences of the elders.

Evidence is somewhat consistent that number of children is positively associated with the probability of co-residence and negatively related with the risk of living alone (Avery et al., 1989; Soldo et al., 1990; Spitze et al., 1992). The number of living adult children not only increases the elders' chance of living with at least one of them, but also indicates that more resources are available from children to support the aged parents. However, some suggest that there may not be a significant difference between having more than two children and having two children in regard to the influence on living arrangements, because usually only one child is mainly responsible for the physical care of the older parents (Velkoff & Lawson, 1998).

CARE NEEDS

Chronic diseases have become the primary focus of health and health care in later life. Chronic conditions often require not only medical care, but also support for emotional, social, and personal care for long periods of time. As the older population increases, the number of people with chronic conditions is expected to increase as well. Some older people find that they are limited in their ability to live independently due to chronic illness or disability. Recent estimates indicate that about 20% of those age 65 and older have either some limitation in at least one activity of daily living or are living in an institution (Federal Interagency Forum on Aging-Related Statistics, 2004). The most common limitation among those living in the community is the ability to get outside, followed by walking and bathing. An inability to feed oneself and problems with toileting are most likely to lead to institutionalization, and so are less likely to be found among those in the community.

Family members are important sources of support to frail or disabled older adults. Those without family support are at risk of being institutionalized when they are unable to care for themselves. Family members provide a wide range of assistance to their kin: transportation, help with household chores, cooking, and shopping. Increasingly, as the use of outpatient treatments and procedures increases, family members are responsible for providing health care as well. Families also assist in more direct personal care on a day-to-day basis: help with dressing, feeding, bathing, and toileting activities. Obviously, this high level of care can be physically and mentally challenging.

Although many family members may share in some of the care tasks, most of the family care provided to an older person comes from a single primary caregiver. Caregivers are usually chosen from close family members, with the spouse being the primary caregiver, especially for older men. If a spouse is not available or is unable to provide care, adult children are likely to become the primary caregiver. Increasingly, adult children are taking on the role of caregiver. Recent research has found that for those over age 70, adult children are more likely to be care providers than spouses (National Academy on an Aging Society 2000), a contrast to earlier studies of caregiving (Stone, Cafferata, & Sangl, 1987). In the absence of formal support, kin assistance is the only constant source of support for older adults.

Just as with living arrangements, demographic characteristics, such as age, gender, and race/ethnicity, influence care arrangements. The oldest old are most likely to be widowed, living alone, or vulnerable to institutionalization. Women report higher risk of chronic illness and functional disability than men in old age. Older women are generally poorer and more economically dependent due to cumulative disadvantages through market and employment systems (O'Rand, 1996). Therefore, older women have higher needs for sick care and financial support in later life, especially after the loss of a spouse, which contributes to their higher likelihood of co-residence with children.

Children's characteristics also shape care arrangements. Overall, compared to sons, daughters are more likely to provide care to older family members (Soldo et al., 1990). However, the role of sons in caregiving is not inconsequential (Laditka & Laditka, 2001). Sons are more likely to take on the roles of organizing care, dealing with financial and legal issues, and performing household repairs and maintenance. Of great concern for the future of family caregiving is the effect of continued increases in the rate of labor force participation by women. As women are more likely to work, and to work more hours, their ability to be primary caregivers for their parents may decrease (Sarkisian & Gerstel, 2004).

Separate living arrangements do not necessarily mean the end of exchange between children and parents. Besides a spouse or co-resident children, a complex web of support mechanisms exists, sometimes referred to as "intimacy at a distance" (Rosenmayr & Kockeis, 1963, p. 418; Wolf, 1994). There is a marked tendency for children to settle near their parents' home or the parents to move closer to their children's residence. Nonresidential children can give financial support to their parents and visit their parents frequently to provide physical help and emotional comfort. Martin and Kinsella (1994) argue that there is little difference in the quality of support received between those older adults who co-resided with their children and those who lived alone but were in daily contact with their children. Concern over the increased mobility of the population also seems misplaced. Recent research shows that increased geographic mobility is likely not a reason to worry about the ability of families to provide care to older adults (Wolf & Longino, 2005).

A number of factors will be important for understanding the future of family care. Demographic changes in family structure will affect the availability of family members, lower fertility rates mean fewer children, and increases in divorce create more tenuous ties among family members. As more recent cohorts reach old age with histories of divorce and remarriage, sociologists will continue to study the effects of these changing family forms on caregiving. The increased participation of women in the paid labor market has created changes in family life even before old age. Given these trends, it is not clear whether women will turn more caregiving duties over to men and if men will take on these new roles.

MACRO-LEVEL INFLUENCES

In addition to the demographic changes, several other forces work at the macro-level in American society to influence the living and care arrangements of older adults. These include social welfare policies of the nation and state, housing resources, and cultural norms influencing filial responsibility. The effects of these changes are often interrelated, as policies shift to accommodate changes in preferences and resources, and the private sector looks to fill gaps in services provided by the state. The United States has a complicated system of federal, state, and local programs designed to assist the older adult population. Some programs, like Social Security and Medicare, are entitlement based and depend strictly on age, marital status, and participant contributions; others are based on financial or medical need, including Medicaid, Supplemental Security Income, and subsidized housing. There is no single comprehensive program that encompasses both the housing and care needs of the older adult population. Medicare, the primary insurer for most older adults, has limited coverage for skilled nursing care and home health aide services and does not cover custodial or nonskilled care, which is the assistance and support for activities of daily living like dressing, bathing, and using the bathroom, which is most often needed by older adults. Medicaid may cover some additional care services, but it is available only to those who qualify based on their low income. As a result, older adults who need assistance must organize and arrange ways to meet their living and care needs on their own by bringing together formal support through home health aides, visiting nurses, or nursing home care, with informal support provided through family and friends.

The resulting system in the United States places a heavy dependence on families to provide care, either directly or through the purchase of services. Since nearly 20% of older adults have some personal care needs, the demand on families and programs can be great. The cost of long-term care is significant; the Congressional Budget Office estimates that the total cost of long-term care in 2004 will reach $135 billion, excluding the value of donated care by family and friends (Congressional Budget Office, 2004). Medicaid and out-of-pocket payments each account for about one-third of this total, and Medicare contributes an additional one-quarter. The remaining expenditures come from private insurance and other sources. If the value of informal care were included, it would exceed the contributions of any other source and contribute nearly as much as Medicare and Medicaid combined. The combination of informal care and out-of-pocket payments is over one-half of the value of long-term care services.

Besides the policy and housing environments, cultural norms are another macro-level influence on living and care arrangements. Sociologists have long observed that the level of care provided by adult children to parents cannot be explained strictly by economic models of investment or insurance. Instead, some portion of the support is the result of altruistic values and a sense of filial duty (Silverstein, Conroy, Wang, Giarrusso, & Bengtson, 2002). The role of family in providing support varies across racial and ethnic groups as well. Minority older adults are generally more likely to co-reside with family (Himes, Hogan, & Eggebeen, 1996) and more likely to receive family care compared to White older adults. Two possible explanations are usually presented to explain this finding: either minority families have a strong norm for providing care or they are forced to provide family care due to economic resources or discrimination (Burr & Mutchler, 1992, 1993, 1994).

FUTURE ISSUES

While the studies of living and care arrangements have revealed many patterns and determinants, there is still much to be understood. The changing composition of the older population may alter what we have taken for granted about later life social roles and care arrangements. As a larger number of older Americans reach later life without a spouse, more often due to divorce rather than death, the expectation for independent living is not likely to decline. However, along with changes in divorce is an increasing acceptance of cohabitation of both heterosexual and homosexual couples. We might expect that older adults will also be more open to these living arrangements, but these informal arrangements may be tested as health declines. This raises questions about the rights and responsibilities of partners as compared to spouses and the roles of stepchildren in the care for older parents and stepparents. As a society, we are only beginning to experience the first cohorts of older adults for whom divorce and remarriage was a significant factor. Future research on the strength of filial obligation in the face of divorce will be needed to test the willingness of children to care for noncustodial or stepparents.

The increasing ethnic diversity of the older population also raises new questions. As noted earlier, differences in living and care arrangements exist between ethnic and racial groups. Groups also differ in their patterns of marriage, divorce, and childbearing. How these factors will interact in the future has significant implications for the preference and availability of family care, family coresidence, and the need for formal care. High rates of immigration among some groups mean that a growing group of older adults in the United States have come here from other countries to live with adult children. Their eligibility for formal care services may be lower and their preference for family care heightened.

The trade-offs between the use of formal, paid care and informal, unpaid care are complex but important from a policy perspective. How quickly formal and informal systems can or should adapt to changes in health is one area of investigation. For example, recent work on how changes in disability affect the need for formal and informal care in the home by those living alone shows that once a formal arrangement for assistance with independent activities of daily living is in place, it is likely to continue even if health improves (Freedman, Aykan, Wolf & Marcotte, 2004). This suggests that individuals are receiving different levels of assistance unrelated to their current needs. The interrelationship of policy, family, and individual is likely to become increasingly complex as the demographic characteristics of the older population shift. Gerontologists studying living and care arrangements will need to focus on both macro- and micro-level influences in order to understand the consequences of these changes.

Sociologists interested in later life recognize that social interactions are shaped by early life situations as well as current day-to-day experiences. These interactions are part of a complex structure of social institutions, policies, and demographics. As more Americans live to old age, how the roles of later life shift and adapt will continue to occupy the research interest of social gerontologists. The changing nature of later life will itself change the expectations of future generations for their own social roles.

REFERENCES

Administration on Aging. (2002). *A profile of older Americans: 2002.* Retrieved August 18, 2003, from http://www.aoa.gov/aoa/ stats/profile/default.htm

Avery, R., Speare, A., & Lawton, L. (1989). Social support, disability and independent living of elderly persons in the United States. *Journal of Aging Studies, 3,* 279–293.

Brown, S. L., Bulanda, J. R., & Lee, G. R. (2005). The significance of nonmarital cohabitation: Martial status and mental health benefits among middle-aged and older adults. *Journal of Gerontology: Social Sciences, 60B*(1), S21–S29.

Bryson, K., & Casper, L. M. (1999). *Coresident grandparents and grandchildren.* Current population reports. Special Studies, P23–P198. Washington, DC: U.S. Government Printing Office.

Burr, J. A., & Mutchler, J. E. (1992). The living arrangements of unmarried elderly Hispanic females. *Demography, 29,* 93–112.

Burr, J. A., & Mutchler, J. E. (1993). Nativity, acculturation, and economic status: Explanations of Asian American living arrangements in later life. *Journal of Gerontology: Social Sciences, 48,* S55–S63.

Burr, J. A., & Mutchler, J. E. (1994). Ethnic living arrangements: Cultural convergence or cultural manifestation? *Social Forces. 72,* 169–180.

Cherlin, A. (2004). *Public and private families.* New York: McGraw-Hill.

Clark, W. A. V., & Dielman, F. M. (1996). *Households and housing: Choices and outcomes in the housing market.* New Brunswick, NJ: Center for Urban Policy Research.

Congressional Budget Office. (2004). *Financing long-term care for the elderly.* Washington, DC: Congressional Budget Office.

De Jong, G. F., Wilmoth, J. M., Angel, J. L., & Cornwell, G. T. (1995). Motives and geographic mobility of very old Americans. *Journal of Gerontology, 50B,* S395–S404.

Federal Interagency Forum on Aging Related Statistics. (2004). *Older Americans 2004: Key indicators of well-being.* Washington, DC: U.S. Government Printing Office.

Fields, J. (2004). *America's families and living arrangements: 2004.* Current Population Reports, P20-P553. Washington, DC: U.S. Census Bureau.

Freedman, V. A., Aykan, H., Wolf, D. A., & Marcotte, J. E. (2004). Disability and home care dynamics among older unmarried Americans. *Journal of Gerontology: Social Sciences, 59B,* S25–S33.

Gendell, M., & Siegel, J. S. (1992, July). Trends in retirement age by sex, 1950–2005. *Monthly Labor Review,* 22–29.

Golant, S. M. (1992). *Housing America's elderly: Many possibilities/few choices.* Newbury Park, CA: Sage.

Goldstein, J. R., & Kenney, C. T. (2001). Marriage delayed or marriage forgone? New cohort forecasts of first marriage for U.S. women. *American Sociological Review, 66,* 506–519.

Harrington Meyer, M., Wolf, D. A., & Himes, C. L. (2005). Linking benefits to marital status: Decreasing access to social security spouse and widow benefits in the U.S. *Feminist Economics, 11,* 145–162.

Harrington Meyer, M., Wolf, D. A. & Himes, C. L. (2006). Declining eligibility for spouse and widow social security benefits in the U.S.? *Research on Aging, 28,* 240–260.

Himes, C. L. (1992). Future caregivers: Projected family structures of older persons. *Journal of Gerontology: Social Sciences 47,* S17–S26.

Himes, C. L., Hogan, D. P., & Eggebeen, D. J. (1996). Living arrangements of minority elders. *Journal of Gerontology: Social Sciences, 51B,* S42–S48.

Laditka, J. N., & Laditka, S. B. (2001). Adult children helping older parents: Variations in likelihood and hours by race and family role. *Research on Aging, 23,* 429–456.

Martin, L. G., & Kinsella, K. (1994). Research on the demography of aging in developing countries. In L. G. Martin & S. H. Preston (Eds.), *Demography of aging.* Washington, DC: National Academy Press.

Mutchler, J. E., & Burr, J. A. (2003). Living arrangements among older persons: A multilevel analysis of housing market effects. *Research on Aging, 25,* 531–558.

National Academy on an Aging Society. (2000). *Caregiving: Helping the elderly with activity limitations.* Washington, DC: National Academy on an Aging Society.

O'Rand, A. M. (1996). The precious and the precocious: Understanding cumulative disadvantage and cumulative advantage over the life course. *Gerontologist, 36,* 2030–2038.

Quinn, J. Burkhauser, R., Cahill, K., & Weathers, R. (1998). *Microeconometric analysis of retirement decision: United States.* Paris: Organization for Economic Co-operation and Development.

Riley, M. W., Foner, A., & Waring, J. (1988). Sociology of age. In N. Smelser (Ed.), *Handbook of sociology* (pp. 243–290). Newbury Park, CA: Sage.

Riley, M. W., & Riley, J. W., Jr. (1994a). Age integration and the lives of older people. *Gerontologist, 34,* 110–115.

Riley, M. W., & Riley, J. W., Jr. (1994b). Structural lag: Past and future. In M. W. Riley, R. L. Kahn, & A. Foner (Eds.), *Age and structural lag: Society's failure to provide meaningful opportunities in work, family, and leisure* (pp. 15–36). New York: Wiley.

Rosenmayr, L., & Kockeis, E. (1963). Propositions for a sociological theory of ageing and the family. *International Social Science Journal, 15*(3), 410–426.

Sarkisian, N., & Gerstel, N. (2004). Explaining the gender gap in help to parents: The importance of employment. *Journal of Marriage and Family, 66,* 431–451.

Silverstein, M., Conroy, S., Wang, H., Giarrusso, R., & Bengtson, V. L. (2002). Reciprocity in parent-child relations over the adult life course. *Journal of Gerontology: Social Sciences, 57B,* S3–S13.

Silverstein, M., & Marenco, A. (2001). How Americans enact the grandparent role across the family life course. *Journal of Family Issues, 2,* 493–522.

Soldo, B. J., Wolf, D. A., & Agree, E. M. (1990). Family, households, and care arrangements of frail older women: A structural analysis. *Journal of Gerontology: Social Sciences, 45,* S238–S249.

Spitze, G., Logan, J. R., & Robinson, L. (1992). Family structure and changes in living arrangements among elderly nonmarried parents. *Journal of Gerontology, 47,* S289–S296.

Stone, R., Cafferata, G., & Sangl, J. (1987). Caregivers of the frail elderly: A national profile. *Gerontologist, 27,* 616–626.

Szinovacz, M. E. (1998). Grandparents today: A demographic profile. *Gerontologist, 38,* 37–52.

Thornton, A., & Young-DeMarco, L. (2001). Four decades of trends in attitudes toward family issues in the United States: The 1960s through the 1990s. *Journal of Marriage and the Family, 63,* 1009–1037.

Treas, J., & Torrecilha, R. (1995). The older population. In R. Farley (Ed.), *State of the Union: America in the 1990s* (Vol. 2). New York: Russell Sage Foundation.

U.S. Bureau of the Census. (2001). *Census 2000: Profiles of general demographic characteristics.* Washington, DC: U.S. Department of Commerce.

U.S. Bureau of the Census. (2004). *Housing vacancies and home ownership 2003.* Retrieved December 17, 2004, from http://www.census.gov/hhes/www/housing/hvs/annual03/ann03ind.html

U.S. Bureau of Labor Statistics. (2005). *Employment situation.* Retrieved September 1, 2005, from ftp://ftp.bls.gov/pub/suppl/empsit.cpseea13.txt

Velkoff, V. A., & Lawson, V. A. (1998). *Gender and aging: Caregiving. U.S. Census Bureau, International Brief.* Washington, DC: U.S. Census Bureau.

Wilmoth, J. M. (1998). Living arrangement transitions among America's older adults. *Gerontologist, 38,* 434–444.

Wilmoth, J. M. (2000). Unbalanced social exchanges and living arrangement transitions among older adults. *Gerontologist, 40,* 64–74.

Wister, A. V., & Burch, T. K. (1987). Values, perceptions, and choice in living arrangements of the elderly. In E. F. Borgatta & R. J. V. Montgomery (Eds.), *Critical issues in aging policy* (pp. 180–198). Newbury Park, CA: Sage.

Wolf, D. A. (1994). The elderly and their kin: Patterns of availability and access. In L. G. Martin, & S. H. Preston (Eds.), *Demography of aging* (pp. 146–194). Washington, DC: National Academy Press.

Wolf, D. A., & Longino, C. F., Jr. (2005). Our "increasingly mobile society"? The curious persistence of a false belief. *Gerontologist, 45,* 5–11.

Wolf, D. A., & Soldo, B. J. (1988). Household composition choices of older unmarried women. *Demography, 25,* 387–403.

CHAPTER 15

Politics and Policy in the Lives of Older Americans

Robert B. Hudson

The modern era has seen extraordinary changes in the size, makeup, and needs of the older population in the United States. Today's well-known new realities include the absolute and relative growth in the number of older Americans, increasing intrapopulation diversity along a host of critical dimensions, and an unprecedented presence of the old in all facets of American life.

An arena receiving perhaps less attention than those centered on social relationships and economic well-being is that of government and public policy. The contribution of public sector initiatives in establishing the enormous institutional presence of the contemporary aged population is rivaled only by long-term growth in the American economy and population-wide advances in nutrition and public health. Absent critical public policy initiatives, older people would not enjoy the overall economic and social standing that they do today.

As do the earlier contributions to Part IV, this chapter explores both the needs and interests of older people and the manner in which those needs and interests have been addressed. In the case of politics and public policy, these are especially interesting and iterative questions. There is no doubt that public policy has been a major contributor to meeting the needs of many older people, and it is now abundantly clear that the political interests of older people have clearly been piqued by what public policy has accomplished. Yet in tracing how these needs have been addressed, there is more at work than just the presence and interests of older people themselves. In the American political context, other factors have led to both the major interests of older people and to the major policies for older people that occupy a dominant position in American social policy today.

SOCIAL POLICY: THE AMERICAN WAY

Public policies at the federal level for older Americans, as for most other Americans, were slow to develop. Compared to the experiences of other countries, the role of the federal government in labor and social legislation was so limited that scholars have long referred to a pattern of "American exceptionalism" (Lipset, 1997). The historically modest scope of social welfare policy and expenditures has, in turn, generated references to "America's reluctant welfare state" (Wilensky & Lebeaux, 1958) or to its being, in cross-national perspective, "a welfare laggard" in developing such policies (Orloff, 1988).

Development of American Social Policy: An Overview

With the notable but isolated exception of Civil War pensions (Skocpol, 1992), the federal government essentially had no presence in social welfare prior to the twentieth century. Local and state government had limited and often punitive roles through such institutions as asylums, sanitariums, poor houses, reform schools, and state mental hospitals (Katz, 1986). Charity offered in community rather than institutional settings (so-called outdoor relief) was the exclusive province of private philanthropy throughout the 1800s. Modest expansion of public activity took place in the early 20th century, principally through regulatory efforts associated with the Progressive movement, which focused on child labor, and the mothers' pension movement, which provided support directed principally to widows with young children.

The New Deal of the 1930s brought government into the business of social welfare on an unprecedented scale. For the first time, the federal government became involved in the provision of public relief, job creation, economic development, and financial market regulation. The Social Security Act was the social policy hallmark of the New Deal, with the federal government launching programs for the aged, the unemployed, and mothers and children. However, the period that followed—from the late 1930s to the early 1960s—saw only modest increases in federal social welfare activity, including expanded social security coverage for survivors and additional workers and new initiatives for the disabled.

Initiatives of the Kennedy and Johnson years generated a host of federal and federal-state social welfare programs. Using a services strategy, these so-called Great Society programs targeted a number of problems (e.g., manpower training, area and community development, education) and a number of populations (e.g., the poor, the sick, the unemployed, the old) for public support. Medicare for the old and Medicaid for the categorically poor ultimately emerged as the two biggest and longest lasting of this large set of programs (Sundquist, 1968).

Developments beginning in the 1970s have led to a fundamental reassessment of the wisdom, size, and purpose of public sector intervention in American social welfare policy. High levels of unemployment and inflation ended what had been the remarkable period of sustained economic development enjoyed during the quarter-century following World War II. Criticisms of the Great Society programs and the emergence of conservative journals and think tanks generated a serious challenge to the intellectual foundations of liberal social welfare policy (Mead, 1986; Davies, 1996). And demographic trends raised, among other concerns, questions about the long-term viability of age-based programs such as Social Security and Medicare (Samuelson, 1978; Peterson, 1996).

As a result of these trends, the past 25 years have seen a growing intellectual and policy stalemate between forces that would expand and contract federal social programs. During the Reagan, George H. W. Bush, and even Clinton years, there were few legislatively enacted expansions of federal social policy, although expenditures have continued to rise, largely due to eligibility and benefit provisions written into current law (Weaver, 1988). One potentially expansive piece of legislation, the Medicare Catastrophic Coverage Act of 1988, was repealed 2 years after its enactment due to opposition from older people, a portion of whom were being taxed to pay for the new benefits contained in the law (Himelfarb, 1995). President Clinton's major national health insurance initiative failed in the early 1990s (Skocpol, 1996), although he was successful in seeing the modest Family and Medical Leave Act enacted (Bernstein, 1997). Perhaps best illustrating the tensions rising around social policy was the failed effort by Republicans in Congress to cut $270 billion from Medicare and $180 billion from Medicaid in the mid-1990s (Smith, 2002).

Today, long-standing and growing tensions about the role of the public sector in social welfare policy provision are at front and center stage. Pressing his vision of "the ownership society," President George W. Bush has called for government to provide more incentives to private sector entrepreneurship through lower taxes and lessened government regulation (Economist, 2005). The president has also encouraged faith-based social service provision to augment or supplant services provided through more secular private nonprofit groups.

After a hiatus of some 20 years, the reluctant aspect of America's attitudes toward the welfare state has gained renewed recognition. The Bush administration has pressed for private entities to take over responsibility from public ones and for individuals and families to assume or maintain roles in the absence of new or increased public support. These initiatives are affecting social policy across the board, including, as we will see, for older people.

Approaches to Understanding American Social Policy Development

Political scientists and other scholars have invoked a number of explanatory arguments in accounting for America's relatively distinct pattern of social policy development. One such argument centers on what is seen as America's unique political culture. Historical attachments to individualism, hard work, self-reliance, voluntarism, free markets, and Protestantism generated enormous resistance to governmental activity in general and governmentally sponsored social benefits in particular (Rimlinger, 1971; Lipset, 1997). Until the late 19th century, poverty and ill health were attributed to individual failings and immoral behavior, a diagnosis that left little room or justification for government involvement (Rosenberg, 1962). To be eligible for public benefits, one usually had to be both demonstrably needy and a member of "the worthy poor." In early New England, "potential recipients of relief included the sick, the disabled, widows with children, and the aged . . . but not the able-bodied poor, who received harsher treatment" (Quadagno, 1988, pp. 24–25).

The salience of work and employment was critical to the enactment of early social security programs, ones that seemed radical innovations to many in the 1930s. Social security benefits would be available only to those who had worked and who then found themselves unable to work due to specific contingencies, specifically, old age, unemployment, and, later, disability (Ball, 2000). Only under these circumstances would erstwhile workers become worthy beneficiaries of this new social insurance program. Of particular note is that this list of contingencies did not extend to absence from the labor force due to illness or the time needed to raise young families. Elsewhere, formal recognition of these burdens yielded national health insurance and family allowance programs still not seen in the United States.

A second historical argument employed by scholars to explain America's limited social welfare policy posture centers on political structure. As is well-known to most high school students, the founding fathers drafted the Constitution with grave concern about the possible excesses of concentrated governmental power. Federalism, the electoral college, a divided Congress, the presidential veto, staggered elections, and the Bill of Rights are each predicated at least in part on that overarching concern (Cochran & Malone, 1999).

Among other consequences, these formal checks and balances create innumerable veto points in American politics, allowing opponents of a given action multiple opportunities to derail legislation they oppose (Schattschneider, 1960; Dye, 1984). Key social policy episodes in which opponents have succeeded include Harry Truman's attempts to pass a national health insurance proposal, Richard Nixon's attempt to reform the Aid to Families with Dependent Children program, and Bill Clinton's inability to move the country in the direction of national health insurance.

Analysts invoking structural arguments to explain policy activity also note that much enacted legislation often mimics the responsible structures and channels by being fragmented, inconsistent, and limited in scope. Analysts see numerous well-intentioned social programs on the books, many enacted during the Kennedy and Johnson years, that are narrow, categorical, and subject to the "special interest" opprobrium directed at much contemporary American social policy. Long ago, Douglass Cater (1964) spoke of "subgovernmental structures" and Theodore Lowi (1967) of "iron triangles" to depict how symbiotic relationships among like-minded public and private actors led to the enactment of large numbers of small programs in the United States.

NEEDS OF OLDER PEOPLE IN AMERICAN SOCIAL POLICY DEVELOPMENT

The needs of seniors have occupied a very important place in this context of American reluctance to enact broad and inclusive social policies. With relatively rare exception, programs for the old came sooner, were funded more generously, and grew faster than social welfare programs addressing other populations or problems. Most obviously at work is that the aged historically have been understood to be a legitimately needy population and one possessing few economic resources given the many vicissitudes workers may have faced earlier in life. As such, old age was "the final emergency" (Rubinow, 1934).

Policies Addressing the Needs of Older Americans

As these comments suggest, the historical great fear of old age was outliving one's income. In the absence of individual wealth or family supports, people in old age were left to the mercies of private charity or public alms. At the time of enactment of the New Deal, it was estimated that three-quarters of older people were poor and that just over half of their income came from their adult children (Upp, 1982). Even as recently as the late 1950s, nearly 40% of all older Americans fell below the official (and very low) poverty line.

Illness and disability were a second great concern of the old, both because they made work difficult or impossible and because there were few health and social supports available to address them. Roughly half of older people had no form of health insurance whatsoever at the time of Medicare's enactment in 1965. In the case of chronic illness and disability, older people were reliant principally on the care of family and friends, with those of modest means occasionally gaining access to early mom-and-pop nursing homes (Vladeck, 1980).

Third, there was a presumption that older people either could not work (due to illness) or should not work (so that younger people might have jobs). That numbers of older people did work was frequently seen as unfair to them, inefficient for employers, and unjust for unemployed younger workers. Thus, there were multiple pressures at work to ease older people of out the labor force. Until very recently, in fact, a major function of both public and private pension policies has been to force or induce older workers into retirement (Graebner, 1980; Quinn, 1997).

This sympathetic case for elderly people, juxtaposed with the ingrained American expectation that the young and middle-aged should be able to fend for themselves (and their children), has contributed to both the absolute and relative generosity of contemporary social programs directed toward the aged in the United States. There is much that these programs do not do or do not do adequately (Harrington Meyer, 2005), but the benefits associated with them far exceed what is available to younger Americans.

The relative prominence of older people in American social policy can be seen in three important instances in which policy advances were made on their behalf when they might have or, indeed, actually had been directed toward other policy constituencies. They were centrally featured in the enactment of Social Security, with Title I being Old Age Assistance (OAA) and Title II being Old Age Insurance (OAI). As a federal-state public assistance program, OAA recognized the dire straits in which millions of low-income elders found themselves during the Great Depression. Not only were older people seen as not responsible for their plight, OAA was employed in part as a sweetener to generate support for more controversial titles of the original act. OAI, the cornerstone of today's Social Security program, was of importance for both being the nation's first social insurance program (based on no means testing and a contributory funding stream) and for being administered exclusively (and ultimately universally) by the federal government (Skocpol, 1995) The original Social Security Act also included a complicated federal-state unemployment insurance program, a public assistance program for dependent children, and a modest maternal and child health program. But in both scope and concept, none of these equaled OAI.

The prominence of the needs of older people was placed in even sharper relief in the road to Medicare's enactment in 1965. Then and now, national health insurance (NHI) has been too contested to become law in the United States. Franklin Roosevelt dropped such a proposal from his original social security legislation, and Harry Truman attempted but failed to get an NHI proposal through Congress in the early 1950s. Trying to devise an at least partial strategy that would move the country toward NHI, reformers and advocates in the 1950s and 1960s turned their attention to a population around whom little controversy would swirl: the aged. Older people were ill, poor, and largely without private health insurance coverage. Thus, they were featured in the protracted battle that led to Medicare's enactment (Marmor, 1970).

Finally, passage of Supplemental Security Income in 1972 resulted from a failed initiative undertaken by Richard Nixon in the late 1960s to reform the Aid to Families with Dependent Children program. His remarkable attempt to provide a (modest) guaranteed income to low-income mothers and children, termed "Nixon's Good Deed" by Burke and Burke (1974), failed in the Senate Finance Committee. Proponents, trying to rescue something from this failure, turned to the so-called adult categories under the public assistance titles: the poor aged, disabled, and blind. Because there was much less controversy surrounding providing benefits to this group, Congress enacted and Nixon signed the SSI legislation providing, as the name implies, a supplement to the Social Security benefits of those low-income individuals.

In each of these legislative episodes—early Social Security, Medicare's enactment, and passage of SSI—the singular and universally acknowledged needs of the aged were on full display.

Political Understandings of the Needs of Older People

This special needs–based historical standing of the old has been incorporated into theoretical constructs in policy studies. While the tone of such writing is occasionally grudging—Why are the old indulged while other groups are ignored?—the pattern leading toward what is often referred to today as America's old age welfare state is important theoretically as well as substantively.

In studying policy formation, analysts want to know who held power and what individuals or groups were most influential in the policy process. Students of social policy formation in the period building up to and following the New Deal have centered much attention on so-called policy elites. They have done so because these elite-level actors were often well positioned and active in the policymaking process and because the larger public, interest groups, and lobbyists were not much in evidence during these early policy episodes (Witte, 1962; Derthick, 1979).

In the case of aging, a critical connection emerged between the influence of the elites, on the one hand, and the needs and policy legitimacy of the old, on the other. This combination is seen in each of the three legislative episodes recounted above. In each instance, the policy elites who were involved were hoping to push forward a broad policy agenda—one that would ultimately involve far more than the aged. From their perspective, the role of the aged was that of a policy loss leader—in other words, a group you would get the consumer (in these cases, Congress) to buy, hoping that they would also buy something different or bigger (e.g., unemployment insurance, national health insurance).

These accounts of early Social Security, Medicare, and SSI enactment reveal the political role played by small numbers of elite actors and their careful use of the needs of the elderly in trying to move their agendas forward. In the case of Social Security, the larger strategy worked in that the other titles were enacted and more radical approaches to old age income protection were defeated. In the case of Medicare, the larger strategy failed since we are still without national health insurance. As for SSI, the poor aged, blind, and disabled served as a fallback after the original proposal failed, and—most dramatic—welfare policy has since gone in a far different direction, with the Temporary Assistance to Needy Families program invoking mandatory work strictures rather than providing guaranteed cash benefits. The aged, however, were well served by the policy outcomes, if not necessarily by the denigrating and utilitarian attitude displayed by some of the inside actors trying to move these agendas forward (Binstock, 1983).

Heightening the role of older people in social welfare policy development is that the standing of many other groups and social problems in American political circles is less legitimate than theirs. Thus, a major school of thought in cross-national welfare state studies holds that the strength of labor unions, social democratic parties, and social movements—instilled with notions of working-class consciousness—have generated broader-based welfare state policies. Such organizations, being large in size and high in cohesion, press their case with employers, the government, and the public at large (Esping-Andersen, 1985; Myles, 1984). Social democratic movements may stand for election and put forth their own policies, as in the cases of Sweden and Austria. Alternatively, as occurred in Great Britain and Germany, respectively, they may convince more conservative governments that they will win over their voters if no action is taken or that their discontent may undermine conservatives' traditional authority if welfare provisions for workers are not put in place (Rimlinger, 1971; Pampel & Williamson, 1989).

The point here is that this kind of broad-based pressure failed to materialize in the United States. The United States has never witnessed a sizable and enduring socialist movement despite much activity around the turn of the twentieth century; labor unions have been more center-left than left (e.g., the American Federation of Labor opposed unemployment insurance during the early years of the depression), and there has not been much expression of class consciousness, due to both ethnic and racial divisions and the decentralized and federal nature of the American political system.

It is in this "exceptionalist" (Lipset, 1997) context that again one finds political opportunities for a group such as older people. Since it appears to social welfare policy proponents that little can be done for others, rationales and tactics change dramatically. Rather than being able to pressure for population-wide policy innovations, reformers settled on a strategy in which the vulnerable status and consequent political legitimacy of older people obviated their need for demonstrable political power (Hudson, 1978). The result has been that in the American context, seniors have fared better than other populations—notably, young families, the sick, and the unemployed. In comparative perspective, it should be noted that even America's elders fare less well than do their counterparts in many European nations; however, in this same cross-national perspective, America's children fare far worse (Smeeding, Torrey, & Rein, 1988).

TRANSFORMING NEEDS INTO INTERESTS: OLD AGE POLICY TODAY

Beginning in the 1970s, the ground began shifting under social policy for seniors. Decades of sustained economic and income growth came to an end, and a new era of conservative political thinking began emerging. Tied to these developments, fundamental questions about the direction of age-based policy arose as well. Both the costs (current federal expenditures) and the benefits (heightened well-being among the old) tied to the policy expansion of the 1960s and 1970s were becoming increasingly apparent. Intergenerational concerns centered on having to meet aging baby boomers' pension and health care obligations also caught policymakers' attention. From a political perspective, the irony of these twin developments was that external pressures began building on these programs at the time that their very success was also subjecting the singular neediness of seniors to new scrutiny.

Policies Reflecting the Interests of Seniors

It is under these circumstances that the longstanding politics based on the unquestioned *needs* of the aged has been augmented by a newer politics increasingly involving the *interests* of the aged. In contrast to the long history in which addressing the plight of the elderly was largely the business of reformers, advocates, and other elite-level actors, the post-1970s period has seen the rise of seniors as a political constituency in their own right, promoting and defending their self-perceived collective interests. Today's aging politics is notably less about what we should do to help senior citizens than it is about what seniors are doing to articulate and press their own concerns.

It is aging-related public policy—both the rising costs and the notable accomplishments—that lies at the heart of this transformation. The story is by now familiar, and Table 15.1 displays the magnitude of the increase in federal expenditures on behalf of older people. As these data and the ongoing debate over the future of Social Security make clear, the costs associated with an aging population are now front-burner political items. In much debate, concern about meeting the needs of older adults has now been supplanted by worry about paying the costs for the growing older adult population.

But also of political importance is the increase in elders' well-being that these expenditures have brought about. These benefits have been individual, societal, and political. On the individual level, the data present an impressive and improving picture. Poverty rates among the old have dropped from 35% in 1959, to 15% in 1982, to just 10.2% in 1995. Median household income, which stood at $16,882 in 1974, rose to $25,152 by 2002 (both measured in 2002 dollars) (Federal Interagency Forum on Aging-Related Statistics 2004). Social Security has been a major factor behind these income increases, with average benefits having risen from $278 in 1952, to $877 in 2005 (U.S. Social Security Administration, 2005). Again, the period of the late 1960s to early 1970s was the most notable. Table 15.2 shows the remarkable increases in social security benefits that were enacted during those years. (Subsequent increases were indexed to the cost of living, beginning in 1975). A series of other indicators of elders' well-being also improved over this time period, including life expectancy, health status, and median net worth (Federal Interagency Forum on Aging Related Statistics, 2004).

On the societal level, the changed place of seniors in American society was one of the most striking developments of the twentieth century. Public policy has contributed centrally to old age having been elevated from a residual to an institutional status in American life. Whereas prior to the 20th century, attaining old age was "nowhere a majoritarian real-

TABLE 15.1   Estimated Federal Spending for the Elderly Under Selected
Programs, 1971–2010 (by fiscal year, in billions of dollars)

	1971	1980	1990	2000	2010 (Projected)
Mandatory programs					
Social security	29	85	196	307	471
Federal civilian retirement	2	8	21	33	50
Military retirement	1	2	7	14	21
Annuitants' health benefits	*	1	2	4	9
Benefits for coal miners/black lung	*	1	1	1	1
Supplemental Security Income	1	2	4	6	10
Veterans' compensation and pensions	1	7	4	9	14
Medicare	8	29	96	189	377
Medicaid	2	5	14	33	77
Food stamps	*	1	1	1	1
Total	44	137	348	597	1,026
Discretionary programs					
Housing	*	2	4	7	10
Veterans' medical care	1	3	6	9	13
Administration on Aging programs	*	1	1	1	1
Low-income energy assistance	n.a.	*	*	*	1
Total	1	6	11	17	24
Total of all federal spending on people age 65 and over	46	144	360	615	1,050
Relative magnitude of spending					
Federal spending on people 65 and over					
As a % of the budget	21.7	24.3	28.7	34.8	42.8
As a % of gross domestic product	4.2	5.3	6.3	6.4	7.1
Per elderly person (in 2000 dollars)	8,896	11,839	15,192	17,688	21,122

Source: Congressional Budget Office (2002).
Notes: * = less than $500 million; n.a. = not applicable.

ity" (Laslett, 1987), attaining old age is today considered the norm, not
the exception. In Martin Kohli's (1988) words, old age has become a
"distinct phase of life." The uniquely modern institution of retirement has
been the culminating event bringing together the demographic, economic,
social emergence, and distinctiveness of the senior population. In a manner largely unknown 75 years ago, it is now expected that most older

TABLE 15.2   Social Security Benefit
Increases, Select Years

Year	Percentage Increase
1968	13
1970	15
1971	10
1972	20
1974	11

Source: United States House of Representatives,
Committee on Ways and Means, *Green Book,*
1998, Table I-1.

people will spend an extended period of time in advanced age outside the workplace. In some ways, of course, this is old news as emergent realities are calling for "retirement reconsidered" (Morris & Bass, 1988), but the emergence of retirement as a major social construct is beyond question. In fact, reconsidering retirement is nothing less than pondering what to make of the presence of a large older population whose existence is defined centrally neither by work nor by illness.

Political Understandings of the New Standing of Seniors

This review raises important questions for both contemporary social policy and gerontology. As seen, older people have benefited from past policy enactments along a number of economic, health, and social dimensions. But they have also benefited along a political dimension: having become actors in the political system rather than merely being (favored) objects of the political system. In the past, other players were overwhelmingly responsible for policy benefits accruing to older people, ones that clearly improved their standard of living. In the wake of the reform activities of the New Deal era, there existed a 20-year period dubbed by Henry Pratt (1976) as "the dismal years" in aging policy, one finally brought to an end by the initiatives of the Kennedy/Johnson years. But it was the remarkable initiatives of the 1960s and early 1970s leading to the improvements in well-being that also activated older people and helped create them as an identifiable and vaunted political constituency. And today, as the political environment has become more threatening to aging-related policy benefits, that constituency can now mobilize to protect and maintain the very aging-related programs that have helped render older people a potent political presence.

In the political science and policy literature, these developments were initially viewed largely in terms of a conventional model of the political system in which voters and interest groups mobilize, make demands on decision makers in Washington, and often see legislation enacted on their behalf. In the case of aging, notice was taken of the development of new groups, some of which were mass-based membership groups and others of which were constituted by social welfare, medical, and other professionals organized on behalf of seniors. Many of the initial organizing efforts were attached to the struggle to enact Medicare. In that campaign, retired union workers came together to form Senior Citizens for Kennedy, a movement that became the National Council of Senior Citizens (NCSC) in the wake of Medicare's passage (Pratt 1983). The best known of the mass-based organizations, the American Association of Retired Persons (AARP) was slower to enter the advocacy arena; indeed, it opposed a proposal to increase Social Security benefits by 20 percent in 1971 as "too inflationary" (Pratt 1976).

Yet as the story unfolds, the two mass membership groups, AARP and NCSC, were actively lobbying by the late 1970s. By this time, they had been joined by a number of organizations of professionals, academics, and public officials, all seeking to expand aging programs relevant to their respective areas of work. Such groups included the National Council on the Aging, Green Thumb, the National Association of State Units on Aging, and the Gerontological Society of America, among others. By the 1980s, there were so many such groups that a new organization, the Legislative Council on Older Americans, was formed in which these groups, today numbering 51, are themselves the members (Binstock, 2005).

While the presence and activities of these organizations have grown impressively, their actual role in the policy process has been subject to some misunderstanding or at least to a too-limited understanding. While the prevailing "pressure" model has held that the massive expansion of aging-related benefits seen over the past 30 years is largely the result of actions by these groups, recent scholarship suggests that it has been the presence of the policies themselves that has served to energize and, in some cases, effectively create these groups. In the contemporary jargon of political science, this phenomenon is referred to as "policy creating politics" or, more formally as "path dependency" (Pierson 2000). Rather than simply being the product of the political process, this body of research suggests that policy itself has a major role in shaping political activity or, looking at the policy process longitudinally, policy at an earlier time period can be an independent factor in shaping subsequent political activity and, in turn, policy at a subsequent time period.

The pathbreaking exploration of this activity originated with Theodore Lowi (1964), who noted how, in the case of business, policy provisions shaped and constrained later lobbying activity and policy outcomes by business interests. Building on this insight, Lowi (1964) and James Q. Wilson (1973) developed policy typologies showing how policy options containing different distributions of gains and losses generated very different styles of political action by interested parties. A yet broader attack on the pluralist-pressure model came from a group labeled the new institutionalists, who argued that the independent role of the state (i.e., governmental institutions) had been badly underestimated by a generation of political scientists and sociologists transfixed by larger social and political forces (Skocpol, 1985). And, in "bringing the state back in," these analysts were also bringing in the product of the state, that is, public policy.

This line of reasoning was applied to aging policy in the early 1980s by Jack Walker of the University of Michigan. In making the larger theoretical case about the role of policy, he found that more than half of the 46 aging-related groups were formed after 1965, the year in which both Medicare and the Older Americans Act were enacted. From his study, Walker concluded:

> In all of these cases, the formation of new groups was one of the *consequences* of major new legislation, not one of the *causes* of its passage. A pressure model of the policymaking process in which an essentially passive legislature responds to petitions from groups of citizens who have spontaneously organized because of common social or economic concerns must yield to a model in which influences for change come as much from inside the government as from beyond its institutional boundaries. (1983, p. 403, emphasis in the original)

The most direct piece of evidence in support of policy's independent role in aging politics was the creation of two trade associations whose members were literally brought into existence by federal legislation. The Older Americans Act mandated creation of State Units on Aging across the country in 1965, and amendments passed in 1973 required the creation of substate planning bodies, designated as Area Agencies on Aging. Within a few years, both the National Association of State Units on Aging and the National Association of Area Agencies on Aging had offices in Washington through which they continued to bring the social service needs of elders to the attention of Congress and federal agencies (Hudson & Strate, 1985).

The most compelling application of this model to aging policy highlights the role of Social Security in helping to create a sense of political identity among older people themselves. In her book, *How Policies Make Citizens: Senior Political Activism and the American Welfare State* (2003), Andrea Louise Campbell establishes a clear connection between the dramatic expansion of Old Age and Survivors Insurance benefits under Social Security and heightened participation by older Americans in the political process. Campbell juxtaposes Social Security liberalization of both eligibility for benefits and benefit increases against measures of participation such as voting, contributing, campaign work, and contacting. She finds increases in each of these types of activity in the wake of Social Security expansion and, more recently, in response to perceived threats to existing Social Security benefits. While broadening concern from a few score groups to millions of individuals, Campbell's conclusions are very reminiscent of Walker's:

> Absent Social Security, senior citizens are a disparate group of people whose common characteristic, age, has little political meaning. Once governmental benefits are conferred, however, the group has political relevance and is ripe for mobilization by policy entrepreneurs, interest groups, and political parties. (2003, p. 36)

CONCLUSION

This chapter has focused directly on the policy needs and interests of older people and how they are addressed in American politics. In this application, an important distinction has emerged between needs and interests, one that sheds considerable light on the emergence of older people as major participants in American politics and as major beneficiaries of the American welfare state. The acknowledged needs of older people extend back centuries and were critical to the emergence of social policies for older people in the early and middle years of social policy development in the United States. Indeed, many such needs continue to be present within the older population, especially among older populations of color and very old women.

Yet the policy accomplishments and the concrete benefits that accompanied them—animating interest groups and providing the political resources of income, leisure time, and self-identify to older people themselves—have served to transform needs into interests. The success of public policy in bringing a modicum of security and well-being to late life also, in Campbell's words, made citizens out of a population that in the early years of American social policy had been only the object of others' compassionate concerns.

REFERENCES

Ball, R. (2000). *Ensuring the essentials.* New York: Century Foundation.

Bernstein, A. (1997). Inside or outside: The politics of family and medical leave. *Policy Studies Journal, 25,* 87–99.

Binstock, R. H. (1983). The aged as scapegoat. *Gerontologist, 23,* 136–143.

Binstock, R. H. (2005). The contemporary politics of old age policies. In R. B. Hudson (Ed.), *The new politics of old age policy* (pp. 265–293). Baltimore: Johns Hopkins University Press.

Burke, V., & Burke, V. (1974). *Nixon's good deed: Welfare reform.* New York: Columbia University Press.

Campbell, A. L. (2003). *How policies make citizens: Senior political activism and the American welfare state.* Princeton, NJ: Princeton University Press.

Cater, D. (1964). *Power in Washington: A critical look at today's struggle to govern in the nation's capital.* New York: Random House.

Cochran, C., & Malone, E. (1999). *Public policy: Perspectives and choices* (2nd ed.). New York: McGraw-Hill.

Davies, G. (1996). *From opportunity to entitlement: The transformation and decline of great society liberalism.* Lawrence: University Press of Kansas.

Derthick, M. (1979). *Policymaking for social security.* Washington, DC: Brookings Institution.

Dye, T. (1984). *Understanding public policy* (5th ed.). Englewood Cliffs, NJ: Prentice-Hall.

Economist. (2005). Seeking freedom, at home and abroad: George Bush's second term. January 20, 2–3.

Esping-Andersen, G. (1985). *Politics and markets: The social democratic road to power.* Princeton, NJ: Princeton University Press.

Federal Interagency Forum on Aging-Related Statistics. (2004). *Older Americans 2004: Key indicators of well-being.* Washington, DC: Author.

Graebner, W. (1980). *A history of retirement: The meaning and function of an American institution, 1885–1978.* New Haven, CT: Yale University Press.

Harrington Meyer, M. (2005). Decreasing welfare, increasing old age inequality: Whose responsibility is it? In R. B. Hudson (Ed.), *The new politics of old age policy* (pp. 65–89). Baltimore: Johns Hopkins University Press.

Himelfarb, R. (1995). *Catastrophic politics: The rise and fall of the Medicare Catastrophic Care Act of 1988.* University Park: Penn State University Press.

Hudson, R. B. (1978). The "graying" of the federal budget and its consequences for old-age policy. *Gerontologist, 18,* 428–440.

Hudson, R. B., & Strate, J. (1985). Aging and political systems. In R. H. Binstock & E. Shanas (Eds.), *Handbook of aging and the social sciences* (2nd ed., pp. 554–585). New York: Van Nostrand Reinhold.

Katz, M. (1986). *In the shadow of the poorhouse: A social history of welfare in America.* New York: Basic Books.

Kohli, M. (1988). Ageing as a challenge for sociological theory. *Ageing and Society, 8,* 367–394.

Laslett, P. (1987). The emergence of the third age. *Ageing and Society, 7,* 133–166.

Lipset, S. M. (1997). *American exceptionalism: A double-edged sword.* New York: Norton.

Lowi, T. (1964). American business, public policy, case-studies, and political theory. *World Politics, 16,* 677–715.

Lowi, T. (1967). *The end of liberalism: Ideology, policy, and the crisis of public authority.* New York: Norton.

Marmor, T. (1970). *The politics of Medicare.* London: Routledge and Kegan Paul.

Mead. L. (1986). *Beyond entitlement: The social obligations of citizenship.* New York: Free Press.

Morris, R., & Bass, S. (1988). *Retirement reconsidered: Economic and social policies for older people.* New York: Springer Publishing.

Myles, J. (1984). *Old age in the welfare state: The political economy of public pensions.* Boston: Little, Brown.

Orloff, A. S. (1988). The political origins of America's belated welfare state. In M. Weir, A. S. Orloff, & T. Skocpol (Eds.), *The politics of social policy in the United States* (pp. 37–80). Princeton, NJ: Princeton University Press.

Pampel, F., & Williamson, J. (1989). *Age, class, politics, and the welfare state.* New York: Cambridge University Press.

Peterson, P. (1996). *Will America grow up before it grows old? How the coming social security crisis threatens you, your family, and your country.* New York: Random House.

Pierson, P. (2000). Increasing returns, path dependence, and the study of politics. *American Political Science Review, 94,* 251–267.

Pratt, H. (1976). *The gray lobby.* Chicago: University of Chicago Press.

Pratt, H. (1983). National interest groups among the elderly: Consolidation and constraint. In W. P. Browne & L. K. Olson (Eds.), *Aging and public policy: The politics of growing old in America* (pp. 61–92). Westport, CT: Greenwood Press.

Quadagno, J. (1988). *The transformation of old age security.* Chicago: University of Chicago Press.

Quinn, J. (1997). Retirement trends and patterns in the 1990s: The end of an era? *Public Policy and Aging Report, 8,* 10–14.

Rimlinger, G. (1971). *Welfare policy and industrialization in Europe, America, and Russia.* New York: Wiley.

Rosenberg, C. (1962). *The cholera years: The United States in 1832, 1849, and 1866.* Chicago: University of Chicago Press.

Rubinow, I. (1934). *The quest for security.* New York: Arno Press.

Samuelson, R. (1978). Busting the U.S. budget: The costs of an aging America. *National Journal, 10,* 256–260.

Schattschneider, E. E. (1960). *The semisovereign people: A realist's view of democracy in America.* New York: Holt, Rinehart, and Winston.

Skocpol, T. (1985). Bringing the state back in: Strategies of analysis in current research. In P. Evans, D. Rueschemeyer, & T. Skocpol (Eds.), *Bringing the state back in.* New York: Cambridge University Press.

Skocpol, T. (1992). *Protecting soldiers and mothers: The political origins of social policy in the United States.* Cambridge, MA: Belknap Press of Harvard University Press.

Skocpol, T. (1995). *Social policy in the United States.* Princeton, NJ: Princeton University Press.

Skocpol, T. (1996). *Boomerang: Clinton's health security effort and the turn against government in U.S. politics.* New York: Norton.

Smeeding, T., Torrey, B., & Rein, M.. (1988). Patterns of income and poverty: The economic status of children and the elderly in eight countries. In J. L. Palmer, T. Smeeding, & B. Torrey (Eds.), *The vulnerable* (pp. 89–119). Washington, DC: Urban Institute Press.

Smith, D. (2002). *Entitlement politics: Medicare and Medicaid, 1995–2001.* New York: Aldine de Gruyter.

Sundquist, J. (1968). *Politics and policy: The Eisenhower, Kennedy, and Johnson years.* Washington, DC: Brookings Institution.

U.S. Social Security Administration. (2005, August). *Monthly statistical snapshot.* Retrieved October 3, 2005, from www.ssa.gov/policy/docs/quickfacts/stat_snapshot/index.html

Upp, M. (1982). A look at the economic status of the aged then and now. *Social Security Bulletin, 45,* 16–22.

Vladeck, B. (1980). *Unloving care: The nursing home tragedy.* New York: Basic Books.

Walker, J. (1983). The origins and maintenance of interest groups in America. *American Political Science Review, 77,* 390–406.

Weaver, R. K. (1988). *Automatic government: The politics of indexation.* Washington, DC: Brookings Institution.

Wilensky, H., & Lebeaux, C. (1958). *Industrial society and social welfare.* New York: Russell Sage Foundation.

Wilson, J. Q. (1973). *Political organizations.* New York: Basic Books.

Witte, E. (1962). *The development of the Social Security Act.* Madison: University of Wisconsin Press.

CHAPTER 16

Afterword

The Gerontological Imagination

Kenneth F. Ferraro

The contributors to this book have considered the major questions posed by scholars studying aging and given a sense of how it is that gerontologists think about aging. In the process, they have helped us to see the elements of the emerging paradigm for the scientific study of aging. The purpose of this chapter is to make these elements explicit—to articulate a gerontological imagination.

It has been commonplace for scholars interested in research on aging to claim that gerontology is a field of study that lacks a paradigm, a fundamental image of its subject matter (Achenbaum, 1987, 1995; Maddox, 1987). The claim was reasonable and may be so to this day, but there are also seeds of the development of a paradigm for gerontology. The lack of a paradigm is not unusual for social sciences, but it is not as common in the physical sciences (Ritzer, 1975). In a situation in which there are several paradigms in a field, there is competition and intellectual conflict among scientists as to the fundamental image of the subject of study. Despite considerable divergence within a field characterized as a multiple paradigm science, there are obviously many unifying concepts, methodologies, and strategies for interpretation. Yet these do not necessarily constitute a shared paradigm.

It is widely recognized that gerontology is a multidisciplinary enterprise, but problems arise in the articulation of its basic image of aging. This chapter identifies some of the key elements in the conceptual framework used in the scientific study of aging. In addition, it seeks to stimulate thought in the field of gerontology toward developing a paradigm within the field and to provide the basic ideas and themes that currently guide scientific research on aging.

To approach this task from a different perspective, one might ask, What is a gerontologist? Although many would agree that a gerontologist is a person who engages in the scientific study of aging, there is still no consensus as to what constitutes professional education for gerontologists. Indeed, there have been heated debates about efforts to standardize the curriculum for preparing a gerontologist. Although the Association for Gerontology in Higher Education has vigorously pursued the development of curriculum standards, certification, and a "program of merit" designation, others have countered that such endeavors are ill advised, for a couple of reasons. First, because we do not yet have a paradigm for gerontology, it is unlikely that we can effectively shape educational standards for this field. In other words, perhaps the paradigm should precede the educational standards. Second, some would argue that there is no such professional role properly labeled *gerontologist*. Rather, because gerontology is multidisciplinary, and must remain so, what we want to aid is professional development in those primary disciplines—sociology, psychology, nursing, and social work, as examples—with accompanying expertise in gerontology.

I choose to sidestep the issue of whether gerontologists do or should exist in order to focus on the more relevant question in the development of gerontology: What fundamental image needs to be fostered for anyone studying aging, regardless of his or her professional background or aspirations? That is, can biologists, sociologists, health educators, and political scientists find some common ground for their intellectual work? Ideally, we want a set of axioms from which other thoughts and ideas can be developed.

When we think of the possibility of a paradigm for gerontology, we are not implying that all the details of this emerging science are known. Rather, a paradigm describes a way of thinking or general organizing principles that map the field. At its broadest level of conceptualization, Ritzer (1975, p. 5) states that a paradigm serves several functions:

1. It defines what entities are (and are not) the concern of a particular scientific community.
2. It tells the scientist where to look (and where not to look) in order to find the entities of concern to him.
3. It tells the scientist what he can expect to discover when he finds and examines the entities of concern to his field.

Within sociology, the field of my disciplinary training, C. Wright Mills (1959) attempted to carve out a way of thinking about social life.

His book *The Sociological Imagination* is not an encyclopedia of sociology, but it remains one of the finest treatises on how sociologists think about the social world. In other words, a clearly articulated paradigm is the most efficient way of coming to understand a field. Also, as Kuhn (1962) and Ritzer (1975) pointed out, a clearly articulated paradigm aids the cumulative development of a science, by either incremental development or revolution.

Although paradigms change, the goal here is to articulate an analytic framework for the study of aging so that it may be challenged, strengthened, or refocused. This effort is purposively integrative. As Boyer (1990) asserted, this type of integrative work emphasizes the need for scholars to give meaning to isolated facts, placing them in perspective. "By integration, we mean making connections across the disciplines, placing the specialties in larger context, illuminating data in a revealing way, often educating nonspecialists, too" (p. 18).

The analytic framework developed here may be described as a *gerontological imagination*. The gerontological imagination is an awareness of the process of human aging that enables one to understand the scientific contributions of a variety of researchers studying aging. In addition, this awareness allows people (not just gerontology scholars) to comprehend the links among biological, behavioral, and social structure factors that influence human aging. It is, by definition, a multidisciplinary sensitivity to aging that incorporates the common stock of knowledge from the core disciplines engaged in research on aging.

The basic elements of a gerontological imagination can be viewed as representative of a culture of scientific thinking on aging. This scientific culture has changed and will continue to change, as described earlier in chapter 2. Moreover, my articulation of the gerontological imagination has also changed since I first wrote about it in 1990. Some tenets remain, but others have been added or substantially revised. Recognizing that paradigms evolve, I offer seven tenets to elucidate what I mean by a gerontological imagination. I reiterate that these are working ideas about our current state of knowledge. They will merit revision as knowledge about aging, especially human aging, accumulates.

ELEMENTS OF A GERONTOLOGICAL IMAGINATION

Aging and Causality

Aging is not a cause of all age-related phenomena. Thus, gerontologists maintain a healthy skepticism for what are attributed to be age effects.

One of the basic ideas in the study of research methodology is that certain conclusions can be drawn only from certain types of research activities. Readers familiar with the logic of experimental designs will recognize that there are special problems with the conclusion that correlated variables have a causal relationship in one direction or the other. While the details of that epistemological issue are not relevant for our current concerns, we should be cautious about interpreting age-related phenomena as being caused by age.

Within gerontology there is widespread dissatisfaction with the use of age as a causal independent variable. This is especially the case in developmental research. Age is a very important marker of life events, life transitions, social context, and resources, but age in and of itself is an impotent causal variable. Jack Botwinick (1978, p. 307) stated this most eloquently:

> Age, as a concept, is synonymous with time, and time in itself cannot affect living function, behavior or otherwise. Time does not "cause" anything; it does not have physical dimensionality to impinge upon the sensorium. . . . Time is a crude index of many events and experiences and these indexed events which are "causal."

Even at the biological level, aging is usually seen as an impotent causal variable. It is not the passage of time that causes cellular or organic changes. Consider the classic Hayflick (1965) experiments on normal diploid human cells. Hayflick observed that regardless of the age of the donor, such cells could proliferate in culture for only a finite number of times. In other words, it was not aging per se that was related to cell structure and reproduction but the number of passages such cells underwent. Cunningham and Brookbank (1988) sum it up nicely: "The limit on the number of cell doublings in vitro implies that there may be a predetermined life span of cells outside the body that *is independent of changes occurring with time* in the body as a whole" (p. 64, emphasis added).

Another way to consider this issue is that aging frequently gets a bad name for things it did not cause. Aging is often considered a gremlin that steals vitality and intellectual power from individuals. As Willott (1997) observed, it is not the passage of time—directly related to chronological aging—that causes various declines in human performance. Rather, there are other processes, whether biological, neuropsychological, or social, that are the true explanatory variables in understanding age-related changes. Although many people will continue to conceptualize aging as a gremlin or thief of human vitality and performance, there is now a considerable body of research indicating that this gremlin may be tamed or subdued through interventions of various sorts.

When one is interested in identifying aging effects, one of the first considerations that a good gerontologist raises is the possibility of cohort (or generational) effects that are known to be age related. (A cohort refers to a set of people born or experiencing some other event at the same time.) It may not be growing older per se that brings about differences in the degree of political conservatism in a given society; perhaps the time at which individuals were born is more important in shaping these dispositions. People who experienced the politically formative years of 18 to 27 during the Great Depression of the 20th century in America are probably going to have a different political and economic outlook from those who experienced those same politically formative years during the times of economic prosperity in the 1950s and 1960s.

Before jumping to the conclusion that a cohort is a better variable to explain age-related differences, however, it should be pointed out that cohort, in and of itself, is similar to aging in that it is limited to marking or indexing events in gerontological research. Knowing when a person was born does not give us a wholly adequate picture of the causal relationships among these variables. Cohort indexes certain life events, historical experiences, and cultural forms that are probably the real causal agents. In that sense, discerning differences among age, period (sometimes referred to as time of measurement), and cohort effects is vital to our understanding of human aging. At the same time, one should maintain a healthy skepticism about attributions of certain changes in human performance or social relationships to aging. In summary, age is a useful categorizing variable in age-related differences for any phenomenon under study. Such knowledge of age differences is important in the cumulative development of knowledge on a subject. Knowledge that age is related to certain criteria however, is not satisfactory in an explanatory scientific enterprise. A gerontological imagination can grow only when there is a healthy skepticism about age as a causal variable.

A corollary of this first tenet is that aging is a life process, not a death process. It is clear that aging is related to mortality, but death often gives aging a bad name. Many might regard such a statement as humorous, but it is nonetheless true. It is vitally important to be able to separate death processes from life processes in studying the process of aging. Failure to do so is to attribute to aging what is actually due to death or dying. In historical perspective, the high prevalence of death among older people is a relatively recent trend among modern societies. I conceptualize aging as a life process primarily because of the need to distinguish various types of causal effects in age-related research.

An excellent illustration of how dying may make the aging process look bad derives from the concept of terminal drop. Kleemeier (1962) pioneered this concept by studying the relationship between test performance and survival. He observed declines in test scores of men on several occasions over the course of 12 years; however, what was most striking was that the decline was much greater for those who died after one of the data collection periods than for those who survived during that same interval.

Contemporary gerontologists have come to identify terminal drop (or terminal change) as referring to decrements in social, psychological, or biological functioning that are not functions of time since birth—age—but of the amount of time before death. Researchers hold that terminal drop indicates that there is a determinant chain of behavioral changes that are really due to a death process (Ferraro & Kelley-Moore, 2001; Riegel & Riegel, 1972). Distinguishing between aging effects and terminal drop is critical for our image of the aging process, especially during the later years. Riegel and Riegel suggested that if we eliminate people who do not survive at least five years after testing from the analysis of age differences, many of the so-called age declines derived from cross-sectional research would disappear (see also Botwinick, 1977; White & Cunningham, 1988).

Thanatology, the study of death and dying, is an intellectual enterprise separate from gerontology. Although it is helpful to be aware of death and dying in the study of aging, we are not primarily interested in those processes. Instead, we are interested in distinguishing between aging and death processes in order to better understand each one.

Aging as Multifaceted Change

> Aging involves biological, psychological, and social changes in individuals at varying rates. The transitions associated with growing older are probably not linearly related to chronological age, and the process of aging itself is also multidimensional in nature.

The approach to the study of aging must recognize the dynamics of aging and the multidimensionality of this dynamism. Nathan Shock, the pioneering biologist of aging, felt that "aging is a dynamic equilibrium. The rates of aging differ for various systems in any given organism, however, it is the whole organism that ages and dies" (see Baker & Achenbaum, 1992, p. 262). We see an aging organism, but there are many systems that are aging at different rates (i.e., multifaceted change).

Drawing from a sociological framework, Featherman and Petersen (1986) reached a parallel conclusion by noting that there are special problems in attempting to mark or track individual aging. First, they note that growing older is rife with change. Aging entails changes, but not all of these changes are either progressive or detrimental. Second, "aging is a process that reflects duration in state" (1986, p. 342). Thus, while aging is a lifelong process, from birth to death, the transitions identified throughout the life course are held for certain periods of time. In other words, we should be interested in the length of time that individuals occupy certain states or possess certain qualities. According to Featherman and Petersen, recognizing such duration dependence gives us a better sense of the pace of individual aging within the various spheres of human life, whether biological, psychological, or social.

In addition, aging is a process of embedded dynamisms because biological and psychosocial aging occur interactively. The changing organism faces social and cultural context that also changes. This leads Featherman and Peterson (1986) to conclude that "there are many clocks that time us" (p. 343). It is intriguing how similar this sounds to the statement by the biologist Nathan Shock, but sociologists obviously focus more on population processes that encompass interindividual commonality and diversity. There are indeed elements of common intellectual ground, and this is one tenet on which there is considerable agreement.

Genetic Influences on Aging

> The imprint of genetics on development and aging is substantial. Genetics influences not only longevity but biological and behavioral processes across the life course.

Although the influence of nature and nurture on aging has long been debated, evidence from studies with a variety of organisms, from yeast to humans, shows clearly that genetic influences on the aging process are undeniable. In human populations, the evidence comes primarily from two types of studies: genealogical or family lineage and twins. Studies of centenarians and nonagenarians reveal that they often have family members who also achieved exceptional longevity (Perls et al., 2002). Twin studies compare people who are genetically identical (monozygotic twins), including those reared apart, and people who are fraternal twins (dizygotic twins). The evidence is fairly consistent that the longevity of identical twins is more similar than is the case for fraternal twins. The emerging consensus is that genes account for about 25% of what determines longevity (Cournil & Kirkwood, 2001; Martin, Austad, & Johnson, 1996; Vijg & Suh, 2005).

The link between genes and longevity is likely through modifications in metabolism and resistance to oxidative stress (Vijg & Suh, 2005). It appears that the genetic determinants of longevity are principally those that affect cellular maintenance and repair, either directly or indirectly (Kirkwood, 2002). For instance, genes may help blunt the impact of oxidative damage on the organism. Moreover, evidence from the Human Genome Project reveals that genes play a critical role in enabling the organism to avoid diseases, including cancer and cardiovascular disease. Indeed, some have argued that it is not that genes program for longevity per se, but that some genes help organisms avoid disease, thereby lengthening life. It is also possible that genes may confer beneficial effects for selective survival, even if they eventually have deleterious effects on the organism—what is referred to as *antagonistic pleiotropy* (Kirkwood, 2002; Williams, 1957).

A gerontological imagination requires an awareness of genetic destiny in the way in which an organism ages. This is not to privilege genetics above environmental or behavioral factors because there is ample evidence that environments substantially influence the actions of genes. Rather, the value of genetic awareness is that there may be limits to an organism's ability to benefit from lifestyle changes or environmental improvements. Some diseases, for instance, sickle cell anemia, are strongly influenced by genetics. The prevalence and course of other diseases may be only partially shaped by genetics. Gerontology is enhanced by the systematic consideration of the role of gene-environment interactions in the course of human aging.

Aging and Heterogeneity

Age is positively associated with heterogeneity in a population.

George Maddox (1987), in his Kleemeier lecture to the Gerontological Society of America, considered the heterogeneity of the older adult population to be one of the fundamental axioms in his study of aging. Although it is convenient to use age as the categorizing variable for analyzing human life, just because people are the same age does not necessarily mean that they have many things in common. This is especially the case as we consider the life course, because many scholars have come to agree that people become less alike as they grow older. In statistical terms, means (averages) of traits may vary over the life course, but standard deviations on such traits will often be larger in the advanced years. Childhood and youth are extremely age-graded times of life. While we all experience various normative life events, the nonnormative events accumulate over time and are often quite influential in shaping lives, creating more diversity between individuals.

The fact that older people are a diverse population has led one social scientist to caution investigators about the use of the mean, or average, to describe older adults. As Quinn (1987) so aptly states, "The most important characteristic of the aged is their diversity. The average can be very deceptive, because it ignores the tremendous dispersion around it. Beware of the mean" (p. 64).

Empirical illustrations of this phenomenon abound. Maddox demonstrates this phenomenon in several ways in health research, most recently by studying trajectories of functional impairment in later life. Hayslip and Sterns (1979) examined a number of tests for age differences in crystallized and fluid intelligence and problem solving. While some age differences occurred across the ages, showing older adults with lower levels, the striking finding of their research was that the standard deviations on almost all of the measures examined were much greater for older adults than for younger ones. Methodologically, we should be sensitive to differences in the variance of scores across age groups as well as to differences in mean scores. Current cohorts of older adults are very diverse, and there is little reason to expect that such diversity will shrink in future years.

Although there is a tendency toward certain functional declines with aging, there are substantial individual differences in the rate of such declines. In addition, many functional abilities can be strengthened or maintained with intervention. One should not conclude that age inevitably brings a decline in human structure and function. Willott, Jackson, and Hunter (1987) present evidence that aging does not always lead to a decline in the size of neurons, as is commonly believed. Instead, they found that no inevitable change in neuronal size need occur and some neurons actually increase in size with aging.

The concept of normal aging has gained considerable currency in gerontology, but it also has its limitations. It is valuable for distinguishing normal aging from age-related changes that are pathological in origin. Just as we noted that aging is a life process and that we must distinguish it from death processes, so also we must distinguish aging from disease processes. The insightful work of Rowe and Kahn (1987) indicates that "the emphasis on 'normal' aging focuses attention on learning what most older people do and do not do, what physiologic and psychologic states are typical. It tends to create a gerontology of the usual" (p. 143, emphasis added). Rowe and Kahn assert that we are ready for a new conceptual distinction to move the field of gerontology forward. They feel that the distinction between aging caused by pathological factors and normal aging is a useful one, but they assert that the normal-aging concept is quite broad in and of itself.

Some of the weaknesses in the term *normal aging* are a neglect of (1) heterogeneity among older people undergoing normal aging, (2) the implication of risk or harm associated with normal aging, and (3) what is modifiable within the sphere of normal aging (Rowe & Kahn, 1998). Therefore, they recommend the division of normal aging into *successful aging* and *usual aging*. They note that there are certain tendencies toward functional declines with aging, but that there are individuals who have grown older without such functional declines. They suggest that these individuals might be regarded as aging successfully with regard to the particular trait or characteristic under study. By contrast, people who show typical nonpathological, age-linked losses would be characterized as experiencing usual aging.

There are problems with their proposed conceptual distinction; chief among them is that the term *usual* is seen as describing the residual of successful aging. Does *usual aging* mean "unsuccessful aging?" Regardless of the preferred terms to describe the phenomenon, Rowe and Kahn should be commended for emphasizing the heterogeneity observed in older adult populations as well as the recognition that many traits can be modified through appropriate interventions. The concept of modifiability is directly linked to the heterogeneity of a population, as Maddox (1987) points out: "Heterogeneity constitutes prime evidence of the modifiability of aging processes and hence the potential for intentional modification of these processes" (p. 562). Hence, heterogeneity of older adult populations and modifiability of the aging process may be two sides of the same coin.

Evidence now abounds from research on information processing that older adults can perform well on many intellectual tasks they were previously thought unable to do. Baltes (1993) concluded from an extensive review of research on the aging mind that for some types of cognitive function (i.e., cognitive pragmatics), "there is evidence for stability and positive change in persons who reach old age without specific brain pathology, and who live in favorable circumstances" (p. 580). Other research shows the value of intervention on cognitive functioning, such as in the case of being offered special instructions or coaching. Suffice it to say that many of the assumptions we have had about performance decrements over the life course are neither pathologically induced nor necessarily "normal." If appropriate interventions can be modeled, many of the so-called declines in psychological and biological functioning can be abated (Baltes, 1993). By Willott's (1997) analogy, the gremlin can be slain, tamed, or at least caged. This also suggests the value of searching for the origins of heterogeneity among the events and experiences earlier in the life course.

Aging and Life Course Analysis

Aging is a life-long process, and using a life course perspective helps advance the scientific study of aging.

As noted earlier, Shock advocated for studies over the entire life span (Baker & Achenbaum, 1992). Both developmental psychologists (e.g., Baltes, Reese, & Lipsitt, 1980) and sociologists (e.g., Elder, 1994; Riley, 1987) helped build this emphasis on study of the life span or life course as an entity. And as Waters showed in Chapter 4, many biologists use animals with a short life span to study development and senescence. Life course studies are helpful in their own right, but are they an integral part of the gerontological imagination? Why is the life course perspective relevant to gerontologists?

Aging involves a series of transitions from birth to death, with both advantages and disadvantages. According to Riley (1985), "Aging is a lifelong process of growing up and growing *older* from birth to death, moving through all the strata in society; it is not simply growing *old* beyond some arbitrary point in the life course" (p. 374). As noted earlier, gerontology as a field has changed from just studying older people to studying the process of growing older. Critical to the gerontological imagination is an awareness that aging is a lifelong process involving transitions from birth to death (Elder, 1994). This has become widely recognized in psychology as the *life span perspective* or *life span developmental perspective on aging*. Sociologists prefer to use the phrase *life course perspective*, in part because the concept of life span is widely used in biology to refer to maximum longevity. Although the preferred phrase may be debated, gerontologists who do not use a life course or life span framework may be disadvantaged in their conceptual and empirical endeavors. Why? Because if there are early origins of the heterogeneity observed in older adult populations, then failure to adopt a longer or life course perspective may lead to a gerontology of temporal proximity.

Aging in society involves numerous transitions, as others expect certain things of individuals at certain ages. Certain roles must be taken up, while other activities and roles are laid down. Thus while age, as a variable measured in chronological years, increases at equal intervals, aging, as a life process involving transitions, is not necessarily linear. Rather, much of what we know about the life course is at certain seasons of an individual's life, and certain ages play more pivotal roles than others in shaping the individual's biological, psychological, and social life.

Turning 16, 21, 50, 65, or 100 all have special meanings in American society, and there are other ages throughout the world that are similarly recognized as pivotal in the life course. On the biological side, there are important life stages related to reproduction. It is hard to overstate the importance of puberty, fertility, and menopause as markers of key life course stages shaping the way we age. If we are interested in the process of growing older, we would be wise to recognize earlier transitions in a person's life, as well as the environmental context of these transitions. Moreover, the very process of aging varies in sociocultural space and time (Elder, 1994).

The stock of knowledge in gerontology shows clearly the utility of information from earlier life in predicting attitudes, personality, behavior, or health in later life. The emergent life course epidemiologic perspective seeks to identify the early origins of disease and disability (Lynch & Smith, 2005). For health gerontology, the idea is that the best models of health in later life will incorporate elements of early life—from birth and middle age to the early periods of later life. According to Wadsworth (1997), there is growing interest in taking a "lifetime view of the natural history of some common serious illnesses which usually begin in middle or later life" (p. 860).

The logic of life course analysis applies to many fields of inquiry besides health. It is clear that studies of asset accumulation also reveal the value of a good start in the race toward economic well-being. Studies of health and wealth are adding to the orientation that studying aging as a process from birth to death is scientifically advantageous. There is still value in what might be described as cohort-centric studies, those that examine selected age groups such as those over age 65 or over age 75, but the recognition is growing among gerontologists that the logical next step after the cohort-centric studies is to conduct panel studies of multiple cohorts.

Aging and Cumulative Disadvantage

> Disadvantage accumulates over the life course, thereby differentiating a cohort over time.

Research on a wide array of topics shows the importance of early advantage or disadvantage on the aging process (Dannefer, 2003; O'Rand, 1996). Gerontology benefits from recognizing how disadvantage accumulates over the life course, for studying both intraindividual change and cohort differentiation (Dannefer, 1987).

Life course studies point to a wide array of biological and social forces that differentiate a population over time, but the concept of cumulative disadvantage helps one to see how trajectories arise from early inequalities. This view of the life course typically shows that some persons are advantaged in their early years, and this advantage compounds over time. Others are disadvantaged because of genetic or environmental factors, and these disadvantages also accumulate. They might compensate for the early disadvantage by working harder or enduring more, but the challenges they face are clear.

In a sense, disadvantages may scar the person's life chances (Preston, Hill, & Drevenstedt, 1998), and many of the inequalities observed in later life were actually established earlier. For instance, racial inequalities in health do not emerge during later life. There are well-documented racial differences in health at birth, in infancy and childhood, and throughout most of adulthood (Ahmed, 1994; Ferraro & Farmer, 1996; Ferraro, Thorpe, McCabe, Kelley-Moore, & Jiang, in press). If gerontologists systematically examine the accumulation of disadvantage—whether it is oxidative damage or financial stress—they will be better positioned to observe how heterogeneity results in part from early inequalities. Gerontology is not simply the study of older people, but includes research on how early disadvantage shapes later life. It is incumbent on gerontologists to consider using a wide-angle lens to identify the accumulation of risk factors across the life course.

At the same time, one should not accept a simple model of determination due to the accumulation of early adverse experiences. Gerontologists look for early origins of the outcomes under consideration, but the effects of early disadvantages are not inexorable; instead, trajectories have a certain degree of plasticity. Some people experience adversity and are scarred; others experience adversity and emerge strengthened or weathered by the experience, perhaps helping them to deal with a future adverse event (Elder, 1974).

Studying such life course challenges and adjustments also enables one to examine the possibility that feedback mechanisms and cyclical change often occur over the life course. The growing use of longitudinal data is pointing precisely to such mechanisms of spiral decline. The key is to examine the long-term antecedents of declines in later life.

Aging and Ageism

There is a propensity toward ageism in modern societies; ageism may also exist among elderly people or those who work with or for elderly people. Even scholars interested in aging may manifest ageism.

Gerontologists should be aware of the prejudice and discrimination directed toward older people. The emergent paradigm of the gerontological imagination is dependent upon the social and intellectual climate.

Achenbaum (1987) claims that gerontology should be comparative in nature; thus, it is important to note that societies and social structures have different images of, and norms regarding, growing older. Several scholars have noted, when comparing societies, a tendency toward ageism in modern societies (e.g., Fry, 1997).

A stunning illustration of the problem of ageism in American society as well as other modern societies was offered by Pat Moore in a three-year participant observation study. Moore, a 26-year old industrial designer at the time, disguised herself as an older person to more fully experience what it means to be an older person in America. Perhaps the reader will recall the potent revelations of Griffin (1960) in the book *Black Like Me*, an account of white man who underwent cosmetic changes to make himself look black and then experienced the cultural and social life of being in a minority group. Just as Griffin staged a racial transition, Moore staged an age transition. With the help of a professional makeup artist, she disguised herself as an older person and traveled throughout the United States and Canada over several years in a variety of settings. She varied the "old" Pat Moore by portraying different levels of social standing: a poor old woman, a middle-class old woman, and a relatively wealthy old woman.

Moore's reflections regarding this experience, described in her book *Disguised* (1985), are most illuminating for understanding ageism in modern societies. She was both loved and hated, welcomed and spat on. Some individuals recognized her situation and in some cases her plight and offered assistance unconditionally. Others found her easy prey for mugging or did not extend common courtesies shown to others. In one situation, she purchased a typewriter ribbon from the same store on two consecutive days, but on one day she was the older Pat and one the younger Pat. She acted identically on both days, and even wore the same dress on the two occasions. Mouthing the same words, one day and the next, appearing as the older Pat Moore and then as the younger Pat Moore, she received incredibly different reactions from the same clerk. The clerk was condescending and curt with the older Pat but affable and gracious with the younger Pat.

Lest we think that businessmen and teenage gangs are the only ones who have ageism in their veins, Pat Moore also visited conferences on aging, where other gerontologists, social scientists, and planners were in attendance. As an older person in the midst of a gerontology conference, she frequently experienced exclusion and neglect. Ageism runs deep, and unfortunately, it continues to reemerge despite efforts to eradicate it.

People who contact or work on a daily basis with impaired older individuals or those suffering from various forms of disadvantage may be particularly likely to be ageist in their orientations. Such ageism may not turn into discriminatory actions but rather spur kindness and self-sacrifice for the older adult. Clinicians frequently see those with serious problems; thus, the clinical perspective in gerontology can be misleading if it leads to a mind-set of aging as steady progress toward disease, disability, and death. Older adults are a diverse population. The majority of older adults in America are relatively healthy, relatively independent, vibrant, and alert. If all service professionals do is work with older adults who do not commonly display these characteristics, we may fail to recognize the diversity within this population. The relatively healthy and independent older adults are the so-called *invisible elders*. The ones who receive the most media attention are the more extreme cases—usually the extremely disadvantaged, but occasionally the exceptionally successful older adult.

One thing that sociologists have taught us regarding racism, sexism, and ageism is that they are institutionally based phenomena. In other words, social structures may exist that maintain or reinforce ideas and actions based on some form of prejudice or discrimination (Minkler, 1990). Because these phenomena are institutionally based, it is entirely conceivable that members of minority statuses will hold some of the same ideas and may in fact also engage in discriminatory behaviors. Women are often held captive to the vestiges of sexism in society. African and Hispanic Americans may similarly be victims of ideas and actions that devalue their status. It is most unfortunate when these phenomena are internalized by the individuals to whom they are directed so that they exhibit them as well. Ageism may be lodged most deeply in the minds of individuals who are approaching advanced ages. Self-effacing behavior on the basis of age by older adults is just one illustration of the depth of the problem.

We expect certain behaviors of individuals at certain ages, and these constrain opportunities in social life. Fortunately, there are some signs that as a society, we are becoming more willing to accept asynchronization over the life course. While age norms are still structured in the very early ages, we are growing more tolerant of people in middle and later life engaging in behaviors atypical for their age.

As I mentioned earlier, ageism is unfortunately reappearing in new forms. Gerontologists and activists for older adults often felt that they had made great strides in stemming the tide of ageism in American society. One must watch recent developments in social policy, however, to see if ageism is lodged within positions on social issues. For example, discussions of rationing health care may devalue medical care for older adults due to perceived length of life. A second example of potentially ageist policy initiatives can be seen in the activities of groups touting generational equity. For medical care as well as for employment opportunities and Social Security, the generational equity debate often pits the needs of children against the needs of older adults. Gerontologists understand the gravity of neglecting children's needs, but they also understand that one cannot dismiss an entire population group just because of age.

A FLUID IMAGINATION

There is no claim to a reified gerontological imagination here; rather, this chapter has attempted to articulate the major tenets of a gerontological imagination. Such an imagination will, of course, undergo change, and that is a healthy process. This book is intended to help shape a gerontological imagination and work toward the definition of a paradigm in the study of aging. To this end, I welcome challenges or additions to this definition of a gerontological imagination. The intellectual climate for this discussion is vibrant, and the policy issues before us demand vigorous attention. I hope that this chapter and this book will serve to clarify our fundamental image of what aging is and what we can do to enhance the experience of those fortunate enough to grow older.

REFERENCES

Achenbaum, W. A. (1987). Can gerontology be a science? *Journal of Aging Studies, 1,* 3–18.

Achenbaum, W. A. (1995). *Crossing frontiers: Gerontology emerges as a science.* New York: Cambridge University Press.

Ahmed, F. (1994). Infant mortality and related issues. In I. L. Livingston (Ed.), *Handbook of Black American health: The mosaic of conditions, issues, policies, and prospects* (pp. 216–235). Westport, CT: Greenwood Press.

Baker, G. T., III, & Achenbaum, W. A. (1992). A historical perspective of research on the biology of aging from Nathan W. Shock. *Experimental Gerontology, 27,* 261–273.

Baltes, P. B. (1993). The aging mind: Potential and limits. *Gerontologist 33,* 580–594.

Baltes, P. B., Reese, H. W., & Lipsitt, L. P. (1980). Life-span developmental psychology. *Annual Review of Psychology, 31,* 65–110.

Botwinick, J. (1977). Intellectual abilities. In J. E. Birren & K. Warner Schaie (Eds.), *Handbook of the psychology of aging* (pp. 580–605). New York: Van Nostrand Reinhold.

Botwinick, J. (1978). *Aging and behavior.* New York: Springer Publishing.

Boyer, E. J. (1990). *Scholarship reconsidered: Priorities of the professoriate.* Princeton, NJ: Carnegie Foundation for the Advancement of Teaching.

Cournil, A., & Kirkwood, T. B. (2001). If you would live long, choose your parents well. *Trends in Genetics, 17,* 233–235.

Cunningham, W. R., & Brookbank, J. W. (1988). *Gerontology: The psychology, biology and sociology of aging.* New York: Harper.

Dannefer, D. (1987). Aging as intracohort differentiation: Accentuation, the Matthew effect, and the life course. *Sociological Forum, 2,* 211–236.

Dannefer, D. (2003). Cumulative advantage/disadvantage and the life course: Cross-fertilizing age and social science theory. *Journal of Gerontology: Social Sciences, 58B,* S327–S337.

Elder, G. H., Jr. (1974). *Children of the Great Depression: Social change in life experience.* Chicago: University of Chicago Press.

Elder, G. H., Jr. (1994). Time, human agency, and social change: Perspectives on the life course. *Social Psychology Quarterly, 57,* 4–15.

Featherman, D. L., & Petersen, T. (1986). Markers of aging: Modeling the clocks that time us. *Research on Aging, 8,* 339–365.

Ferraro, K. F., & Farmer, M. M. (1996). Double jeopardy to health hypothesis for African Americans: Analysis and critique. *Journal of Health and Social Behavior, 37,* 27–43.

Ferraro, K. F., & Kelley-Moore, J. A. (2001). Self-rated health and mortality among Black and White adults: Examining the dynamic evaluation thesis. *Journal of Gerontology: Social Sciences, 56B,* S195–S205.

Ferraro, K. F., Thorpe, R. J., Jr., McCabe, G. P., Kelley-Moore, J. A., & Jiang, Z. (in press). The color of hospitalization over the adult life course: Cumulative disadvantage in Black and White? *Journal of Gerontology: Social Sciences, 61B.*

Fry, C. L. (1997). Cross-cultural perspectives on aging. In K. F. Ferraro (Ed.), *Gerontology: Perspectives and issues* (pp. 138–154). New York: Springer Publishing.

Griffin, J. H. (1960). *Black like me.* New York: Signet.

Hayflick, L. (1965). The limited in vitro lifetime of human diploid cell strains. *Experimental Cell Research, 37,* 614–636.

Hayslip, B., & Sterns, H. L. (1979). Age differences in relationships between crystallized and fluid intelligences and problem solving. *Journal of Gerontology, 34,* 404–414.

Kirkwood, T. B. L. (2002). Evolution of ageing. *Mechanisms of Ageing and Development, 123,* 737–745.

Kleemeier, R. W. (1962). Intellectual change in the senium. In *Proceedings of the Social Statistics Section of the American Statistical Association* (122nd annual meeting), 290–295.

Kuhn, T. (1962). *The structure of scientific revolutions.* Chicago: University of Chicago Press.

Lynch, J., & Smith, G. D. (2005). A life course approach to chronic disease epidemiology. *Annual Review of Public Health, 26,* 1–35.

Maddox, G. L. (1987). Aging differently. *Gerontologist, 27,* 557–564.

Martin, G. M., Austad, S. N., & Johnson, T. E. (1996). Genetic analysis of aging: Role of oxidative damage and environmental stresses. *Nature Genetics, 13,* 25–34.

Mills, C. W. (1959). *The sociological imagination.* New York: Oxford University Press.

Minkler, M. (1990). Aging and disability: Behind and beyond the stereotypes. *Journal of Aging Studies, 4,* 246–260.

Moore, P. (1985). *Disguised.* Waco, TX: Word Books.

O'Rand, A M. (1996). The precious and the precocious: Understanding cumulative disadvantage and cumulative advantage over the life course. *Gerontologist, 36,* 230–238.

Perls, T. T., Wilmoth, J., Levenson, R., Drinkwater, M., Cohen, M., Bogan, H., et al. (2002). Life-long sustained mortality advantage of siblings of centenarians. *Proceedings of the National Academy of Science, 99,* 8442–8447.

Preston, S. H., Hill, M. E., & Drevenstedt, G. L. (1998). Childhood conditions that predict survival to advanced ages among African Americans. *Social Science and Medicine, 47,* 1231–1246.

Quinn, J. F. (1987). The economic status of the elderly: Beware of the mean. *Review of Income and Wealth, 33,* 63–82.

Riegel, K. F., & Riegel, R. M. (1972). Development, drop, and death. *Developmental Psychology, 6,* 306–319.

Riley, M. W. (1985). Age strata in social systems. In R. H. Binstock & E. Shanas (Eds.), *Handbook of aging and the social sciences* (pp. 369–411). New York: Van Nostrand Reinhold.

Riley, M. W. (1987). On the significance of age in sociology. *American Sociological Review, 52,* 1–14.

Ritzer, G. (1975). *Sociology: A multiple paradigm science.* Boston: Allyn & Bacon.

Rowe, J. W., & Kahn, R. L. (1987). Human aging: Usual and successful. *Science, 237,* 143–149.

Rowe, J. W., & Kahn, R. L. (1998). *Successful aging.* New York: Pantheon.

Vijg, J., & Suh, Y. (2005). Genetics of longevity and aging. *Annual Review of Medicine, 56,* 193–212.

Wadsworth, M. E. J. (1997). Health inequalities in the life course perspective. *Social Science and Medicine, 44,* 859–869.

White, N., & Cunningham, W. R. (1988). Is terminal drop pervasive or specific? *Journal of Gerontology: Psychological Sciences, 43,* 141–144.

Williams, G. C. (1957). Pleiotropy, natural selection and the evolution of senescence. *Evolution, 11,* 398–411.

Willott, J. F. (1997). Neurogerontology: The aging nervous system. In K. F. Ferraro (Ed.), *Gerontology: Perspectives and issues* (pp. 68–96). New York: Springer Publishing.

Willott, J. F., Jackson, L. M., & Hunter, K. P. (1987). Morphometric study of the anteroventral cochlear nucleus of two mouse models of presbycusis. *Journal of Comparative Neurology, 260,* 472–490.

Subject Index

Name Index